The Web Server Handbook

The Web Server Handbook

Pete Palmer
Adam Schneider
Anne Chenette

For book and bookstore information

http://www.prenhall.com

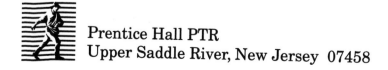

Prentice Hall PTR
Upper Saddle River, New Jersey 07458

Editorial/production supervision: *Craig Little*
Manufacturing manager: *Alexis R. Heydt*
Acquisitions editor: *Mark L. Taub*
Cover design: *Defranco Design Inc.*
Cover design director: *Jerry Votta*

The publisher offers discounts on this book when ordered in bulk quantities.
For more information, contact:

Corporate Sales Department
Prentice Hall PTR
1 Lake Street
Upper Saddle River, NJ 07458

Phone: 800-382-3419; Fax: 201-236-7141
email: corpsales@prenhall.com

Adobe Illustrator, Adobe Photoshop, PageMaker, and PostScript are trademarks of Adobe Systems, Inc. America Online is a service mark and WebCrawler is a trademark of America Online, Inc. Apple, AppleTalk, Macintosh, Macintosh Quadra, and QuickTime are registered trademarks and AppleScript, Mac, MacOS, MacTCP, Power Macintosh, ResEdit, SimpleText, Sound Manager, System 6, System 7, and TeachText are trademarks of Apple Computer, Inc. BBEdit is a trademark of Bare Bones Software, Inc. Chameleon and NetManage are registered trademarks of Net-Manage, Inc. Cheetah Web Server is a trademark of TGV, Inc. ClarisWorks is a trademark of Claris Corp. Compaq is a registered trademark of Compaq Computer Corp. CompuServe is a registered trademark of CompuServe, Inc. CorelDRAW and Word Perfect are trademarks of Corel Corp. Cray is a trademark of Cray Computer Corp. Ethernet is a trademark of Xerox Corp. Eudora is a registered trademark of Qualcomm, Inc. EWAN is a trademark of Zandata. Free Agent is a trademark of Forte, Inc. Freehand is a trademark of Altsys Corp. IBM and OS/2 are registered trademarks and PowerPC is a trademark of International Business Machines Corp. Pentium is a registered trademark of Intel Corp. Lotus is a trademark of Lotus Development Corp. Lycos is a trademark of Lycos, Inc. MacSLIP is a trademark of Hyde Park Software. Microsoft and MS-DOS are registered trademarks and Excel, Internet Explorer, Microsoft Network, Visual Basic, Windows, Windows 95, Windows NT, and Word are trademarks of Microsoft Corporation. Motorola is a registered trademark of Motorola Corp. Netscape is a trademark of Netscape Communications Corp. Nisus is a registered trademark of Nisus Software, Inc. Paint Shop Pro is a trademark of JASC, Inc. PKZIP and PKUNZIP are trademarks of PKWARE, Inc. Prodigy is a trademark of Prodigy Services Co. QuarkXPress is a registered trademark of Quark, Inc. Quarterdeck is a registered trademark of Quarterdeck Corporation. Silicon Graphics is a registered trademark of Silicon Graphics, Inc. Java, OpenWindows, Solaris, Sun, and SunOS are trademarks of Sun Microsystems, Inc. SPARCstation is a registered trademark of SPARC International, Inc. Stacker is a registered trademark of Stac, Inc. StarNine is a registered trademark and WebSTAR is a trademark of StarNine Technologies, Inc. StuffIt, StuffIt Expander, and StuffIt Spacesaver are trademarks of Aladdin Systems, Inc. Trumpet Winsock is a registered trademark of Peter R. Tattam and Trumpet Software International Pty. Ltd. TurboGopher is a trademark of the Regents of the University of Minnesota. UNIX is a registered trademark in the United States and other countries licensed exclusively through X/Open Company, Ltd. WebSite is a trademark of O'Reilly & Associates, Inc. WS_FTP is a trademark of Ipswitch, Inc. X Window System is a trademark of the Massachusetts Institute of Technology. Yahoo! is a trademark of Yahoo, Inc.
    All other trademarks and service marks are the property of their respective owners.

Printed in the United States of America
10 9 8 7 6 5 4 3 2 1

ISBN 0-13-239930-X

Prentice-Hall International (UK) Limited, *London*
Prentice-Hall of Australia Pty. Limited, *Sydney*
Prentice-Hall Canada Inc., *Toronto*
Prentice-Hall Hispanoamericana, S.A., *Mexico*
Prentice-Hall of India Private Limited, *New Delhi*
Prentice-Hall of Japan, Inc., *Tokyo*
Simon & Schuster Asia Pte. Ltd., *Singapore*
Editora Prentice-Hall do Brasil, Ltda., *Rio de Janeiro*

Contents

Preface   **xix**

Introduction   **xxi**

THE STORY OF BOB   xxi
  The Hobby Server: Bob Serves Up a Little Fun   xxi
  Bob Expands To a Small Business Server   xxii
  Bob's Mid-Size Business Server   xxiii
  "Webmaster Bob" and His Large Business   xxiv

ORGANIZATION OF THIS BOOK   xxv

CONVENTIONS USED IN THIS BOOK   xxvi
  Italics   xxvii
  Constant Width ("Computer" Font)   xxvii
  Constant Width Italics   xxvii
  Square Brackets   xxvii

KEEPING CURRENT   xxvii

ACKNOWLEDGEMENTS   xxviii

ABOUT THE AUTHORS   xxviii

CHAPTER 1
The Internet And The World Wide Web   **1**

NETWORKS AND INTERNETS   1

THE INTERNET   4
 The Internet Before the World Wide Web   5
 Prehistory of the World Wide Web   7

THE ORIGINS OF THE WORLD WIDE WEB   8

CHAPTER 2

Overview Of The World Wide Web   11

EXPLORING THE WEB   12
 Pages & URLs   12
 Links   12
 HTML   18
 New Developments   19

SUMMARY   20

CHAPTER 3

Why You Should Create A Web Server   23

WEB SERVERS   23

HOME PAGES   24

THE WEB SOLUTION   27

WHAT YOU CAN DO WITH THE WEB   28
 Multimedia Presentation   28
 Databases   31
 Software   33
 Communications   36

CHAPTER 4

Quick Start Guide To The Internet And The Web   39

TYPES OF INTERNET SERVICE PROVIDERS   39
 Educational Accounts   40
 Employer Accounts   40
 FreeNets and BBSs   40
 Commercial Services   40
 Local Internet Service Providers (ISPs)   41

TYPES OF ACCOUNTS   41
 Shell Accounts   41
 SLIP/PPP Accounts   42

CHOOSING A PROVIDER   44

ACCOUNT REQUIREMENTS   45
 Electronic Mail (E-Mail)   45
 Usenet News   45
 FTP   46

Telnet   46
Gopher   46
World Wide Web   46

STEP-BY-STEP EXAMPLE   47
Testing Your Hardware Setup   47
Finding an Internet Service Provider   48
Getting Going — Using Your ISP's System   49
Testing the Account   50
Creating a Home Page on the Web   50

BEFORE YOU MOVE ON   57

CHAPTER 5

Web Server Fundamentals

59

FILE SERVERS   59

WEB SERVER COMPUTER HARDWARE   60
Base Computer   61
Memory   62
Disk Space   63
Modems   63
Processor Speed   64

WEB SERVER SOFTWARE   64
Operating Systems   64
TCP/IP Software   66
HTTP Software   67

CHAPTER 6

Connecting To The Internet

69

INTERNET SERVICE PROVIDERS   69

DATA COMMUNICATIONS SERVICES   72
Traditional Phone Lines   72
Digital Data Connections   73

GETTING YOUR OWN DOMAIN NAME   74
Domain Name Conventions   75
DNS Servers   76
Registering Your Domain Name   76

GETTING YOUR OWN IP ADDRESS   83

CHAPTER 7

Setting Up A UNIX Web Server

85

PREREQUISITES   86
An Internet Connection   86
UNIX Hardware   87

UNIX Software   87

HTTPD SOFTWARE PACKAGES   88

GETTING THE SERVER SOFTWARE   88
An Example of Downloading a Server Package   89

INSTALLING THE SOFTWARE   92

BUILDING HTTPD FROM SOURCE   93

CONFIGURING YOUR SERVER   95
Editing the Configuration Files   96
Main Server Configuration   96
Server Resource Map   99
File Type Mapping   106

ACCESS CONTROL CONFIGURATION   107
Types of Access Control   107
Editing Access Control Files   108
Access Control Directives   108
User Authentication   112
Access Control Examples   114

TESTING YOUR SERVER   118

CGI AND UNIX   119
Scripts   119
Image Maps   120

HELPER APPLICATIONS   121
XV   121
XAnim   122
Mpegplay   122
Ghostview   122

WEB DEVELOPMENT TOOLS   122
HoTMetaL Free   123
Mapedit   123

CHAPTER 8

Setting Up A Windows Web Server   125

PREREQUISITES   126
An Internet Connection   126
PC Hardware   127
PC Software   128

GETTING THE SOFTWARE   129
Windows 3.1 TCP/IP Socket Software   129
PKZIP   130
Web Browser   130
Web Server Software   131

INSTALLING THE WINDOWS HTTPD PROGRAM   132

PREPARING YOUR SYSTEM   133

Time Zone   134
Setting Your Command Environment Size   135
Installing VBRUN300.DLL   135
Creating the Httpd Clickable Icon   135
Starting Up Your Server   136

CONFIGURING YOUR SERVER   136
Editing the Configuration Files   138
Main Server Configuration   138
Server Resource Map   140
File Type Mapping   144

ACCESS CONTROL CONFIGURATION   145
Types of Access Control   145
Editing Access Control Files   146
Access Control Directives   146
User Authentication   151
Access Control Examples   153

TESTING YOUR SERVER   157

CGI WITH WINDOWS HTTPD   158
Windows CGI   158
MS-DOS CGI   159
Perl   160

GETTING PROGRAMS FROM THE INTERNET   161
A Brief Word About Shareware   162

INTERNET APPLICATIONS   163
WS_FTP   163
EWAN   164
Pegasus Mail   164
Free Agent   164
WS_Gopher   165

HELPER APPLICATIONS   165
PKZIP   165
GraphX Viewer   166
WHAM   166
QuickTime for Windows   166
Mpegplay   166

WEB DEVELOPMENT TOOLS   167
HoTMetaL Free   167
Mapedit   168
WebImage   168
Paint Shop Pro   168

WINDOWS 95 AND WINDOWS NT   169
Server Software Packages   169
WebSite   169
Running Your WebSite Server   175

CHAPTER 9

Setting Up A Macintosh Web Server   **177**

PREREQUISITES   178
   An Internet Connection   178
   Macintosh Hardware   179
   Software   180

GETTING THE SERVER SOFTWARE   181
   MacHTTP vs. WebSTAR   182
   Downloading MacHTTP   183
   Paying for MacHTTP   184

INSTALLING MACHTTP   184
   The MacHTTP Application & Documentation   185
   MacTCP & AppleScript   186
   Your Web Pages   187
   Crank It Up!   188
   Your Home Page   189

CONFIGURATION: THE MACHTTP.CONFIG FILE   191
   Version   192
   Default Files   192
   Connection Settings   193
   File Type Mapping   195
   Security Settings   197

CONFIGURATION: MACHTTP MENU ITEMS   199
   Realm Passwords   199
   The Options Menu   199

SECURITY TIPS   201
   ALLOW and DENY   201
   Realms   201
   Running Multiple Servers on Different Ports   202

TESTING YOUR SERVER   203

CGI ON A MACINTOSH   204
   Macintosh CGI Applications   204
   AppleScript   204
   Perl   205

RECOMMENDED CGI APPLICATIONS   207
   Kelly's Error   207
   Mac-ImageMap   208
   MapServe   208
   Count WWWebula   208
   ServerStat   209
   Annotate   209

INTERNET APPLICATIONS   210
   Internet Config   210
   Anarchie   211
   Fetch   211
   NCSA Telnet   211
   Eudora Light   212

NewsWatcher   212
TurboGopher   213
IP Monitor   213

HELPER APPLICATIONS   214
Stuffit Expander   214
DropStuff with Expander Enhancer   214
Tex-Edit Plus   215
JPEGView   216
Jade   216
SoundApp   217
Fast Player   217
Sparkle   218
uuUndo   218
Mpack   218
Tar   218
ZipIt   219

WEB DEVELOPMENT TOOLS   219
HTML Helpers   219
Graphic Converter   220
Clip2gif   221
Transparency   221
WebMap   221
SoundEffects   221
QuickEditor   222
Progressify   222
ProJPEG   222
ResEdit   223

CHAPTER 10

How To Create Spiffy Web Pages   225

PAGE CONTENT   226
Bigger Is Not Better   226
Good Writing Counts   228
Don't Let Your Site Get Stale   229

PAGE LAYOUT   231
Simplicity   231
Anchors and Links   232
Signatures   233
Headings   234
White Space: The Good, the Bad, and the Ugly   236
Tables   237
Consistency   240
A Real Layout Template That You Can Use   240

IMAGES   242
Number and Size of Images   242
Thumbnails   243
Height and Width Attributes   245
File Formats   247
Organizing Your Images   250

SOUNDS AND MOVIES   251
    Sound Formats   251
    Sampling Rates   252
    RealAudio and Xing StreamWorks   252
    Movies   253

COMPATIBILITY   254
    General Web Compatibility Issues   255
    Graphical vs. Non-graphical Browsers   257
    Netscape   259
    Your Site and the Future of HTML   263

DOING BUSINESS ON THE WEB   263
    Give Something Back   263
    Selling Merchandise on the Web   264
    Catalogs   265
    The Worldwide Market   266

SUMMARY   266

CHAPTER 11

Publicizing Your World Wide Web Site   267

NETIQUETTE   267

ADVERTISING OUTSIDE THE WEB   270
    E-mail   270
    Usenet   270

ADVERTISING ON THE WEB   273
    Yahoo   274
    Lycos   276
    WebCrawler   279
    Alta Vista   281
    Submit It   281
    "What's New" Pages: Mosaic and Netscape   282
    ALIWEB   283
    Point's "Top 5%" Awards   284
    Other Indexes and Lists   285
    Other People's Pages   287

KEEPING TRACK OF YOUR SUCCESS   288
    Graphical Counters   288
    The Server Log   289
    Feedback   290

CHAPTER 12

Running CGI Programs On Your Web Server   291

WHAT YOU CAN DO WITH CGI   291

OVERVIEW OF CGI   292
    How a "Normal" URL Is Processed   292

How a CGI URL Is Processed   292
Understanding a CGI URL   294
CGI Programming Languages   296

USING CGI PROGRAMS   296
Executing Other People's Programs   296
Finding CGI Programs   297
Installing CGI Programs on Your System   298

CREATING CGI PROGRAMS   299
A Simple Example: A Personalized Poem   299

HTML FORMS: AN OVERVIEW   302
The <FORM> Tag   303
The <INPUT> Tag   303
The <SELECT> Tag   306
The <TEXTAREA> Tag   307

TESTING YOUR CGI SCRIPTS   309
Check Your Setup   309
Check Your Forms   310
Run Programs Locally   310
Check the HTTP Header   310

CGI SECURITY   311

JAVA AND JAVASCRIPT   311

CONCLUSION   313

CHAPTER 13

A Bunch Of Perl Scripts   315

AN HTML MAD LIB   315

A POP-UP MENU   320

MORE MAD LIBS   322

A PERL GUEST BOOK   328

AN ORDER ENTRY SYSTEM   337

A SEARCHABLE INDEX   345

CHAPTER 14

Web Server Security And Maintenance   351

KEEPING YOUR SERVER RUNNING   351
Buy a Reliable System   352
Be Familiar with Your System   352
Backup, Backup, Backup   352
Have a Substitute Server Available   353
Have a Reliable and Supportive Provider   353
Keep Your Software Updated   353

Read the Web Newsgroups for Your Platform   354
Beware of Viruses   354

MANAGING USERS   354
Network Firewalls and Proxies   355

SELECTING A SERVER PACKAGE   356

PROTECTING YOUR DATA   356
File Space   356
CGI   357
Server-Generated Indexes   357
Symbolic Links   357
Port Numbers   357
UNIX Server Processes   357
User Authentication   358
Other Internet Services   358
Message Encryption   359

RECOVERING FROM A BREAK-IN   359

COMMERCIAL ACTIVITY   360

APPENDIX   A
HTML Quick Reference Guide   361

STRUCTURAL TAGS   362
<HTML>...</HTML>   362
<HEAD>...</HEAD>   362
<TITLE>...</TITLE>   362
<ISINDEX>   362
<BODY>...</BODY>   362

TEXT STYLES   362
<EM>...</EM>   363
<STRONG>...</STRONG>   363
<CODE>...</CODE>   363
<ADDRESS>...</ADDRESS>   364
<I>...</I>   364
<B>...</B>   364
<TT>...</TT>   364
<PRE>...</PRE>   364
<H1>...</H1>, <H2>...</H2>, etc.   364

PAGE LAYOUT   364
<P>   364

   365
<BR clear={left,right,all}>   365
<HR>   365
<BLOCKQUOTE>...</BLOCKQUOTE>   366

LISTS   366
<UL>...</UL>   366
<OL>...</OL>   366

<LI> 366
<DL>...</DL> 366
<DT> 366
<DD> 367

IMAGES 367
 Src="*filename or URL*" 367
 Alt="*alternate text*" 367
 Align=*{top,middle,bottom,left,right}* 367
 Ismap 367

LINKS AND ANCHORS 368
 <A href="*filename or URL*">...</A> 368
 <A name="*nametext*">...</A> 368

SPECIAL CHARACTERS 369

NETSCAPE 1.1 EXTENSIONS TO HTML 370
 Tables 370
 <CENTER>...</CENTER> 370
 <BLINK>...</BLINK> 371
 <BASEFONT size=*n*> 371
 <FONT size=*{n,+n,-n}*>...</FONT> 371
 <NOBR>...</NOBR> 371
 <WBR> 371
 <HR size=*n*> 371
 <HR width=*{n,n%}*> 372
 <HR align=*{left,right,center}*> 372
 <HR noshade> 372
 <IMG align=*{texttop, absbottom, absmiddle, baseline}*> 372
 <IMG width=*{n,n%}*>, <IMG height=*{n,n%}*> 373
 <IMG border=*n*> 373
 <IMG hspace=*n*>, <IMG vspace=*n*> 373

NETSCAPE 2.0 EXTENSIONS TO HTML 373
 Superscripts and Subscripts 374
 <BIG> and <SMALL> 374
 Divisions and Aligned Paragraphs 374
 Frames 374
 Client-Side Image Maps 375

APPENDIX B
UNIX Quick Reference Guide **377**

GETTING STARTED 378
 Logging In 378
 Changing Your Password 378
 Setting Your Terminal Type 379
 Characters: Backspace, Special Characters, etc. 379
 Determining Your Shell 379
 Logging Out 380

NAVIGATING AROUND A UNIX SYSTEM 380
 UNIX File Systems 380
 UNIX Path Names 381

Listing the Contents of a Directory   381
Changing Directories   382
Finding the Current Directory   382
Finding Your Home Directory   383
Creating Directories   383
Removing Directories   383

FUN WITH FILES   384
Creating Files   384
Moving and Renaming Files   385
Copying Files   385
Deleting Files   385
Changing Files   386
File Permissions   386
File Compression   387

NETWORK COMMANDS   388
FTP   388
Telnet   390
Rlogin   391

SHARING FILES   392
Sending and Receiving E-Mail   392
Uuencoding   393
Tar   393

EDITING TEXT FILES WITH THE VI EDITOR   394
Invoking The VI Editor   394
Modes   395
Moving Around a File   395
Inserting and Appending Text   396
Deleting Text   396
Changing Text   396
Undoing Changes   396
Importing Text   397
Saving Text   397
Getting Out of the VI Editor   397

GETTING MORE INFORMATION: THE "MAN" COMMAND   397

APPENDIX C

Perl Quick Reference Guide   401

INTRODUCTION TO PERL   402
Perl Release Status   402
Obtaining Perl and Its Documentation   402

PERL BASICS   403
How to Run Perl Programs   403
File Naming Conventions   404
Program Format   404
Required First Line   405

VARIABLES   405
Simple Variables (Scalars)   405

Normal Arrays   407
Associative Arrays   408

OPERATORS   409
True and False in Perl   409
Arithmetic Operators   410
Relational Operators   410
File Test Operators   411
Miscellaneous Operators   412

SPECIAL VARIABLES, FILEHANDLES, & "HERE" DOCUMENTS   413
Predefined Variables   413
Special Arrays   414
Filehandles   414
"Here" Documents   415

COMPOUND STATEMENTS AND FLOW CONTROL   415
If Statements   415
While Statements   416
Foreach Statements   416
Until Statements   417
Unless Statements   417
The ǀǀ Operator as Flow Control   417

STRING OPERATIONS   417
Pattern Matching   418
Regular Expressions   418
String Functions   419

OTHER PERL FUNCTIONS   420
Input/Output Functions   420
Miscellaneous Functions   421
Platform-Specific Functions   421

SUBROUTINES   422

DEBUGGING   422

CONVERTING OTHER SCRIPTS TO PERL   424

PERL LIBRARIES   424
Installing and Using Perl Libraries   424
Cgi-lib.pl   425
Other Libraries   426

SECURITY ISSUES ON UNIX SYSTEMS   426
External Programs and Shell Meta-Characters   426
Root Permissions   427
Perl Taint Checking   427

APPENDIX D
Networks And TCP/IP   429

HISTORY OF NETWORKING   429
The Need for Compatibility   429

NETWORKING TODAY   430

OSI AND TCP   431
   The OSI Reference Model: Layers   431
   TCP and Datagrams   433

IP AND MESSAGE ROUTING   434
   IP Addresses   434

SUMMARY   434

APPENDIX E

The CD   437

WEB PAGES AND PERL SCRIPTS   437

UNIX   438

WINDOWS   439

MACINTOSH   439

Index   441

Preface

*A*s you can see by browsing through any magazine these days, just about anyone can "surf" the World Wide Web. But many people assume that if you want to put your *own* information on the Web, you need to spend lots of money on a specialized computer and hired networking consultants.

The truth is that with the right knowledge, *anyone* can put information on the Web for others to see. This book gives you that knowledge, and you may very well be able to do it with equipment that you already own. We will show you how to create a World Wide Web server that can provide information — text, graphics, sound, and more — on demand, to anyone on the Internet, anywhere in the world. (A "Web server" is simply the computer that is home to one or more Web "sites," which are collections of Web "pages" and supporting software.)

We will teach you the basics of the Internet and World Wide Web, so that you have a greater understanding of the workings of the Web. Then we will walk you through the process of setting up a World Wide Web site on *your* computer, and we will recommend a number of useful programs — many of which are available for free — and tell you exactly how to get them. Finally, we will give you some advice about proper Web site design and maintenance, and we will show you how to add more complicated elements — such as interactive forms — to your pages to increase their usefulness and appeal.

This book is not biased toward or against any type of computer or operating system. One of the most exciting features of the Web is its amazing compatibility with different platforms, and we have fully embraced this ideal. Macintosh, Microsoft Windows, and UNIX users each have their own specialized chapter, but the rest of the book applies to *everyone*.

We'll provide step-by-step instructions, along with practical tips based on our extensive Web experience, but we won't overload you with unnecessary details. We will also give you an overview of helpful background material, plus numerous pointers to more information. And, unlike the template-based books and software currently being sold for Web server creation, this book gives you the information you'll need to customize *your* server for *your* needs.

Why should you create a Web site? Aside from the obvious academic benefits that everyone can reap from this global network, the Web opens up whole new markets, and gives rise to business opportunities that are only possible in cyberspace. If you have an organization that needs a way to spread information around the country or around the world, or if you own a business of any kind, you can use this electronic frontier to bolster your membership or gain an edge over your competition. Or you can just have fun. No matter what your motives, this book can help.

This is *not* a book on surfing the Web. There are already many books and magazine articles on this topic, as well as tons of free information on the Web itself. We provide the basic steps for getting you on the Web, then point you toward the latest Web information to learn more.

This is *not* a book on the latest "hot spots of the Internet." Such information goes out of date much faster than it can be printed. It is far more effective to use the Web-based tools to find these sites; we'll tell you how.

This is also *not* a book on writing HTML (the language used to write Web pages). There are several good books about HTML, but these books do not explain how to build your own Web server from scratch, like we do. This book *does* provide enough information about HTML to get you going — the basics of HTML and a quick reference guide. We also give recommendations for our favorite Web sources of HTML information.

Finally, this is not a book on how to market your services on the World Wide Web. We'll leave the marketing advice to the pros. However, we will give you some essential information on Internet conventions and "netiquette," as well as some valuable tips on how to advertise your Web server most effectively.

This book is for beginners and experienced Internet users alike. The material covered here has no prerequisites, other than a general understanding of your computer and a desire to learn more. Setting up your Web site will take some effort — but probably not as much as you might think — and keeping it going will require a commitment on your part, but we think you will find the end result rewarding and worthwhile.

Introduction

*T*his section provides an introduction to Web servers by telling the story of an average guy and his experience with an ever-expanding Web site. We will also summarize this book's contents and organization, and we will explain some of the conventions used throughout.

THE STORY OF BOB

To introduce you to the wonderful world of running a Web site, we would like to tell you a story about Bob, a fictional friend of ours. Bob knows about the World Wide Web through his daughter, who uses the Web in the computer lab at her grade school.

Bob's daughter has told him about the many fantastic things she has found on the Web. Not wanting to feel behind the times, Bob decides to see what all the fuss is about. He gets an Internet account through a local Internet service provider and has his daughter show him around. After surfing the Web for a while, he decides he likes it so much that he wants to do something more. He wants to create his own Web server.

The Hobby Server: Bob Serves Up a Little Fun

Bob is an avid fan of the St. Paul Saints minor league baseball club; he decides that a great use for his server would be to set up an unofficial Web page about his favorite team. He has a Macintosh home computer and not much money budgeted for this venture. Bob plans on creating Web pages that include standings, seasonal statistics, and newspaper stories about his team, as well as links to the official Saints Web site. He has already scanned in pictures of Municipal Stadium, the star players, the manager, and Saint the Pig (the team mascot). His Mac has all of the resources necessary to manage the files, and he has set up and configured MacHTTP (Chapter 9 will tell *you* how to do this on a Mac; Chapters 7 & 8 deal with UNIX systems and Windows, respectively).

To keep things as inexpensive as possible, Bob decides not to put a second phone line into his house; his pages will only be available to the Web from nine o'clock until midnight each night. Bob figures that other Saints fans won't care about the limited hours because that may be when they will be browsing the Web anyway (except perhaps on game nights).

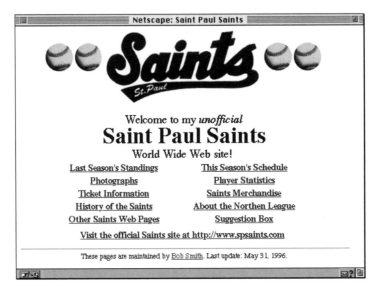

Bob's hobby server, with information about his favorite baseball team, the St. Paul Saints.

Bob finds a reputable local Internet service provider (ISP) and talks things over with a sales support employee. Bob's best option turns out to be a 14.4k bps PPP connection. This way, he won't have to buy any additional equipment; Bob's computer came with a modem, although he never really used it until now. While this isn't the speediest connection in the world, his fellow fans don't care. His little server's traffic is mostly limited to Saints fans in the Twin Cities area, so his computer isn't going to be swamped. The only practical option cheaper than this would have been to log in as a user on one of the provider's computers and put his files there, but since Bob is becoming as much of a computer enthusiast as he is a Saints fan, he wants to do it himself.

Bob Expands To a Small Business Server

Having had so much fun with his hobby server, Bob decides to put his small business — an independent insurance agency — on the Web, for increased advertising exposure. Now, he has more things to worry about. First, the server has to be running day and night. He also needs to have the data move faster, because his insurance customers are far less patient than Saints fans. Bob plans on showing his rates, his picture, various insurance plans for his customers, and so on. Bob is so excited about the idea that he's already used his home computer to create a page for his business; now it needs a permanent home.

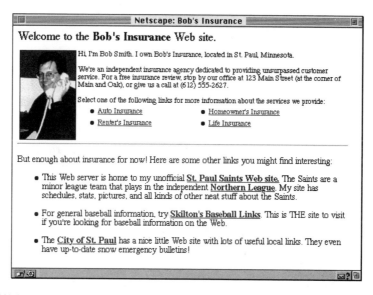

The Web page that Bob has created for his insurance office. In addition to insurance information, he has included some other things to make it more interesting.

Once again, Bob confers with his Internet service provider for options. The best option turns out to be a 28.8k bps modem connection with a dedicated phone line. This means that Bob will have to get a new modem and install an additional phone line in his office, which the computer gets to use 24 hours a day; his ISP in turn has a line set aside for the incoming connection from Bob's computer. Bob also gets his own domain name; this means that people who want to connect to Bob's business' server can look for it under an easy-to-remember name, such as "bobs-insurance.com."

Bob's Mid-Size Business Server

Thanks to the popularity of his Web site, Bob's business has grown exponentially, and he has had to hire a dozen new employees to handle all of the customers. Bob puts together a LAN (local area network) at his office and buys a Sun SPARCstation to be his file server and Web server. The traffic is way beyond what his 28.8k connection can handle, so Bob calls up his ISP for more advice.

This time he is told that a 56k connection will serve his needs, but he will have to upgrade his phone line and his modem to a more expensive one in order to handle the amount of data flow. Bob realizes that this step may be adequate for the time being, but the cost is high enough that he should really start think-ing about investing for future growth. So he forgoes the 56k line and jumps to the next level of service, which is a high-speed digital line (ISDN). This will not only give his dedicated server the bandwidth it needs for now and into the near future, but it can also be used for the voice communications of the employees in his office.

"Webmaster Bob" and His Large Business

Bob's business grows so much after getting the ISDN connection that he makes enough money to purchase many of his competitors in the area and expand to other states. Bob himself has quit personally selling insurance and now dedicates all of his time to the network needs of all of his new branches. Bob and his new computer-junkie employees decide that each office should have a dedicated Web server connected to Bob's Insurance, Inc. headquarters through a leased ISDN network. At headquarters, Bob has installed a router (a computer device that does nothing but route data to and from systems on a network) that has an ultrafast T1 connection to MRnet, a non-profit company with even bigger connections to the main Internet hub network.

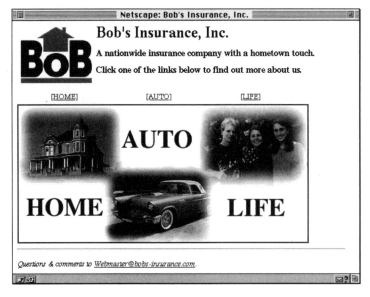

Bob's business has grown so much that he has overhauled both the hardware used to run his Web site and the pages themselves. His baseball information is still on his Web server somewhere, but Bob, Inc. is the real focus of the site.

Finally, thanks to the overwhelming success of Bob's Web site and his com-pany, he moves to a warmer climate and manages his business over the Net. Plus, he is able to realize a life-long dream: he buys his *own* minor league base-ball team!

ORGANIZATION OF THIS BOOK

This book will tell you how to do just about everything Bob did. The first four chapters provide an introduction to the Internet and the World Wide Web. The next five chapters describe basic Web server information that is common to all computing platforms, as well as specific instructions for your platform. Finally, the last five chapters will show you how to create an attractive Web site, tell the world about it, and then make it even better.

- Chapter 1 is an overview and history of computer networks, the Internet, and the World Wide Web — what they are, how they were developed, and how they work.
- Chapter 2 provides a brief introduction to *using* the World Wide Web, for those who are new to cyberspace.
- Chapter 3 answers the burning question, why should *you* create a Web server? To give you some ideas, it also shows you some examples of interesting things people have put on the Web.
- Chapter 4 is the "quick start" chapter, with a step-by-step procedure for getting an account on the Internet and learning your way around, plus how to get started creating your own Web pages.
- Chapter 5 covers the fundamentals of Web server hardware and software, and explains some of the terminology used on the Internet.
- Chapter 6 describes the details of data communication services, such as the different types of phone lines and modems. It also explains Internet domain names in detail, tells you why you should get one, and walks you through the process of doing so.
- Chapters 7 through 9 are really the heart of the book. They provide simple yet comprehensive procedures for installing and configuring a Web server on a Macintosh, a PC running Windows 3.1 or Windows 95, or any system running the UNIX operating system (including IBM-compatible PCs). They also include pointers to our favorite freeware and shareware programs that will work with your server.
- Chapter 10 covers good Web site design and presentation, to make your Web pages as attractive, useful, and *compatible* as possible; we'll show you how to tame some oft-abused features of HTML. The most powerful server in the world is useless if nobody wants to look at what's on it.
- Chapter 11 gives you practical and proven advice on publicizing your server throughout the world, and how to find the best audience for your needs.
- Chapter 12 teaches you about CGI: how to install customized applications that work with your server to perform specialized functions such as information gathering, personalized display, and database retrieval. In other words, more than just serving pictures and text.
- Chapter 13 walks you through the basics of creating a few CGI programs from scratch, using the Perl programming language.
- Chapter 14 gives some basic tips for maintaining your Web server while ensuring its security.

At the end of the book are five appendixes which go into a little more detail about some topics that are touched on in Chapters 1 through 14.

- Appendix A is an HTML quick reference guide. You'll probably need to read a couple of Web pages to learn how to string it all together, but this appendix will come in handy when you need to look something up quickly.
- Appendix B is a UNIX quick reference guide. It contains everything you need to know to get *started* using UNIX, and tells you how to find more information. When you first get on the Internet, it is likely that you will have a UNIX account.
- Appendix C is a Perl quick reference. Because of its amazing cross-platform compatibility, Perl is the language you'll use to create customized CGI programs. This appendix is not comprehensive, but it contains enough information to get you going, even if you haven't done any serious programming before.
- Appendix D describes the details of networks and the TCP/IP protocols that are used to construct the underpinnings of the Internet. This information is useful and interesting, but not required reading.
- Appendix E tells you exactly how to install and use the software on the CD that comes with this book.

You can use our CD in any Macintosh, IBM-compatible PC, or UNIX system that has a CD-ROM drive. A number of files on the CD are organized into a miniature Web that you can read locally with your favorite Web browser. The complete contents of the CD are as follows:

- Pages with links to all the Web sites mentioned in the book.
- A nice HTML page that you can use as a template for creating your own pages; see Chapter 10 for details.
- All the sample Perl scripts used in Chapters 12 and 13, and Perl software for Macintosh, Windows, and UNIX.
- Dozens of useful shareware and freeware programs, ready for use on your computer.

If you don't have access to a CD-ROM drive, the CD's Web pages are also on our book's companion Web site, which is available to any Internet user at the following URL:

```
http://www.prenhall.com/~palmer/handbook.html
```

CONVENTIONS USED IN THIS BOOK

In this book, we have adopted a consistent and uniform set of notation conventions. For easy reference, we summarize these notation conventions here.

Italics

Names of variables, or "placeholder names," which you substitute with specific values in your system, are generally shown in *italics*. Emphasized or new terms are also in italics.

Constant Width ("Computer" Font)

Information displayed on your computer's screen is shown in a `constant width font (Courier)`. This includes command lines, file and directory names, e-mail addresses, URLs, and HTML tags.

Constant Width Italics

Variable names or information within constant width font that is changed when a user types it is shown in `constant width italics`. For example, in a definition of the syntax for a UNIX command, the arguments specified by the user ("file1"and "file2") are shown in constant width italics:

```
ls -l file1 file2
```

Square Brackets

Optional portions of a command (such as UNIX command line options or arguments) are enclosed in [square brackets].

KEEPING CURRENT

Most of the illustrations in this book were made by taking "snapshots" of the screens of our computers while engaged in various Web-related activities. In the text of the book, we recommend a number of useful resources on the Web, and we include the specific addresses (URLs) of these sites so that you can visit them for yourself. Chapters 7 through 9 mention several shareware and freeware applications, and we list their prices and locations.

To keep our information as fresh as possible, we checked and double-checked all the illustrations and references right up to our last deadline, to ensure that everything was still in the same place it was when we started writing. However, the Web is growing and changing so fast that some of the sites that we show you may have moved or disappeared, and the prices of the software that we recommend may have gone up (or down).

We apologize in advance, but don't be too disappointed. Chances are that there will be even more and better information on the Web by the time you read this book.

If sites have moved, you should be able to find their new homes, either by messages left at the previous location, or by using one of the many helpful searching mechanisms that we describe in the book (see the sections in Chapter 11 about Yahoo, Lycos, WebCrawler, and Alta Vista).

Better yet, we will always have the most up-to-date information available on our book's Web site, which anyone can access 24 hours a day:

```
http://www.prenhall.com/~palmer/handbook.html
```

Send us some e-mail if you like the book!

ACKNOWLEDGEMENTS

Thanks to the following for their valuable contributions:

Jonathan Rice, Robert Denny, Doug McIntyre, Paul Palmer, John Cope, Mike Crowley, Gordon Fink, Jeff Pomeroy, Chris Palmer, Steven Brenner, Brian Alton, Carrie Helgeson, Holly Moe, Mary Alton, Winternet, McDonald's on Stinson Boulevard, Perkins on Riverside Avenue, and the authors of all the freeware and shareware programs on the CD.

We would also like to extend special thanks to Linda Link for her artwork, and Doug Rau for his technical input.

ABOUT THE AUTHORS

Pete Palmer is a graduate of Ohio State University. He has been a technical writer and programmer in the mainframe computer industry for the past nine years. When not working with computers, he enjoys watching trains with his daughters.

Adam Schneider graduated from the University of California at Santa Cruz and does research in cognitive psychology. He also does independent consulting of various kinds, specializing in Macintosh applications. In his spare time, Adam fiddles around with his guitar and looks for any excuse to play softball.

Anne Chenette has a degree in Russian language and a minor in computer science. She has been a technical writer and UNIX system administrator for 13 years, and has been an active member of the Internet community since 1984. Anne's claims to fame include tap-dancing on the radio and conducting the Minnesota Orchestra.

The Internet And
The World Wide Web

As the Internet grows in size and popularity, it's a good idea to look at what it is and where it came from. This chapter provides you with key conceptual information and a brief history of the Internet. It gives you some perspective about the role your server can play in this new community of computers and networks. You will also see just how significant the introduction of the World Wide Web has been. If you are familiar with this sort of information, or if you are impatient and want to set up your Web server immediately, you can move on to the later chapters.

1.1 NETWORKS AND INTERNETS

A computer network is simply a set of computers and related equipment, linked by some means of communication, and assisted by software that can take advantage of those links. An essential characteristic of a network is that each device, or node, attached to the network has an address. Just as each house, apartment, and office on a street has a distinct address so that mail can be properly delivered to the intended recipient, each network node has an address to which data can be delivered.

A typical office network consists of desktop workstations, printers, and file servers (computers with large, fast disks) linked by cables that run through the building. These might be fiber optic lines, coaxial cable, or "unshielded twisted pair" telephone wiring.

As nodes are added to the network, it soon becomes impractical for each node to have a direct connection to each other one. This is why network planners usually choose one of two other ways of organizing nodes so that their interconnections are indirect. The way in which a network's physical connections are organized is called the network topology.

In the first networking scheme, each computer is connected to its two nearest neighbors (Fig. 1–1). To deliver data from one node to another — for example, a file being fetched from a file server — each node on the network has to pass the information along to its neighbor until the recipient is reached. It's as if the post office delivered all mail for each street to house number 1, and each family had to sort out their own mail and pass the rest of the bundle on to the next house.

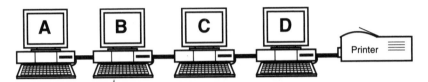

Fig. 1–1   A simple, linear network. If computer A wants to print something, the data must pass through B, C, and D to get there, which requires four hops along the network.

In another common configuration, each node is connected to a central facility, called a hub (Fig. 1–2). Here, it is the job of a central node to act as dispatcher for all of the network traffic.

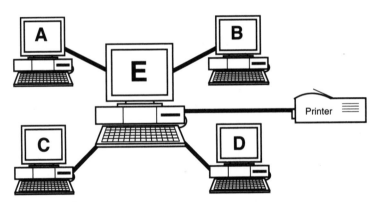

Fig. 1–2   A hub network. If computers A, B, C, or D want to use the printer, they send the data to E, which acts as the network's hub. Any information passed between nodes has to take no more than two steps.

Networking software running on each computer manages the shared resources of the network. One of its principal tasks is to protect end users from the details of node addressing; network resources are presented in a more familiar and consistent way. For example, one job of the networking software might be to make a shared file server appear to each workstation as if it were a local disk drive.

The need often arises for information to be shared among computer networks. It's easy enough to do if the two networks concerned are small, close to each other, and managed by the same organization — you simply hook them together into a single, larger network, and carry on as before.

But if the two individual networks are large; or if they run different network operating systems; or if one is all UNIX workstations and one is all PCs running Windows; or if they're in buildings half a mile or half a continent apart, then it may be difficult to merge them in any coherent way. And if one network is managed by Human Resources and one is managed by Engineering, there may be even more daunting political or organizational difficulties.

The answer in such cases is often to establish an *internet*. (Hey, there's that word that everyone is talking about!) An internet is a link between networks that is analogous to the link between nodes in a network (Fig. 1–3). And, just as there may be many nodes in a network, there may be many smaller networks within an internet. A local network allows information and services to be shared among computers; similarly, an internet allows sharing among networks. There are two important ways, however, in which an internet — a network of networks — is not like a local network of computers.

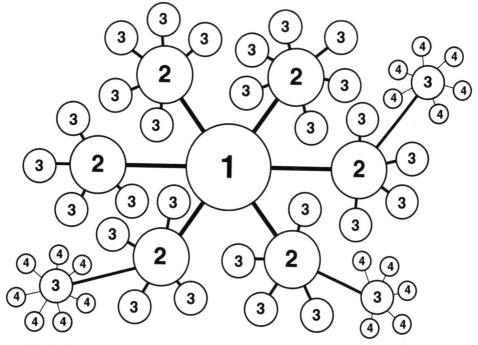

Fig. 1–3 A schematic diagram of an oversimplified internet. Each circle represents a network of some kind. The largest (1) represents the hub of a powerful network of medium-sized networks (2). These in turn have smaller subnetworks branching off of them (3), and some of those are divided even further (4). Eventually, you would get down to small networks that look like Figure 1–1 or Figure 1–2. In a real internet, there would also likely be some connections between the "branches."

First, local computer networks commonly rely on a permanent physical connection — cables running from desk to desk, or from desk to hub. Internet connections may also be "hard wired," especially when the networks are physi-cally close to each other. But, more typically, internet connections involve high speed phone lines leased from common carriers, routed through the public tele-phone network — sometimes these are the same lines you use with your voice telephone, and sometimes they are special high-capacity digital lines.

Second, the aim of a local network is often to make all network facilities available to all users. The design of an internet connection may focus instead on specific services that are required. For example, it may be that the internetwork-ing needs of a firm are limited to e-mail among sales offices; there is never a requirement for someone in the Paris office to use a printer in the New York office. When establishing an internet, the administrators of each network must agree on how tightly enmeshed they will be, and which services will be made available.

1.2 THE INTERNET

In general, an internet is *any* connection among disparate networks that pro-vides an agreed-upon set of facilities and services. Change "an" to "The," how-ever, and suddenly you're not talking about how your co-worker's PC in St. Paul is sharing files with your Macintosh in Minneapolis. You're talking about The Internet, spoken as well as written with capital letters — "The Net," as long-time users call it.

The origin of the Internet can be traced back to the 1960s, when the United States Department of Defense's Advanced Research Projects Agency (ARPA) determined that it would be advantageous for its contractors to communicate in a standard way. Starting at UCLA in 1969, it established an internet of networks at government, university, and commercial sites involved in defense research projects. That internet grew into the Internet of today.

By 1973, the ARPA sites had devised a networking protocol, TCP/IP, that was not tied to a particular computer vendor or platform. TCP/IP was, and remains, the lingua franca of the Internet; implemented on every computer from Compaq to Cray, it provides a common way to pass information from machine to machine.

By the late 1970s, a basic set of Internet services had also been settled upon. These services included the ability to log on to a remote computer system (if one had an account there), a mechanism to transfer files to and from other sites, and electronic mail.

The Internet as we know it today owes much of its universal nature to the merging of the mighty ARPA internet with a more grassroots effort. Usenet, as it came to be called, began in 1979 as a public conference system, similar to private computer bulletin boards, on a few linked sites in North Carolina. Usenet offered a way for people on the Net to exchange information, opinions, and diatribes on a wide variety of subjects. Once Usenet was hooked up to the ARPA sites, it exploded in popularity; now almost anyone could participate in worldwide dis-cussions, not just those involved with defense contracts. Usenet (a.k.a. "Net-

News") now includes thousands upon thousands of discussion topics; so many sites are now hooked up to the former ARPAnet that its military roots are mostly forgotten. The Internet exists as an entity in and of itself.

One of the most fundamental, and, to newcomers, most perplexing characteristics of the Internet is that no single organization manages it. Lotus founder Mitch Kapor calls it "one of the largest successful anarchies" in the world. While ARPA funded and encouraged initial development, the Internet has never been a government-run network — it is a voluntary association of mutually interested sites. Today, ARPA and its successor in Internet history, the National Science Foundation, are out of the picture entirely. The commercial, educational, and government sites on the Internet each fund their participation in whatever way suits them.

There is *some* central planning: the Internet Architecture Board and The Internet Society help to guide the development of Internet standards and protocols, and InterNIC (Network Information Center) makes sure that Internet sites around the world have unique addresses. But there is no central authority; rather, proposed changes and new standards are published to the Internet at large, and anyone is welcome to comment. It is revealing that Internet standards are identified by the letters RFC and a number; a "Request For Comment" is the closest thing to a decree that the worldwide community of sites is willing to produce.

Today, more than 100 countries and territories have full access to the Internet; at least 50 more have electronic mail systems reachable from the Internet. Because there is no central authority, there is no "official" count of the number of people who use the Net, but reasonable estimates (as of early 1996) are in the range of thirty million people. (Estimates that this number could reach 100 million by the turn of the century may sound extreme, but they are not insupportable.) The Net was once oriented very much toward research and education, but at least two thirds of Internet sites are now commercial organizations.

The most striking development in the recent history of the Internet, however, is not its growth in sites and users, nor the astounding exposure it has had in the mainstream press since 1992. It is instead a very subtle shift in the roles of Internet site administrators and users. That shift changed the way that information is discovered and disseminated on the Net, and holds the promise of being as sweeping and unpredictable an innovation as moveable type.

The engine of that change is called the World Wide Web.

The Internet Before the World Wide Web

Let's start by looking at the state of the Internet in 1992, just before the World Wide Web crept in with its subtle paradigm shift. The principal services that people used were:

- Telnet, rlogin, and rsh — programs that allowed authorized users to log in to remote computer systems.
- UUCP and FTP — facilities for transferring files between systems.
- Usenet — the topic-specific discussion "newsgroups."

Suppose you had access to the Internet from your desktop computer, and you wanted to find, for example, the U.S. Consumer Price Index for the past ten years. What would you do?

Odds are that telnet or rlogin wouldn't be of any help. Unless you happened to have an account at a remote site that was a repository of economic data, the ability to log in to a distant computer wouldn't be useful.

File transfer facilities might be useful, though. Because most Internet sites allow access to some files without prior account validation — a practice known as *anonymous FTP* — getting a file from another Internet site is fairly simple to do. All you need to know is the Internet address of the remote site, and the name of the file you want — in this example, the Consumer Price Index history.

Therein lies the difficulty. Of the thousands of Internet sites, which ones store historical economic data on-line, in that portion of their file systems accessible to anonymous FTP? We don't know that *any* do! In the unregulated community of Internet sites, there is no true index, no scheme for browsing. Without a site address and a file name, FTP is powerless.

Usenet might provide some relief, provided that you can find a newsgroup applicable to your quest. There are at least eight newsgroups related to economics, so one of them might offer some tips (but which one?). Many newsgroups include Frequently Asked Questions articles, posted regularly — perhaps one of those will include pointers to FTP sites with Consumer Price Index data.

So, on the Internet before the World Wide Web, our example quest boils down to this: if there is an applicable Usenet news group, and if you can find an article that pertains to the subject of interest (or if you can post a specific question and get a prompt, correct answer to it); or if there is an Internet site that maintains the data you want, and if it offers anonymous FTP, *and* the data is in a format that your system can use; then you're in luck.

That's difficult enough. Now suppose that, having gone through this entire process just to look at the U.S. Consumer Price Index, you decide that you'll need to compare that with, say, the rise and fall of the Japanese yen. Does all your work buy you anything?

The answer *might* be yes. If the same FTP site at which you discovered the price index data happens to be a repository of other economic data, and if you are able to discover, merely by browsing cryptic file names, the new information you seek, all is well. But if not, the process by which you discovered one repository of economic history gained you little or nothing, for by knowing one source you are no further along the road to finding others.

Finally, consider the flip side of the research problem: publication. Suppose that you have just finished your thesis on pulsars, or a list of recommended software for preschool children, or a new home finance utility for Windows. How do you use the Internet to make your information available to others? Where do you put it? How do you let others know that it's there?

In theory, of course, you could just place the information in files accessible by anonymous FTP from your own Internet site, and then mention their availability on an appropriate Usenet newsgroup. But, in practice, many sites do not allow non-administrative users to place files into their FTP areas. And, because Usenet articles are short-lived, your mention of an interesting program or research paper today won't help someone looking for it a month from now.

Sound frustrating and confusing? It *is*! The problems, then:

- Information is hard to locate.
- Successfully locating one piece of information does not reduce the difficulty of locating other, related ones.
- Publication of new information may be restricted.
- There is no permanent way to advertise that certain information exists.

Prehistory of the World Wide Web

Vannevar Bush, science advisor to President Roosevelt, published an article in the July, 1945 issue of *Atlantic Monthly* entitled "As We May Think," a futurist's vision of developments in the process of thinking. He wrote:

> When data of any sort are placed in storage, they are filed alphabetically or numerically, and information is found (when it is) by tracing it down from subclass to subclass.... The human mind does not work that way. It operates by association. With one item in its grasp, it snaps instantly to the next that is suggested by the association of thoughts, in accordance with some intricate web of trails carried by the cells of the brain.

Bush envisioned a way for everyone to construct a personal library of information. With computers still several years ahead of him, Bush imagined a mechanical desk, called a "memex," that would allow its owner to store microfilm images of interesting books, magazines, and papers, and to link them according to the user's whim — in other words, the relationships between various sources of information, originally present only in the mind of the reader, could be captured, saved, and used again. This vision reflects a deep understanding of how information becomes knowledge: through experience, embodied as relationships among disparate data.

Consider, for example, the human librarian in today's paper library. What makes a librarian useful? Not just the ability to locate a certain book on a given topic, for that's a task that can be largely automated — most modern libraries do, in fact, use computers for cataloging. But a good librarian might say, "If you found that book interesting, here's another one you probably should read." He or she adds their knowledge and experience to raw information.

Vannevar Bush's memex, by treating links on equal footing with information, was an early vision of today's World Wide Web. He proposed that "wholly new forms of encyclopedias will appear." He said that with an interlinked system of information, "the patent attorney," for instance, "has on call the millions of issued patents, with familiar trails to every point of his client's interest." These are exactly the kinds of resources now exploding onto the Web; it merely required fifty years for technology to catch up with Bush's imagination.

The term "hypertext" was coined in 1965 to describe this notion of text containing straightforward links to other information. A better term is "hypermedia," since the linked information need not be text (although the terms are often used interchangeably). In the following years, various applications of hypertext were tested in the computer world, out of sight of most of the general public. Its first use in a non-technical setting was Apple Computer's HyperCard software for the Macintosh, introduced in 1987. HyperCard allowed users to select links in "stacks" of cards that contained information; these links led to other, related cards. It was even possible for Macintosh users to easily create their own HyperCard stacks. However, despite the fact that Apple shipped HyperCard with their system software, it wasn't the revolution they hoped it might be.

1.3 THE ORIGINS OF THE WORLD WIDE WEB

The World Wide Web (also called "WWW" or "The Web"; the terms are used interchangeably) was conceived at CERN, a prestigious particle physics laboratory in Geneva, Switzerland. In 1990, CERN employees Tim Berners-Lee and Robert Cailliau proposed hooking up all the networked computers to a hypertext-based information system. The information would be organized using documents that contained links to related pages, either in the same computer or on another system elsewhere at CERN.

Berners-Lee and Cailliau contrived the system because the massive amounts of data at CERN were accessible to all, but largely unorganized. With hypertext-based information servers and "browser" programs on all CERN workstations, any researcher could quickly and easily access experimental data, software help files, addresses of other personnel, and so on. They called their project the "World Wide Web" because they envisioned that high-energy physics researchers from around the globe would be able to access to files at CERN as well as set up their own servers. Like the Internet at large, there would be no one central computer, no hierarchy; it would be generally anarchistic in form. (Don't picture the World Wide Web as an elegant spider's web, with evenly-spaced, radial spokes; if a spider created the model for the World Wide Web, she must have done it drunk or blindfolded!)

The links on the Web are accomplished by the creation of documents written in the HyperText Markup Language (HTML). HTML is, roughly, a subset of a larger standard called the Standard Generalized Markup Language (SGML). What distinguishes HTML documents from other file formats is that layout of an HTML page is largely determined by the viewing program, not by the author of the document. HTML also allows pictures to be placed among the text, but most importantly, it allows a document to contain "hyperlinks" that point to other HTML documents or even non-HTML files, such as text, pictures, sounds, and movies. An international committee decides on the exact format of HTML directives (actually called "tags"), and they periodically update the HTML standard to incorporate new features.

One of the important characteristics of the newborn World Wide Web was — and is — that the files accessible on the Web can be of almost any format. The server simply sends a file in raw form, and the browser takes care of any conversion. This means that enormous collections of existing material could be placed on the Web with minimal effort. Often, an HTML index file is manually created, but even that is not necessary; a Web server can simply list all the files in a directory and automatically create links to each file.

After CERN built its prototype Web, a few non-physics sites gradually joined the network, and by early 1993 there were a few dozen Internet sites with HTTP servers (HTTP stands for HyperText Transfer Protocol, the file transfer method used with HTML documents). In February of 1993, a team of programmers at NCSA (the National Center for Supercomputing Applications), led by Marc Andreesen, introduced a program called NCSA Mosaic for the UNIX X Windows system (not to be confused with Microsoft Windows; X Windows is the workstation management software used by many programmers). Mosaic made browsing the Web so easy that even people who had little or no experience with computers could do it. More importantly, other information systems, including FTP and Gopher, were accessible with Mosaic; it was "one-stop shopping" for Internet information.

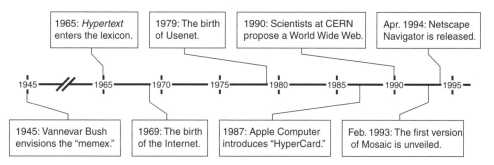

Fig. 1–4   The pre-history and history of the Web, in timeline form.

With the advent of Mosaic for X Windows, the World Wide Web's growth picked up; in June of 1993, there were more than 100 Web servers. Of course, relatively few people had even heard of X Windows, let alone used it, so most people expected interest in the Web to fade. That never happened, however, because in September of 1993, NCSA introduced Mosaic for the Macintosh and Microsoft Windows operating systems. Suddenly, countless people with Internet connections at home, work, and school could access the information on the Web. Many of these people started providing their own informational pages, and more and more sites added servers to store the new influx of data. By the end of 1993, the number of WWW-accessible sites had tripled, and in September of 1994 — one year after the introduction of Mosaic for Windows and the Mac — there were about 4000 HTTP servers around the world, and an estimated two million people were browsing the Web.

In October of 1994, Mosaic got some major competition. By April of that year, Marc Andreesen and some of his NCSA comrades had joined with Jim Clark of Silicon Graphics, Inc., and set up camp in Mountain View, California. Their goal was to provide services related to the World Wide Web, and to create a new and better browsing program, called Netscape. Released in October of 1994, Netscape quickly became by far the most common browser used to navigate the Web. Two strategies helped Netscape accomplish this coup: first, they gave their program away to almost anyone who wanted it; second, they introduced new extensions to HTML that only Netscape could understand. If you wanted to see the latest and greatest Web pages in all their glory, you *had* to use Netscape. The worldwide consortium in charge of writing HTML standards was somewhat annoyed by Netscape's nonconformity, but there was little they could do. Netscape has become the standard Web browser for most users; hence, this book will take most of its "screen snaps" from Netscape, and we will cover many of the Netscape HTML extensions.

Our discussion of World Wide Web browsers thus far has focused on NCSA Mosaic and Netscape; that's because these two programs have been most influential in shaping the Web's initial growth and evolution. It is worth noting that there are a number of other programs out there as well. Most notably, Lynx (pronounced "links" — get it?) is used on many UNIX systems, and is the most common text-based browser; Lynx users cannot view any pictures or other multimedia items contained in Web pages.

In early 1996, Microsoft's Internet Explorer software became freely available to users of most platforms; it is similar in size and scope to the latest versions of Netscape, in that it encompasses Internet services other than just the World Wide Web. Time will tell whether Microsoft can successfully penetrate the Web software market, having entered the playing field so late in the game.

There are also a number of smaller free or inexpensive browser programs, such as MacWeb and Cello, for Macintosh and Windows systems. Their main advantage is that they take up less disk space and memory than the "big" browsers like Netscape. Try them out and decide for yourself which one you want to use.

Overview Of The World Wide Web

Now that you've been introduced to the ideas that led up to the birth of a World Wide Web, we'll take you through a little tour of the things you'll find there. This chapter is meant as a quick introduction for those who are brand new to the World Wide Web. In the next chapter, we'll dig a little deeper and show you some more interesting Web sites; the gory details of how *you* will place information on line will be covered after that.

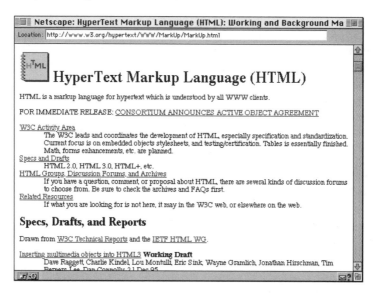

Fig. 2–1 A World Wide Web page. The underlined words and phrases are links.

2.1 EXPLORING THE WEB

Many people like to say that they "surf the Web." That's not really a good analogy, except that Web surfing is somewhat like "channel surfing" with a TV remote control. "Exploring" or "wandering" are better verbs; there's so much material there that it's easy to be led astray, and you'll never find *all* of it. Onward ho!

Pages & URLs

The Web's most important unit is the *page*. A Web page is an HTML document that shows up in a Web browser just like an ordinary document would show up in a word processor. If the page requires more than one screenful of space, you can scroll down using arrow keys or your mouse to see more. Your browser will let you set the default font and size in which you view most of the text on Web pages, but pages can contain instructions to make that text larger or smaller. You can also choose whether you wish to see the images that are embedded in the page, or whether you want the images to be represented by placeholders (usually because you don't want to take the time to download the pictures). There are many files on the Web, such as certain animation or sound formats, which your Web browser will not be able to view at all; however, you can tell your browser which of your programs *can* view those files, and the browser will either save the files for later viewing or launch the appropriate display program.

Every Web page has a *URL*. This stands for Uniform Resource Locator, and it is like the page's address or phone number. Every file — of any kind — has a *unique* URL, and all Web browsers interpret them the same way. Figure 2–1 shows a World Wide Web page; its URL is in the "Location" box near the top of the browser window: `http://www.w3.org/hypertext/WWW/MarkUp/Markup.html`. This URL says, in English, "Please use the HyperText Transfer Protocol (`http`) to access the server run by the World Wide Web Consortium (`www.w3.org`); look in the directory entitled `/hypertext/WWW/MarkUp`, and retrieve the file named `Markup.html`."

Files that are accessed via anonymous FTP also have URLs; they are essentially identical to WWW URLs, except they begin with "`ftp`" rather than "`http`." Even Gopher, Usenet, and telnet services can be accessed via URLs. Compared to "the old days" on the Internet, URLs are truly a wonderful thing. In the past, you had to go through a detailed description of the search process just to tell someone else about a file on the Internet. Now, you can simply give them the URL, and they will have no trouble finding it.

Links

A typical page will have a descriptive title or header that tells you its purpose — if it has one — and it will probably contain a number of words, phrases, or images that are highlighted and/or underlined. These are links, and selecting one will send you to another location; sometimes you will end up at a different point within the same document, or, more likely, you will receive a different document, perhaps halfway around the world. If your destination is a non-HTML file, the file will be displayed or saved by your browser in whatever way is appropriate; but if you follow a link to another HTML file, you might find even more links. After a few clicks, you may find yourself on a page completely unrelated to what you originally set out to find, and you will come to appreciate the size and range (and lack of organization) of the Web.

The following illustrations show how quickly you can get off track. Let's say you just got hooked up to the Internet, and you managed to get a hold of a copy of Netscape that you can run on your Macintosh. And let's say you're interested in comtemporary American folk music; you might first visit a well-known page called "FolkBook," located at Ohio State University. You see that there's a lot of useful stuff here, but the first thing that comes to your mind is, perhaps, "What kind of people would bother to take the time to put this stuff up on the Web?" You see a link that says "Acknowledgements," so you click on it. Figure 2–2 shows what you see.

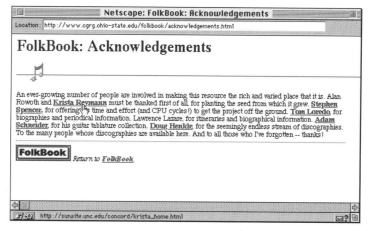

Fig. 2–2   The FolkBook acknowledgements page.

Since you're new to the Web and extremely nosy, you might try clicking on Krista Reymann's name; you will be taken to her personal "home page" (which is in North Carolina, even though Krista lives in California). This is a page that Krista has put together which tells a little bit about her and includes links to some of her interests. Since one of Krista's hobbies is flying, she has included some aviation links on her home page (Fig. 2–3).

Clicking on Krista's "Palo Alto Airport" link takes you, not surprisingly, to a page all about the airport in Palo Alto, California (Fig. 2–4).

From there, you can click on the "Current weather" link, which shows you the latest weather observations in Palo Alto, stored on a Web server in Michigan (Fig. 2–5). The picture at the bottom of the window is a map of North America.

If you were to explore the Interactive Weather Browser page a little further, you would find that you could easily call up the weather for your hometown, or

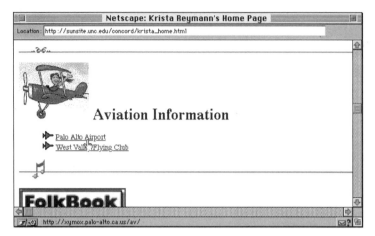

Fig. 2–3   Part of Krista Reymann's home page.

Fig. 2–4   The Palo Alto Airport page.

for anywhere else in the U.S. or Canada. So, although you originally were seek-
ing information about folk music on a server in Ohio, you've traveled to the East
Coast, the West Coast, and then back to Michigan, where you can find out the
current temperature in the Yukon Territory — all from the comfort of your living
room! Personal home pages like Krista Reymann's are an important part of the
Web because they often encompass many different topics; they will expose you to
information you didn't even know you wanted to find.

As you explore, you can usually keep track of where you've been. You can
always go "back" to a page you were on before. Most programs also allow you to
save "bookmarks" or a "hot list" of your favorite Web sites; simply selecting an
item from a list is much easier than remembering URLs.

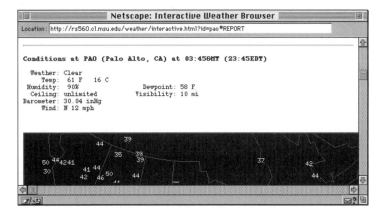

Fig. 2–5 The weather in Palo Alto, California.

Some of the simplest Web pages contain little more than text, pictures, horizontal dividers, and links to other pages. But as the Web continues to grow, and as HTML continues to expand (including the Netscape extensions), more and more World Wide Web developers are creating pages that include such elements as:

- Tables, with columns and rows separated by three-dimensional borders (Fig. 2–6).

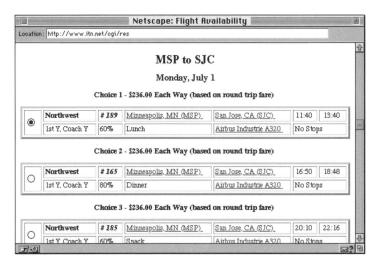

Fig. 2–6 A table in Netscape. This is from a travel-oriented Web site that finds the best air fare for you.

- Input forms with buttons and check boxes for collecting information from Web users (Fig. 2–7).

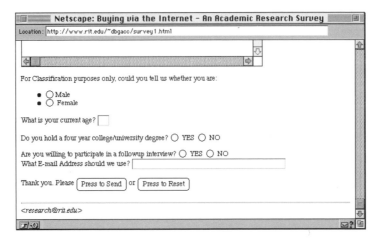

Fig. 2–7 Radio buttons and text forms are one way to collect information from people on the Web.

- Links to programs that return information according to user-specified parameters (Fig. 2–8 and Fig. 2–9).

Fig. 2–8 Clicking the button ("Generate a Generic Country Song") runs a program on a remote site.

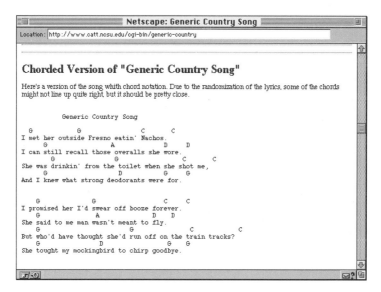

Fig. 2–9 And just for fun, here are the results of clicking the "Generate" button in Figure 2–8!

- Background images or textures (Fig. 2–10).
- Complex layouts that allow text to flow around pictures (Fig. 2–11).

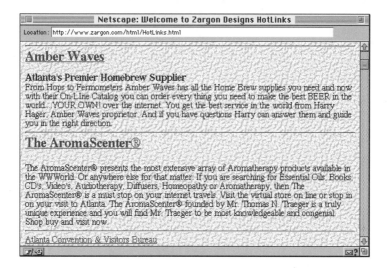

Fig. 2–10 The texture on this page is a "background" image; text and other pictures are placed on top of the texture. This page also demonstrates one of the current trends in Web site development: on-line shopping!

Fig. 2–11   Text flowing around an embedded image. This very nice feature used to be limited to Netscape, but it is now standard.

This list of features is not exhaustive by any means; in fact, the biggest constraint on the appearance of any given Web page is the imagination of the page's author!

HTML

Everything on a Web page is controlled by a *source* HTML document, and your browser will allow you to look at the source of any page you call up. HTML contains special instructions, called *tags*, which are always enclosed in angular brackets (for example, <I>). HTML tags specify all the special attributes of a page, such as links, text styles, image placement and borders, dividers, form input boxes, buttons, and colors. The text itself is the only thing on a web page that is not enclosed in brackets.

Here is a very brief example of what HTML looks like, and what it produces, included here only to give you a sense of what on earth we're talking about:

Source:

```
HTML can easily create <I>italics</I>
and <B>boldface</B> type, as well as
<TT>typewriter-<WBR>style</TT> text.
```

Output:

HTML can easily create *italics* and **boldface** type, as well as `typewriter-style` text.

To a novice browsing the Web, HTML tags are meaningless, and you never have to see them if you do not want to. Of course, if you want to create your own Web pages, you need to learn some HTML, but it is not very difficult. In fact, there are even inexpensive programs available to help you create HTML documents from existing files, quickly and easily. We will cover many details of Web publishing in Chapter 10, and a quick reference guide to HTML tags is available in Appendix A.

New Developments

In addition to the millions of HTML pages on the World Wide Web, browser programs also allow point-and-click access to all the Usenet newsgroups, Gopher servers, and FTP archives, often through HTML interfaces that are much less intimidating than the "old" days of indecipherable file names and command prompts (see Fig. 2–12). You can also send e-mail through your browser, and newer versions of Netscape even allow you to retrieve and store messages!

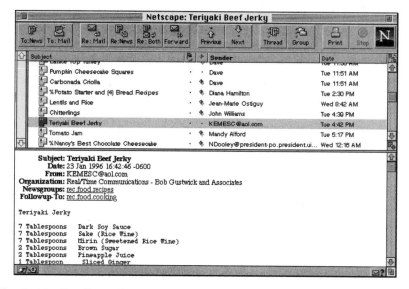

Fig. 2–12   Reading a Usenet newsgroup with the Netscape Web browser.

While we were writing this book, new features were emerging on the horizon. Some of them have already established a firm foothold on the Web, and some have yet to prove their staying power. Here are some interesting items to keep your eye on:

- **Java**: An object-oriented programming language that creates small application programs that can be downloaded and run by Web browsers. See page 311 for more information.
- **JavaScript**: A scripting language in which the code is embedded in HTML files and is interpreted by the browser, allowing the browser to perform tricks like scrolling banners across the bottom of the screen.

- **Plug-ins**: Third-party extensions to browsing software that allow browsers to display multimedia "Live Objects" such as MIDI files, animation, and speech.
- **Scratch 'n' sniff Web pages**: Just kidding.

2.2 SUMMARY

Now you've seen how the World Wide Web started, and what it was supposed to accomplish. You've been given a brief introduction to how it works. So, what have you learned? Is the Internet really that much better, now that we have this new tool for organizing and exploring it? Recall the four problems with pre-Web Internet access that we mentioned in Chapter 1 (page 7); while the Web has not completely eliminated these issues, it has certainly provided some solutions, and it holds the promise of helping even more in the future:

- *Information is hard to locate.* The World Wide Web offers a number of indexing or "yellow pages" services, as well as several that will search more than 90% of the Web for key words or phrases. If it's out there, chances are you'll be able to track it down. (See Chapter 11, pages 274-278, for details about some of these searching mechanisms.)
- *Successfully locating one piece of information does not reduce the difficulty of locating other, related ones.* On the Web, one relevant piece of information almost always leads to related sources, and those sources lead to others. Now, the problem is not that information is hard to find, but rather that resources explode exponentially as one follows link after link.
- *Publication of new information may be restricted.* Almost all commercial Internet service providers allow ordinary users to create Web pages, accessible from anywhere. If your provider doesn't have Web space for you, it's easy to find one that does.
- *There is no permanent way to advertise that certain information exists.* There are a number of services whose sole purpose is to catalog the Web (see Chapter 11); these same services are where you look to find things. Once the existence of a Web page has been advertised, links to it will be forged by other people with a common interest. And, because other links point to those links, new pages are fully incorporated into the Web with astonishing speed. Everyone who shares your interests becomes a potential advertiser of your information.

The World Wide Web has made its revolutionary mark through small changes in the character of the Internet — first, by granting every *user*, not just every site administrator, the ability to publish as well as to seek information; and second, by exposing and emphasizing relationships among data.

The Internet user no longer needs to know where to go to find something out. It is sufficient to know simply where to find some related information, another Internet user with a similar interest, or an index or search service. Once you find what you're looking for, you can relate it to your own special knowledge and interests. And you can publish that relationship on your own Web pages, so that the next person to search is rewarded by your added insight. Vannevar Bush would undoubtedly be impressed that his vision of an information system based on relationships rather than categories has been more or less realized. He might even say that exploring the World Wide Web, with all its dead ends, tangents, and unexpected rewards, is not unlike navigating the pathways of the human mind itself.

Why You Should Create A Web Server

*T*here are as many different uses of a Web server as there are sites on the Internet. Web pages are used by individuals, organizations, small businesses, and multinational corporations alike to disseminate and gather information. A page on the World Wide Web can reach millions of people around the world, at a comparatively small cost. And this potential audience continues to grow at unbelievable rates.

3.1 WEB SERVERS

A Web server is simply any computer, hooked up to the Internet (or sometimes a local network), that is running software that allows it to dispense and receive data using the HyperText Transfer Protocol.

There are two primary ways to make information available on the Web. The difference between these two methods is like the difference between renting an apartment and buying a house. When you rent, you don't have to do as much maintenance, but you have to abide by certain rules, and you can always be evicted. When you own a house, you have to fix the roof, mow the lawn, and do other maintenance, but you have that comfortable feeling of having a place of your own, and you can do whatever you want — you can paint it pink and green and add on a five-car garage, if that's what you really want.

If you want to "rent," you sign up with a company that provides Internet services, and you get to keep a directory full of Web pages on their system. This method is easier and cheaper, and you can let someone else worry about all the technical details of running a Web server. But what fun is that?

The "buying" method involves creating a Web server of your own. When you own the server, you are responsible for its upkeep, but you are free to do whatever you want with it. You don't have to follow anyone's policies, and you can even choose your own URLs (within certain constraints). We think this is the better way to go, because you will learn a lot about computers and the Internet, and it's a lot more fun.

Actually, to follow this housing analogy all the way through, running your own Web server is probably more like living in a condominium than buying a house, since you still need to go through a service provider to get connected to the Internet (more about this in later chapters).

3.2 HOME PAGES

The most basic use of a Web site is the personal home page. Creating a home page is the logical first step of any Web provider. As you can see in Figure 3–1, a home page can convey any personal and professional information that an individual wants to offer. In this case, Chuck Griffith — an Internet user from Minneapolis — includes links to pages relating to his life, opinions, and interests, as well as a "Reference" page that includes links to sites that many other people might find useful.

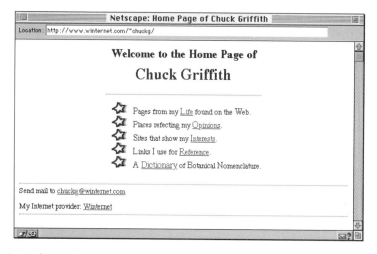

Fig. 3–1   Chuck Griffith's home page.

Another simple example is the Web page of a small business, or a small part of a larger business or organization. Figure 3–2 shows the top of the home page of the St. Croix River Valley Railroad, a passenger rail excursion service operated by the Minnesota Transportation Museum. This page provides a description of the service, links to pictures of the locomotives, a complete schedule of departures, and even a map for getting to the station (Fig. 3–3).

Of course, you may want to drum up business using the Web by actually showing your products and prices. Keeping with the transportation theme, Figure 3–4 shows a page for buying and leasing box cars and parts.

If you need something a little bigger than a railroad car, like maybe a 747, you could try Boeing (Fig. 3–5). Note that while Chuck Griffith, R. G. Mrotek,

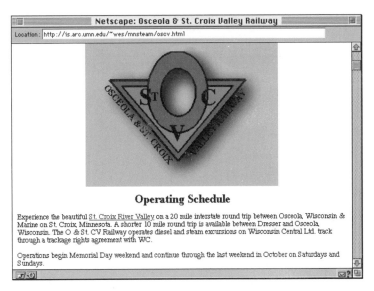

Fig. 3–2 The St. Croix River Valley Railroad's home page.

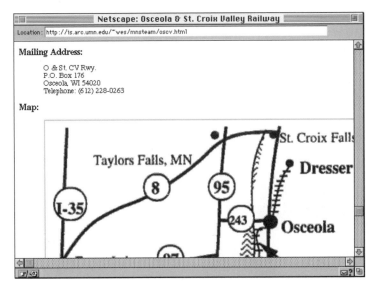

Fig. 3–3 More of the railroad's home page.

and the railroad are all using someone else's system, the URL of Boeing's home page is simply `http://www.boeing.com/`. Boeing has their own Internet domain, and they run their own server. In fact, the Web's influence has become so significant that many large companies pay consulting firms or their own employees specifically to create and maintain their Internet presence.

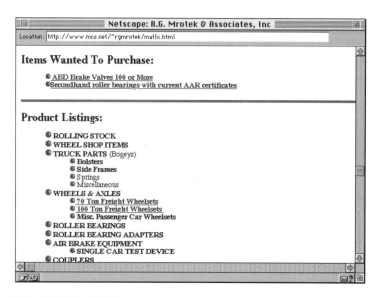

Fig. 3–4   R. G. Mrotek's box car page.

Fig. 3–5   Boeing's home page.

The next section explains the benefits of creating your own personalized Web presence, and all without paying a consultant to do it for you. You'll see examples of effective pages and learn ideas for attracting users to your Web site.

3.3 THE WEB SOLUTION

The World Wide Web is huge, and it is growing all the time. As of early 1996, it was estimated that at least two million people were *directly* connected to the Internet and browsing the Web; you can bet it's a lot more than that now! With the addition of the indirectly-connected users on the major commercial services like America Online, CompuServe, Prodigy, and the Microsoft Network, the number is more like ten million. If you place a page on the Web, every one of those people will be able to view it. (The trick is to make them *want* to view your page; we will discuss this later in this chapter and in Chapter 10.)

If you simply have personal information available that you think other people might like — maybe you have some poetry, reviews, or photographs that you'd like to share — then reaching the maximum number of people may not be your goal. You just want to point interested parties in the right direction. The Web can do that for you. Give the URL of your self-portrait to a pen-pal in New Zealand who wants to know what you look like, and he or she will have no trouble finding your pages. Tell the readers of the Usenet group `rec.climbing` that you have some tips on rock climbing in the Cascades on your pages, and they will get there. If no one ever reads your pages, it's disappointing but not devastating. At least it's good to know that you have contributed something to the world-wide body of knowledge, your little roadside stand on the information superhighway.

But if you own a business, you want to reach as many people as possible. You would love it if all ten million Web surfers stopped by your site every day to see what you had to offer. You can publish your complete catalog of products or services on your Web pages, and you can even take credit card orders. The Web can take your business into new markets you never even considered; people in Miami don't read the Denver yellow pages, but there's no reason for them to only shop at local Web sites. You may even need to consider how you're going to handle all those international orders!

The World Wide Web is well-suited for customer service. If your business runs a "help line" related to your products or services, you may have noticed that the same questions get asked over and over. If you publish the answers to those frequently asked questions on a Web page, you won't have as many people calling your support line; this could save you time and money. Moreover, the Web is accessible 24 hours a day, 365 days a year (as long as the server is running!). And the information can be changed continually, so it will never be out of date. If people have further questions, you can set up a form that they can e-mail to you. If people have suggestions, you can make it very easy for them to give their input; people are more likely to send comments via e-mail than by regular mail or by phone. In short, the World Wide Web makes it much easier for businesses and organizations to communicate with their customers and members. And the communication is instantaneous, inexpensive, and international.

Of course, it is important to remember that while the Web might offer you time- and money-saving conveniences, it will cost you — in technology and labor — to get a Web site up and running. You should think about how in-depth you want your Web presence to be, and how much you are willing to do to keep it going.

Many businesses are simply renting disk space on someone else's Web server to publish single-page advertisements, which don't generate much interest — if any — in repeat visits. You want your Web presence to be better than that. Having a single Web page is like having a small one-line entry in the phone book. To really grab people and make them want to visit your site, you need to do more. You need good-looking pages that give something back to the reader. You want people to tell their friends and colleagues about your pages.

Your goal is to end up as a link on other pages, even pages that have nothing to do with your business. Let's say that you own a company that makes fishing equipment. Now let's say there's a Web-browsing real estate agent in Little Rock who likes to go fly fishing. If your company puts together a fantastic page devoted to fly fishing, including "how to catch 'em" tips and links to other fishing-related sites — as well as information about ordering from your company — our hypothetical angler might add your page to her list of "favorite links" on her home page. Now, anyone looking to buy a house in Arkansas might discover your pages, and if they like what they see, you'll end up on *their* lists as well.

The fastest-growing portion of the World Wide Web is businesses setting up home pages. If you are wondering whether it is worthwhile to get started right now on putting together a Web site, just remember that you probably have a lot of competitors who are wondering the same thing. It is in your best interest to get on the Web as soon as possible. But it's more important to do it well.

3.4 WHAT YOU CAN DO WITH THE WEB

In later chapters, you'll learn how to get an Internet account that will let you browse the Web, how to install the necessary hardware to have your own server, and how to build an effective set of pages. For now, we will provide some examples of what you can do with the World Wide Web.

Multimedia Presentation

We have already shown you Web pages that display text and pictures. Figure 3–6 shows a page that has more complex multimedia links. If you click on the musical note icon, you will download a half-minute audio sample of a Patty Larkin song. Similarly, clicking on the movie camera will get you a clip from a music video. If you have your Web browser configured properly, and have the necessary software, you can view these clips as soon as they have finished downloading.

The Patty Larkin page happens to illustrate still another graphical element found on World Wide Web pages: the group of arrow buttons on the left is an *image map*. An image map appears on the screen just like any other linked image, but different parts of the image send you to different places.

Figure 3–7 is a very literal example of an image map. Clicking on the map will get you a list of publicly available NASA Space Shuttle photographs of

Fig. 3–6 A record company's page that advertises musician Patty Larkin's *Angels Running* album.

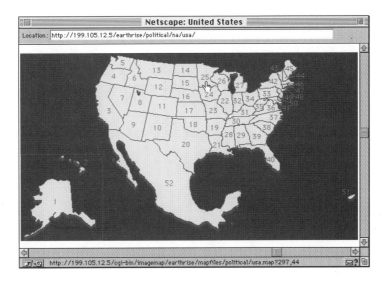

Fig. 3–7 A clickable image map of the United States.

whichever state you clicked on; in this example, we have clicked on the authors' home state of Minnesota. Figure 3–8 shows the list of images.

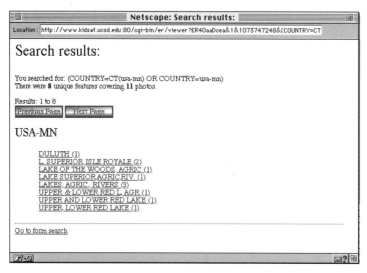

Fig. 3–8   The list of Space Shuttle photographs of Minnesota. We were led to this page after clicking on the outline of Minnesota in Figure 3–7.

Image maps are a clever way to present various kinds of multimedia information, but they are also an example of a simple software program running on a Web server. We will have more to say about programs like this after the following section on databases.

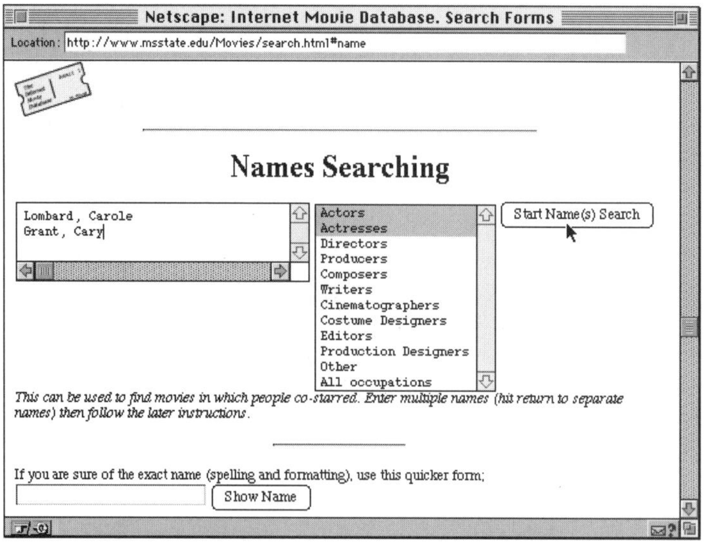

Fig. 3–9   The search form for the Internet Movie Database.

Databases

If you have a large amount of information in a database, you might want to set up a Web page that includes an interface to search that information. The "Internet Movie Database," pictured in Figure 3–9, is a good example. Type the name of any person in the movie industry, click a couple buttons, and you are shown a list of every film they were involved with. In our example, we've selected two names, Carole Lombard and Cary Grant.

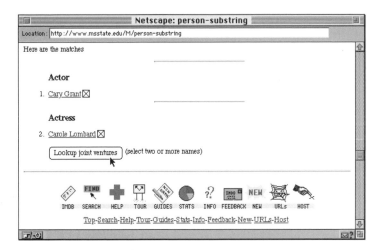

Fig. 3–10   The Internet Movie Database search process.

When we click on the "Start Name(s) Search" button, we are given the search results (Fig. 3–10), with an option to cross-reference the actors by selecting both check boxes. A program on the remote Web server checks through the entire database and quickly returns a list of links to three movies that starred both Grant and Lombard (Fig. 3–11). Finally, we can view all kinds of information about any of the films on the list (Fig. 3–12).

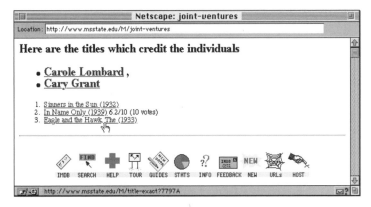

Fig. 3–11   Results of a search in the Internet Movie Database.

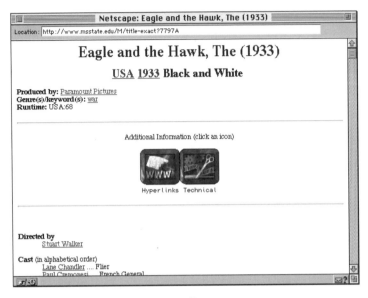

Fig. 3–12   An Internet Movie Database film entry.

Another well-known and widely-used example of an existing database on the World Wide Web is the HTML interface to Webster's Dictionary (Fig. 3–13). You can look up any word in the dictionary, and when the definition comes back (Fig. 3–14), you can click on any of those words as well. You could follow the links all the way through the entire English language!

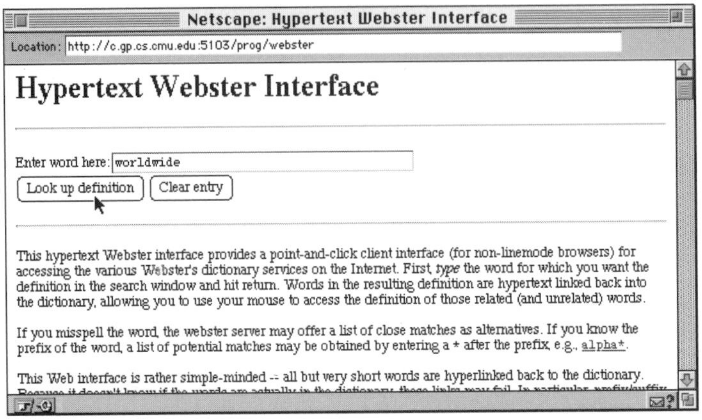

Fig. 3–13   WWW interface to Webster's Dictionary.

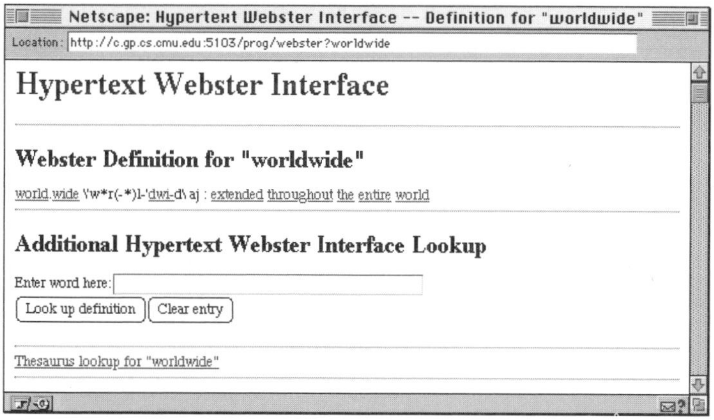

Fig. 3–14 The results of looking up the word "worldwide" in the on-line Webster's Dictionary.

Software

There are literally unlimited ways to make software available on the World Wide Web, so a discussion of all applications would be impossible. However, we will show you two examples of businesses with software on the Web. In your explorations, you will doubtless find many more.

Since World Wide Web browsers can access FTP archives as well as hypertext pages, users of the Web can access incredible amounts of data in the form of documents and software programs that they can download and use on their personal computers. But, as mentioned in Chapter 1, finding a file in an FTP site is often an arduous journey; using the Web, you can spare people from the maze of directories and incomprehensible file names like "`pw31_06.rev`" that make up many archives. If you have software that you want to make available, you can allow people to download it simply by clicking a link on a Web page.

If you would rather leave your software in an FTP site, so that it is accessible via "normal" FTP functions as well as Web browsers, that's fine. You can still provide user-friendly Web links to the files. Even a single hypertext page that does nothing but serve as an introduction and index — a "front door" — to an FTP site is preferable to making someone plunge straight into an archive.

Another way to use software on the Web is to allow people to use the programs without actually downloading a copy. You can set up pages that send instructions to your Web server to run a program under certain parameters. The output of the program is then sent back to the user on a new hypertext page.

As an example, Letraset, a graphic supplies company, has a Web site that allows you to download a "free font of the month" to use on your computer (Fig. 3–15). They have created an excellent Web site that gives something back to the Internet community. Furthermore, because they change the free font every month, people will return to their site in the future — it is a safe bet that people

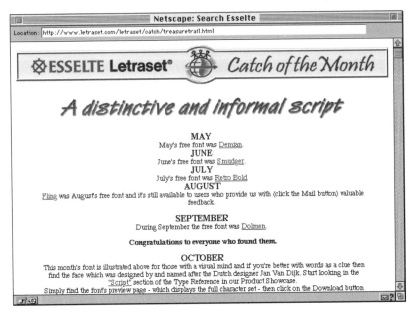

Fig. 3–15 Letraset's "Catch of the Month" page.

Fig. 3–16 Letraset's "Ripper" program that allows you to see how some of their fonts look.

having no official connection to Letraset have added this nifty site to their hot lists and home pages.

If the free font wasn't enough, they also allow you to try out a number of their typefaces by displaying text of your choice in that font (Fig. 3–16). It is a very fancy example of running a remote program via an interface on a Web page.

Our second illustration of software on the Web is a mortgage company in New York. Their site is somewhat different from Letraset's, because while they have software to download and use on their pages, they are not in the business of selling software; they are simply using it as an effective marketing tool. They also differ from Letraset in that they do not run their own server; they are using space on www.moran.com. (Smaller businesses are more likely to take this route.)

On one page in Spectrum's Web site, there is a detailed form where you list your income, your debt, your taxes, etc. (Fig. 3–17). After you submit the form, their computer will send you e-mail with an analysis of the kind of mortgage you can obtain.

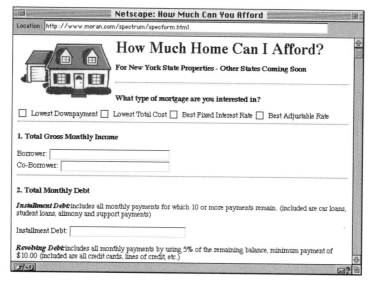

Fig. 3–17   Spectrum Mortgage's customized financial analysis.

Another page contains a DOS-compatible program called the "Loan Prepayment Analyzer." You can click on the disk icon to download the program and later run it on your personal computer (Fig. 3–18).

Spectrum has even thoughtfully provided the utility ("PKZip") needed to unpack their software, in case you did not already have it (Fig. 3–19). By providing so many helpful tools, they ensure that people will visit their site and recommend it to others.

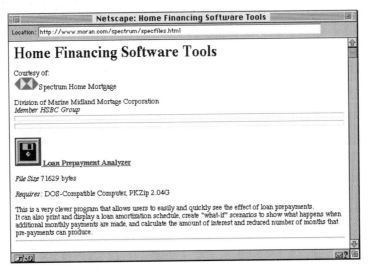

Fig. 3–18   Spectrum Mortgage's software, which they have made available for downloading.

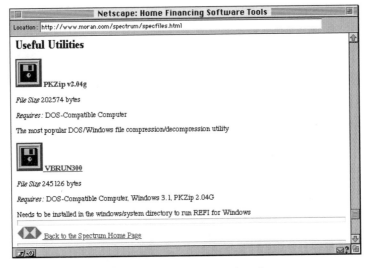

Fig. 3–19   Helper utilities for Spectrum Mortgage's software.

Communications

Talking about "communication" on the Internet may seem redundant, since the core of everything on the Net boils down to communication. But here we are referring to personal communications. As we have briefly seen already (in Figure 3–17 above, and Figure 2–7 on page 16), you can set up forms and buttons to collect information from people. But you can also use Web pages to send e-mail messages, virtual postcards, or whatever else creative Web designers have dreamed up.

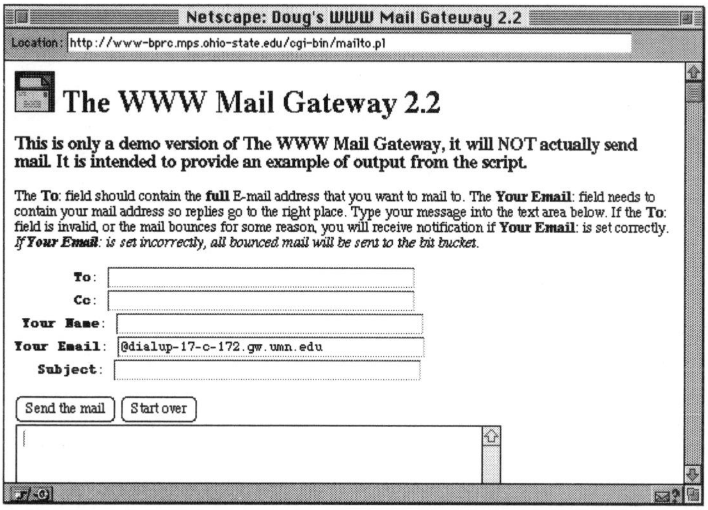

Fig. 3–20 Doug's WWW Mail Gateway.

There are many ways to use the Web as a messaging system, but we will illustrate the idea with one particular example. "Doug's WWW Mail Gateway" (Fig. 3–20) is a program — written in the Perl programming language — that anyone can use to send mail to anyone else. It used to be that you didn't even need to have the program on your own server — you simply created a link on your Web pages that specified the sender, the recipient (it doesn't even have to be you) and the subject of the message, and you could use Doug's server to run the program. Unfortunately, Doug's server got a little overwhelmed by people all over the world using it, so you now have to copy the program onto your own server. This is actually quite easy; we will tell you exactly how to set up Perl scripts on your system later in this book.

If Doug's program doesn't meet your exact needs, there are many others like it that are available for free or for a nominal charge. You could even write your own!

As we have seen, the World Wide Web presents a wonderful opportunity for you or your organization to present yourself to the world. The next chapter will walk you through the major steps toward actually establishing yourself on the Internet and the Web.

Quick Start Guide
To The Internet
And The Web

*I*f you are new to the Internet and the World Wide Web, the first thing you should do is get a user account with an Internet service provider. While this book is focused on serving information rather than retrieving information, the only real way to know what you can provide to the rest of the world is to become familiar with this dynamic new frontier.

This chapter will walk you through the basic steps for getting your feet wet on the Web. If you already have an account with full Internet access, you can skip over this section or use it as a refresher.

Once you have become acquainted with the contents of this chapter, you will be more than ready to present information on the Web through a user account on an Internet provider's system. Keep in mind that this is not the same as having a dedicated Web server, but you will need to understand all of the information presented here when you create your own server.

Of course, you could *immediately* buy all of the necessary computer equipment, software, phone connections, and so on to become a Web server, but this would be very difficult even for the most industrious individual. The best approach is to follow a step-by-step plan that will educate you as you go and spare you unnecessary expenses.

4.1 TYPES OF INTERNET SERVICE PROVIDERS

Unless you currently have your own direct connection to the Internet, you will need to get a user account from an Internet service provider (ISP). There are many, many different types of accounts available from various types of companies. As you read in Chapter 1, there is no "Internet, Inc.," or central organization. Users "get on the Net" through independent providers that have an

Internet connection of some sort. You will be a user on their computer system, connected via modem from your own system.

These days, there are a variety of ways to get an Internet account. An account can range from a simple e-mail address and access to Usenet newsgroups (more on that later) all the way to an unlimited, real-time Internet connection. Of course, you usually pay proportionately for the increase in features.

Educational Accounts

If you are affiliated with a college or university, contact your school's computer center and inquire about account availability. Most institutions of higher education have full Internet connections, and many schools give free accounts to students and employees; this is the cheapest way to get hooked up. If you have graduated, you may be able to purchase an account at a good price — ask your school's computer center or the alumni association. Also, more and more high schools and even some elementary schools are getting Internet access.

Employer Accounts

If you are not involved with an educational institution, see if accounts are available at your place of employment. There has been tremendous growth in the number of businesses that offer Internet services to their employees. It is very common these days for business cards to include not only a person's name and phone number, but also an e-mail address.

FreeNets and BBSs

The next cheapest way to get a basic account is through a FreeNet or a Bulletin Board Service (BBS). FreeNets are popping up in many major markets; to see if there is one in your area, call your local library. Libraries are usually among the first sites on a community-based FreeNet. Almost every community has a number of BBSs, and many of them are listed in the yellow pages. Pick one, and dial it up with your modem. It is customary for BBSs to keep a list of all of the other BBSs in the area, so you can print out the list and then pick and choose. Most BBSs offer only very limited Internet services, but the cost is quite reasonable.

Commercial Services

Perhaps the easiest (though not the cheapest) way to get an account is through a major commercial provider. Companies such as CompuServe, America Online, Prodigy, and the Microsoft Network are in business to provide you with easy, friendly, and well-supported user accounts. The down side is that if you spend any appreciable amount of time on line, you may end up paying much more than you would with a local, independent provider.

Local Internet Service Providers (ISPs)

Local Internet service providers serve the same purpose as the major commercial services, but they typically cover a much smaller geographical area and have far fewer users. Almost every major population center has a few providers to choose from, and more are popping up every day, even in small towns. Local ISPs give you a choice of various kinds of accounts, with varying prices. Many will also let you get a "dedicated" line through their system; this is more expensive than a regular account, but it is the cheapest way to turn your system into a full-time Web server. (We will have much more to say about ISPs and dedicated lines in the next chapter.)

To find some ISPs in your area, try calling a local college or university's computer science department. Even if they can't help you, they'll know someone who can. If you already have an account that lets you browse the World Wide Web, see if you can track down a complete list of local ISPs; if they're smart, they will all have Web pages about themselves, and most of them will list their rates and terms right up front. You might also want to check out "The List" (`http://www.thelist.com`), which provides information about ISPs all around the world (see page 71).

4.2 TYPES OF ACCOUNTS

A simple user account with a service such as CompuServe or America Online allows you to log into your provider's computer and do things like read your e-mail, read Usenet newsgroups, and surf the Web. An expanded account lets you use your provider's computer as your own (to various degrees). This means that your provider sets aside data storage space that you and other people around the world can access at any time, night or day. You are still using your provider's equipment and programs, but you can learn a lot about the fundamentals of being an information server.

Shell Accounts

The most common expanded user account is a shell account. If you are connecting to one of the common commercial services from your home computer, you may not even know that you have a shell account, because you are given interface software to run on your Windows or Macintosh system that protects you from all the crude commands of the provider's computer. Nonetheless, you are a still a remote user logged into your provider's computer (see Figure 4–1 for a illustration of this process).

Because most ISPs use some variety of the UNIX operating system, you will need to become familiar with UNIX basics. But don't worry, you will really only need to learn a few commands for copying, editing, and transferring files to and from your own computer. For your convenience, we have included a UNIX quick reference guide in Appendix B of this book.

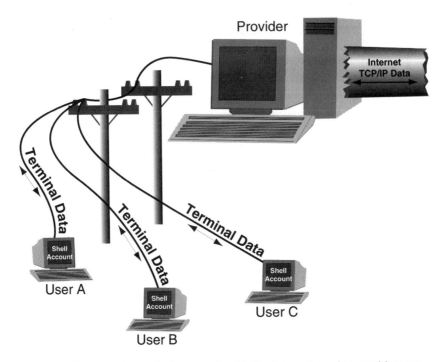

Fig. 4–1 The users have shell accounts with the Internet service provider; programs are run on the provider's system, and no matter how powerful the computers on the other end are, they act as "dumb terminals."

When you log into a shell account, you are initially placed in your *home directory*. Your provider usually sets aside a certain amount of disk storage space for you to use, probably in the range of two to five megabytes (your mileage may vary). This is where you will keep your files.

If you are an MS-DOS user, you are already familiar with command line prompts and hierarchical file systems (although you should note that UNIX uses a "front" slash, not a backslash, to separate directories). Macintosh and Windows users may need a little more time to become acclimated to text-based directories rather than graphical folders. Figure 4–2 shows a sample of a session in a UNIX shell account.

Learning to use a shell account may seem at first glance like a lot of work. But the best way to understand all of the Internet user programs and utilities is to explore beyond the fancy interface — look under the hood! All the time you spend futzing around with your shell account will be a valuable education.

SLIP/PPP Accounts

The latest services gaining popularity are SLIP (Serial Line Internet Protocol) and PPP (Point-to-Point Protocol). The two protocols are extremely similar and provide essentially the same type of connection.

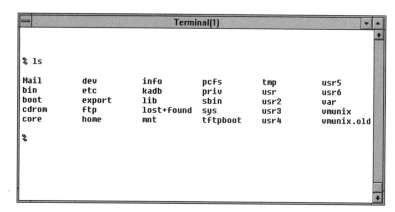

Fig. 4–2 A UNIX shell account. The `ls` command that has been typed here is equivalent to `dir` in MS-DOS.

There is a big difference between a shell account and a SLIP/PPP account. With a shell account, you are a remote user on another computer system. Except for your terminal emulation software, you use the computing resources of that other system. Nothing runs locally on your machine. When you ask for a directory listing, the result is a list of files in the current directory on the other computer, not your own. It is very important to understand this.

With a SLIP/PPP account, your provider simply gives you a connection, or pipe, to the rest of the world (using the TCP/IP standard, which we describe in Chapter 6 and Appendix D). This means that all of the computing work is done on *your* system, not your provider's. You need to have all of the required software on your own computer. Your provider simply plays the role of "data traffic cop" — all of the information that you and your computer request from or provide to other computers around the world is passed through your provider's lines (Fig. 4–3). Keep in mind that your provider probably has another provider upstream from them, who, in turn, has a provider upstream from *them*, and so on.

When you create your own Web server, it is likely that you will have a SLIP or PPP connection, at least for prototyping your system. Most SLIP/PPP accounts also come with a shell account, so you get "the best of both worlds."

Using a SLIP/PPP connection is popular among Net users partly because it is faster than being a remote user on another system, and partly because people are much happier using their systems' graphical interfaces than the text-based UNIX environment. There is already user-friendly, feature-filled, stable software for every popular computing platform.

While SLIP/PPP accounts have many advantages for creating, running, and accessing a server, they are not very well suited for learning the detailed technical skills necessary for developing the server. This might sound odd, but your best learning path is to use your shell account and see what is in the guts of a fully functional Web server, before you configure your own computer system and plug it into the world.

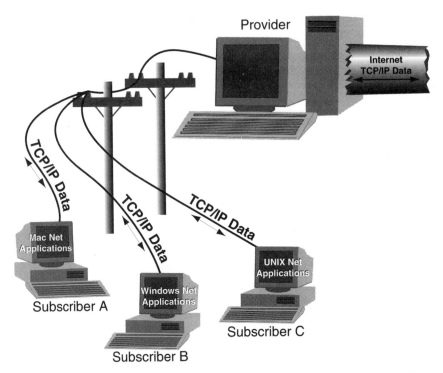

Fig. 4–3 The users have SLIP/PPP accounts with the Internet service provider. Programs are run on the users' systems; the provider simply transmits TCP/IP data back and forth.

4.3 CHOOSING A PROVIDER

If you can get an account for free, be it through school, work, or a FreeNet, you might as well do it. Spend some time getting acquainted with e-mail, Usenet, and whatever other features your account includes. With a free account, you have nothing to lose by doing a little research before you get yourself fully connected. But you will probably soon "outgrow" your limited account. You may be able to set up Web pages using a student or employer account, but you will not be able to use their system as a full-time server. Not only is this technically difficult or impossible, it may also be against their "acceptable use" policies.

Eventually, you will need to go through an Internet service provider and get an expanded account that includes *at least* a shell and probably SLIP or PPP. For financial reasons, a local commercial provider is probably your best bet. Many of these providers allow you to pay a flat monthly fee for unlimited connect time. This is what you want; any metered service adds up *very* quickly. When you do your "shopping," find out what their exact rates are, which Internet services are available, and how much space they will give you to store your files. (Chapter 6 has more information on the services you need to support a Web server.)

4.4 ACCOUNT REQUIREMENTS

No matter which provider you sign up with, you should be sure that your first account has the services listed below (at the very least). This is essential for a couple of reasons:

- These services are the basic tools for using the Internet. If you don't know how to use them, you will severely limit your ability to access all of the information available to you.

- These services are incorporated into virtually all World Wide Web navigation programs. Knowing the function of each of them will maximize your options when you go to create Web pages.

If, once you get an account, you need help finding or using these tools, look for on-line help or ask your system administrator to point you in the right direction. There are also many books, available at any library or bookstore, that will walk you through the details of these basic Internet services.

Electronic Mail (E-Mail)

This is the most basic and universal of all Internet services. E-mail is simply a letter typed into a computer and sent to another user on the Internet. By definition, every account on the Net has an e-mail address (which looks something like `yourname@your-provider.com`) and a means to send and receive mail.

Usenet News

To recap the brief description from Chapter 1, Usenet is a hierarchically organized collection of thousands of "newsgroups," each of which is devoted to a single topic; some groups cover a broad range of subjects, while others have a very specific focus. Some groups are "moderated," meaning that all articles must by screened by someone before they are released to the world. But most are unmoderated; anyone with an Internet connection can post articles to these groups.

Because there is so little control over the content, many newsgroups tend to have a very low "signal-to-noise" ratio. But some newsgroups are better than others, and many contain interesting and worthwhile discussions. Usenet newsgroups are also great places to go to request information, but only if you've already exhausted other resources, such as the World Wide Web; Usenet readers get very irritated when newcomers ("newbies") ask simple questions that they could have easily answered themselves if they looked hard enough, especially in the Frequently Asked Questions (FAQ) files.

For a tongue-in-cheek introduction to proper Internet decorum, look up "Emily Postnews" on the Web at `http://www.clari.net/brad/emily.html`. We will have more to say about "netiquette" in Chapter 11.

FTP

An account with FTP (File Transfer Protocol) capability will let you connect to any FTP site in the world and download files of all kinds, including software that you can run on your machine. Once you know how to use FTP, you can download anything else you might possibly need. For instance, if you started with nothing but a terminal emulation program, you could dial in to your shell account, then use FTP to download software that would let you use SLIP or PPP. Once you have SLIP or PPP, you could use an FTP program on your own system to copy files from around the world directly onto your hard drive.

Telnet

Telnet allows you to log in to other computers, usually using an account on the remote system. If you start with a SLIP/PPP account, you will most likely use a telnet program to get into your shell account. There are a few services you can access via telnet that do not require a login name and password (for instance, weather forecasts), but those are becoming increasingly rare as information is made available on the World Wide Web.

Gopher

Like some telnet services, Gopher is quickly being driven into the background by the Web. It is a text-based, menu-driven system that allows easy access to large amounts of information in the Internet. Many schools and companies have set up Gopher servers devoted mostly to information about themselves, but with some menu items pointing to other Gopher servers around the world. Your provider's Gopher server, if it has one, is often a good source for help files and phone numbers. Generally, individual users are not allowed to make files available in Gopher, so its scope is somewhat limited.

Having access to Gopher is not really a prerequisite to being an information provider, but it can't hurt — you want to be able to learn about as many facets of the Internet as possible.

World Wide Web

To start establishing your presence on the Web, you *must* get an account with a provider that will give you "Web space" on their system: a place to store files that can be accessed by people around the world using HTTP. If you are getting a shell account only, be sure that you will be able to use a text-based Web browser such as Lynx. (With a SLIP or PPP account, you will use your own browsing software that runs on your personal computer.)

4.5 STEP-BY-STEP EXAMPLE

Now that you are familiar with all of the basic concepts leading up to providing information to the Web, let's walk through an actual start-up procedure. The following steps are explained in this section:

1. Testing your hardware setup
2. Finding an Internet service provider
3. Getting going — using your ISP's system
4. Testing your account
5. Creating a home page on the Web

For this sample, we assume that you have a personal computer, a modem, and at least one local Internet provider in your area, but no account yet.

Testing Your Hardware Setup

Our personal computer in this example is an MS-DOS-based PC with a 486 processor and a 14.4k bps modem. We must confirm that our equipment setup is functioning properly by using our communications software to connect to a known, free location. To do this, we call up the St. Paul Public Library's on-line catalog (Fig. 4–4); you can find your library's dial-up number in your local phone book. To ensure that our terminal emulation software is functioning properly, we perform a title search. Figure 4–5 shows the results of that session.

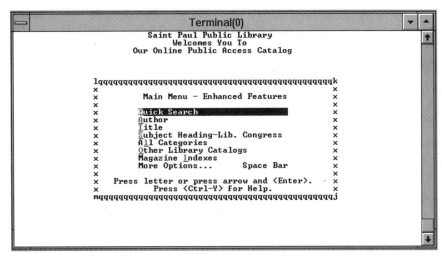

Fig. 4–4 The St. Paul Public Library's on-line catalog.

Now that we are satisfied that our communications system is fully functional, we can move on to the next step.

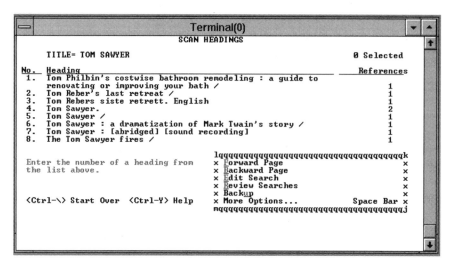

Fig. 4–5   The title search for Tom Sawyer at the St. Paul Public Library.

Finding an Internet Service Provider

We took our own advice about finding an ISP — we located a system administrator at the University of Minnesota by simply calling the Computer Science Department. Of course, it took a few transfers and a few minutes on hold, but we finally reached the right individual, and we asked him if he had the names and numbers of any local Internet service providers. He gave us a few numbers to call.

We talked to each of the ISPs using our "checklist" of required services from section 4.4. We told them we were looking for an expanded user account that provided a command shell, e-mail, and Usenet news, as well as telnet, FTP, and WWW services. We also asked about the availability of file storage space on their system (to allow others access to our files via FTP or the Web). All three providers had these services at about the same price. We chose Winternet because they were highly recommended by the system administrator at the University.

Winternet allowed us to log into their system as a guest to sign up for an account (Figure 4–6). This took only a few minutes. Upon receiving our application, a Winternet operator called us back and told us that in 15 minutes our account would be ready to use. We gave them an initial password that we liked (of course, we changed it as soon as we logged in, to keep it secret), and we were finished.

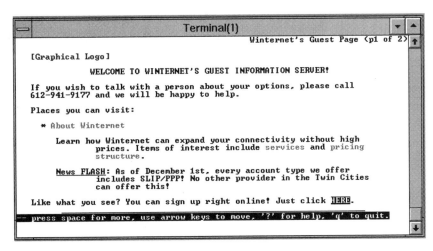

Fig. 4–6 The sign-up option from Winternet's guest menu.

Getting Going — Using Your ISP's System

Once signed up, we dial Winternet's number with our terminal program; after our modem negotiates a connection, we are immediately prompted for our login name and password (Fig. 4–7).

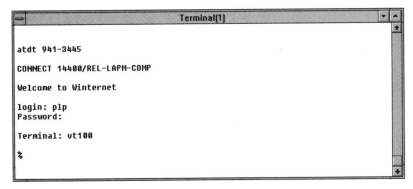

Fig. 4–7 Logging into an Internet service provider's system from a PC.

We are then given a UNIX prompt from our command shell. When we originally signed up, we were given a choice between the most common UNIX command shells. We choose the C shell because it looks and acts much like the MS-DOS command line environment.

At this point, we should point out that we are familiar with the basic commands and utilities available on a UNIX system. If you are not, Appendix B should get you started; if you want to know more, a quick trip to your library or bookstore for a basic primer on UNIX is all you will probably need. Your provider will also have some on-line documentation, and if your account is through work or school, they may have packets of information that you can pick up. It is important to remind you that this exercise is designed to prepare you for learning the fundamentals of creating your own server, not for Net surfing (though you can use your account to do this as well), so we won't be using pretty graphical interfaces here. This is the real thing.

Testing the Account

Because we chose the C shell, we are given the C-shell command prompt when we log in. (In our case, the prompt is simply a percent sign; yours may be different.) We want to make sure that our login name is known to rest of the system. To do this, we send some mail to our own e-mail address (Fig. 4–8). Because we didn't get a message from the system saying "user unknown," we know that it worked.

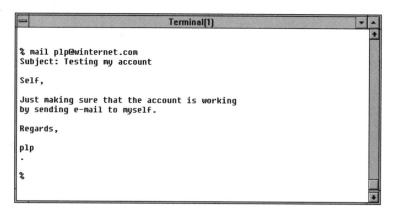

Fig. 4–8 Sending mail to ourselves.

Now, let's see if our account can get out to the world. We will use the UNIX `ping` command. All this command does is check to see if our system can communicate with a specified site on any network we are connected to. We decided to "ping" the White House (Fig. 4–9).

We now know that our account can maneuver around the world. (It's possible that `ping` won't work on your system; if it doesn't, type `finger president@whitehouse.gov`. You should see the message shown in Figure 4–10.)

We'll assume for this exercise that all of the other services are working correctly. But just to be sure, we call up the Lynx WWW browser and connect to our favorite World Wide Web starting point, `www.yahoo.com`. Once again, everything checks out just fine (Fig. 4–11).

Creating a Home Page on the Web

As you recall, one of our account requirements was to have storage space on our provider's system so that we could maintain some files for others around the

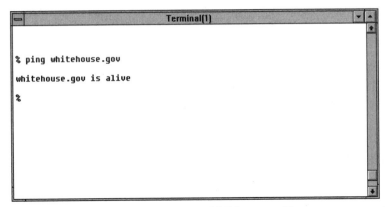

Fig. 4–9 Pinging the White House from a UNIX system. The response says that whitehouse.gov is "alive," so we know that we have made at least one connection across cyberspace.

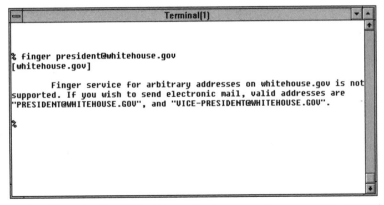

Fig. 4–10 Fingering the White House. If ping doesn't work, try this instead.

world to access. You will probably want to start by creating a simple "home page" for yourself. In the short time that the Web has existed, there has arisen a tradition for users to create an initial page associated with themselves. People may provide a personal profile, a résumé, simple links to their own areas of interest, or something completely weird and unrelated to anything! Of course, a business' home page is usually more official.

In our case, our provider has created a directory called WWW. Files in this directory can be accessed by the entire Internet. We can move into that directory by typing cd WWW.

Now we want to create a file in the WWW directory for all the Web to see. You can either learn how to use a basic UNIX text editor, or you can create the file on your personal computer and upload it to your shell account. You could also create the file on your computer and then cut-and-paste the text into a UNIX

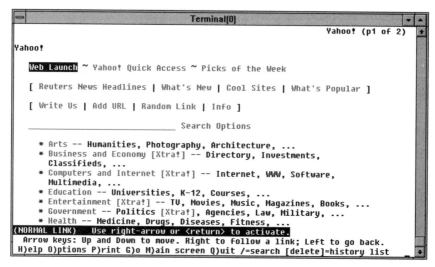

Fig. 4–11 Yahoo as seen from the Lynx browser, which is available in most UNIX shell accounts. (The formatting might look different on your system.)

text editor running on your terminal emulation program; this is *our* favorite method.

This is a good time to point out that no matter what method you use to enter text files, you should become proficient in uploading and downloading files between your system and your provider's system. This is because you probably don't want to — and shouldn't — use access time doing things that could just as easily be done on your own computer, like typing up Web pages. Also, the odds are that your more interesting files, like images and sounds, will be produced on your computer for use on your Web pages.

Getting back to our home page, we create a file called `hello.html` by invoking the `vi` text editor (see Appendix B) and typing the following text:

```
<HTML>
<HEAD><TITLE>Hello World</TITLE></HEAD>
<BODY>
<P>Hello, World!
<P>Welcome to my first Web Page.
</BODY>
</HTML>
```

The file that we just created is written in HTML, the HyperText Markup Language. To learn more about writing in HTML, see the URLs at the beginning of Appendix A. The appendix itself is just a quick reference guide that will teach you the syntax of the most commonly used tags.

You may need to take one more step to make *your* `hello.html` file available to other users on the World Wide Web. Files on a UNIX system can either be "public" or "private"; you can decide whether you want other people to be able to see them. To make sure `hello.html` is accessible to everyone, just type

chmod 644 hello.html at your shell prompt (chmod stands for "change mode").
Typing chmod 600 hello.html would *hide* the file from everyone but you.

Figure 4–12 shows what the rest of the world is going to see using the
Netscape browser. Voila, our first Web page! It's not much, but we have established a presence on the Internet.

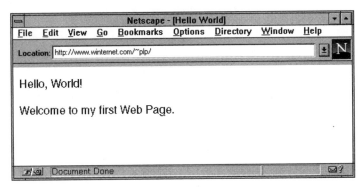

Fig. 4–12   The "Hello World" page, as seen from Netscape.

Just to make this sample a bit more fun for ourselves and anyone accessing
our page, we will add links to some of our own material and some other information on the Web. The additional HTML element that we will use is the hypertext
reference tag, which is used for creating a link to the file, picture, sound, or program to which we want to point Web browsers. A simple hypertext reference is
coded as follows:

```
<A href="thing">link text</A>
```

So, let's copy our "Hello World" page into a file called index.html, add some
words, and point to some things out on the Web. The command to create a copy of
the file with a new name will look like this (note that the percent sign is just our
command prompt; the actual copy command begins with cp):

```
% cp hello.html index.html
```

We then edit the newly created index.html so that it looks like this:

```
<HTML>
<HEAD><TITLE>Hello World</TITLE></HEAD>
<BODY>
<P>Hello, World!
<P>Welcome to my first Web Page.
<P>I would like to tell you about my
   <A href="interests.html">interests</A>.
</BODY>
</HTML>
```

The new line has a hypertext reference to the non-existent file
interests.html, located in the same directory as index.html. Let's look at this
line by itself:

```
<P>I would like to tell you about my
   <A href="interests.html">interests</A>.
```

Anything following the `<A href>` tag but before the `</A>` tag is selectable text that is highlighted by all browsers. By clicking on the highlighted word "interests," a user tells the browser to retrieve our file `interests.html` and display it. Figure 4–13 shows what our new file, with its hypertext link, will look like.

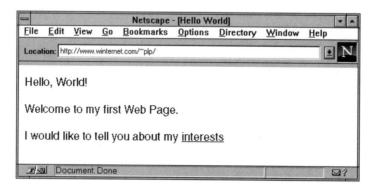

Fig. 4–13   Our enhanced "Hello World" page. It now includes a link, which is underlined.

Of course, we now have to create the file `interests.html`. To prepare for this, we poke around the Web and write down the URLs of our favorite Web sites (URLs are the "things" found in `<A href>` tags). If you are following along at home, you should surf the Web a little bit so that you can replace the links in our sample with your own. If you're looking for something specific, try a search mechanism like `http://www.yahoo.com/` or `http://www.lycos.com/` (for more information about searching the Web, see pages 274-281 in Chapter 11).

Here is the HTML source of *our* `interests.html` page, which is pictured in Figure 4–14:

```
<HTML>
<HEAD><TITLE>Interests</TITLE></HEAD>
<BODY>
<P>I like old movies, especially those starring
<A href="http://parkweb.com/carole/clombar4.gif">
   Carole Lombard.</A>
<P>I believe in
   <A href="http://www.armory.com/~jon/hs/HomeSchool.html">
   home schooling </A> my children.
<P>I also love to play the guitar. I have spent many, many
   hours learning hundreds of new songs at
   <A href="http://www.olga.net/">
   OLGA</A>, the On Line Guitar Archive.
</BODY>
</HTML>
```

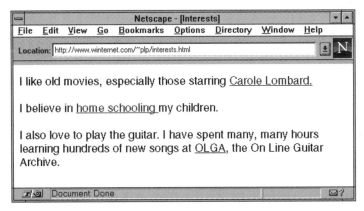

Fig. 4–14 Our `interests.html` page. Each paragraph contains one link to another page somewhere on the World Wide Web.

Note that in the HTML file, the indents on the left are there simply to make it easier for us to read what we've typed; Web browsers ignore carriage returns and treat multiple spaces as if they were a single space. Figures 4–15 through 4–17 show the destination pages of our links.

Fig. 4–15 The Carole Lombard link from `interests.html`.

This simple example should help get you started. The best way to learn how to write Web pages is to look at the source HTML of other documents while you are browsing the Web. You can also refer to Appendix A of this book for more

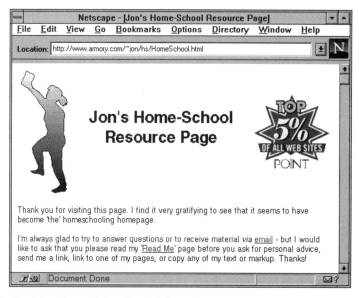

Fig. 4–16   The Home Schooling link from `interests.html`.

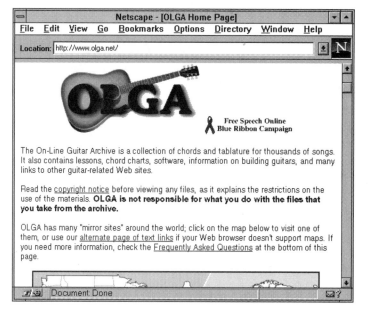

Fig. 4–17   The OLGA link from `interests.html`.

information on HTML tags, and to Chapter 10 for tips on good page design. It is likely to be far easier than you imagined.

4.6 BEFORE YOU MOVE ON

Before you go on to the next chapter, where you'll learn about the hardware needed to set up your own Web server (finally!), spend some time with your user account. Surf the Web, send e-mail, read Usenet newsgroups, download some files. Create a home page, and link it to lots of other pages. If you have access to a scanner, scan in some pictures and put them on your pages. If you don't have a scanner, draw your own pictures, or use FTP or the Web to find some nice public domain graphics; or go to a place like Kinko's Copy Centers, where you can use a scanner for an hourly fee. Give some thought to how you want to organize your site, and how you want your pages to look. For now, have fun; the hard work will come soon enough. When you feel comfortable as a competent member of the worldwide on-line community, read on.

## CHAPTER 5

Web Server
Fundamentals

A Web server at its most basic level is simply any computer system connected to the Internet with industry-standard Web server software. There is really no such thing as a "typical" Web server. Your server requirements depend upon a number of factors, such as the type of connection you have, the number of files you will make available, and the types of programs you will be running. The requirements of a personal hobby server will be completely different from those of a business with an on-line order entry system. However, there are many things that are common among every server.

This chapter describes what you will need, in terms of both hardware and software, to create a functioning Web server. The next chapter will cover more details about network connections in general, and how this applies to the Internet in particular.

5.1 FILE SERVERS

To understand how a Web server works, and what you need to transform your desktop computer into one, it is helpful to understand some broader concepts about *file servers*. A file server can be thought of as a networked repository for files; it is simply a computer system that is connected to other computers for the purpose of providing and managing files and programs to multiple users.

This setup maximizes the ability of users to share valuable resources. Keep in mind that while many users can access a file server, not all the files are necessarily "public" files that can retrieved by any user. The security protections provided by your operating system allow the owner of a file or program to determine who can retrieve the file.

In small networks — such as those found in a small office or college department — the file server usually has a lot of disk storage space and printers, and is attached to various other peripherals such as magnetic tape backup systems. This server would store the large programs that are commonly used.

For example, a college department's network may consist of a dozen PCs located in different offices. The users of these PCs are faculty and graduate students who are primarily involved in research. They all use a program such as WordPerfect for documenting their research, and CorelDRAW for creating illustrations. Both of these programs require a lot of disk space, so it would be very inefficient to keep separate copies on each of the PCs. Each time someone wants to use WordPerfect, the file server sends a copy of the program across the network to the requesting PC. This copy of the program is available to the user of that PC for one session only, after which it is discarded. The next time he or she wants to use WordPerfect, a new copy is sent from the file server. The various users are also freed from worrying about software maintenance such as upgrades and fixes. If the system administrator upgrades WordPerfect to a new version, all users of that file server will have immediate access to that version.

In a larger network with hundreds of users, multiple file servers are often used, each dedicated to a specific set of tasks. For example, one server could be used to store and manage all of a network's e-mail, another for the files owned by users with names beginning with A–N, another server for users with names beginning with O–Z, and yet another for application software.

A common variant of a file server is the print server, which manages the printing chores of numerous users on a network. Instead of print jobs being sent directly to a specific printer, these jobs are sent to the print server which, in turn, sends it to any printer on the network. This is especially useful for a network that has a lot of printing activity. If one printer has a lot of backed-up traffic, other printers can be used to ease the load. Also, users can send their draft printing jobs to the more inexpensive draft printer and send their desktop publishing work to the more expensive printer.

The Web server that you are creating is essentially a file server that can potentially be accessed by anyone on the Internet who has Web browsing software. The work performed by a Web browser is primarily file retrieval. As a Webmaster, you must configure your system to allow these browsers to access your information flawlessly.

This does *not* mean that you need to go out and buy a second computer to begin serving information to Web browsers. In fact, your home computer will work just fine if you have the right hardware and software setup. See the platform-specific chapter for your system (7, 8, or 9) for specific requirements.

5.2 WEB SERVER COMPUTER HARDWARE

This section describes computer architectures, memory, disk space, processor speed, and so on. When you start planning your Web server, the obvious first step is to be sure you have the right computer. Having a good hardware setup from the beginning will save you from constantly having to make costly upgrades as your Web server's needs grow.

While you certainly do not want to have more expensive components than you need, you also do not want a system that is too limited for your requirements. You must strike a balance between economy and power.

Base Computer

Almost all major types and brands of computers can be used as Web servers, from desktop PCs to the largest supercomputer. The odds are that your current computer system can be used in one fashion or another as a Web server. Some are better suited than others for this type of service. In later chapters, we will teach you the specifics of setting up a complete server on a Microsoft Windows-based PC, Apple Macintosh, or any computer that can run the UNIX operating system.

Although this is not a complete list, the following computer architectures are capable of being Web servers:

UNIX and LINUX Almost all of the early development of the Internet was done on computers that run the UNIX operating system. To this day, most computer scientists use UNIX, and most of the Internet backbone systems use some flavor of UNIX. For this reason, UNIX servers are still the most popular on the Net. Systems running the UNIX operating system can be purchased from any number of computer vendors, because UNIX describes system software, not hardware.

The UNIX workstation is also currently the most popular type of Web server. This may change in years to come, now that very good Web server software is available for the Macintosh and for Windows; but for now, UNIX servers have proven to be the ideal machines for the job.

Unfortunately, workstations are relatively expensive. An alternative that has proven to be successful for many Webmasters is to put a free version of UNIX, known as LINUX, on their relatively inexpensive IBM-compatible PCs. When configured correctly, LINUX can be as stable as any implementation of UNIX, so you should seriously consider this option if you have an IBM-compatible system and are willing to spend a little extra time and effort to set up LINUX on your machine.

Macintosh The best reason to set up a Web server on a Macintosh is the same one that attracts people to Macs in the first place: it's very easy to do, especially if you are already familiar with the Macintosh environment. The TCP/IP software is built into the System 7 software and very reliable; the server software is readily available and fairly inexpensive; and becoming a Web server is as easy as double-clicking an icon. Unfortunately, Macintoshes don't have the raw processing power of a UNIX system, and they are slightly more expensive than comparable IBM-compatible PCs. Because Mac Web servers are less common than UNIX and LINUX, there are not quite as many choices in the way of *free* software that will work with your server program, but what's available is very good, so don't let that stop you.

PCs Running Windows   Microsoft Windows 3.1 and Microsoft Windows 95 offer many of the advantages that a Macintosh server does, such as a user-friendly graphical user interface. Primarily, the server packages are very easy to install for the experienced Windows user, and the territory is very familiar. If you don't need the raw processing power of a UNIX system, and you already use Windows regularly, then this is the platform for you.

Memory

As with all of the components described in this section, your memory (RAM) requirements will depend upon the type of computer you are using, the size of the programs you are running, the size of the files you will be serving to the Web, and the number of simultaneous users you expect to be accessing your system. No matter which system you use, one thing is true: It is easy to have too little memory, and you can never have too much.

To evaluate your specific requirements, you will probably need to do some guesswork. Here are a couple of examples that show how radically requirements can vary:

A SPARCstation running the Solaris operating system needs at least 16 MB of memory to function smoothly as a single-user workstation. If this system doubles as a networked file server in a small office, you can count on needing a minimum of 32 MB. Now, let's say we start using it as the department's Web server on an ISDN connection with a fair amount of consistent traffic. To keep the users of the system content with the computer's usual functions, we would need to add enough additional memory to support all of the Web activity. You could easily need at least 64 MB, and would probably do better with 128 MB, before you have reached the practical limitations of the computer's processing ability. This is, of course, an extreme example and can get very expensive.

Now, compare this to a 486 PC running Windows 95. Let's say that this system is used almost exclusively as a Web server, and it is connected to a 28.8k bps phone line. The basic Windows 95 system functions adequately with 8 MB of memory, and since it is not used for anything except a Web server, the additional activity may only require an additional 4 to 8 MB to handle all requests through the 28.8k connection. A 680x0 Macintosh used only as a simple Web server would probably be fine with only 8 MB of memory. These are not an unlikely scenarios for an economy-class server.

The price/performance debates are constantly raging in the Usenet news-groups, with no one system emerging as the clear "winner." As with many things in life, you often get what you pay for.

Of course, the type of work being performed by your server will affect all of this. If your Web server performs extensive database searches on your system, or crunches numbers for sophisticated mathematical operations, you would need whatever memory you would ordinarily need to do this in *addition* to the memory needed for the Web server software. Because your Web server is unique, you will need to carefully calculate your own requirements.

Disk Space

The total amount of disk space that you require obviously depends on the number and size of the files you will have. Your best bet for calculating this is to create an imaginary Web file system on paper with some reasonable estimates of the sizes of each file. While not totally accurate, it will give you an idea of the number of bytes you are dealing with.

Unlike RAM, disks are inexpensive and always getting cheaper. You will be doing yourself a favor by getting as much disk space as you can afford, within reason. When we calculate our disk space requirements for any given project, we usually end up using double or triple our initial estimates. This is probably a good rule of thumb. Be very careful when doing this, especially if you plan to have a lot of graphics files and large databases.

While transparent background file compression software (e.g., Stacker or StuffIt SpaceSaver) may look like an inexpensive way to get more space out of your hard drive, it is probably not a good idea for your Web server. When the decompression software "unpacks" these for use, it puts an additional load on your server, and if you have many people accessing your server at once, this could be significant. You are better off buying an additional drive. (However, compressing large *individual* files is a good idea, because it speeds up transmission times.)

It is also a good idea to have more than one physical drive on your system for backup and recovery purposes, especially if your server is going to be on line at all times. Having a second drive with copies of *all* of the files on your primary drive allows you to easily and reliably keep your server running with only a minimal interruption in service, should your first drive fail. Without a backup drive, you run the risk of losing all of the data since your last backup to tape or floppy disks. Also, you would have to be off line for however long it takes to restore all of your files and repair or replace the damaged drive.

Modems

Your modem should match or exceed the speed of the connection with your Internet service provider; the various types of connections are described in detail in Chapter 6. Once you have decided on the type of connection you are going to have, you may want to ask your provider for recommendations concerning specific brands of modems, because there are many differences between manufacturers. If a modem adheres to established standards (such as V.34 bis for 28.8k bps modems), then it will communicate with another modem adhering to this standard at some minimum level. But, there are some features, such as different types of data compression, that are not available with every modem. By matching non-standard features, you can really boost the efficiency of your modem connection.

You should get the fastest modem that your budget can handle (and that is supported by your provider). No matter which modem you choose, you should be sure that it has a minimum speed of 14.4k bps. It would be impractical to consider running even the smallest Web server at a slower speed than this. Another consideration is your modem's ability to negotiate a connection speed at regular intervals rather than only at startup time and times when your phone line has experienced some form of degradation. Inexpensive modems simply lower their connection speed — or drop their connection — when a line gets dirty (that is, full of unwanted line noise), even if it is just a temporary situation. More expensive, full-featured modems poll the connection regularly to see what the condition of the line is and how to make to the speediest data transfer rates. Having this feature could save you a lot of time by not forcing you to reboot your system every time your modem gets lazy.

Another thing to consider is whether to get an internal or external modem. There is little or no difference in the performance of internal versus external varieties of a given model of modem. However, an external modem usually has an LCD display or status lights that let you know how your modem is performing. Additionally, external modems are easier to install and replace than internal modems. Therefore, it may be worth the few extra dollars to purchase an external modem.

Processor Speed

Again, this issue is platform-dependent. The computer makers of the world are obsessed with processor speed, and while it is important to have the speed you need, it isn't the end-all of an efficient server. It is argued in many quarters that efficiency is more of an equation of memory size than of processor speed. This is because even the fastest disks are very slow when compared with the speed of RAM. No matter how fast your processor is, it can move data only as fast as the storage device can, unless the files are in memory. More importantly, a blindingly fast processor won't help at all if you have a relatively slow phone connection. So, a possible rule of thumb for processor speed is to get as fast a processor as you can afford, after you have gone overboard on memory and gotten a decent modem.

5.3 WEB SERVER SOFTWARE

The specific Web server packages that are available for your type of computer are described in detail in Chapters 7 through 9. For the general discussion in this chapter, you need only to understand that there are three major types of software that every server must have: an operating system, a TCP/IP software package, and an HTTPD program.

Operating Systems

Your operating system is the software layer that directly manages your hardware and allows your programs to function on that hardware. The most common operating systems on the PC are MS-DOS and Microsoft Windows. On the Mac, it is System 7, and on numerous other systems it is UNIX. All of these operating systems support Web server software to one extent or another. This subsection focuses on the key features of operating systems with regard to Web servers.

Multi-User vs. Single-User Until recently, there were two distinct classes of operating systems: single-user and multi-user. Operating systems such as MS-DOS are assumed (correctly, in this case) to be single-user. You don't log into a running system and start your session, like on a mainframe; you simply power up the machine and start working (or playing). An operating system like this is fine for performing one task at a time very quickly and effectively. However, it is not well suited at all to being a Web server, where multiple users doing multiple tasks all at once are the reality.

A multi-user operating system has built-in features that make the resources of the computer available on an equal basis to a variety of users. UNIX was designed with this in mind. More and more, Mac and PC software developers recognize that these "personal computers" are often networked and are accessed by a number of users. This is why many of the significant new features associated with MacOS and Microsoft's Windows 95 are in the area of networking.

Multitasking Another important feature for Web servers is *multitasking*. This term describes an operating system's ability to do more than one thing at a time. Performing seemingly concurrent operations is crucial to a Web server. The reason is that if your server is open to the world, a single-threaded operating system will service only one user request, in its entirety, before moving on to the next request. Therefore, someone retrieving a large graphic file would have exclusive access to the server until the file was completely downloaded while, say, 20 users wait with simple requests for tiny text files. Fortunately, all Web server software insists that your operating system either perform real multitasking (UNIX), or reliably fake it (Windows and Macintosh).

UNIX was designed to be a multi-user, multitasking operating system. Every request for the computer to do something is turned into "processes." These processes are then queued and managed by elaborate scheduling software that maximizes the efficiency of the computer in relation to the users and available system resources. With these features solidly built into the software, it is little wonder why UNIX is so popular among Web server programmers. Many of their worries are taken care of in the operating system, freeing them from working process management into their application software.

MS-DOS is not a multitasking operating system. It completes a user request in its entirety before moving onto the next one. It assumes that there is only one user on the system doing one thing at a time. Windows 3.1, which runs on top of MS-DOS, has the ability to have more than one program active at a given time. However, it is not considered to be "true multitasking" because of the way it does this. Windows 3.1 stops a running program (and remembers where it stopped) and starts another program (or restarts the one it stopped). The PC is still doing one "thing" at any given moment. This is not the best use of available hardware resources, and may cause your system to completely freeze up when it is not implemented correctly. However, there are some very good Windows 3.1 Web server packages that are reported to function very reliably. The programmers obviously worked through a lot of these issues, especially in the area of having multiple users.

The Macintosh operating system does not perform true multitasking, but it does have the ability to run programs "in the background" when the frontmost application will allow this. Apple's Thread Manager system extension makes this quasi-multitasking more efficient, and more and more programmers are writing applications that take advantage of this "threading" of processes. Fortunately, the software needed to use a Mac as a Web server runs very well in the background.

TCP/IP Software

Every Web server is a computer that is connected to the Internet either directly or through other computers "upstream." This server must communicate using a protocol suite called TCP/IP, which is the standard format of data transmission on the Internet. This is how it is possible for various types of dissimilar computers to exchange information. Every server converts its information to TCP/IP packets and then sends them out to the world. The computer receiving this information then converts it to something it understands before processing the actual data. TCP/IP is described in detail in Appendix D.

A good analogy is the international aircraft control system. The accepted standard language of communication between pilots and controllers is English. A pilot may discuss flight details with the co-pilot in, say, Italian. Once they have decided on a message for the controller, they translate their message into English and radio it in. Now, if they are landing their plane in Tokyo, the Tokyo controller hears the radio message in English and then translates it into Japanese for internal communication in the control tower. In cyberspace, TCP/IP conversion software sits behind every computer's interface to all other networks, including the Internet. This is why your computer has to have a TCP/IP software package up and running before your other Web server software can function. You will find more information about the TCP/IP software available for your system in Chapter 7, 8, or 9.

The TCP/IP suite supports these well-known Internet services:

FTP   File Transfer Protocol (FTP) allows the user of one computer to connect to another computer for the purpose of transferring files. While connected, the user can exchange files between the two computers as well as navigate around the other computer's file system.

SMTP   The Simple Mail Transfer Protocol (SMTP) provides the mechanism for sending mail between systems. This protocol does two things: first, it makes a connection from one computer to another, requesting that a second connection be made for the transfer of mail message data. Once the second connection is made, the data (simple ASCII text) is sent. Upon completion, both connections are terminated.

NNTP The Network News Transport Protocol (NNTP) is similar to the SMTP protocol, but it works only with Usenet news articles. There are also a small number of commands available with this protocol that update newsgroup lists, article headings, and news articles themselves.

Telnet The network terminal protocol (telnet) allows you to become a user on a remote computer. Once you have connected, your computer effectively becomes a terminal directly connected to the other computer. In this way, a user with a login name and password on a system connected to the Internet can work from anywhere in the world as easily as working from a hard-wired terminal.

NFS The protocol for network file systems (NFS) allows one computer to connect to another computer and make the files on the other computer available to users of the first computer; it is a similar concept to a file server. When the remote file system is mounted, a user does not need to know that some (or all) of the available files actually reside on another computer.

HTTP Software

The Web's communication mechanism is HTTP, the latest addition to the TCP/IP world. The HTTP software package is what turns your fully functional TCP/IP system into a Web server. On many platforms, this package is called "HTTPd"; the "d" stands for *daemon* (on the Net, a daemon is a system program that runs in the background and automatically handles certain system operations).

HTTP is a file transfer protocol that — when it comes to serving many individual files to many people — works more efficiently than FTP. This is because connections between computers are made for the sole purpose of retrieving a specific, named file. All of the command-level overhead that exists with FTP (allowing the user to navigate around the other system, get directory listings, and so on) is not included with HTTP. A user requests a named file on the other system and either gets that file (and only that file) or receives an error message (indicating why the file could not be retrieved), and nothing else. The computers are only connected long enough for the single transaction to take place. The server is then free to process the next request. This protocol maximizes the potential use of the available resources on both systems.

HTTP is the transfer protocol that you will need to be most familiar with, because any computer accessing your Web server will be making its requests for information via HTTP.

Appendix D describes in detail how information requests are made using TCP/IP standards; having this knowledge, you should be able to more easily fix things when they don't work like you expect them to.

If you're not interested in the nitty-gritty details of multilayered data transactions, forget about Appendix D and move on to the next chapter. In Chapter 6, you'll learn how to find a place in cyberspace to set up shop. After that, we'll finally help you *build* the shop.

Connecting To
The Internet

Once your Web server has all of the hardware in place, it is time to get connected to the Internet. There is nothing magical about this, but there are things you need to consider as you take each step.

There are many different types of Internet connections, and you need to find the one that best suits the needs of your server. This chapter describes physical data connections, modems, and Internet service providers, and it will show you how to get your own Internet domain name.

6.1 INTERNET SERVICE PROVIDERS

An Internet service provider is a business that connects your computer or computer network to the Internet. (You many also encounter references to "Internet access providers"; "ISP" and "IAP" are used more or less interchangeably.) As discussed in Chapter 4, ISPs offer a wide range of options and features. Your Web server primarily needs the provider to do one thing: route TCP/IP data to and from your system. Remember, your Web server is a *host* system on the Net. Your system manages all of its own information and information processing. At the most basic level, the ISP serves the function of "traffic cop," guaranteeing that your packets make it to the rest of the world, and that their packets make it you (Fig. 6–1). Of course, most ISPs offer far more than this, such as a shell account and file space on their computer, mail forwarding, domain name services (DNS), and a Usenet news feed. However, all your server really needs is just a clean and open "pipe" to all the other computers on the Internet.

If your Web server is going to be connected through your place of employment or your college, you should work with the system administrator to get all of your connection options. This may be as simple as getting a hard-wired network connection to an existing network, or a dial-up phone number to a network that is already connected to the Internet. You should still read this section to get an

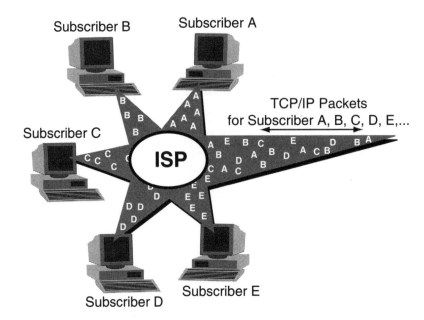

Fig. 6–1 The Internet service provider moves TCP/IP packets between its subscribers and the rest of the Internet.

idea of how this all works, so you can make the most of the options available to you.

Keep in mind that even if you can set up a simple Web server through work or school, they probably will not allow you to leave it connected and running twenty-four hours a day. If this is the case, or if you do not have an existing connection at all, you are going to need to shop around for an ISP.

Almost every town has some sort of access to the Internet. In major cities, there is now heavy competition between many different providers. The first thing that you need to do is find out which services are available to you in your community, the prices for these services, and the level of support a provider is going to give you. If you are new to the Net, or are using a proprietary national service like AOL or CompuServe, you will need to poke around to find out who the providers are in your area. You can do this by asking your local library or college for a list of providers.

If you have access to the World Wide Web already, via your own or a friend's Internet account, find a non-biased Web site dedicated to local information. You should be able to find such a site using Yahoo. (For example, Figure 6–2 shows a Web page that lists ISPs in the Washington, D.C. area; we found it with Yahoo). There is also a wonderful site called "The List" (http://www.thelist.com) that covers Internet service providers around the country and around the world (Figure 6–3), but a local site might be able to give you more details about Internet services in your community. Another way to find out about local ISPs is through a local newsgroup. For example, in Minnesota there is a newsgroup explicitly for this type of discussion called `mn.online-service`. But be ready for heated arguments, as many users are very loyal to their provider.

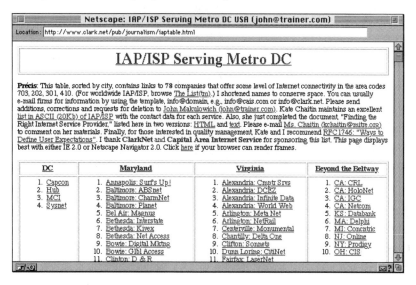

Fig. 6–2 A helpful list of ISPs in and around Washington, D.C.

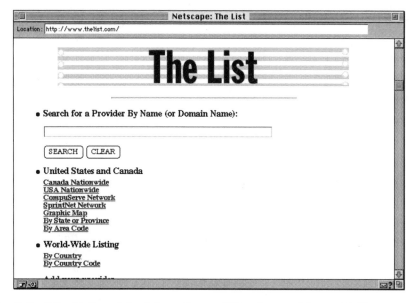

Fig. 6–3 "The List" contains information on ISPs all around the world. You can search by country, state, or area code.

Keep in mind that you may have to change providers early on if your first choice disappoints you. This is an emerging industry and there are some inept companies as well as some fabulous ones. This is very similar to the competition among long distance providers a few years back, when it seemed that there were hundreds of companies fighting for your business. Over time, the shoddy ones are discovered and put out of business by the natural market forces.

In Chapter 4, we walked you through a real example of signing up with a service provider. Before you proceed, you may want to review this information, as well as the "Web Server Fundamentals" discussion in Chapter 5.

6.2 DATA COMMUNICATIONS SERVICES

In the previous chapters, we described all of the components that you need to have a working Internet host. Now it is time to get that server connected so that data can flow to and from your system.

You know that you need a data connection through an ISP to manage your Internet data flow. Now you must figure out what sort of connection you will need. The services you purchase will depend on the demands of your server, the options available to you from your provider, and the amount of money you are willing to spend. There is a large range of features available (see Table 6–1).

Table 6–1   Connection Types

Connection	Speed	Description
2400 baud modem	2,400 bits/sec	Analog
14.4k baud modem	14,400 bits/sec	Analog
28.8k baud modem	28,800 bits/sec	Analog
56k digital line	57,600 bits/sec	Digital
ISDN	128,000 bits/sec	Digital
T1	1,544,000 bits/sec	Digital

Deciding on the type of connection for your server is probably the biggest issue that you will need to resolve. You want the maximum potential throughput that your budget can handle.

To have a legitimate presence on the Web, you will want to have your system connected twenty-four hours a day. Unless you accomplish this by simply using space on your provider's server, this will require a dedicated phone line in your home or office and, of course, an agreement with your provider for data services.

Traditional Phone Lines

Traditional phone lines have limited bandwidth — they can not carry a tremendous amount of computer data — but they may be sufficient if you are running a small server or want to stay within a budget. The main advantage to using traditional phone lines is the cost. The modems that you can use with this basic connection are 14,400 bps (bits per second) and 28,800 bps. Anything less than 14.4k bps is not feasible for the amount of data that even the smallest server will be handling. The theoretical maximum amount of data that can be sent over a phone line is 31k bps. This means that the current 28.8k bps modems come very close to the limitations of the standard phone wire.

You can use any of the inexpensive modems available at your local retail computer store; the prices get cheaper every month. You simply install either an internal modem card or an external modem unit, along with a modular phone connector, and you are ready to connect. A more expensive modem will have better error-checking and a better chance of staying connected if the phone line gets fuzzy, but it won't give you more speed.

For 14.4k and 28.8k connections, there are two protocols that you can use to connect your Web server to the world: Serial Line Internet Protocol (SLIP) and the Point-to-Point Protocol (PPP). While these are distinct protocols, they perform the same function: facilitating TCP/IP data transfer from one point to another. These protocols are ideal for modem connections over a standard phone line.

While SLIP has been common for some time now, PPP is gaining popularity and is the de facto Internet standard for simple point-to-point connections. The best way to decide which one to use is to evaluate for yourself how user-friendly each protocol's software is on your platform. Or ask your Internet service provider for advice.

Digital Data Connections

If you want more data throughput for your system than SLIP or PPP can provide, then you must upgrade your phone system to support a digital connection. The details of installing and configuring a high speed connection are far beyond the scope of this book and are best left up to a trained network administrator, but you should be familiar with the general concepts.

Regular telephone lines are analog devices. This means that sounds are converted to electrical *waves* that move across a wire. Your computer data is converted into sound by your modem and sent as electricity across the line. Digital lines, on the other hand, use variations in voltage to represent numeric data. Simply put, you are sending *discrete numbers* rather than smooth waves. This is obviously more efficient for devices that communicate with numeric data anyway.

There will likely be many different types of digital connections available to you through your provider or the phone company; a phone call or two should give you an overview of the types of connections available in your area. To get a quick look at some of the equipment requirements for digital connections (CSU/DSU boxes, routers, and so on), point your Web browser at the following URL:

```
http://www.mot.com/MIMS/ISG/Products/
```

56k Line   This is the first step into the digital data communication world. A 56k line requires a special connection from the phone company. It consists of two line pairs (transmit and receive) that are connected with a *terminating box* — usually a unit called a CSU/DSU (channel service unit/data service unit) — and a *router*.

ISDN   The Integrated Services Digital Network (ISDN) is the hottest thing going these days in the area of Internet connectivity. Besides offering 128k throughput, you can also use your ISDN connection for your office phone services. ISDN consists of a pair of phone wires that facilitate one or two logical circuits. This allows you to have one voice connection and one data connection, or two voice connections, or two data connections operating simultaneously.

T1   T1 connections are expensive (although far less so than they used to be). These lines are used by big networks and usually require a CSU/DSU box and a router. If your bandwidth demands are this great, you probably should talk to a networking consultant.

Frame Relay   Like ISDN, frame relay is another hot connection type on the Net today. Your digital information leaves your system and goes to the phone company where it moves in a congested cloud of other connections. Your connection to another location is a virtual connection, rather than a physical one. This is accomplished by dividing your information into parcels, or frames, which are reassembled at the destination. (This is somewhat similar to the concept of TCP datagrams; see Appendix D.) Your information makes it from point A to point B through arbitrary routes in a phone company system. You are billed based on your usage of the type of virtual connections you use. Once again, the actual details are far outside the scope of this book, and you probably will not be using this type of connection. But if you would like to, talk to your provider or your phone company.

6.3 GETTING YOUR OWN DOMAIN NAME

Every Internet host has an IP address associated with it, consisting of four numbers separated by periods. Computers love IP addresses; what could be more fun than parsing through a series of numbers separated by periods? Human beings *don't* like IP addresses. We like words, names, and identifiers. We would rather send something to "Time Magazine" than 198.4.180.242.

Domain names — non-numerical addresses — are necessary when we throw humans into this computer networking mix. A domain name is simply a name, composed mostly of letters rather than numbers, that is associated with a given IP address (for example, www.time.com = 198.4.180.242). We don't name our pets Cat 1 and Cat 2, or Fish 6 and Fish 7, so why should we name the components on our network 123.456.78.9? This section explains the conventions used on the Internet, plus how you can get your own domain name.

Domain Name Conventions

There are hierarchical rules and conventions for domain names. This is why you always see xxx.com or yyy.edu, for example. By the way, it is important to note that the *words* in a domain name do not correspond directly to the numbers in an IP address. For example, there is no IP number that specifically translates to .com, and none that means www. Never, ever try to *guess* an IP number from a domain name, or vice versa.

Let's say you will be setting up a Web server through an Internet service provider. Chances are that your provider has a stock of IP addresses. You are given one of these IPs when you establish your account, and the IP number you get is, for example, 208.241.61.22. This is *the* unique identifier that your server has on the Net. All packets destined for your machine must have this in the header. But you certainly want to have a human face for this number, so you should register a domain name as well. Not only does it make it easier to remember, but you can take your domain name with you even if your IP address changes.

If we are setting up a Web server for our company, Wizbang Widgets, we will definitely want Wizbang in the first part of our domain name, if it is available; this part must be unique. The last part must follow the domain conventions of the Internet. These conventions, at least for sites based in the United States, are as follows:

.com	Commercial enterprises, such as cnn.com
.org	Organizations, such as boy-scouts.org
.net	Network providers and internet maintenance sites
.edu	Four-year and higher learning institutions
.gov	Federal government agencies
.us	Local government entities, such as courthouses and libraries (for example, stpaul.lib.mn.us is the St. Paul Public Library)
.*country*	Nations other than the United States, where *country* is a unique, two-letter country code, such as .fr for France or .il for Israel

Wizbang Widgets is a "for profit" business (hopefully!), so we will get a .com domain (*your* server will almost certainly have either .com or .org). Since we chose "Wizbang" as our unique name, we will have the domain name wizbang.com. If our Webmaster's name is Hector, his e-mail address will probably end up being hector@wizbang.com.

Many Web servers are named *www*.something.com; the www is not actually part of the registered domain name. It is simply a useful convention that ensures that HTTP requests are sent only to a machine in that domain which is running Web server software. Talk to your provider about whether your site can include the www prefix; in most situations, this is easily accommodated.

DNS Servers

The rest of the world needs to know which IP number to put in their packets, in order to get data to or from `wizbang.com`. This is done through a domain name services (DNS) server. Long ago, each main host on a network connected to the Internet kept a map of which name was associated with which IP address; this is still done on many local subnets. But more likely, your software asks a DNS server to resolve the address for you. Your provider or your provider's provider probably maintains a DNS server. These servers have programs that regularly ask other DNS servers or the main registry services for new or updated domain name/IP associations. They also maintain a cache of recently satisfied name requests, which speeds up the resolution process.

Registering Your Domain Name

Once your computer or network has its own IP address and is ready to be connected to the Internet, it's time to get that domain name you've always wanted. IP addresses and domain names are assigned by InterNIC for most of the world, RIPE Network Coordination Centre for Europe, and the Asian Pacific Region Internet Registry (APNIC) for the Pacific rim. (There will soon be a separate registry service for Australia as well.) Figures 6–4, 6–5, and 6–6 represent InterNIC's, RIPE's, and APNIC's home pages, respectively.

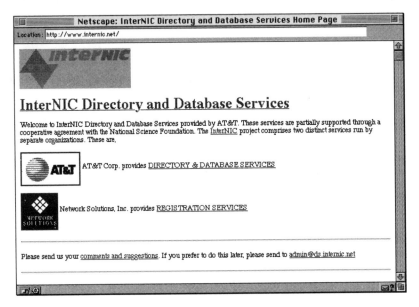

Fig. 6–4   InterNIC Directory and Database Services
(`http://www.internic.net/`).

In most cases, you will apply for a numerical address through your ISP, not directly to InterNIC. When you contact your ISP to get the actual connection to

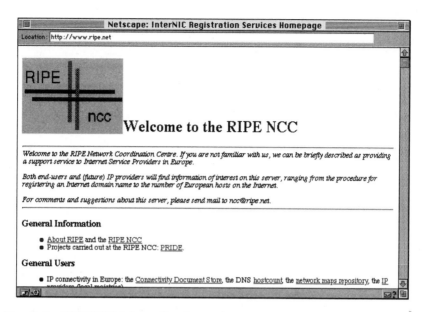

Fig. 6–5 RIPE NCC Information Server (`http://www.ripe.net/`).

your server, the provider can also do all of the registration for an IP address and domain name — usually for a fee. Not only is this an advantage for you, but it actually benefits the provider (who usually manages the blocks of IP addresses) and the folks at InterNIC (who like having experts fill out the requests).

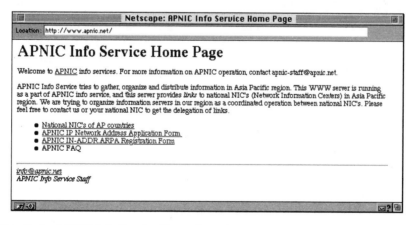

Fig. 6–6 APNIC Info Service Home Page (`http://www.apnic.net/`).

If, however, you decide to apply directly to InterNIC (because you are a system administrator or you just want to save money), here is the procedure for doing so:

- Think up a domain name that you want to register. Remember that you must follow certain naming conventions when choosing a domain name (see the list on page 75).
- Point your Web browser at http://www.internic.net/
- Click on "Registration Services"; this will take you to InterNIC's domain name registration server (Fig. 6–7).

Fig. 6–7 InterNIC's domain name registration page.

- Check that your desired domain name is available and not registered to another site. Click on the link that says "Whois query form." In the box that appears, enter the name that you want to register. If your name has been taken already, think of a new one. (For example, enter parkweb.com. You can see that this name has already been taken, so try something else.) Once you find an unused name that you like, return to the "Registration Services" page.

You now need to fill out the application form. You have two choices here: you can fill out the form on line using your Web browser by clicking on "Templates (WWW)." Or, you can download the application by clicking on "Templates (Text)"; then download and save domain-template.txt, and fill it out using your favorite text editor or word processor.

Here is what the actual application template looks like. You can find it at this URL: ftp://rs.internic.net/templates/domain-template.txt.

```
************* Please DO NOT REMOVE Version Number *************
Domain Version Number: 2.0
********** Please see attached detailed instructions **********
** Only for registrations under ROOT, COM, ORG, NET, EDU, GOV **

0.    (N)ew (M)odify (D)elete...:

1.    Purpose/Description.......:

2.    Complete Domain Name......:

Organization Using Domain Name
3a. Organization Name..........:
3b. Street Address.............:
3c. City.......................:
3d. State......................:
3e. Postal Code................:
3f. Country....................:


Administrative Contact
4a. NIC Handle (if known)......:
4b. Name (Last, First).........:
4c. Organization Name..........:
4d. Street Address.............:
4e. City.......................:
4f. State......................:
4g. Postal Code................:
4h. Country....................:
4i. Phone Number...............:
4j. E-Mailbox..................:

Technical Contact
5a. NIC Handle (if known)......:
5b. Name (Last, First).........:
5c. Organization Name..........:
5d. Street Address.............:
5e. City.......................:
5f. State......................:
5g. Postal Code................:
5h. Country....................:
5i. Phone Number...............:
5j. E-Mailbox..................:
```

```
Billing Contact
6a. NIC Handle (if known)......:
6b. Name (Last, First).........:
6c. Organization Name..........:
6d. Street Address.............:
6e. City.......................:
6f. State......................:
6g. Postal Code................:
6h. Country....................:
6i. Phone Number...............:
6j. E-Mailbox..................:

Primary Name Server
7a. Primary Server Hostname....:
7b. Primary Server Netaddress..:

Secondary Name Server(s)
8a. Secondary Server Hostname..:
8b. Secondary Server Netaddress:

Invoice Delivery
9.  (E)mail (P)ostal...........:
```

The following list explains what you need to provide on each line:

0. **(N)ew (M)odify (D)elete:** Enter the selection that applies to you. You will probably be registering a new domain name, so enter N.

1. **Purpose:** Write the reason that you are applying for a domain name. For example, you could enter, *"I need a domain name for my new Web server. This server will be used to provide information about my insurance company."*

2. **Complete Domain Name:** Enter in the unique domain name that you are requesting (for example, `bobs-insurance.com`).

3. **Organization Using Domain Name:** Enter all of the requested information. For example, Bob enters the following:

```
Organization Using Domain Name
3a. Organization Name..........: Bob's Insurance, Inc.
3b. Street Address.............: 1234 Main St.
3c. City.......................: St. Paul
3d. State......................: MN
3e. Postal Code................: 55108
3f. Country....................: USA
```

4. **Administrative Contact:** This is the person who represents the organization. This is not necessarily the person who will be running the computer system; it is simply the organization's spokesperson. For example, CEO Bob Smith of Bob's Insurance, Inc. may be this administrative contact, even though he has nothing to do with the company's computers. Since this is a new application for `bobs-insurance.com`, line 4a should be left blank. Once the application is approved, Bob Smith would be given a *NIC handle* (a unique identifier) which he could use for future applications. In that case, Bob Smith would only have to enter his NIC handle in 4a and leave the rest of section 4 blank.

```
Administrative Contact
4a. NIC Handle (if known)......:
4b. Name (Last, First).........: Bob Smith
4c. Organization Name..........: Bob's Insurance, Inc.
4d. Street Address.............: 1234 Main St.
4e. City.......................: St. Paul
4f. State......................: MN
4g. Postal Code................: 55108
4h. Country....................: USA
4i. Phone Number...............: 612-555-1000
4j. E-Mailbox..................: bobsmith@winternet.com
```

5. **Technical Contact:** This is similar to section 4, except that the technical contact is the person who handles the networking details of the system. For example, the network administrator at Bob's Insurance, Inc. is Bob's wife, Sue Smith. So, section 5 of the Smiths' application would look like this:

```
Technical Contact
5a. NIC Handle (if known)......:
5b. Name (Last, First).........: Sue Smith
5c. Organization Name..........: Bob's Insurance, Inc.
5d. Street Address.............: 1234 Main St.
5e. City.......................: St. Paul
5f. State......................: MN
5g. Postal Code................: 55108
5h. Country....................: USA
5i. Phone Number...............: 612-555-1000
5j. E-Mailbox..................: suesmith@winternet.com
```

6. **Billing Contact:** This section has the same fields as the previous two sections. In our example, let's assume that Sue also pays all of the bills at Bob's Insurance, Inc., so their application would look like this:

```
Billing Contact
6a. NIC Handle (if known)......:
6b. Name (Last, First)........: Sue Smith
6c. Organization Name.........: Bob's Insurance, Inc.
6d. Street Address............: 1234 Main St.
6e. City.....................: St. Paul
6f. State....................: MN
6g. Postal Code..............: 55108
6h. Country..................: USA
6i. Phone Number.............: 612-555-1000
6j. E-Mailbox................: suesmith@winternet.com
```

7. **Primary Name Server:** To provide this information, you need to do a lit-tle checking around. Ask your provider (or the administrator of the system you are connecting to) for the name and IP address of the active domain name server that will serve as the home of your domain name. For example, `bobs-insurance.com` will be using a local provider called Winternet whose name server is `ns.winternet.com`; its IP address is `198.168.169.5`. This is how it would look on the form:

```
Primary Name Server
7a. Primary Server Hostname....: ns.winternet.com
7b. Primary Server Netaddress..: 198.168.169.5
```

8. **Secondary Name Server:** This section is for the domain name and IP address that will be used if the primary domain name server is unavailable for some reason. Again, ask your provider for this information. Winternet's backup name server is `ns1.iaxs.net`. This is how it would look on the form:

```
Secondary Name Server
8a. Secondary Server Hostname..: ns1.iaxs.net
8b. Secondary Server Netaddress: 198.168.100.1
```

9. **Invoice Delivery:** This is where you tell the NIC whether you want to be billed by e-mail or postal mail:

```
Invoice Delivery
9.  (E)mail (P)ostal..........: E
```

Once you have completed the form, submit it through your browser or e-mail it to `hostmaster@internic.net`. Be sure to get the address right, as there is a NIC parody site at `internic.com`. Don't send it there by mistake!

Once the application is processed (usually in a week or so), you will be sent a confirmation message. At this point, your server will be accessible by name on the Internet. Shortly after this you will be billed $100 for your first two years. You will then get a bill each year for $50.

6.4 GETTING YOUR OWN IP ADDRESS

While getting your own domain name is a fairly easy process, getting a unique IP address is more complex these days. InterNIC is placing restrictions on who can get their own dedicated IPs. The reason is obvious: an IP address is made of four numbers that can range from 0 to 255. Therefore, there can not possibly be more than 256^4, or around 4 billion, unique IPs. At the current rate of growth of the Internet, even that seemingly inexhaustible supply could be in jeopardy! This should be of little concern to the readers of this book, because we are assuming that you are going to set up your server using an existing provider already connected to the Internet. This is why we recommend that you get your IP address through your provider or the system administrator of the network you are connecting to.

In the "old" days, any network administrator could request a block of IP addresses, whether or not this network was going to be connected to the Internet itself. Now, you can get unique addresses only for systems that directly connect to the Internet, or for network gateways that connect with systems that are directly connected.

Because you will most likely be using one of a specific pool of IP addresses that your provider has already registered with InterNIC, you will have to give up that IP if you ever switch providers — which may be a necessity if you move to a different city or state. But your domain name will stay with you for the rest of your life, as long as you keep paying the bill. When you move to a new provider who has a new block of IPs, you just inform InterNIC of the change, and within a few days, no one will ever know you moved. Because it is the domain name that stays with you and not the numerical address, you should *not* advertise your IP address.

If you really want to bypass your service provider and apply directly to InterNIC for an IP address, the application process is very similar to the domain name registration process. Keep in mind that InterNIC has set aside a block of IPs for internal routing (`192.168.`*xx*`.`*yy*). Use addresses in this range if you are not going to connect to the Net, for whatever reason.

Here is the procedure for getting an IP address from InterNIC:

1. Direct your Web browser to `http://www.internic.net/`
2. Click on "Registration Services" (this takes you to Figure 6–7 again).
3. Click on "Templates (WWW)" and follow the instructions. Or, click on "Templates (Text)," download `internet-number-template.txt`, and fill out the application off-line.

Once again, we must emphasize that InterNIC does not like to give out IPs to individuals unless there is some important reason that you need to have one independent of your provider or network.

If you have followed this book chapter-by-chapter, you should now be ready to install, configure, and use the Web server software for your system. The following three chapters are platform-specific, so you can ignore the ones that do not apply to you (although you may want to read them anyway, so that you understand what everyone else is going through). This is the fun part; good luck!

CHAPTER 7

Setting Up A
UNIX Web Server

*T*he UNIX operating system is the most popular platform for World Wide Web servers. It holds this distinction because it meets the demands of networked information serving very well. Moreover, most Web software was initially developed on the UNIX platform and later ported to other environments.

Unlike other operating systems (such as MS-DOS, Windows, Macintosh, and OS/2), UNIX is hardware independent. This means that its exact implementation varies from system to system. UNIX also comes in many different flavors. The name "UNIX" is owned by Open Systems, Ltd. The actual source code for the UNIX operating system is currently owned by the Santa Cruz Operation. Well, it was last Wednesday, anyway; in the past few years, UNIX has changed hands many times.

By design, UNIX is customized for the hardware platform upon which it is being installed, so the features and capabilities can vary greatly between distributions. However, there are general capabilities common to all UNIX systems. This means that the Web server software described in this chapter should be installable on virtually all implementations of UNIX with little or no modification.

If you are a PC user planning to set up a dedicated server, you should seriously consider installing a version of UNIX that will run on your IBM-compatible system, since UNIX is far better suited for networked file serving than MS-DOS or Windows. The basics of installing UNIX on your computer are fairly easy to learn.

7.1 PREREQUISITES

Before you start, there are a few things you need to have. At a minimum, they are a network and/or an Internet connection, a computer running some flavor of UNIX with TCP/IP properly configured, and an IP address.

It is possible that your system is currently connected to a network; many UNIX systems are. Furthermore, it is possible that you want to create a Web server that will only be used by your internal network. While the instructions in this chapter assume that you will be connected to the Internet, they apply to local TCP/IP networks as well (in most cases).

An Internet Connection

To set up an Internet Web server on a UNIX system, you need to have an Internet connection from your machine that gives your computer a unique IP address that can be accessed from anywhere on the Internet.

If you are already connected to a UNIX TCP/IP network, contact your system administrator to see what sort of Internet connection (if any) your network has. If you are the system administrator of a UNIX TCP/IP network that is not currently connected to the Internet, you need to follow the instructions in Chapter 6 to get a domain name and a block of IP addresses from InterNIC.

You can connect to an Internet service provider (ISP) through your system's modem or terminating device (for digital connections). Because of the way UNIX systems depend upon configuration files to perform any type of networking, it's probably a good idea to get a static IP address from your provider (rather than a dynamic IP address, which will be different each time you connect).

You should also register a domain name that always translates to your current IP address (see Chapter 6). This way, even if you switch providers — and therefore IP addresses — people will still be able to locate your server by name. Besides, it is much easier to remember "`parkweb.com`" than "`204.246.64.26`"!

If your server really takes off, you will want to get as fast a modem as possible and a dedicated phone line for it. This way, your server can run 24 hours a day, and it won't interfere with the phone habits of your office or family. Beyond that, you could get a faster digital connection. Talk to your service provider about your available options.

For stand-alone systems or low volume networks, a SLIP/PPP account is not very expensive at all. You should be able to find a provider who will give you limited access (usually around 100 hours per month) for less than $30 per month; see Chapter 4 for details. If you are setting up a server for a business, and you do it right, it will probably be worth the cost; consider it a part of your advertising expenses. For a "hobby server," a non-profit organization, or a business with a small budget, you should still get a static IP address with a domain name, but the dedicated line might be optional. If you decide not to get one, consider leaving your server on during certain hours each day, and advertise those hours so people know when you are "open."

UNIX Hardware

Because UNIX is hardware independent and can be configured with any number of features for any number of users, it is impossible to give any estimates of how much disk space and memory you will need, how fast your processor should be, or how big of a connection you will need. But at a bare minimum, even a desktop LINUX system should probably have at least 8 megabytes of RAM, unless you want to use X Windows, which requires an *additional* 8 megabytes. The actual httpd programs are very small — around 250K — and will not have a significant impact on your memory requirements. However, the additional files and programs, as well as the TCP/IP traffic, will affect all of your hardware requirements. A very common message one receives these days on the Web is "Please be patient, we will be upgrading our Web server very soon." You should try to anticipate your future hardware needs so that people don't have to put up one of those messages on your system.

UNIX Software

There are a number of commercial versions of UNIX packages available from Sun Microsystems, SCO, and BSDI. There are also freeware packages, known as LINUX and FreeBSD, which run on any PC with an Intel-compatible 386 processor (or better), and which are arguably as stable and versatile as their commercial counterparts. The sample server used throughout this chapter and much of the book is an AMD 486/40 system running the LINUX operating system. Since we like to promote as many free things as possible in this book, here are some sites where you can get LINUX and FreeBSD:

- LINUX: `http://sunsite.unc.edu/pub/Linux/welcome.html`
- FreeBSD: `http://www.freebsd.org/`

The server programs mentioned in this book should work on any of the popular flavors of UNIX. These programs do not rely on any particular shell or require any window-driven system. In most cases, you don't even need to have a C compiler available (though it's always a good idea to have one around). What you do need is to have TCP/IP built into your kernel, along with the supporting network configuration files.

UNIX httpd Program   This is what transforms your UNIX system from just another computer with an IP address into one that can serve information to people all around the world. Web server software monitors your Internet connection for incoming messages via the HyperText Transfer Protocol, interprets the requests, and sends out files if the requests are valid. The server software is the heart of your Web site, and it will be the focus of this chapter.

Web Browser   You will need a functioning Web browser to successfully install and test your server. If you don't have one installed, now is a good time. To obtain the Netscape browser, use an FTP program to connect to `ftp.netscape.com`, and go to the directory of the release level you want to download. There are plenty of other browsers available; we just chose to use Netscape in our examples.

7.2 HTTPD SOFTWARE PACKAGES

The essential piece of software for a UNIX Web server is the HTTP daemon (httpd). A daemon is a program that runs in the background, waiting for the operating system to give it something to do. The httpd program answers any HTTP request that it receives. How the specific HTTP request gets to the httpd program is discussed in the configuration section.

All of the server packages described in this section are available on the Internet. The odds are that if you are ready to install Web server software, you are familiar with getting software from sites on the Internet. See section 7.3 for information on downloading files using the `ftp` command or your Web browser.

It seems that every week, a new UNIX Web server package is introduced on the Internet. The following is a list of some of the more popular packages, and where to get them.

- NCSA HTTPd:
  `http://hoohoo.ncsa.uiuc.edu/`

- W^{3}C httpd (formerly known as CERN httpd):
  `http://www.w3.org/pub/WWW/Daemon/`

- Netsite:
  `http://www.netscape.com/comprod/server_central/`

- Apache:
  `http://www.apache.org/apache/`

This chapter focuses on the NCSA HTTPd server program. The specific examples are performed on a LINUX system, but they will be generally applicable to all UNIX platforms.

7.3 GETTING THE SERVER SOFTWARE

The obvious first step in creating a Web server on your UNIX system is to download a server package. This is the easy part. The difficult part is deciding which package to choose. You need to read about the various software releases, using your Web browser to visit the URLs listed in the previous section. You need to consider things like the security requirements of your site and whether you want "freeware" or a commercial product.

You also need to consider whether to get a *binary release* or a *source release*. A binary release is a precompiled program that can be run on your system. A source release consists of the source files necessary for compiling the httpd program on your system. Unless there is some reason you need to insert local code or make a customized version of the server software, you should use the binary release (if there is one available for your system).

An Example of Downloading a Server Package

Let's run through an example of downloading the NCSA server. The downloading procedures are the same for source and binary releases. The first thing you need to do is become acquainted with the software's features and capabilities. Point your favorite Web browser at NCSA HTTPd's home page (Fig. 7–1); the URL is `http://hoohoo.ncsa.uiuc.edu/`.

Fig. 7–1   The NCSA HTTPd Home Page.

NCSA has a wonderful feature that allows you to fill in a form with your system type and a few configurable items (Figures 7–2 and 7–3). This instantly gets you the correct executable binary for your system with an initial configuration that is ready to use. If you are doing an initial installation, this is the way you should go. There is no reason to edit the configuration files by hand when this facility is provided for you. (If you are performing an upgrade for a server that is currently up and running, go to the "Precompiled Executables" link off of the main NCSA server page.)

To get the correctly customized package for your system, go to the "OneStep Downloader" link from the main NCSA HTTPd page. You will see a page that asks you a number of questions (Fig. 7–2); we will walk you through these and suggest some answers.

Initial: Operating System   Select the actual version of UNIX that you are using. If you are not sure exactly which version you have, use your system's `uname` command with the `-a` option, like so:

```
% uname -a
```

The reply on our system was `LINUX 1.2.13`. Therefore, this is the selection we made in NCSA's form (Fig. 7–2).

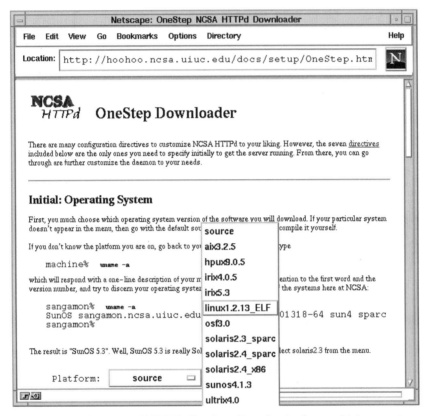

Fig. 7–2   The first part of NCSA's OneStep Downloader form, which prompts you for the name of your operating system.

Directive 1/7: Process type   You have two choices here, `standalone` or `inetd`. Unless you have some particular requirement for putting the HTTP daemon in your initialization process, just use `standalone`. This way, it is much easier to stop, restart, and monitor the daemon. Besides, using `inetd` slows down your system.

Directive 2/7: Binding port   This is the software port that your server listens to. Unless otherwise stated in the URL, all incoming HTTP requests try to connect to port 80. Leave it as this unless you want to test your server or keep other people away from it; if this is the case, any port number above 1024 will work.

Directive 3/7: Server user identity This gives the server a user ID when servicing requests. Use nobody if you don't want to worry about the permissions on individual files and programs. Set up a user account for the server, such as www or JoBlo, if you want to maximize security. This way, you can give your server only the access that you would give to any common user.

Directive 4/7: Server group identity This is the same as Directive 3/7, except that it applies to group ownership. Once again, use nobody, or give the server its own group, such as www.

Directive 5/7: Server administrator e-mail address This is the full e-mail address of the person who is responsible for the server.

Directive 6/7: Location of server directory This is where you want your server space to exist. Leave it as /usr/local/etc/httpd unless you have a particular need.

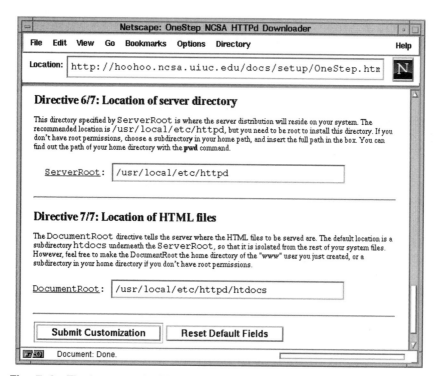

Fig. 7–3 The last part of NCSA's OneStep Downloader form.

Directive 7/7: Location of HTML files   This is your HTML document directory tree. Once again, leave it as `/usr/local/etc/httpd/htdocs` unless you have a compelling reason to change it.

Submit your information by clicking the "Submit Customization" button at the bottom of the form (Fig. 7–3). The NCSA server creates a customized package with the information you just provided for your system. You will be given a link to download this package within 15 minutes of submission.

The file you receive is a compressed archive; this means that there are a number of files merged into a single file and then compressed. You will need to have the `uncompress` command (for uncompressing files ending in `.z`), and the `tar` command (for unbundling the resulting tape archive file); your UNIX software probably came with these commands.

7.4 INSTALLING THE SOFTWARE

Once you have a compressed archive of httpd software that you want in a local directory, it's time to uncompress it and unbundle the individual files in the package. The following example uses the binary release of the NCSA HTTPd package (the LINUX 1.2.13 example that we downloaded in the previous section). The uncompressing and unarchiving procedure is exactly the same for the source release, but the individual files will be different. Let's walk through the necessary steps.

1. Change the awful file name to something usable, like `linuxhttpd.tar.z`, and move it to the `/usr/local/etc/` directory.

2. Uncompress the file:

   ```
   % uncompress linuxhttpd.tar.Z
   ```

   This leaves you with a tar file called `linuxhttpd.tar`.

3. Unbundle the files in the tar file. To do this, use the `tar` command with the extract option (`x`), the file option (`f`), and the verbose (`v`) option so that you can see what's going on. For example:

   ```
   % tar xvf linuxhttpd.tar
   ```

   This gives you output looking something like this:

   ```
   .httpd_1.5a-export/BUGS, 145 bytes, 1 tape blocks
   x httpd_1.5a-export/CHANGES, 9137 bytes, 18 tape blocks
   x httpd_1.5a-export/COPYRIGHT, 3251 bytes, 7 tape blocks
   x httpd_1.5a-export/CREDITS, 4880 bytes, 10 tape blocks
   x httpd_1.5a-export/Makefile, 1838 bytes, 4 tape blocks
   x httpd_1.5a-export/README, 3341 bytes, 7 tape blocks
   x httpd_1.5a-export/conf, 0 bytes, 0 tape blocks
   ```

```
x httpd_1.5a-export/conf/access.conf-dist, 1549 bytes, 4 tape blocks
x httpd_1.5a-export/conf/httpd.conf-dist, 9681 bytes, 19 tape blocks
x httpd_1.5a-export/conf/localhost_srm.conf-dist, 1497 bytes, 3 tape blocks
x httpd_1.5a-export/conf/mime.types, 3319 bytes, 7 tape blocks
.
```

4. Rename the directory `httpd_1.5a-export` to simply `httpd`:

```
% mv httpd_1.5a-export httpd
```

(Of course, you may need to change the above statement slightly to account for newer version numbers.)

5. Voila! You have a new directory tree for NCSA HTTPd, which should contain the following:

```
cgi-bin/
cgi-src/
conf/
httpd
icons/
src/
support/
```

For the NCSA binary package, the server software is installed at this point. If you happened to put the new directory tree in some directory other than `/usr/local/etc`, you will need to update the configuration files in the server's `conf` subdirectory.

7.5 BUILDING HTTPD FROM SOURCE

This section describes how to build an httpd program from a source release. If you are going to use the binary release for your system (which we *highly* recommend), then you can skip this section altogether. The NCSA HTTPd program is used in these examples. However, the general approach are very similar with other packages.

This is a straightforward procedure, but it does require some understanding of compiling C programs on a UNIX system, or at least a familiarity with the `make` command. You also need to be sure your have a C development environment available on your system.

The first thing you need to do is download the source package. To do this, point your browser at `http://hoohoo.ncsa.uiuc.edu/docs/Overview.html` and select "Downloading." From there, select "compile a binary." You are then given the screen shown in Figure 7–4. Download the source and read the instructions for editing the `Makefile`; this is a plain text file that contains some variables that you will need to adjust for your system.

There are three source directories in which you will want to build binaries: `src`, `cgi-src`, and `support`. To compile the programs in the `cgi-src` and `support` directories, simply go to that directory (`cd cgi-src` or `cd support`) and type

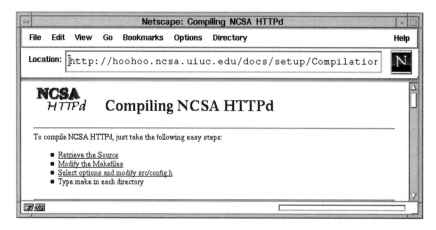

Fig. 7–4   NCSA's page that shows you how to download the source code and compile it on your system.

`make` with your system name. For example, to compile the source on our LINUX system, we use the following command:

```
% make linux
```

To compile the binaries in the `src` directory, you need to edit the file named `Makefile` by *un*commenting lines that pertain to your system (you uncomment a line by removing the # character). In most cases, you should only need to edit the `AUX_CFLAGS` and `EXTRA_LIBS` section. The following chunk of text is how `/usr/local/etc/src/Makefile` looks on our LINUX system; note that the *only* line we have uncommented is the one right beneath the line that says `# For Linux`.

```
# NCSA HTTPd 1.5
#
.
.
.
# AUX_CFLAGS are system-specific control flags.
# NOTE: IF YOU DO NOT CHOOSE ONE OF THESE, EDIT portability.h AND CHOOSE
# SETTINGS FOR THE SYSTEM FLAGS. IF YOU DON'T, BAD THINGS WILL HAPPEN.
#
# For SunOS 4:  Only use uncomment EXTRA_LIBS if you want to circumvent
# NIS and /etc/hosts file.
# AUX_CFLAGS= -DSUNOS4
# EXTRA_LIBS= -lresolv
# For Solaris 2.x
# AUX_CFLAGS= -DSOLARIS2
# EXTRA_LIBS= -lsocket -lnsl
```

```
# For SGI IRIX. Use the EXTRA_LIBS line if you're using NIS and want
# user-supported directories
# AUX_CFLAGS= -DIRIX
# EXTRA_LIBS= -lsun
 .
 .
 .
# For Linux -m486 ONLY IF YOU HAVE 486 BINARY SUPPORT IN KERNEL
AUX_CFLAGS= -DLINUX
# For NetBSD 1.0
# May not need -lcrypt if its included in your libc
# AUX_CFLAGS= -DNetBSD
# EXTRA_LIBS = -lcrypt
# For FreeBSD 2.0.5
# AUX_CFLAGS= -DFreeBSD
# For A/UX
# AUX_CFLAGS= -DAUX -D_POSIX_SOURCE
# EXTRA_LIBS= -lbsd -lposix -s
# DBM_LIBS= -ldbm
 .
 .
 .
#
#
```

Once you have adjusted your `Makefile`, you compile with the `make` command and a system name, just like before:

```
% make linux
```

When the new binaries are created, they are automatically moved into the correct directories. If all goes well (and it probably will), you should have all the files necessary to move on to the configuration process.

7.6 CONFIGURING YOUR SERVER

The NCSA HTTPd program requires that you have certain items defined in plain-text configuration files. When you first install your software, these files contain default values set by the program's author. These defaults may very well be sufficient for some users, but it is likely you will want to customize your server in one way or another.

There are two main areas of configuration for the NCSA HTTPd package: server configuration and security configuration. To change any of the default settings, you have to edit the configuration text files that are in the `/usr/local/etc/httpd/conf` directory. The important files are:

- `httpd.conf` – main server configuration file
- `srm.conf` – server resource map
- `access.conf` – access configuration file (described in section 7.7)

These files serve a number of purposes. They tell the server program where to find files, which files and directories can be accessed, who can access them, and the location of programs that can be executed through the server. This gives you the flexibility of having the server do everything you want it to, and *only* what you want it to.

Editing the Configuration Files

All of your NCSA HTTPd files should be in a directory called `/usr/local/etc/httpd/`. To save space and make this section a little easier to read, we will sometimes refer to `/usr/local/etc/httpd/` as simply `httpd/`. If you have made your `ServerRoot` equivalent to some other directory, simply replace `/usr/local/etc/httpd` with the location you have chosen.

If you choose to change the configuration, it is important to edit the file correctly. Lines that begin with the # character are ignored, and are therefore useful for inserting comments. Directory paths use directory names separated by slashes; if you are used to using MS-DOS, this may take some adjustment, since MS-DOS uses backslashes instead. And UNIX paths do *not* start with the name of a disk, like the `c:` found in MS-DOS.

When editing the configuration files, be sure to use a text editor that does not always use internal formatting characters. This is very important. An ideal editor for this sort of operation is `vi`, which is available on most implementations of UNIX. We have included some `vi` basics in Appendix B. If you decide you don't like `vi`, or you are already accustomed to using a different text editor, that's fine; just make sure you save the files as plain text.

One more note: the configuration files are case sensitive, so you should type in the names of the directives exactly as they appear here. The values that you assign to those directives (options, file names, on and off, etc.) should be lowercase.

Main Server Configuration

The main server configuration file (`httpd/conf/httpd.conf`) defines several major server options, which are described below. Most of them come with preconfigured default values. Unless you know that you really need to change any of these items, it's probably best to just use the default values. The following list describes the configurable parameters in the `httpd/conf/httpd.conf` file. You should print out a copy of your `httpd.conf` file and follow along, so that you can see the exact syntax and default value for each directive. Note that the list of directives here might not exactly match what you have on your system, because each successive version of HTTPd uses a slightly different organizational scheme and a slightly different inventory of directives.

- **ServerType**   This indicates how the server will be started on your system. It can be either `standalone` (the default) or `inetd`. Using `standalone` is the preferred method because it is easier to kill, restart, and monitor. Unless you have some specific reason for running your server from `inetd`, you should use `standalone`.

- **Port**   This is the software port number that httpd is listening to. The default is port 80. You can change it to any number above 1024 that you want. In fact, many Webmasters use port 8080 for testing the server. Using a number other than 80 disallows access to your server to any clients that do not specify the port number in the URL.

- **StartServers**   This is the number of servers to start when NCSA HTTPd initially executes; the more servers you have, the more HTTP requests you can process at once. The default setting is `5`.

- **MaxServers**   When traffic gets heavy, HTTPd launches additional server processes. This directive sets the maximum number of servers that are allowed on your system. The default setting is `20`.

- **Timeout**   This is the amount of time (in seconds) that the server will wait for a request after an initial connection is made. The default is 1200 seconds, which should be more than enough for any connection. If a client needs more than twenty minutes for an HTTP call, there are probably other problems with the connection.

- **User**   This sets the user ID for the server when it processes requests. This directive can only be used if you are running with the `ServerType` set to `standalone` and initially executed by `root`. You give this directive a user name (such as `www` or `nobody`, if you have previously created this user) or a user number (such as `#-2`). The default is `User #-1`.

- **Group**   This sets the group ID for the server when it processes requests. This directive can only be used if you are running with the `ServerType` set to standalone and initially executed by `root`. You give this directive a group name (such as `wwwgroup`, if you have previously created this group) or a group number (such as `#-2`). The default setting is `Group #-1`.

- **IdentityCheck**   This is an obscure remote-user logging directive. Unless you are a seasoned network administrator, you should keep this set to `Off`, or leave it commented.

- **ServerName**   This is your server's fully qualified domain name; this is the name that the rest of the world uses to access your server (for example, `www.parkweb.com`). Your provider and/or your DNS service need to know about any change from your registered domain name.

- **ServerAdmin**   This is an e-mail address that identifies the server's administrator. Put in a full e-mail address for the individual you want to receive comments sent from users of the server. For example, our domain name is `parkweb.com`, so we filled in `webmaster@parkweb.com`.

- **ServerRoot**   This is the directory where the httpd program lives. The default setting for `ServerRoot` is `/usr/local/etc/httpd/`. Don't change this item unless you have some very special requirement. The entire directory tree that you extracted from your tar file is built from this starting point, so if you change this parameter, you must make a similar change in your `access.conf` file.

- **ErrorLog**   This sets the name of the file where errors are logged. The default value is `logs/error_log`. This file is listed relative to the directory you gave in the `ServerRoot` statement, so the real path of the log file listed here is `/usr/local/etc/httpd/logs/error_log`.

- **TransferLog**   This is the name of the file where client accesses are logged. The default value is `logs/access_log`.

- **AgentLog**   This is the name of the file that records the software product used by the client. The default value is `logs/agent_log`.

- **RefererLog**   This is the name of the file where *referers* are logged; a referer is the page or program that led someone to your server. For example, `http://www.lycos.com/cgi-bin/namesearch?guitar/` (Lycos' search program) could be the referer to the ParkWeb guitar page. The default value for `RefererLog` is `logs/referer_log`.

- **PidFile**   If you are running your server in standalone mode, the HTTP daemon has a process ID. This directive identifies a log file that will record this ID. A possible setting might be `PidFile logs/pid_log`.

- **TypesConfig**   This is the location of the MIME types configuration file (`mime.types`). It works just like the previous two variables, so you can use a relative (`conf/mime.types`) or full (`/usr/local/etc/conf/mime.types`) path name.

- **AccessConfig**   This is the location of the Global Access Configuration file (`access.conf`). You can use the path name relative to the directory defined with `ServerRoot` (for example, `conf/access.conf`) or a literal path name (`/usr/local/etc/conf/access.conf`).

- **ResourceConfig**   This is the location of the Server Resource configuration file (`srm.conf`). As with the `AccessConfig` directive, you can use the path name relative to `ServerRoot` (`conf/srm.conf`) or a literal path name (`/usr/local/etc/conf/srm.conf`).

- **LogOptions**   This allows you set up your logging mechanism. The syntax is `LogOptions` *option1 option2*. The options are:

- **combined** Puts the logging information that would normally go into the Referer Log and the Agent Log into the Transfer Log.
- **separate** Keeps the logging information for agents and referers in their own log files.
- **date** Adds the date to each line of the Agent Log and the Referer Log, which otherwise don't have them. (This only works if you have separate listed as one of your logging options.)

- **BindAddress** This tells the server to respond to requests either from one specific IP address (for example, BindAddress 204.246.64.26), or from any IP address (BindAddress *), which is the default.

Additional Directives As we mentioned at the top of this list, you may see some additional directives included in the distribution package that you receive. Most of them relate to virtual hosts. The virtual host feature allows your server to respond to multiple IP addresses or domain names. This way, you can have a single NCSA HTTPd daemon fielding requests for different "servers," even though these servers are physically located on your UNIX system. In fact, you can set up different file space (different document roots) for each of these virtual hosts. Keep in mind that you must have additional domain names properly registered with your provider.

Your NCSA HTTPd configuration files will also contain a few directives regarding the KeepAlive feature, which allows more than one file or program transaction to occur within a single connection. There may also be directives related to features that have not even been implemented at the time we are writing this book. But have no fear; any new directives should be documented in the new versions of the server package.

Server Resource Map

The primary responsibility of the server resource map file is to let the server know where to find files, programs, and icons to satisfy requests from clients. The map file should be named /usr/local/etc/httpd/conf/srm.conf; once again, only change the items that you really need to change.

To see what the default values are for any of these directives, take a look at the default server resource map file that comes with your NCSA HTTPd package.

- **DocumentRoot** This line tells NCSA HTTPd in which directory your *document root* begins. When someone requests a file, your server looks for it by interpreting the file name as relative to the document root. The default DocumentRoot setting is /usr/local/etc/httpd/htdoc, so a file named /usr/local/etc/httpd/htdocs/funfile.html would be accessed with this URL: http://your.server.name/funfile.html. If you had a subdirectory called trains, the literal path of the directory on your hard disk would be

`/usr/local/etc/httpd/htdocs/trains`, but the URL would be as follows: `http://your.server.name/trains/`.

- **UserDir**   This identifies the name of a directory in a user's home directory where he or she can put files that can be accessed by the server. The default is `public_html`. So, user `marypoppins` would put her Web files (including any subdirectories she wants to create) in the directory called `/home/marypoppins/public_html`. The URL for her home page would then be `http://www.nanny.com/~marypoppins/`.

- **Redirect**   If you used to have files on your server that have been moved to a completely different site, you can have people automatically sent to the new location, no questions asked, using the `Redirect` directive. (Of course, you can use this directive for other purposes as well; use your imagination.) The syntax is:

```
Redirect  oldfilename  newURL
```

  The *oldfilename* must be a complete path (starting from your server's document root), and the *newURL* must be a full URL, usually starting with `http:`. You generally should *not* use `Redirect` to point to files on your own server; for that you can use the `Alias` directive.

- **Alias**   Aliasing simply gives an alternative name to an existing item on your server; you can alias up to 20 items. For example, if all of your graphics exist in the directory `/home/www/art`, you could use the following line to simplify the URLs for clients:

```
Alias  /art/  /home/www/art/
```

  This means that when someone visiting your site requests the URL `http://your.server.name/art/monalisa.gif`, they will get the picture `monalisa.gif` from the `/home/www/art/` directory.

- **ScriptAlias**   This is similar to the `Alias` directive, except that it applies to scripts (programs) that your server can invoke. For example:

```
ScriptAlias  /cgi-bin/  /usr/local/etc/httpd/cgi/
```

  This redirects HTTP calls for `/cgi-bin/` to `/usr/local/etc/httpd/cgi/` instead.

- **DirectoryIndex**   This line identifies the *default page* for any and all directories in your document tree. This file is automatically retrieved by the server if the HTTP call is made to a directory. By Web convention, the default value is `index.html`. This allows users to simply point their browsers at the URL of a directory, with no file name specified (for example, `http://your.server.name/trains/`); people accessing your site don't need to know the names of any files, just directories.

- **IndexOptions** This directive tells the server which indexing options you want active. The syntax is as follows:

  ```
  IndexOptions option1 option2 option3 ...
  ```

  There are a number of features that you can invoke with the `IndexOptions` directive. They are:

  - **FancyIndexing** If you want the server to automatically generate an HTML-formatted index — including icons — of any directory where there is no default page, then include `FancyIndexing` in `IndexOptions` (see Figure 7–5 for an example). If you leave out `FancyIndexing`, the index will appear as a plain list of files, as in Figure 7–6.

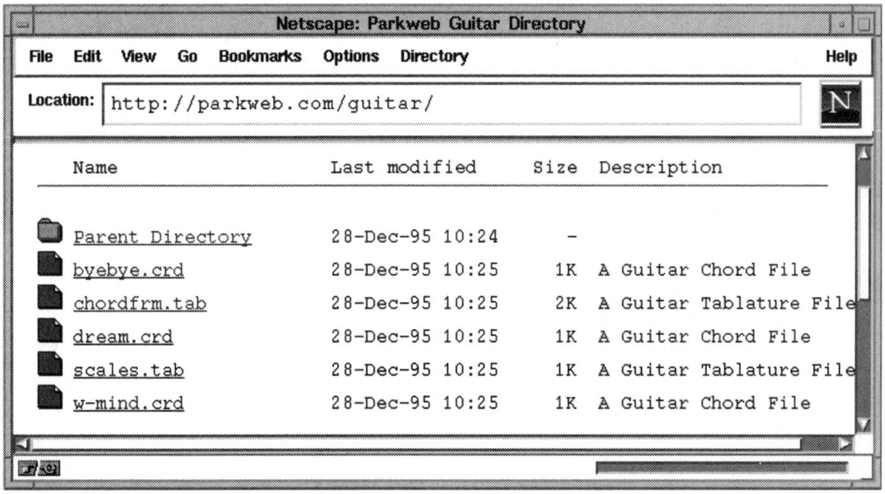

Fig. 7–5 In this server-generated index, `FancyIndexing` has been activated.

  - **IconsAreLinks** Allows users to click on a listed file's icon, as well as the descriptive text, to retrieve the file.
  - **ScanHTMLTitles** If there is no description associated with HTML files (see the `AddDescription` directive on page 103), the title inside of the HTML file is put in the description field.
  - **SuppressLastModified** Hides the date that the file was last modified.
  - **SuppressSize** Hides the size of the file.
  - **SuppressDescription** Hides all of the files' descriptions.

- **AddIcon** Allows you to specify the icon to be displayed in server-generated indexes for a given file type. If you have the `FancyIndexing` directive turned on, icons will appear next to the individual file entries in the automatically generated index. The usage is:

  ```
  AddIcon iconfile filetype1 filetype2 ...
  ```

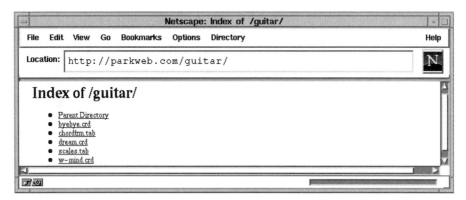

Fig. 7–6 Here, `FancyIndexing` has been turned off.

For example:

```
AddIcon  /icons/monalisa.gif  .jpg .gif .bmp
```

This assigns the `monalisa.gif` icon to JPEG, GIF, and BMP image files (which have `.jpg`, `.gif`, and `.bmp` extensions, respectively) in server-generated indexes. If you do not give any `AddIcon` directives, each file will simply get the icon defined by `DefaultIcon`.

- **AddIconByType**   This directive also affects the appearance of server-generated indexes; it is similar to the `AddIcon` directive, except that it reads files' MIME types, rather than their suffixes. For example:

```
AddIconByType  /icons/monalisa.gif  image/*
```

This assigns the `monalisa.gif` icon to files whose MIME type is defined as `image` in the MIME types definition file (`mime.types`). Additionally, you can use `AddIconByType` to define three-letter identifiers that will be used in indexes requested by text-based browsers; the syntax for this feature is `(ALT, icon)`, where `ALT` is the identifier and `icon` is the icon's file name. For example:

```
AddIconByType  (IMG,/icons/monalisa.gif)
```

- **AddIconByEncoding**   This is the same as `AddIconByType`, except that it defines an icon based on the file's encoding type (MIME subtype), which is defined in the MIME types file. For example:

```
AddIconByEncoding  /icons/gzip.gif  x-gzip
```

This directive would assign the `gzip.gif` icon to any file identified as having been compressed with the `gzip` command.

- **DefaultIcon** Specifies the icon file that will be used in server-generated indexes for *undefined* file types. Here is the usage:

```
DefaultIcon  iconfile
```

If you have your icon path aliased to another directory, use the alias name here, not the literal directory. The following line assigns the `question.gif` icon to any undefined file:

```
DefaultIcon  /home/www/icons/question.gif
```

- **AddDescription** This directive allows you to add a descriptive comment in server-generated indexes for specified file types in the controlled directory. The usage is:

```
AddDescription  'a descriptive statement'  fileidentifier
```

For example, if you want your server-generated indexes to denote that all files with the suffix `.crd` contain guitar chords, and all files with the suffix `.tab` contain guitar tablature (as in Figure 7–7), you would use the lines:

```
AddDescription  'A Guitar Chord File'  .crd
AddDescription  'A Guitar Tablature File'  .tab
```

- **ReadmeName** Specifies the name of the file that contains description text for server-generated indexes. The usage is:

```
ReadmeName filename
```

The server really wants to add some descriptive text to the server generated index. First, it looks for an HTML file named *filename*`.html`; if this file exists, its contents will be appended to the index, and the contents of the file's `<TITLE>` tag will appear as *filename*`.html`'s description in the listing (see Figure 7–7). If the `.html` file is not there, the server will look for simply *filename* instead (no `.html` suffix), and put its plain-text contents below the listing.

- **HeaderName** Specifies the name of the file that appears at the top of a server generated index and serves as a title or header. The usage is:

```
HeaderName filename
```

This directive works the same as `ReadmeName`; the server wants to add a header or title to the server generated index. First, it looks for an HTML file named *filename*`.html`; if this file exists, its formatted contents will be placed at the top of the page, before the actual index items (Fig. 7–8). If the `.html` file is not there, the server will look for *filename* instead (no `.html` suffix), and put its plain-text contents above the listing.

- **IndexIgnore** You can use this directive to hide certain file names from people visiting your site. This is especially useful for keeping files like access

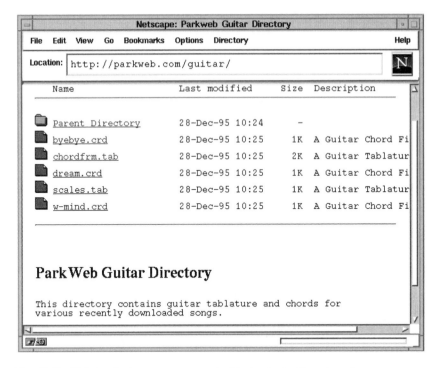

Fig. 7–7 This is what a server-generated index looks like when the
`ReadMeName` directive is used. Everything from the big "ParkWeb Guitar Directory" heading on down is actually `readme.html`.

control files away from nosy people. You can use an asterisk (`*`) character as a wild card identifier with `IndexIgnore`. The format for this directive is:

```
IndexIgnore   file1 file2 file3 etc.
```

For example, here is what you would use to hide the file `.htaccess`, any file with the `.old` extension, and any file with the `report` prefix:

```
IndexIgnore   .htaccess   *.old   report.*
```

- **DefaultType** This line tells the server which file type (text file, graphic, program, etc.) to assume if there is no file name extension that identifies its type. See page 106 for more information on file type mapping. For now, here is an example of a typical `DefaultType` setting:

```
DefaultType   text/plain
```

- **AddType** Defines the type of the specified file extension. This overrides the existing type definition for files with this extension, if one has been previously defined in the MIME types file. This is useful if you have unique type requirements for certain groups of files. The usage is:

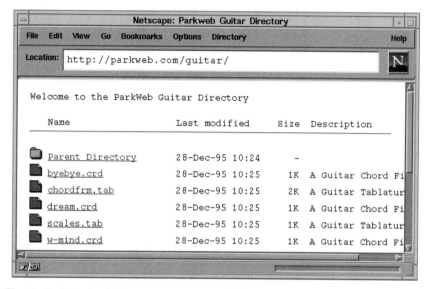

Fig. 7–8 This is what a server-generated index looks like when the HeaderName directive is used. The line at the top of the page ("Welcome to the ParkWeb Guitar Directory") is actually header.html.

```
Addtype    type/subtype    .extension
```

For example, if you want the server to deliver all of the files with the .tab extension as plain text files, you would add the line:

```
AddType    text/plain    .tab
```

Again, see page below for further explanation of MIME types and subtypes.

- **AccessFileName**   This directive defines the name of the access control file in any directory you want to protect. The default setting is .htaccess. We will explain access control files later, so read section 7.7 before you change this line.

- **ErrorDocument**   This directive allows you to create your own error messages or to run a CGI script when an error would normally be returned to the user. The syntax is:

```
ErrorDocument    type    fullpathname
```

For example, if you created your own error message, entitled getlost.msg, that will be used whenever there is a 403-FORBIDDEN offense, you would use this directive:

```
ErrorDocument    403    errormessages/getlost.msg
```

Where errormessages/getlost.msg is the path from your document root (not your server root) to your error message for 403 errors. Similarly, you could invoke a script instead of printing a message:

```
ErrorDocument   403   /cgi-bin/getlost.pl
```

File Type Mapping

When someone requests a document from your server, they don't necessarily know what *type* of file they are going to get. When NCSA HTTPd serves a file, it attaches an *HTTP header* that tells the Web browser what's coming so the browser will know what to do with it. An HTTP header must include a *MIME type*. (MIME stands for Multipurpose Internet Mail Extensions; the MIME standards were originally developed with e-mail in mind.)

Every file transmitted via HTTP has a MIME type and subtype. The MIME type is a general category such as `text`, `image`, or `audio`, and the subtype is something like `html`, `jpeg`, or `x-aiff`. A list of file type "mappings" in the `httpd/conf/mime.types` file tells NCSA HTTPd which MIME types and subtypes should be mapped to which files.

NCSA HTTPd looks at a file's suffix, or extension (the end of the file's name, usually beginning with a period) and goes to the MIME types file to determine its type. For instance, an ASCII text document with the `.txt` extension typically has type `text` and the subtype `plain`.

The format of the file type mapping lines in the `mime.types` file follows this pattern:

```
type/subtype  .ext1  .ext1  .ext3
```

If it doesn't find a suffix it recognizes, it looks at the `DefaultType` directive in the server resource configuration file (`httpd/conf/srm.conf`), and uses that instead. Here are some actual file mapping statements from the `mime.types` file that comes with your NCSA HTTPd package:

```
text/html                     html htm
text/plain                    txt
text/richtext                 rtx
text/tab-separated-values     tsv
image/gif                     gif
image/ief                     ief
image/jpeg                    jpeg jpg jpe
image/tiff                    tiff tif
application/x-bcpio           bcpio
application/x-cpio            cpio
application/x-gtar            gtar
application/x-shar            shar
application/x-sv4cpio         sv4cpio
application/x-sv4crc          sv4crc
application/tar               tar
application/x-ustar           ustar
```

```
audio/basic                    au snd
audio/x-aiff                   aif aiff aifc
audio/wav                      wav
```

There are an infinite number of possible file type mappings, but you will probably find that you don't need to change the defaults much at all. The list that comes with NCSA HTTPd is pretty comprehensive, and you probably will only need to add items if you have binary file types that are not on this list, or if you want to use slightly different suffixes.

7.7 ACCESS CONTROL CONFIGURATION

Now that your server has been successfully installed with a basic configuration, it's time to think about security. By setting up access control mechanisms, you can control not only who can access your server, but also what information these users can get. You wouldn't want just anybody navigating around your entire hard disk or network.

For example, you may have a server containing private business plans that you want to make available to only a select number of employees in different parts of the country. On this same server, you may have personal movie reviews that you want available to the world. This section explains the various ways in which you can control situations such as this.

Types of Access Control

There are two types of controls that you can implement on your server: *global access control* and *directory access control*. Each of these mechanisms use configuration files — known as *access control files*, or ACFs — that set up rules for access. In these configuration files you give directives that the server knows how to use; all of the supported directives are described in this section.

Global Access Control   Limits who can use the server and its files. The global access rules are given in the file `httpd/conf/access.conf`. If, for some reason, you want to rename or move this file, change the value of `AccessConfig` in your `httpd/conf/httpd.conf` file to reflect the new file name. The `access.conf` file defines the access rules for the file tree that makes up your server, which keeps people from accessing files on your system that are not part of the server file space; it defines the directories that can be accessed within the file tree; it defines the extent to which local directory access control feature can limit user access; and it limits which users (or groups of users) can use the server.

Directory Access Control   Limits who has access to files and programs in *any individual directory* in the server file space. This is done by placing a file called `.htaccess` in the directory to be controlled. The access rules defined in a given directory apply to all the subdirectories of that directory as well, unless they in turn have their own `.htaccess` files. Note that `.htaccess` files should *not* include the `<Directory>` sectioning directive (see below).

Editing Access Control Files

Access control configuration files are similar to the general configuration files described in section 7.6 (such as `httpd/conf/httpd.conf`), in that they are text files consisting of lines of ASCII characters. The only exception comes when issuing the `Directory` and `Limit` directives. They are *sectioning directives* that require you to nest other directive information within them. You must *open* a sectioning directive and then *close* it; this is similar to the syntax of HTML tags. For example, in the global ACF (typically named `httpd/conf/access.conf`), you may have the following directive:

```
<Directory /usr/local/etc/httpd/htdocs/>
Options Indexes
</Directory>
```

As you can see, we opened the `Directory` directive with:

```
<Directory /usr/local/etc/httpd/htdocs/>
```

We then set certain options in the `Directory` directive with:

```
Options Indexes
```

And we closed out the `Directory` directive with:

```
</Directory>
```

This will make more sense as we explain each of the directives and their available options.

Access Control Directives

Now that you know the basic concepts behind access control files, let's take a look at what you can do with them. The following list describes the directives that are allowed in these files. Most of these directives can be used in either the global ACF or the directory ACF. Some of these directives call for password information about users and groups. This is explained in detail in the section on user authentication (page 112).

- **Directory**   Identifies a directory within the server file space that is subject to access control. You may only use this sectioning directive in the global ACF. For example, you could put the following line in your `httpd/conf/access.conf` file:

   ```
   <Directory /usr/local/etc/httpd/htdocs>
   Options All
   ```

```
</Directory>
```

This says that the `Options All` directive applies to the directory `/usr/local/etc/httpd/htdocs/` and all of its subdirectories. This enables *all* of the server features for the `htdocs` directory tree unless limitations are placed on the directory level, using `.htaccess` files.

- **Options** Controls the availability of server features for any directory (and its subdirectories); you can either put it in a particular directory's `.htaccess` file, or you can include it in a `Directory` directive in your global ACF. You can assign the following values to this directive:

  - **None** Don't enable *any* server features in the directory.
  - **All** Enable all server features in this directory.
  - **FollowSymLinks** Following symbolic links is permitted.
  - **SymLinksIfOwnerMatch** Following symbolic links is only permitted if the owner of the link matches the owner of the file to which it points.
  - **ExecCGI** Executing CGI scripts is permitted in the directory.
  - **Indexes** Allow users to get a server-generated directory index. If you do *not* give the `Indexes` option, users cannot get a directory listing, but all other server features are available.

- **AllowOverride** Allows the global ACF to limit which controls can be overridden by a directory ACF. You only use this directive in the global ACF. If this directive isn't given in the global ACF, directory ACFs can use any and all of the available controls. When you use this directive, you are, in effect, limiting the power of your directory ACFs. Here are the options you can use:

  - **None** Completely disables directory ACFs.
  - **All** Permits directory ACFs to use all access control features (this has the same effect as *omitting* `AllowOverride`).
  - **Options** Permits the use of the `Options` directive.
  - **FileInfo** Permits the use the `FileInfo` directive.
  - **AuthConfig** Makes the following directives available to directory ACFs: `AuthName`, `AuthType`, `AuthUserFile`, and `AuthGroupFile`.
  - **Limit** Permits the use of the `Limit` sectioning directive.

  Here is an example of an `AllowOverride` directive:

  ```
  AllowOverride Options FileInfo Limit
  ```

- **AuthName** Identifies the authorization realm for the directory being controlled. A directory authorization realm is a security mechanism to allow only certain users to access directories or files; it consists of a realm name (defined by this directive), the realm's authorization type (`AuthType` directive), the realm's user/password file (`AuthUserFile` directive), and the realm's optional groups file, which associates user names with group names (`AuthGroupFile`). This directive effectively customizes the authentication dialog box when prompting users for a user name and password. For example, you could put the following directive in the `.htaccess` file in a directory called `trains`:

```
AuthName  LetIn
```

Figure 7–9 shows what a browser's authentication dialog box would look like when this directive is in effect.

Fig. 7–9   This is the dialog box that appears in a Web browser when a server needs a password and user name. Here, the `Authname` directive is set to `LetIn`.

- **AuthType**   This sets the authorization type for the server or directory that you are controlling. This one is easy: only the `Basic` option is supported in the current NCSA HTTPd release. However, you still must have this directive if you are going to do any user authentication. Here's the only acceptable usage:

```
AuthType  Basic
```

- **AuthUserFile**   Identifies the actual password file that will be used for user authentication on the server or in this directory. The usage is:

```
AuthUserFile  passwordfile
```

And here's an example directive:

```
AuthUserFile  /usr/local/etc/httpd/conf/passwd.pwd
```

- **AuthGroupFile**   Identifies the "groups" file to use for user authentication on the server or in this directory. The usage is the same as with the `AuthUserFile` directive.

- **Limit**   A sectioning directive that controls who can access the server, a directory, server files, or server programs. This directive can be used in global ACFs and directory ACFs. It has four subdirectives: `order`, `deny`, `allow`, and `require`. The operations that are permitted or restricted are a client's ability to retrieve information from the server (GET) and to send information to your server application programs (POST). You can include both GET and POST if you so choose.

```
<Limit GET POST>
subdirectives
</Limit>
```

Here is a description of the subdirectives:

- **deny** This denies access to people accessing your server from certain Internet hosts. You can deny users based on their domain name or their IP address. For example, `deny from .aol.com` (always precede the domain name with a period) denies access to any user from America Online; `deny from 204.246.64.26` denies access to any user at parkweb.com, because this is ParkWeb's IP address. You can deny everybody with `deny from all`, or you can deny users based on the first one, two, or three numbers in their IP address (`deny from 204`, `deny from 204.246`, or `deny from 204.246.64`).
- **allow** This permits access to people from specified host addresses. You grant this access based on their domain name or their IP address. The rules and syntax are the same as those for the `deny` subdirective.
- **require** This allows you to limit access to specific users or groups. This means that even users who have passwords for other parts of the server can be denied access to a particular directory based upon their user name (`require username`) or their membership in a named group (`require groupname`). You can also simply require that they have a valid user name and password on the system (`require valid-user`). Note that `valid-user` is what you actually type; don't fill this in with anyone's user name.
- **order** This specifies the order in which the server evaluates other subdirectives. For example, `order deny,allow` tells the server to evaluate the `deny` subdirective *before* the `allow` subdirective; the second subdirective will override the first one.
- **satisfy** If you are using both the `allow` and `require` options, this adds a little more control. Your choices are `any` or `all`. When `satisfy` is set to `all`, someone can access your server only if they meet *all* of the `allow` and `require` conditions. Therefore, if you have included the options `allow from .parkweb.com`, `require user bozo`, and `satisfy all`, the only person who can get in is `bozo` from `parkweb.com`. If `satisfy` is set to `any`, all `parkweb.com` users and all `bozos` can access your server.

See the "Access Control Examples" section, beginning on page 114, for demonstrations of these directives in the context of a real global or directory access control file.

In addition to the directives listed in this section, you can also use the `AddType`, `AddIcon`, `IndexIgnore`, and `DefaultIcon` directives in global ACFs and directory ACFs, in order to override these directives' values in the main server configuration files.

User Authentication

As you saw in the previous section, you can issue directives that restrict access to certain files or directories to authorized users only. This section describes how all of this works.

NCSA HTTPd provides a facility for issuing user names and passwords. Additionally, you can create named groups that consist of a list of registered users. This user/password facility is independent of any other password mechanism currently on your system, and it works only with your server. You, the Webmaster, assign user names and passwords to your Web server in the same way a system administrator does on a multi-user system. Before you learn how to use user and group names in your ACFs, we'll show you how to create a small database of people you want to be able to use your Web server (or whose access you want to restrict).

Password Protection   Your NCSA HTTPd server program comes with a program called htpasswd. If you plan on having controls put on individual directories, you have to create a user/password mechanism that enforces your server security policy. Keep in mind that you will be issuing user names as well as passwords. Take the following steps to install and use the htpasswd command.

First, locate the password program (called htpasswd) in the httpd/support directory of the NCSA HTTPd distribution. Either keep it there or move it to a more convenient location.

At your shell prompt, use the following syntax to create or modify a user/password file:

```
htpasswd [-c] filename user
```

This command tells the program to change the password of *user* in the user/password file which is called *filename*. If the -c option is present, a new file is created. The program then prompts you for a password. You can then add users to the password file by executing the command without the -c option (Fig. 7–10). You can repeat the command for as many users as you want to add to this file.

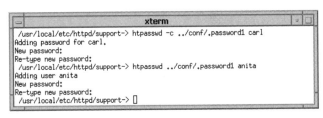

```
/usr/local/etc/httpd/support-> htpasswd -c ../conf/.password1 carl
Adding password for carl.
New password:
Re-type new password:
  /usr/local/etc/httpd/support-> htpasswd ../conf/.password1 anita
Adding user anita
New password:
Re-type new password:
  /usr/local/etc/httpd/support-> []
```

Fig. 7–10   Using the htpasswd command to first create a new password file named .passwd1, with a user named carl; then, user anita is added to the same file. For security reasons, the passwords themselves do not show up when you type them.

The password files you create are referenced by both directory ACFs and the global ACF. The ACF files use the `AuthUserFile` directive to point to a password file that they use for authenticating users trying to access a particular directory or the server itself. It's a good idea to keep these files in one centralized directory in order to keep maintenance easy.

You can call your password files anything you like, but it is wise to give each of them a meaningful name like `/usr/local/etc/httpd/conf/.password1` so as not to confuse yourself. You can also have many different password files. This is not a problem because in any ACF that contains directives pertaining to users/passwords, the password file must be identified with the `AuthUserFile` directive. For example:

```
AuthUserFile /usr/local/etc/httpd/conf/.password1
```

Groups   Now that you know how to create a list of users, let's assign these users to some named groups. This is not mandatory at all; you can control access by listing the individual user names in each of the configuration files. However, if you start accumulating a large number of users, maintenance of these files will soon become a nightmare if you don't organize these names into groups. To create a group file, simply create a text file whose lines have the following syntax:

```
groupname: userA userB userC
```

To assign the group name "siblings" to Carl and Anita (who are brother and sister) and put it into a groups file, you would create a text file — called something like `.groups1` — that includes the following line:

```
siblings: carl anita
```

Now, let's say that you have a few directories that you want to be accessed only by members of a single work department, such as technical writers. By creating a group name for these writers — let's say "techw" — you never have to add or remove names in the directory ACFs as the department roster changes. You only need to keep the single file identifying the "techw" group up-to-date. You can identify as many groups as you like within a single groups file, like this:

```
siblings:  carl anita
techw:  janet carl luis laura
janitor:  bob carol ted alice
managers:  dufus gizmo knowitall
fab4:  john paul george ringo
```

Like password files, you can call your group files anything you like, but you should give them each a meaningful name like `httpd/conf/.groups1`. You can also have many different group files, because, as with password files, any ACF that contains directives pertaining to groups identifies the group file with the `AuthGroupFile` directive. For example:

```
AuthGroupFile /usr/local/etc/httpd/conf/.groups1
```

Access Control Examples

Any access control system will be specific to your site because every server has a unique purpose. Let's look at a few possible scenarios that may be useful to you. In the following examples we will use two people named Carl and Anita to demonstrate access control. In Figure 7–10, we created a password file for them called .passwd1. We also created a group file for them called .groups1 in which their user names were placed in the group siblings (see above). Keep in mind that we need to have the AllowOverride directive set to all so that we can explore the various controls with directory ACFs.

Granting Access to Selected Users
First, we will grant certain privileges to Carl and Anita. As you will see, there are a few ways to do this. Let's grant exclusive global access to the server to Carl and Anita by editing the global ACF (httpd/conf/access.conf). They are permitted to get directory and file information (GET), and to submit information to server application programs (POST). Here is the way the Directory sectioning directive should look in the global ACF (we have added extra comments to explain things as we go along):

```
# This is the defined server space that is being controlled:
#
<Directory /usr/local/etc/httpd/htdocs>

# This is the password file that is going to be used
# to authenticate Carl and Anita:
#
AuthUserFile /usr/local/etc/httpd/conf/.password1

# This is the Authorization realm name that appears on
# the user/password query box:
#
Authname LetIn

# This is the authorization type (only "Basic" is
# currently supported):
#
AuthType Basic

# This opens the Limit sectioning directive. It
# allows the validated users to GET files and
# directories, and lets them submit (POST) data to server
# application programs:
#
<Limit GET POST>

# This tells the server the order in which to evaluate
# Limit subdirectives:
#
order deny,require
```

```
# This directive denies access to everybody:
#
deny from all

# These directives require that your user name be either
# Carl or Anita to access the server:
#
require user Carl
require user anita

# This closes the Limit sectioning directive:
#
</Limit>

# This closes the Directory sectioning directive:
#
</Directory>
```

If we still wanted Carl and Anita to be the only ones able to access our server, but we wanted to deny them the ability to use server programs, we would replace the following line:

```
<Limit GET POST>
```

with:

```
<Limit GET>
```

By denying them the ability to send data to the server application programs, they effectively can't use them. However, they can still get directory information and files. If you wanted to let *anybody* access the server, but fix it so that only Carl and Anita could access a certain directory, you would put the Limit subdirective into a file called .htaccess in the directory you want to protect, and you would remove the Directory lines:

```
<Directory /usr/etc/local/httpd/htdocs>
</Directory>
```

Directory ACFs have much the same function as global ACFs; you can use them to limit certain people's ability to get files and run programs.

Since Carl and Anita have already been assigned to a group called siblings, we can grant them server access on a group basis. To do this, we need to add a line where the AuthGroupFile directive is set to .groups1. Here is what our sample text looks like now in the global ACF:

```
# This is the defined server space that is being controlled:
#
<Directory /usr/local/etc/httpd/htdocs>
```

```
# This is the password file that is going to be used
# to authenticate Carl and Anita:
#
AuthUserFile /usr/local/etc/httpd/.password1

# This is the groups file that is going to be used
# to authenticate members of the siblings group:
#
AuthGroupFile .groups1

# This is the Authorization realm name that appears on
# the user/password query box:
#
Authname LetIn

# This is the authorization type (only "Basic" is
# currently supported):
#
AuthType Basic

# This opens the Limit sectioning directive. It
# allows the validated users to GET files and
# directories, and lets them submit (POST) data to server
# application programs:
#
<Limit GET POST>

# This tells the server the order in which to evaluate
# Limit subdirectives:
#
order deny,require

# This directive denies access to everybody:
#
deny from all

# This directive requires that access is only available
# to the "siblings" group, whose members are Carl and Anita:
#
require group siblings

# This closes the Limit sectioning directive:
#
</Limit>

# This closes the Directory sectioning directive:
#
</Directory>
```

You can see that the only differences between this example and the first one are that an AuthGroupFile directive has been added, and the require user subdirectives (in the `Limit` directive) have been replaced with a single `require group` subdirective.

Carl and Anita have their accounts on the host `parkweb.com`. Since they are such good Net citizens, we decide to grant access to all of their fellow users at ParkWeb. This is where we use the `allow` subdirective. Notice that we no longer have to identify any password files or group names because the `allow` subdirective operates on client domain names and IP addresses.

```
# This is the defined server space that is being controlled:
#
<Directory /usr/local/etc/httpd/htdocs>

# This opens the Limit sectioning directive. It
# allows the validated users to GET files and
# directories, and lets them submit (POST) data to server
# application programs:
#
<Limit GET POST>

# This tells the server the order in which to evaluate
# Limit subdirectives:
#
order deny, require

# This directive denies access to everybody:
#
deny from all

# This directive allows users from ParkWeb (parkweb.com)
# to access the server (This directive could be issued as
# "allow from 204.246.64.26" as well):
#
allow from parkweb.com

# This closes the Limit sectioning directive
#
</Limit>

# This closes the Directory sectioning directive
#
</Directory>
```

Once again, we could put this same text into a directory ACF, except that the `Directory` sectioning directive would need to be removed.

If we wanted to *deny* access to ParkWeb users, we would simply change the lines:

```
order deny,allow
deny from all
allow from parkweb.com
```

to the following lines:

```
order allow,deny
allow from all
deny from parkweb.com
```

Play around with the different access control directives until you have your server access set to exactly where you want it. Once you get the hang of using these directives in various combinations, there is much you can do in protecting your server from unwanted guests.

7.8 Testing Your Server

Once you have your server set up just the way you want it, try to break it! Construct a page that has a dozen different images on it, and see what happens when you try to load them all at once. Get a bunch of friends with Web browsers together, and have them all try to get into your server at exactly the same time. Now have them all load that picture-laden page at once. While all this is going on, you can keep an eye on the server logs to see what's going on.

You should try to hit your server with as many different Web browsers as possible, and make sure they are all seeing the same thing. To make sure the MIME types are being sent correctly, put a large variety of different files in your site and have your friends try to view or download them.

If you have any kind of access control set up, try to access files in the controlled areas and make sure NCSA HTTPd lets you in once you enter the password. More importantly, make sure it keeps you out of places you're not supposed to be in at all. If you have denied access to a certain domain, ask someone in that domain to try to access the server, just to be sure they can't! (An easy way to test your deny directives is to temporarily deny access to yourself.)

While you or other people are accessing your server, try to perform other simple tasks on your system, like reading news, writing a letter, or checking your e-mail. If it's difficult because NCSA HTTPd keeps hogging your system resources, you should think about upgrading your hardware or getting a faster connection.

Once you are convinced that everything is working exactly as it should, and you have tweaked your configuration files as best you can, sit back and admire your accomplishments. You are now officially a UNIX Webmaster! You have created a fully functional World Wide Web site over which you have complete control. You can put anything you want in there, and anyone in the world can connect to your server and see the fruits of your labor.

For more details about server security and maintenance — details which apply to *all* servers, not just UNIX — see Chapter 14.

7.9 CGI AND UNIX

If you have followed the instructions in this chapter up to this point, you should
have a complete World Wide Web file server connected to the Internet. The next
step is to provide people accessing your server with useful programs that run on
your machine. These are commonly called CGI programs or CGI scripts. Setting
up and creating scripts is probably the most complicated part of building a Web
site; you don't *need* to do it at all, but your site will be a lot more interesting if
you do.

When someone accessing your system wants to run a program, they give
the instructions to your server via a URL or a bundle of HTTP data. The server
ensures that they made a valid request, and then it packages the data into a
standard format that the waiting program can understand. No matter what language that program is written in, it must know what the data from the server is
going to look like. The server plays the role of the middleman between the user
and the program being called; this process is called the Common Gateway Interface (CGI). CGI programs and operations are also discussed in some detail in
Chapter 12.

In this section, we will go over the basics of using CGI scripts on your UNIX
server, and we'll give you some URLs that you can look up if you want to know
more.

Scripts

NCSA HTTPd has no built-in facility to run scripts, so it's up to you to have
the right tools accessible to your server and the clients accessing it. The CGI
interface provided with NCSA HTTPd is very versatile and easy to use. Your
exact options depend upon the programming environment on your system. For
example, if you use the popular Perl scripting language for your CGI programs,
you must have the Perl interpreter configured on your system. If it's already
there, then all you need to do is put your programs into the correct directory
(usually cgi-bin) and they should run.

In a UNIX environment, your CGI programs can be shell scripts (such as
those written in sh, ksh, and csh), or programs written in your favorite programming language (such as Perl, C, or FORTRAN). Perl scripts are one of the most
common formats for CGI programs, because the scripts are written in plain
ASCII text characters that can be run on any computer (including non-UNIX
systems) as is; you do not have to compile the script to create an executable
binary program. Shell scripts do not have to be compiled either, but since there
are quite a few different shells in use on UNIX (and other) systems, they are not
entirely universal. Perl is the only widely used scripting language that will work
with all of the widely used computer platforms.

Since anyone can use Perl, it is very well suited to handle Internet interfaces; consequently, there are libraries of Perl routines available on the Net that
provide support for CGI scripts, making the programming tasks much easier. So
easy, in fact, that you can probably set up simple Perl scripts without really

knowing anything about computer programming. If you get lost, or if you want to do some serious programming, there are a lot of on-line reference materials to help you out.

To get started with Perl CGI scripts on UNIX, you really only need two things: a Perl interpreter and a special file named `cgi-lib.pl`. Your UNIX system probably came with a Perl interpreter; if not, you can download it from the Perl archive at `ftp://ftp.cis.ufl.edu/pub/perl/CPAN/src/`. Cgi-lib.pl is a Perl *library* — a collection of subroutines — that allows you to process form data and perform other Web-related tasks with amazing ease (see Chapters 12 and 13 for details). You can get it from `http://www.bio.cam.ac.uk/cgi-lib/`; once you have downloaded it, put it in your Perl interpreter's `lib` directory.

A good way to try out your CGI interface is to run a sample script. Your server may not have included sample scripts in the distribution package, so you may have to find one on the Net or use the simple poem script in Chapter 12 (page 299) or one of the scripts in Chapter 13. Once you successfully run a CGI script from a Web browser, you will know that your environment is correctly configured, and you can start experimenting with additional programs that perform more complex tasks.

Image Maps

You will likely want to use image maps in your Web pages. Since we needed to describe them anyway, we'll do it here to provide an example of using CGI with your server. Your NCSA HTTPd server software comes with a built-in, ready-to-use image map program (called `imagemap`) in the `cgi-bin` directory. To use image maps, simply take the following steps:

1. Add the following line to your MIME types file (usually `conf/mime.types`), if it's not already there:

   ```
   AddType   text/x-imagemap   .map
   ```

   From now on, you should make sure that all map files that you create have the `.map` suffix.

2. Create an image map, preferably using an image map utility such as Mapedit (described on page 123). Save the map definition file — e.g., `mynewmap.map` — somewhere in the server file space, such as in a directory called `/usr/local/etc/httpd/htdocs/maps/`.

3. Take the actual graphic that you used to create the map definition file — e.g., `mypic.gif` — somewhere in the server file space, such as in a directory called `/usr/local/etc/httpd/htdocs/images/`.

4. Add the appropriate code to your Web pages. With the NCSA HTTPd server, there are two ways to reference an image map. In the first scheme, the path to the map file (`maps/mynewmap.map`) follows the name of the map serving program (`cgi-bin/imagemap`):

```
<A href="http://YOURSITE.COM/cgi-win/imagemap.exe/mynewmap">
<IMG src="http://YOURSITE.COM/images/mypic.gif" ismap> </A>
```

Alternatively, you can reference the map definition file directly. Because of the `AddType` directive that we added in Step 1, NCSA HTTPd knows that the `.map` file should be treated as an image map. The server software has built-in code to handle maps, so using the `imagemap` program is not even necessary; just use the following HTMLcode:

```
<A HREF="http://YOURSITE.COM.com/maps/mynewmap.map">
<IMG SRC="http://YOURSITE.COM/images/mypic.gif" ISMAP> </A>
```

7.10 HELPER APPLICATIONS

These are applications that you never knew you needed until you started down-loading files off the Internet, using the Web and FTP. Their purpose is simply to take all kinds of information, created on all kinds of computers, and make it usable on your UNIX machine. You might not *need* all of these programs, but you will probably find them useful.

For each program we describe in this section and the following section, we have listed the URL of a page with more information about the program. If any of these pages have moved, you should be able to find their new location by using one of the Web search mechanisms, such as Lycos or Alta Vista. This is in no way intended to be a *comprehensive* guide to Net-related Windows applications; these are just the ones that we recommend most highly. All the programs listed here are excellent utilities, and more importantly, they're free.

Even if you don't need any specific files, you should check your favorite soft-ware archives regularly to see if anything new has cropped up. When you get to the directory you're interested in, send a `LIST -lt` command from your FTP pro-gram to see a file listing that is sorted by date, so the most recent ones are at the top.

Most of the application software described from this point forward runs in the X Windows environment. None of them require any special flavor of X Win-dows, such as Motif or OpenWindows, so they should work fine no matter what you use. If you don't have X Windows installed on your system, you will need to either install it or do your graphics work on another computer. If you'd like to give it a try, X Windows is available through your UNIX vendor or at various locations on the net. A good starting point is `http://www.x.org/`.

XV

Price: free
URL: `ftp://ftp.cis.upenn.edu/pub/xv`

XV is the most popular graphics viewer/editor package in the UNIX world. It can convert a file from any popular format to any other. It comes with a nice auto-cropping feature and color/contrast manipulation tool. You can also resize and change the graphics aspect ratio with just a few mouse clicks. XV is an almost mandatory utility for any UNIX system.

XAnim

Price: free

URL: `http://www.portal.com/~podlipec/home.html`

XAnim is a free UNIX movie player (as well as a graphics viewer) that supports many movie formats found on the Internet (but not MPEG). The player pops up automatically when you have your Web browser configured to associate it with the various multimedia file types. XAnim is especially valuable because it supports the popular QuickTime movie format.

Mpegplay

Price: free

URL: `ftp://mm-ftp.CS.Berkeley.EDU/pub/multimedia/mpeg/play/`

This is a nice, simple player for movies in the compressed MPEG format. If you set your Web browser to use Mpegplay as your MPEG movie helper, the program will be automatically launched upon the download of a file with the `.mpeg` or `.mpg` suffix. You can run the movie forwards, backwards, or frame-by-frame, or in a continuous loop. Very nice, very free.

Ghostview

Price: free

URL: `http://www.cs.wisc.edu/~ghost/ghostview/index.html`

Many documents on the Web are in PostScript format (usually identified with the `.ps` suffix). These documents are usually typeset text files that are designed to have a nice printed presentation. Ghostview is a freeware program that allows you to see these documents on your screen. You can also print out the document, or a subset of its pages. Note that this is only a viewing program, not a PostScript editor. The only downside is that it has a limited number of display fonts, so what you see is not necessarily what you get.

7.11 WEB DEVELOPMENT TOOLS

This section describes a couple of programs that you will use to create or modify the files that you place on your site. The programs we are describing here are — once again — all available on the Internet. You may want to return to this section after reading Chapter 10, because that chapter contains some information about Web site creation (especially regarding HTML and image formats) that might be useful to know when you are shopping for Web development tools.

If you are using your UNIX machine as a dedicated server, you may actually find it easier and more user-friendly to create your Web files on a separate

Macintosh or Windows system. You can then copy the files over to the computer running UNIX. If this is your plan, refer to the "Web Development Tools" sections on pages 167 and 219, in which we recommend some useful programs for Windows and Macintosh, respectively.

HoTMetaL Free

Price: free
URL: `http://www.sq.com/products/hotmetal/hm-ftp.htm`

HoTMetaL Free is an HTML editor package that ensures you have clean and correct HTML coding. It is great for users who do not want to learn the coding elements in HTML, or users who prefer a graphical interface when editing HTML text files. Graphical tags are shown on the screen to represent the various elements. Inserting and changing elements is done through pop-up menus. These menus are context-sensitive, so only the elements which are legal in that portion of document will be shown on the screen. If you use HoTMetaL Free while your browser is active, you can reload the file each time you save it and see the results of your work. Many Webmasters who provide support for a number of users insist that an HTML editor such as this one be used. This frees everybody from HTML debugging duties. The only downside is that HoTMetaL Free isn't very friendly to imported HTML files that don't follow HoTMetaL's rules. However, you can save these files from your Web browser as simple ASCII text and then tag them with HoTMetaL Free.

There are many HTML editors on the market right now, with a wide variety of prices and features. We've recommended HoTMetaL because it's free, it does a lot, and it forces you to "be good" with your HTML. But you may find that HoTMetaL's HTML enforcement tactics are not for you, or that it does too much or too little for your needs. Since you will probably spend more time with your HTML editor than any other program in this section, you should shop around and find the one that suits you best.

Mapedit

Price: free
URL: `http://www.boutell.com/mapedit`

To use image maps, you must define "hot zones" on the picture which correspond to different links. The zones are regions whose boundaries are written in a map definition file, which can be used with a map serving program such as the `imagemap` program that comes with NCSA HTTPd (see page 120). There are three ways to find the coordinates of the clickable regions: you can guess, you can use a graphics program that will track the coordinates of your cursor (and then jot down the numbers), or you can use a program like Mapedit.

This very useful utility allows you to draw circles, rectangles, and polygons directly onto your graphic (in GIF, JPEG, or PNG formats). The shapes do not stay on the picture; they are just there for your information while creating the map. Mapedit then outputs out your shapes' coordinates to the map definition file, along with the appropriate URLs. It is free, and the author issues frequent updates, so you will probably see new features and bug fixes.

## CHAPTER 8

Setting Up A Windows Web Server

When people think of Web servers, the image of a sophisticated UNIX setup often comes to mind. True, there are inherent advantages to running a multitasking, multi-user system like UNIX or VMS. However, you can set up a very stable, full-featured server under Microsoft Windows 3.1, Windows NT, or Windows 95, running on an ordinary IBM-compatible PC. If you currently are a Windows user, there are numerous advantages to using this platform for your Web server. Here are just a few:

- Familiarity with the graphical user interface
- Preconfigured programs that work with your server
- No need to learn UNIX

The Windows environment is ideal for non-technical users, users with limited server demands, and Windows users wanting to get a server up and running in a hurry. Also, if you are familiar with programming in Visual Basic — which is an increasingly common feature in many Microsoft products — there is a built-in Web server interface for running these programs from your server.

PCs running Windows are no longer the lightweight machines that you might normally think of. In fact, if you have one of the latest, fastest processors running with a lot of memory, your server's performance will be similar to some of the higher-priced workstations that have traditionally been considered to be the minimum for an Internet server.

This chapter describes in detail a wonderful software package called "Windows httpd," written by Robert Denny. This product is actually a version of the very popular NCSA HTTPd package (described in Chapter 7) that has been customized for Windows 3.1. This chapter describes where to get the Web server software, how to install it, and how to configure and use it. Believe it or not, if you currently have a SLIP or PPP Internet account, you should be able to have a server on the air in one sitting.

Windows or UNIX?

If you are planning to use your IBM-compatible PC to run a *dedicated* Web server, you may want to consider installing a PC version of UNIX — such as LINUX, BSDI, or SCO UNIX — on that machine. UNIX offers many advantages over Windows, such as built-in networking, security, and multitasking. Moreover, a UNIX Web server is extremely stable.

The disadvantage of setting up UNIX on your PC — aside from the fact that it's somewhat difficult to install and administer — is that you will lose your friendly, familiar Windows interface, which is why we only recommend this approach if you have a spare computer. Then, you can do all your page development in Windows and use the UNIX system only for file serving. If you want to learn more about the requirements of setting up a UNIX Web server, read Chapter 7.

8.1 PREREQUISITES

Before you start, there are a few things you need to have. At a minimum, they are an Internet connection (a shell account will work, but a SLIP or PPP connection would be better), a PC running some version of Microsoft Windows, and a modem.

An Internet Connection

To set up a Web server on a PC with Windows 3.1, you need to have an Internet account that gives your computer a unique IP address that can be accessed from anywhere on the Internet. This can be accomplished by way of a hard-wired network connection or SLIP/PPP. If you have used a computer that had its own IP address — possibly at a large company or at a university — it was probably a hard-wired network connection. From your home or office, however, you probably will be dialing up using a modem and a Windows socket package (see page 128).

Configuring a SLIP or PPP connection is one of the most difficult parts of hooking up to the Internet, on any platform. We'd love to help, but it seems that every Internet service provider requires a slightly different configuration; your provider will be able to help you with your initial setup.

We cover Internet connections in detail in Chapter 6 and Appendix D, but it is worth a brief review here. When you first start out on the Internet, you will probably have a dynamic IP address; every time you dial into your Internet service provider's system, you are randomly given an IP address from a large pool that is assigned to that provider. This way, thousands of people could share a handful of IP addresses, as long as they did not all try to hook up at once (which they cannot do, since the provider's modem pool is limited).

You *can* run a Web server using a dynamic IP address, but it is not recommended, unless you are still in the testing phase (in which case it doesn't matter, since you are the only one who needs to know your address). But when you decide the time is right to start a public Web server on your own computer — one that you are going to publicize around the world — you will want to upgrade to a static IP address. When you have a static IP, your SLIP or PPP software always uses the same IP address, which is reserved for you by your provider. You should also register a domain name that always translates to your current IP address (see Chapter 6). This way, even if you switch providers — and therefore IP addresses — people will still be able to locate your server by name. Besides, it is much easier to remember "`parkweb.com`" than "`204.246.64.26`"!

If your server really takes off, you will want to get as fast a modem as possible and a dedicated phone line. This way, your server can run 24 hours a day, and it won't interfere with the phone habits of your office or family. Beyond that, you could get a faster digital connection. Talk to your service provider about your available options.

Getting a SLIP/PPP account is not very expensive at all. You should be able to find a provider who will give you nearly unlimited access (around 100 hours) for less than $30 per month. A static IP address is a little more expensive, and a dedicated line (a 24-hour connection) will be much more expensive. If you are setting up a server for a business, and you do it right, it will probably be worth the cost; consider it a part of your advertising expenses. For a hobby server, a non-profit organization, or a business with a small budget, you should still get a static IP address, but the dedicated line might be optional. If you decide not to get one, consider leaving your server on during certain hours each day, and advertise those hours so people know when you are "open."

PC Hardware

The following list describes the basic hardware requirements for a Windows Web server. Keep in mind that these are the requirements for a *dedicated* server (one that is used *only* as a Web server). If you plan to use your PC for other purposes while your server is running, you may need more memory, more disk space, and possibly a faster processor.

Processor   You need to have a PC with a 386, 486, Pentium, or P6 processor (or an equivalent CPU from a non-Intel vendor). If you only have one computer, you can set up your server on that system, meaning you'll have to share its resources with people all over the world while the server is running. You should at least start out this way. Depending on your computer's processor, memory, etc., you might have no problems at all running the server software in the background while you go about your business. But if you do have problems, and you really need to use your server as your day-to-day computer, you'll need to go out and spend some money upgrading your hardware.

Buying a second computer to use as a dedicated server is really the ideal solution. It's expensive, but you can make it a little easier on the pocketbook by tracking down a second-hand PC. Look up "Computers–Used" in the yellow pages, read the classified ads in your local paper, or read the Usenet newsgroup `misc.forsale.computers.pc-specific.systems`.

If you decide to get a dedicated server, you should connect the server's hard drive to your other computer(s) via a simple network. This way, you will be able to manipulate the Web site's file structure without having to disturb the server's computer too much, and you can move files from your other computers to the Web server without having to go through the Internet or walk around with floppy disks.

Memory (RAM)   You should probably have at least 8 MB of RAM if you're planning to run server applications programs or serve large files (like graphics). Otherwise, a minimum of 4 MB should work just fine.

Disk space   The amount of disk space you need completely depends on the number and size of files you are going to have in your Web space, as well as the requirements of the other software and documents currently on your system. However, you will need a minimum of 1.4 MB of disk space free to install the Windows httpd package.

Modem   You must have at least a 14.4k bps modem to have an effective server. Anything less is far too slow. Even if you are just starting out, your best bet is probably to get a 28.8 modem, if your provider supports that speed.

PC Software

Here are the software requirements for a Windows Web server.

Microsoft Windows   Be sure that you are using Windows 3.1 (or Windows for Workgroups 3.11) — *not* Windows 95 — with the Windows httpd software described here. If you are using Windows 95, you cannot use Windows httpd with any reliability. However, Windows 95 and NT users should consider learning all about Web servers with this free package ($99 for commercial use) on Windows 3.1 before paying for the commercial packages available for Windows 95/NT. (Yes, this means temporarily *down*grading to Windows 3.1, but that's actually not too much of an ordeal.)

If you want to go ahead and use a Windows 95/NT server, read section 8.13 — *after* reading the rest of this chapter. In section 8.13, we will describe the installation and configuration of a package called WebSite, which has a similar structure to Windows httpd, but has a friendlier graphical interface. See page 168 for specific instructions.

Winsock   If you are using Windows for Workgroups 3.11, Windows 95, or Windows NT, you already have a socket package available as part of your system software. Windows 3.1 is a single-user operating system. Therefore, you need a TCP/IP socket package for Windows (commonly known as "Winsock"), which provides the necessary software support for you to communicate with other systems on the Internet (or any other TCP/IP network). This software converts your information into TCP/IP packets, and reassembles TCP/IP packets that are sent to you from somewhere else. (TCP/IP software is described in detail in Appendix D.)

A Windows Web Server Package This is what transforms your PC from just another computer with an IP address into one that can serve information to people all around the world. Web server software monitors your Internet connection for incoming messages via HyperText Transfer Protocol, interprets the requests, and sends out files if the requests are valid. The server software is the heart of your Web site, and it will be the focus of this chapter.

8.2 GETTING THE SOFTWARE

There are many Windows socket and server programs on the market today. Some of these packages are available as individual programs, and others are available as part of a suite of products. Shop around and see which one works best for you. The following section includes descriptions of some of these products, and the location on the Internet where they can be found.

Windows 3.1 TCP/IP Socket Software

If you currently have a SLIP or PPP user account with an Internet service provider, then you already have a socket package. If you are starting from a shell account, use the `ftp` command to get your software. Of course, you will need to get a SLIP or PPP account for your server to work on a Net connection; sometimes this requires a slightly different login, and it almost always requires a dialing script; talk to your Internet service provider for details.

The Trumpet Winsock TCP/IP socket software package is available on the Internet and is not packaged as part of a software suite. This is the leading Windows socket package on the market, and it is one reason why SLIP/PPP has been so successful, at least on the Windows platform.

Trumpet is the standard-bearer for all competing socket packages. The price is $25 and it is distributed as shareware, meaning that you can immediately download it for a trial period before paying. You can download it from the Trumpet archive by connecting via FTP to `jazz.trumpet.com.au` and looking in the `/pub/winsock` directory.

Note that the process just described accomplishes the same thing as pointing a Web browser to this URL: `ftp://jazz.trumpet.com.au/pub/winsock`. From now on, we will just give the URL of FTP locations; if you are not using a Web browser, you will need to connect to the site in question, then change directories.

You can also find more about Trumpet by pointing your Web browser at the Trumpet home page (Fig. 8–1): `http://www.trumpet.com.au/`.

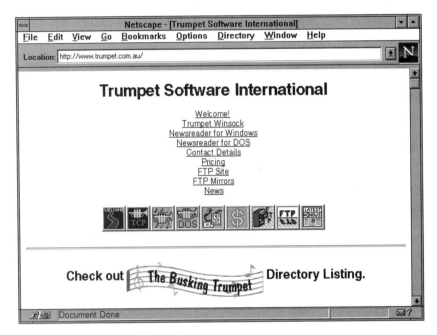

Fig. 8–1   The Trumpet Winsock home page.

PKZIP

Almost any DOS or Windows software that you download from the Internet will have a `.zip` suffix; these files are in a compressed format called ZIP, and you need the PKZIP utility to be able to use them. You may already have PKZIP, but if you don't, refer to page 132 for instructions on downloading it.

Web Browser

You will need a functioning Web browser to successfully install and test your server. If you don't have one installed, now is a good time to do it. To obtain the Netscape browser, use an FTP program to connect to `ftp.netscape.com` and go to the `windows` directory of the release level you want to download. There are plenty of other browsers available; we just chose to use Netscape in our examples. Netscape is free for personal or educational use, but there is a fee for commercial users.

To install Netscape on your system, start up Windows and select the Program Manager group. From there, simply pull down the `File` menu, select `Run`, and enter in the name of the file you just downloaded from the Netscape FTP site.

Web Server Software

There are two categories of Web server software: stand-alone programs, and suites of communications software that include some degree of Web server functionality. The suites also include a number of other programs that range from socket software to e-mail programs and Web browsers.

We recommend that you use a prduct called Windows httpd to set up your server. If you need something bigger or are using Windows 95, then you should check out WebSite (see section 8.13). But you may want to look into the Internet software suites, because they include socket software and many other programs that you will need, such as FTP, telnet, and e-mail software.

Windows httpd This is the product that is described in detail in this chapter. Windows httpd is free for personal and non-commercial use. You can use it on a trial basis for up to 30 days of commercial use. After that, commercial sites must register and pay the $99 fee. To download Windows httpd, point your Web browser at `http://www.city.net/win-httpd/` and read the on-line instructions (Fig. 8–2).

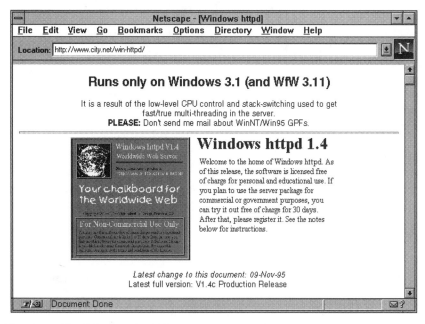

Fig. 8–2 The Windows httpd home page.

WebSite WebSite is a powerful — and more expensive — upgrade to Windows httpd; we will describe it in more detail in section 8.13, where we discuss setting up a Web server in Windows 95 or Windows NT.

Chameleon   This is a suite of Internet-related Windows software packages. Besides the socket program, you get dozens of user programs and utilities. This suite also contains a personal Web server package. You can find this software at `http://www.netmanage.com/` (Fig. 8–3).

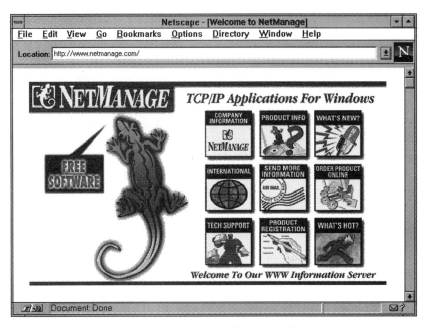

Fig. 8–3   NetManage's Web site (home of Chameleon).

Quarterdeck Internet Suite   This is a multi-purpose software suite of products. It comes with a socket program and various client (user) programs that allow you to read news, log into remote systems, send e-mail, and so on. You can add the separately priced WebServer package (Fig. 8–4) to this suite; it has been very well received by the Windows community. You can find more information about this product at `http://www.qdeck.com/`.

8.3 INSTALLING THE WINDOWS HTTPD PROGRAM

Now that you have downloaded a server software package, it is time to install it on your system. The procedures here describe the installation of Robert Denny's Windows httpd program.

1. Be sure to have a copy of the archiving software called PKZIP, version 2.04g. You can get a shareware copy of this package at the following location, using your FTP software or Web browser:

   `ftp://ftp.pkware.com/pub/pkware/`

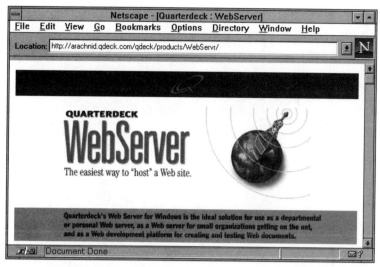

Fig. 8–4 Quarterdeck's WebServer page.

Once you are into that directory, select `pkz204g.exe`. This is a self-extract-ing archive; put the extracted files in a directory called `zip` — and make sure that this directory is in the `path` statement in your `c:\autoexec.bat` file. When you run the program, it creates the `pkzip.exe` and `pkunzip.exe` programs; you can use them by typing simply `pkzip` or `pkunzip`.

2. Create a directory called `c:\httpd`. Be sure to use this exact directory name because many of the files reference this directory name.

3. Find the `whttpd.zip` file that you downloaded, and move it into `c:\httpd`. Move into that directory by typing `cd c:\httpd`.

4. Unzip `whttpd14.zip` in your `c:\httpd` directory, using the `-d` option. It is essential that you use this command option in order to preserve the direc-tory structure of the package.

```
c:\httpd> pkunzip -d whttpd14.zip
```

If the zip file extracts correctly, your `c:\httpd` directory listing should look like Figure 8–5.

8.4 PREPARING YOUR SYSTEM

Once your software is correctly installed in the `c:\httpd` directory, you need to make a few adjustments to your Windows environment in order for your server package to work properly.

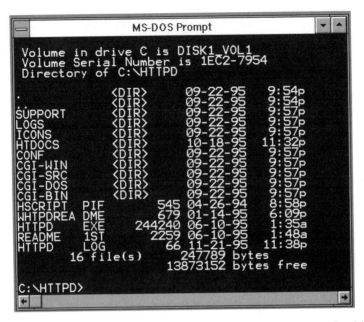

Fig. 8–5 Once you have installed Windows httpd, this is what you should see when you type `dir` in the `c:\httpd` directory.

Time Zone

The first thing you need to do is let the server know which time zone you are in. This is because the Common Log Format used by the server records events using Greenwich Mean Time (GMT). Since the clock on your computer is set to your local time zone, the server needs to make the adjustments to adhere to the standard. To do this, open your `autoexec.bat` file with your favorite editor (you can just type `edit autoexec.bat` from your `C:\>` prompt) and add a line with the following format:

```
SET TZ=zzznddd
```

In this directive, *zzz* is an abbreviation for your standard time zone (for example, EST), *n* is the difference in hours between your standard time zone and GMT, and *ddd* is an abbreviation for your summer daylight saving time. If your part of the world does not have a different time zone in the summer, just leave *ddd* blank. Here are some examples of different time zone settings:

```
SET TZ=EST5EDT   (Baltimore)

SET TZ=CST6CDT   (Kansas City)

SET TZ=MST7      (Phoenix; no daylight saving time)

SET TZ=PST8PDT   (Sacramento)
```

Setting Your Command Environment Size

Many of the example programs and demonstrations described in this chapter use the MS-DOS command environment, which runs beneath Windows. In order for these programs to run correctly, you need to create a sufficient amount of memory space in this environment. To do this, you must add the following line to the [NonWindowsApp] section of the c:\windows\system.ini file.

```
CommandEnvSize=8192
```

Installing VBRUN300.DLL

You need the Visual Basic 3.0 runtime DLL called VBRUN300.DLL in your c:\windows\system directory in order to run Visual Basic CGI programs from your server. This file is *not* required for running the server program itself; however, Visual Basic has become the Windows programmer's language of choice, so it would serve you well to have this file installed in order to use these applications and many others. If you do not already have VBRUN300.DLL, you can find a copy at many of the Windows shareware archives on the Internet, including ftp://igc.org/pub/INTERNET/windows/Misc/. Once you have downloaded it, place it in your c:\windows\system directory.

Creating the Httpd Clickable Icon

With the software on the your system, you are ready to create a clickable icon for Windows httpd. To do this, open up the Windows File Manager program, but make sure you can see the Program Manager in the "background" of your screen. Navigate to the c:\httpd directory, and put your cursor on the httpd.exe file icon. Now, hold down your left mouse button and drag the file icon to the open window or icon of the program group where Windows httpd is going to reside. Let go of the mouse button and the new icon will magically appear (Fig. 8–6).

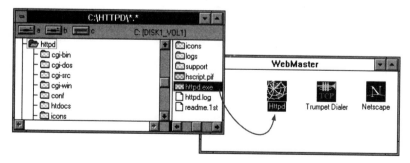

Fig. 8–6 An "Httpd" icon has been created in the WebMaster program group simply by dragging the small icon from the File Manager to the "WebMaster" window.

Starting Up Your Server

Believe it or not, this is the easy part. If all of your software was installed correctly and you carefully performed the system configuration steps, you will be ready to go!

1. Start up your Windows socket program (Fig. 8–7). Run the login script (using the `Dialler` menu) and connect to your provider. Even if you are only going to be testing your system locally without connecting to the Net, you still to have the socket program running before you start up the server program; just don't run any dialing scripts.

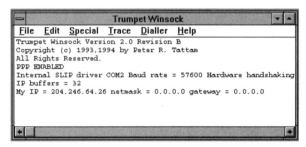

Fig. 8–7   The Trumpet Winsock program.

2. Double-click on the Windows httpd icon. The program will initialize, then automatically minimize into an icon. If you are not connected to the Internet, the initialization window (Fig. 8–8) will stay on the screen for 30 seconds before it minimizes.

3. Fire up your favorite browser and try to access your server. If all is well, you should see Windows httpd's default "Welcome" page, shown in Figure 8–9.

8.5 Configuring Your Server

The Windows httpd program requires that you have certain items defined in plain-text configuration files. When you first install your software, these files contain default values set by the program's author. These may very well be sufficient for some users, but it is likely you will want to customize your server in one way or another.

There are two main areas of configuration for the Windows httpd package: server configuration and security configuration. To change any of the default settings, you have to edit the configuration text files in the `c:\httpd\conf` directory. The important files are:

- `httpd.cnf` – main server configuration file
- `srm.cnf` – server resource map
- `access.cnf` – access configuration file (described in section 8.6)

Fig. 8–8   The Windows httpd initialization screen.

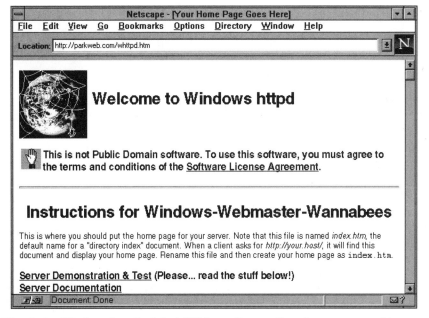

Fig. 8–9   Windows httpd's default "Welcome" page. If you have set everything up properly — but have not added any of your own files yet — this is what you will see if you connect to your own server.

These files serve a number of purposes. They tell the server program where to find files, which files and directories can be accessed, who can access them, and the location of programs that can be executed through the server. This gives you the flexibility of having the server do everything you want it to, and *only* what you want it to.

Editing the Configuration Files

Before you make any changes to the configuration files, make backup copies of the defaults that come with Windows httpd, and then store those backups somewhere safe. We also recommend printing a hard copy of the text of the default files for reference. That way, you can follow along with this book even if your system is not on while you're reading this section.

If you decide to change the default configuration, it is important to edit the files correctly. Lines that begin with the # character are ignored, and are therefore useful for inserting comments. Directory names use a slash character (/) rather the backslash character (\) normally used with MS-DOS. For example, the directory c:\httpd would be written as c:/httpd/ in the configuration file. This is due to the fact that the program originated in the UNIX world, where front slashes are used to separate directory names.

When editing the configuration files, be sure to use a text editor that is able to save text files without any internal formatting characters. This is very important. An ideal editor for this sort of operation is MS-DOS's full-screen text editor (the edit command), which is available in the most recent releases of MS-DOS (version 5.0 and later). However, since most full featured editors give you the option to save your file as plain text, you can probably still use the text editor you normally use, if you prefer not to use edit.

One more note: the configuration files are case sensitive, so you should type in the names of the directives exactly as they appear here. The values that you assign to those directives (options, file names, on and off, etc.) should be lower-case.

Now, grab your printed default files or turn on your system, and we'll walk you through the configuration of your Windows httpd server, describing each option along the way.

Main Server Configuration

The main server configuration file (c:\httpd\conf\httpd.cnf) defines seven major server items, which are described below. Unless you know that you really need to change any of these items, it's probably best to just use the default values. The following list describes the configurable parameters in the c:\httpd\conf\httpd.cnf file:

- **ServerRoot** This is the directory where the httpd program lives. The default ServerRoot is defined as c:/httpd/ (this is actually c:\httpd, according to MS-DOS). Don't change this item unless you have some very special requirement. The entire directory tree that you unzipped is built from this starting point. If you do change this parameter, you will have to make a similar change in your `access.cnf` file.

- **Port** This is the software port number that Windows httpd is listening to. The default is port 80. You can change it to any number above 1024 that you want. In fact, many Webmasters use port 8080 for testing the server. Using a number other than 80 disallows access to your server to any clients that do not specify the port number in the URL.

- **Timeout** This is the amount of time (in seconds) that the server will wait for a request after an initial connection is made. The default is 30 seconds; there's a good chance you'll want to increase this to one or two minutes, depending on the amount of traffic at your site.

- **ServerAdmin** This is an e-mail address that identifies the server's administrator. Put in a full e-mail address for the individual you want to receive comments sent from users of the server. For example, our domain name is `parkweb.com`, so we filled in `webmaster@parkweb.com`.

- **ErrorLog** This is the name of the file where errors are logged. The default value is `logs/error.log`. (Remember to use the slash character rather than the backslash character.) This file is listed relative to the directory you gave in the `ServerRoot` statement, so the real name of the log file listed here is `c:\httpd\logs\error.log`.

- **TransferLog** This parameter tells httpd where to record client accesses. The default value is `logs/access.log`. (Remember to use the slash character rather than the backslash character.) As with the `ErrorLog` setting, this file is listed relative to the directory you gave in the `ServerRoot` statement, so the real name of the file listed here is `c:\httpd\logs\access.log`.

- **ServerName** This is your server's fully qualified domain name; this is the name that the rest of the world uses to access your server (for example, `www.parkweb.com`). Your provider and/or your DNS service need to know about any change from your registered domain name.

Sample Server Configuration File The contents of a real server configuration file (`c:\httpd\conf\httpd.cnf`) are shown below.

```
#-------------------------------------------------------------
#
#   HTTPD.CNF
#
#
ServerRoot  c:/httpd/
#
Port  80
#
```

```
Timeout   30
#
ServerAdmin   webmaster@parkweb.com
#
ErrorLog   logs/error.log
#
TransferLog   logs/access.log
#
ServerName   www.parkweb.com
#-------------------------------------------------------------
```

Server Resource Map

The primary responsibility of the server resource map file is to let the server know where to find files, programs, and icons to satisfy requests from clients. The map file should be named `c:\httpd\conf\srm.cnf`; once again, only change the items that you really need to change.

- **DocumentRoot**   This line tells the server where your server's *document root* begins. The server seeks out files relative to this directory. If you use the default `DocumentRoot` setting (`c:/httpd/htdocs`), a file named `c:\httpd\htdocs\funfile.htm` would be accessed with the following URL: `http://your.server.name/funfile.htm`. If you had a subdirectory called trains, the literal path would be `c:\httpd\htdocs\trains`, but the URL would be `http://your.server.name/trains/`.

- **DirectoryIndex**   This line identifies the *default page* for any and all directories in your server space. This is the file name that is automatically sought out by the server if an HTTP call is made to a directory, but not an individual file. By Web convention, the default value is `index.htm`. This allows users to simply point their browsers at the URL of a directory, with no file name specified (for example, `http://your.server.name/trains/`); people accessing your site don't need to know the names of any files, just directories.

- **AccessFileName**   This directive defines the name of the access control file in any directory you want to protect. The default setting is `#haccess.ctl`. We will explain access control files later, so read section 8.6 before you change this line.

- **Redirect**   If you used to have files on your server that have been moved to a completely different site, you can have people automatically sent to the new location, no questions asked, using the `Redirect` directive. (Of course, you can use this directive for other purposes as well; use your imagination.) The syntax is:

  ```
  Redirect  oldfilename  newURL
  ```

  The `oldfilename` must be a complete path (starting from your server's document root), and the `newURL` must be a full URL, usually starting with `http://`. You generally should *not* use `Redirect` to point to files on your own server; for that you can use the `Alias` directive.

- **Alias** Aliasing simply gives an alternative name to an existing item on your server; you can alias up to 20 items. For example, if all of your graphics exist in the directory `c:\graphics\art\Web`, you could use the following line to simplify the URLs for clients:

```
Alias  /art/  c:/graphics/art/web
```

This means that when someone visiting your site requests the URL `http://your.server.name/art/monalisa.gif`, they will get the picture `monalisa.gif` from the `c:\graphics\art\web` directory.

- **ScriptAlias** This is similar to the `Alias` directive, except that it applies to scripts (programs) that your server can invoke. For example:

```
ScriptAlias  /cgi-bin/  c:/httpd/cgi-dos/
```

This redirects HTTP calls for `/cgi-bin/` to `c:\httpd\cgi-dos`.

- **WinScriptAlias** Same as `ScriptAlias`, except that it defines the real location of Windows server scripts. For example:

```
WinScriptAlias  /cgi-win/  c:/httpd/cgi-win/
```

- **DefaultType** This line tells the server which file type (text file, graphic, program, etc.) to assume if there is no file name extension that identifies its type. See page 143 for more information on file type mapping. For now, here is an example of a typical `DefaultType` setting:

```
DefaultType  text/plain
```

- **AddType** Defines the type of the specified file extension. This overrides the existing type definition for files with this extension, if one has been previously defined in the MIME types file. This is useful if you have unique type requirements for certain groups of files. The usage is:

```
Addtype  type/subtype  .extension
```

For example, if you want the server to deliver all of the files with the `.tab` extension as plain text files, you would add the line:

```
AddType  text/plain  .tab
```

See page 143 for further explanation of MIME types and subtypes.

- **FancyIndexing** If you want the server to automatically generate an HTML-formatted index — including icons — of any directory where there is no default page, give this the `on` value (Fig. 8–10). If you don't want this fancy index to be created, give it the `off` value, and the index will appear as a plain list of files, as in Figure 8–11. The syntax of this directive is very simple:

```
FancyIndex   on
```

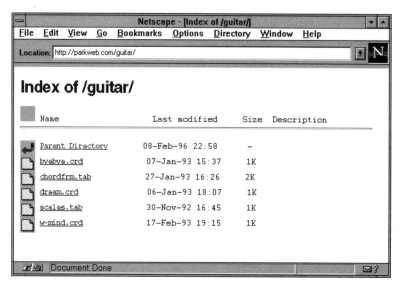

Fig. 8–10   This is what a server-generated index looks like when the FancyIndexing directive is set to `on`.

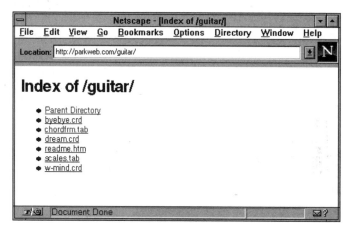

Fig. 8–11   A server-generated index when the FancyIndexing directive is set to `off`.

- **AddIcon** This directive allows you to specify the icon to be displayed in server-generated indexes for a given file type. If you have the `FancyIndexing` directive turned `on`, icons will appear next to the individual file entries in the automatically generated index. The usage is:

  ```
  AddIcon  iconfile  filetype1 filetype2 ...
  ```

  For example:

  ```
  AddIcon  /icons/monalisa.gif  .jpg .gif .bmp
  ```

  This assigns the `monalisa.gif` icon to JPEG, GIF, and Windows BMP image files (which have `.jpg`, `.gif`, and `.bmp` extensions, respectively) in server-generated indexes. If you do not give any `AddIcon` directives, each file will simply get the icon defined by `DefaultIcon`.

- **DefaultIcon** Specifies the icon file that will be used in server-generated indexes for *undefined* file types. Here is the usage:

  ```
  DefaultIcon  iconfile
  ```

  If you have your icon path aliased to another directory, use the alias name here, not the literal directory. The following line assigns the `question.gif` icon to any undefined file:

  ```
  DefaultIcon  /icons/question.gif
  ```

- **IndexIgnore** You can use this directive to hide certain file names from people visiting your site. This is especially useful for keeping files like access control files away from nosy people. You can use an asterisk (*) character as a wild card identifier with `IndexIgnore`. The format for this directive is:

  ```
  IndexIgnore  file1 file2 file3 etc.
  ```

  For example, here is what you would use to hide the file `#haccess.ctl`, any file with the `.old` extension, and any file with the `report` prefix:

  ```
  IndexIgnore  #haccess.ctl  *.old  report.*
  ```

To see the default values for any of these directives, take a look at the default server resource map file that comes with your Windows httpd package (`c:\httpd\conf\srm.cnf`).

File Type Mapping

When someone requests a document from your server, they don't necessarily know what *type* of file they are going to get. When Windows HTTPd serves a file, it attaches an *HTTP header* that tells the Web browser what's coming so the browser will know what to do with it. An HTTP header must include a *MIME type*. (MIME stands for Multipurpose Internet Mail Extensions; the MIME standards were originally developed with e-mail in mind.)

Every file transmitted via HTTP has a MIME type and subtype. The MIME type is a general category such as text, image, or audio, and the subtype is something like html, jpeg, or x-aiff. A list of file type *mappings* in the c:\httpd\conf\mime.typ file tells Windows httpd which MIME types and sub-types should be mapped to which files.

Windows httpd looks at a file's suffix, or extension (the end of the file's name, usually beginning with a period) and goes to the MIME types file to deter-mine its type. For instance, an ASCII text document with the .txt extension typ-ically has type text and the subtype plain.

The format of the file type mapping lines in the mime.typ file follows this pattern:

```
type/subtype   .ext1   .ext1   .ext3
```

If it doesn't find a suffix it recognizes, it looks at the DefaultType directive in the server resource configuration file (c:\httpd\conf\srm.cnf), and uses that instead.

Here are some actual file mapping statements from the mime.typ file that comes with your server package:

```
text/html                        html htm
text/plain                       txt
text/richtext                    rtx
text/tab-separated-values        tsv
image/gif                        gif
image/ief                        ief
image/jpeg                       jpeg jpg jpe
image/tiff                       tiff tif
application/x-bcpio              bcpio
application/x-cpio               cpio
application/x-gtar               gtar
application/x-shar               shar
application/x-sv4cpio            sv4cpio
application/x-sv4crc             sv4crc
application/tar                  tar
application/x-ustar             ustar
#
# Added for PC stuff
#
application/x-lzh               lzh
application/x-gzip              gz
#
audio/basic                     au snd
audio/x-aiff                    aif aiff aifc
audio/wav                       wav
```

There are an infinite number of possible file type mappings, but you will probably find that you don't need to change the defaults much at all. The list that comes with Windows httpd is quite comprehensive, and you probably will only need to add items if you have binary file types that are not on this list, or if you want to use slightly different suffixes.

8.6 ACCESS CONTROL CONFIGURATION

Now that your server has been successfully installed with a basic configuration, it's time to think about security. By setting up access control mechanisms, you can control not only who can access your server, but also what these users can get at. You wouldn't want just anybody navigating around your entire hard disk or network.

For example, you may have a server containing private business plans that you want to make available to only a select number of employees in different parts of the country. On this same server, you may have personal movie reviews that you want available to the world. This section explains the various ways in which you can control situations such as this.

Types of Access Control

There are two types of controls that you can implement on your server: *global access control* and *directory access control*. Each of these mechanisms use configuration files — known as *access control files*, or ACFs — that set up rules for access. In these configuration files you give directives that the server knows how to use; all of the supported directives are described in this section.

Global Access Control   Limits who can use the server and its files. The global access rules are given in the file `c:\httpd\conf\access.cnf`. If, for some reason, you want to rename or move this file, change the value of `AccessConfig` in your server configuration file (`c:\httpd\conf\httpd.cnf`) to reflect the new file name. The `access.cnf` file defines the access rules for the file tree that makes up your server, which keeps people from accessing files on your system that are not part of the server file space; it defines the directories that can be accessed within the file tree; it defines the extent to which local directory access control feature can limit user access; and it limits which users (or groups of users) can use the server.

Directory Access Control   Limits who has access to files and programs in *any individual directory* in the server file space. This is done by placing a file called `#haccess.ctl` in the directory to be controlled. The access rules defined in a given directory apply to all the subdirectories of that directory as well, unless they in turn have their own `#haccess.ctl` files. Note that `#haccess.ctl` files should *not* include the `<Directory>` sectioning directive (see below).

Editing Access Control Files

Access control files are similar to the general configuration files described in section 8.5 (such as `c:\httpd\conf\httpd.cnf`), in that they are text files consisting of lines of ASCII characters. The only exception comes when issuing the `Directory` and `Limit` directives. They are *sectioning directives* that require you to nest other directive information within them. You must *open* a sectioning directive and then *close* it; this is similar to the syntax of HTML tags. For example, in the global ACF (typically named `c:\httpd\conf\access.cnf`), you may have the following directive:

```
<Directory c:/httpd/htdocs>
Options Indexes
</Directory>
```

As you can see, we opened the `Directory` directive with:

```
<Directory c:/httpd/htdocs>
```

We then set certain options in the `Directory` directive with:

```
Options Indexes
```

And we closed out the `Directory` directive with:

```
</Directory>
```

This will make more sense as we explain each of the directives and their available options.

Access Control Directives

Now that you know the basic concepts behind access control files, let's take a look at what you can do with them. The following list describes the directives that are allowed in these files. Most of these directives can be used in either the global ACF or the directory ACF. Some of these directives call for password information about users and groups. This is explained in detail in the section on user authentication (page 151).

- **Directory**   Identifies a directory within the server file space that is subject to access control. You may only use this sectioning directive in the global ACF. For example, you could put the following line in your `c:\httpd\conf\access.cnf` file:

  ```
  <Directory /httpd/htdocs>
  Options All
  </Directory>
  ```

  This says that the `Options All` directive applies to the directory `/httpd/htdocs/` (which is really `c:\httpd\htdocs`) and all of its subdirectories. This enables *all* of the server features for the `htdocs` directory tree unless limitations are placed on the directory level, using `#haccess.ctl` files.

- **Options**   Controls the availability of server features for any directory (and its subdirectories); you can either put it in a particular directory's `#hac-`

`cess.ctl` file, or you can include it in a `Directory` directive in your global ACF. You can assign one of three values to this directive:

- **None** Don't enable *any* server features in the directory
- **All** Enable all server features in this directory
- **Indexes** Allow users to get a server-generated directory index. If you do *not* give the `Indexes` option, users cannot get a directory listing, but all other server features are available.

- **AllowOverride** Allows the global ACF to limit which controls can be overridden by a directory ACF. You only use this directive in the global ACF. If this directive isn't given in the global ACF, directory ACFs can use any and all of the available controls. When you use this directive, you are, in effect, limiting the power of your directory ACFs. Here are the options you can use:

  - **None** Completely disables directory ACFs.
  - **All** Permits directory ACFs to use all access control features (this has the same effect as *omitting* `AllowOverride`).
  - **Options** Permits the use of the `Options` directive.
  - **FileInfo** Permits the use the `FileInfo` directive.
  - **AuthConfig** Makes the following directives available to directory ACFs: `AuthName`, `AuthType`, `AuthUserFile`, and `AuthGroupFile`.
  - **Limit** Permits the use of the `Limit` sectioning directive.

  Here is an example of an `AllowOverride` directive:

  ```
  AllowOverride Options FileInfo Limit
  ```

- **ReadmeName** Specifies the name of the file that contains description text for server-generated indexes. The usage is:

  ```
  ReadmeName filename
  ```

  The server really wants to add descriptive text to server-generated indexes. First, it looks for an HTML file named `filename.htm`; if this file exists, its contents will be appended to the index listing, and the contents of the file's `<TITLE>` tag will appear as that file's description in the listing (see Figure 8–12). If the `.htm` file is not there, the server will look for simply `filename` instead, and put its plain-text contents below the listing.

- **AddDescription** This directive allows you to add a descriptive comment in server-generated indexes for specified file types in the controlled directory. The usage is:

  ```
  AddDescription 'a descriptive statement' fileidentifier
  ```

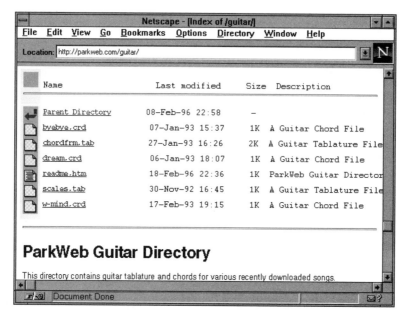

Fig. 8–12 This is what a server-generated index looks like when the `ReadMeName` directive is used. Everything from the big "ParkWeb Guitar Directory" heading on down is actually `readme.htm`.

For example, if you want your server-generated indexes to denote that all files with the suffix `.crd` contain guitar chords, and all files with the suffix `.tab` contain guitar tablature, you would use the lines:

```
AddDescription   'A Guitar Chord File'   .crd
AddDescription   'A Guitar Tablature File'   .tab
```

Figure 8–13 shows the results of these two directives.

- **AuthName** Identifies the *authorization realm* for the directory being controlled. A directory authorization realm consists of a realm name (defined by this directive), the realm's authorization type (`AuthType` directive), the realm's user/password file (`AuthUserFile` directive), and the realm's optional groups file, which associates user names with group names (`AuthGroupFile`). This directive effectively customizes the authentication dialog box when prompting users for a user name and password. For example, you could put the following directive in the `#haccess.ctl` file in a directory called `trains`:

```
AuthName   LetIn
```

Figure 8–14 shows what a browser's authentication dialog box would look like when this directive is in effect.

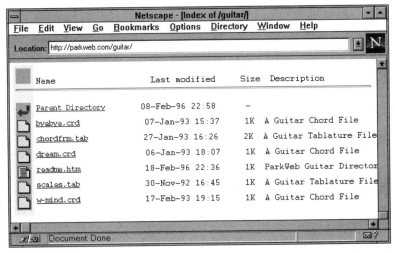

Fig. 8–13 Two `AddDescription` directives have been applied to this server-generated index, so `.tab` and `.crd` files are briefly described on the right side of the listing.

Fig. 8–14 This is the dialog box that appears in a Web browser when a server needs a password and user name. Here, the `Authname` directive is set to `LetIn`.

- **AuthType** This sets the authorization type for the server or directory that you are controlling. This one is easy: only the `Basic` option is supported in the current Windows httpd release. However, you still must have this directive if you are going to do any user authentication. Here's the only acceptable usage:

```
AuthType  Basic
```

- **AuthUserFile** Identifies the actual password file that will be used for user authentication on the server or in this directory. The usage is:

```
AuthUserFile  passwordfile
```

And here's an example directive:

```
AuthUserFile  c:/httpd/conf/passwd.pwd
```

- **AuthGroupFile**   Identifies the "groups" file to use for user authentication in this directory. The usage is the same as the `AuthUserFile` directive:

```
AuthGroupFile  groupfile
```

- **Limit**   A sectioning directive that controls who can access the server, a directory, server files, or server programs. This directive can be used in global ACFs and directory ACFs. It has four subdirectives: `order`, `deny`, `allow`, and `require`. The operations that are permitted or restricted are a client's ability to retrieve information from the server (GET) and to send information to your server application programs (POST). You can include both GET and POST if you so choose.

```
<Limit GET POST>
subdirectives
</Limit>
```

Here is a description of the subdirectives:

- **deny**   This denies access to people accessing your server from certain Internet hosts. You can deny users based on their domain name or their IP address. For example, `deny from .aol.com` (always precede the domain name with a period) denies access to any user from America Online; `deny from 204.246.64.26` denies access to any user at `parkweb.com`, because this is ParkWeb's IP address. You can deny everybody with `deny from all`, or you can deny users based on the first one, two, or three numbers in their IP address (`deny from 204`, `deny from 204.246`, or `deny from 204.246.64`).
- **allow**   This permits access to people from specified host addresses. You grant this access based on their domain name or their IP address. The rules and syntax are the same as those for the `deny` subdirective.
- **require**   This allows you to limit access to specific users or groups. This means that even users who have passwords for other parts of the server can be denied access to a particular directory based upon their user name (`require username`) or their membership in a named group (`require groupname`). You can also simply require that they have a valid user name and password on the system (`require valid-user`). Note that `valid-user` is what you actually type; don't fill this in with anyone's user name!
- **order**   This specifies the order in which the server evaluates other subdirectives. For example, `order deny,allow` tells the server to evaluate the `deny` subdirective *before* the `allow` subdirective; the second subdirective will override the first one.
- **satisfy**   If you are using both the `allow` and `require` options, this adds a little more control. Your choices are `any` or `all`. When `satisfy` is set to

all, someone can access your server only if they meet *all* of the `allow` and `require` conditions. Therefore, if you have included the options `allow from .parkweb.com`, `require user bozo`, and `satisfy all`, the only person who can get in is `bozo` from `parkweb.com`. If `satisfy` is set to any, all `parkweb.com` users and all `bozos` can access your server.

See the "Access Control Examples" section, beginning on page 153, for demonstrations of these directives in the context of a real global or directory access control file.

In addition to the directives listed in this section, you can also use the `AddType`, `AddIcon`, `IndexIgnore`, and `DefaultIcon` directives in global ACFs and directory ACFs, in order to override these directives' values in the main server configuration files.

User Authentication

As you saw in the previous section, you can issue directives that restrict access to certain files or directories to authorized users only. This section describes how all of this works.

Windows httpd provides a facility for issuing user names and passwords. Additionally, you can create named groups that consist of a list of registered users. This user/password facility is independent of any other password mechanism currently on your system, and it works only with your server. You, the Webmaster, assign user names and passwords to your Web server in the same way a system administrator does on a multi-user system. Before you learn how to use user and group names in your ACFs, we'll show you how to create a small database of people you want to be able to use your Web server (or whose access you want to restrict).

Password Protection Your Windows httpd server program comes with a DOS program called `htpasswd.exe`. If you plan on having controls put on individual directories, you have to create a user/password mechanism that enforces your server security policy. Keep in mind that you will be issuing user names as well as passwords. Take the following steps to install and use the `htpasswd` command.

First, locate the password program (`htpasswd.exe`) from the Windows httpd distribution in the `c:\httpd\support` directory. Either keep it there or move it to a more convenient location.

At an MS-DOS prompt, use the following syntax to create or modify a user/password file:

```
htpasswd [-c] filename user
```

This command tells the program to change the password of *user* in the user/password file, which is called *filename*. If the `-c` option is present, a new file is created. The program then prompts you for a password. You can then add users to the password file by executing the command without the `-c` option (Fig.

8–15). You can repeat the command for as many users as you want to add to this file.

Fig. 8–15 Using the `htpasswd` command to first create a new password file named `server1.pwd`, with a user named `carl`; then, user `anita` is added to the same file. For security reasons, the passwords themselves do not show up when you type them.

The password files you create are referenced by both directory ACFs and the global ACF. The ACF files use the `AuthUserFile` directive to point to a password file that they use for authenticating users trying to access a particular directory or the server itself. It's a good idea to keep these files in one centralized directory to keep maintenance easy.

You can call your password files anything you like, but it is wise to give them meaningful names like `c:\httpd\conf\passwd.pwd`, so as not to confuse yourself. You can also have many different password files. This is not a problem because in any ACF that contains directives pertaining to users/passwords, the password file must be identified with the `AuthUserFile` directive. For example:

```
AuthUserFile c:\httpd\conf\passwd.pwd
```

Groups Now that you know how to create a list of users, let's assign these users to some named groups. This is not mandatory at all; you can control access by listing the individual user names in each of the configuration files. However, if you start accumulating a large number of users, maintenance of these files will soon become a nightmare if you don't organize these names into groups. To create a group file, simply create a text file whose lines have the following syntax:

```
groupname: userA userB userC
```

To assign the group name "siblings" to Carl and Anita (who are brother and sister) and put it into a groups file, you would create a file — called something like `groups.grp` — with the following line:

```
siblings: carl anita
```

Now, let's say you have a few directories that you want to be accessed only by members of a single work department, such as technical writers. By creating a group name for these writers — let's say "techw" — you never have to add or remove names in the directory ACFs as the department roster changes. You only need to keep the single file identifying the "techw" group up-to-date. You can identify as many groups as you like within a single groups file, like this:

```
siblings: carl anita
techw: janet carl luis laura
janitor: bob carol ted alice
managers: dufus gizmo knowitall
fab4: john paul george ringo
```

Like password files, you can call your group files anything you like, but you should give them each a meaningful name like `c:\httpd\conf\groups.grp`. You can also have many different group files, because, as with password files, any ACF that contains directives pertaining to groups identifies the group file with the `AuthGroupFile` directive. For example:

```
AuthGroupFile c:\httpd\conf\groups.grp
```

Access Control Examples

Any access control system will be specific to your site because every server has a unique purpose. Let's look at a few possible scenarios that may be useful to you. In the following examples we will use two people named Carl and Anita to demonstrate access control. In Figure 8–15, we created a password file for them called `server1.pwd`. We also created a group file for them called `groups.grp` in which their user names were placed in the group `siblings` (see above). Keep in mind that we need to have the `AllowOverride` directive set to `all` so that we can explore the various controls with directory ACFs.

Granting Access to Selected Users   First, we will grant certain privileges to Carl and Anita. As you will see, there are a few ways to do this. Let's grant exclusive global access to the server to Carl and Anita by editing the global ACF (`c:\httpd\conf\access.cnf`). They are permitted to get directory and file information (`GET`), and to submit information to server application programs (`POST`). Here is the way the `Directory` sectioning directive should look in the global ACF (we have added extra comments to explain things as we go along):

```
# This is the defined server space that is being controlled:
#
<Directory /httpd/htdocs>

# This is the password file that will be used to
# authenticate Carl and Anita:
#
AuthUserFile c:/httpd/conf/server1.pwd
```

```
# This is the Authorization realm name that appears on
# the user/password query box:
#
Authname LetIn

# This is the authorization type (the only valid type
# is "Basic"):
#
AuthType Basic

# This opens the Limit sectioning directive. It
# allows the validated users to GET files and
# directories, and lets them submit (POST) data to server
# application programs:
#
<Limit GET POST>

# This tells the server the order in which to evaluate
# Limit subdirectives:
#
order deny,require

# This directive denies access to everybody:
#
deny from all

# These directives require that your user name be either
# Carl or Anita to access the server:
#
require user carl
require user anita

# This closes the Limit sectioning directive:
#
</Limit>

# This closes the Directory sectioning directive:
#
</Directory>
```

If we still wanted Carl and Anita to be the only ones able to access our server, but we wanted to deny them the ability to use server programs, we would replace the following line:

```
<Limit GET POST>
```

with:

```
<Limit GET>
```

By denying them the ability to send data to the server application programs, they effectively can't use them. However, they can still get directory information and files. If we wanted to let *anybody* access the server, but fix it so that only Carl and Anita could access a certain directory, we would put the Limit subdirective into a file called `#haccess.ctl` in the directory that we want to protect, and we would remove the `Directory` lines:

```
<Directory /httpd/htdocs>
</Directory>
```

Directory ACFs have much the same function as global ACFs; you can use them to limit certain people's ability to get files and run programs.

Since Carl and Anita have already been assigned to a group called `siblings`, we can grant them server access on a group basis. To do this, we need to add a line where the `AuthGroupFile` directive is set to `groups.grp`. Here is what our sample text looks like now in the global ACF:

```
# This is the defined server space that is being controlled:
#
<Directory /httpd/htdocs>

# This is the password file that will be used to
# to authenticate Carl and Anita:
#
AuthUserFile c:/httpd/conf/server1.pwd

# This is the groups file that will be used to
# authenticate members of the siblings group:
#
AuthGroupFile groups.grp

# This is the Authorization realm name that appears on
# the user/password query box:
#
Authname LetIn

# This is the authorization type (the only valid type
# is "Basic"):
#
AuthType Basic

# This opens the Limit sectioning directive. It
# allows the validated users to GET files and
# directories, and lets them submit (POST) data to server
# application programs:
#
<Limit GET POST>

# This tells the server the order in which to evaluate
# Limit subdirectives:
#
order deny,require

# This directive denies access to everybody:
#
deny from all
```

```
# This directive says that access is only available to the
# "siblings" group, whose members are Carl and Anita:
#
require group siblings
```

```
# This closes the Limit sectioning directive:
#
</Limit>
```

```
# This closes the Directory sectioning directive:
#
</Directory>
```

You can see that the only differences between this example and the first one are that an `AuthGroupFile` directive has been added, and the `require user` subdirectives (in the `Limit` directive) have been replaced with a single `require group` subdirective.

Carl and Anita have their accounts on the host `parkweb.com`. Since they are such good Net citizens, we decide to grant access to all of their fellow users at ParkWeb. This is where we use the `allow` subdirective. Notice that we no longer have to identify any password files or group names because the `allow` subdirective operates on client domain names and IP addresses.

```
# This is the defined server space that is being controlled:
#
<Directory /httpd/htdocs>
```

```
# This opens the Limit sectioning directive. It
# allows the validated users to GET files and
# directories, and lets them submit (POST) data to server
# application programs:
#
<Limit GET POST>
```

```
# This tells the server the order in which to evaluate
# Limit subdirectives:
#
order deny,require
```

```
# This directive denies access to everybody:
#
deny from all
```

```
# This directive allows users from ParkWeb (parkweb.com)
# to access the server (This directive could be issued as
# "allow from 204.246.64.26" as well):
#
allow from parkweb.com
```

```
# This closes the Limit sectioning directive
#
</Limit>
```

```
# This closes the Directory sectioning directive
#
</Directory>
```

Once again, we could put this same text into a directory ACF, except that the `Directory` sectioning directive would need to be removed.

If we wanted to *deny* access to ParkWeb users, we would simply change the lines:

```
order deny,allow
deny from all
allow from parkweb.com
```

to the following lines:

```
order allow,deny
allow from all
deny from parkweb.com
```

Play around with the different access control directives until you have your server access set to exactly where you want it. Once you get the hang of using these directives in various combinations, there is much you can do to protect your server from unwanted guests.

8.7 TESTING YOUR SERVER

Once you have your server set up just the way you want it, try to break it! Construct a page that has a dozen different images on it, and see what happens when you try to load them all at once. Get a bunch of friends with Web browsers together, and have them all try to get into your server at exactly the same time. Now have them all load that picture-laden page at once. While all this is going on, you should be watching the Windows httpd icon's status line. This tells you how many connections the server is currently handling.

You should try to hit your server with as many different Web browsers as possible, and make sure they are all seeing the same thing. To make sure the MIME types are being sent correctly, put a large variety of different files in your site and have your friends try to view or download them.

If you have any kind of access control set up, try to access files in the controlled areas and make sure Windows httpd lets you in once you enter the password. More importantly, make sure it keeps you out of places you're not supposed to be in at all. If you have denied access to a certain domain, ask someone in that domain to try to access the server, just to be sure they can't! (An easy way to test your `deny` directives is to temporarily deny access to yourself.)

While you or other people are accessing your server, try to perform other simple tasks on your PC, like writing a letter or checking your e-mail. If it's difficult because Windows httpd keeps hogging your CPU or your modem, maybe you should think about getting a faster PC, a faster line, or even another computer to use as a dedicated server.

Once you are convinced that everything is working exactly as it should, and you have tweaked your configuration files as best you can, sit back and admire your accomplishments. You are now officially a Windows Webmaster! You have created a fully functional World Wide Web site over which you have complete control. You can put anything you want in there, and anyone in the world can connect to your PC and see the fruits of your labor.

For more details about server security and maintenance — details which apply to all servers, not just Windows httpd — see Chapter 14.

8.8 CGI WITH WINDOWS HTTPD

If you have followed the instructions in this chapter up to this point, you should have a complete Web file server connected to the Internet. The next step is to provide people accessing your server with useful programs that run on your machine. These are commonly called CGI programs or CGI scripts. Setting up and creating scripts is probably the most complicated part of building a Web site; you don't *need* to do it at all, but your site will be a lot more interesting if you do. Here, we will go over the basics of what you will need if you want to use CGI scripts on your Windows server, and we'll give you some URLs that you can look up if you want to know more.

When someone accessing your system wants to run a program, they give the instructions to your server via a URL or a bundle of HTTP data. The server ensures that they made a valid request, and then it packages the data into a standard format that the waiting program can understand. No matter what language that program is written in, it must know what the data from the server is going to look like. The server plays the role of the middleman between the user and the program being called; this process is called the Common Gateway Interface (CGI). CGI programs and operations are discussed in detail in Chapter 12.

Because Windows 3.1 runs on top of the MS-DOS operating system, you can run your CGI programs in either the Windows environment or in the MS-DOS environment.

Windows CGI

This is the method recommended by Robert Denny, the author of Windows httpd. The interface he provides with the server is designed to use CGI applications written in Visual Basic. This is why having VBRUN300.DLL available on your system is highly recommended; it is the DLL that allows you to run Visual Basic programs. The Windows CGI environment also supports the server's image feature.

Visual Basic Applications   Because Windows httpd provides extensive support for Visual Basic, there are a number of applications that have been compiled and are ready to use. All you need to do is put a copy of the program in the directory defined by the WinScriptAlias directive in your server resource map configuration file (`c:\httpd\conf\srm.conf`). When the server receives a request for a program in that directory, it automatically invokes the Visual Basic environment, runs the program, and then passes the results back to the requester. You can find some ready-to-use CGI applications in the major Windows software archives (e.g., `http://www.winsite.com`).

Image Maps   You will likely want to use image maps in your Web pages. The `imagemap` program that comes with Windows httpd (in the `cgi-win` directory) is a good example of a Visual basic program using Windows CGI, so we will describe it here. To use image maps, simply take the following steps:

1. Create an image map definition file, preferably using a utility such as Mapedit or WebImage (see pages 167-168). Save the `.map` file to the `c:\httpd\conf\maps` directory.

2. Save the actual graphic file (the one that you used to create the map definition file) somewhere in your server's file space.

3. Add an entry in the image map configuration file (`conf\imagemap.cnf`) that points to the map definition file. For example, if the `.map` file you created is called `newmap.map`, and you want to reference this map as `mynewmap` in a URL, you would type:

   ```
   mynewmap : c:\httpd\conf\maps\newmap.map
   ```

4. Add the following text to an HTML document to call up the map:

   ```
   <A href="http://YOURSITE.COM/cgi-win/imagemap.exe/mynewmap">
   <IMG src="http://YOURSITE.COM/images/mypic.gif" ismap> </A>
   ```

MS-DOS CGI

Windows httpd allows you to run MS-DOS CGI programs in an MS-DOS background shell, known as a virtual machine (VM). The server creates temporary input (`.inp`), output (`.out`), and batch (`.bat`) files. The VM executes the temporary batch file and writes the results to the temporary output file. The server then takes the output file and sends it off across the Web to the browser that requested it. The only problem is that the default setup uses the `command.com` shell in the VM, which is not well suited for CGI applications. It doesn't support complex input/output redirection and can't perform many of the operations supported in popular programming languages. So, to run Perl scripts (recommended in this book) or MS-DOS `.exe` executable programs, you need to make modifications to your default CGI environment. You can get accurate information for making these configuration changes from the following locations:

- Running Perl CGI scripts using John Cope's CGI-DOS wrapper:
  `http://www.achilles.net/~john/cgi-dos/`

- Running MS-DOS .exe files using Mike Crowley's instructions:
  http://130.45.40.46/cgi-dos/topten.exe?/cgihints.htm

Both of these resources are mirrored on our book's Web site at
http://www.prenhall.com/~palmer/cgi-dos.html; look there first.

All of the popular programming languages available for MS-DOS systems
now support CGI applications. However, even if you don't buy the latest-and-
greatest upgrade, you should be able to create CGI programs in your favorite
language. Once you have modified your server's CGI interface, you can run your
.exe CGI programs by simply putting them in your CGI-DOS directory. The
default directory is c:\httpd\cgi-dos.

Perl

If you really want to take advantage of the wealth of programs available for
your CGI environment, you should become acquainted with Perl. It is quickly
becoming a scripting standard in the UNIX world, and it is freely available from
a number of sources on the Internet.

The main advantage to using Perl rather than Visual Basic programs is
that Perl interpreters are available for all commonly used Web server platforms.
So the fantastic Perl script that your UNIX friend wrote will probably work on
your PC, if you set everything up properly. The universality of Perl also means
that there are a *lot* of on-line reference materials to help you out.

Since this book is about World Wide Web servers in general, not just
Microsoft Windows, we have chosen to focus on Perl, since it can be used with
UNIX and Macintosh as well as Windows. Chapter 12 includes a very simple
Perl script that will introduce you to the world of CGI scripting, Chapter 13 con-
tains a few examples of useful Perl scripts that will work with any Perl inter-
preter, and Appendix C is a Perl quick reference guide.

The Windows httpd CGI interface for MS-DOS is not preconfigured for running Perl scripts. The default configuration supports .bat files as CGI programs,
but this is very limiting. Running Perl scripts from Windows on a DOS virtual
machine in the background requires a number of complicated changes. Rather
than reinventing the wheel, we recommend that you follow the steps outlined on
http://www.prenhall.com/~palmer/cgi-dos.html; there, you'll find instructions on how to configure the Windows httpd CGI environment to handle Perl
scripts. The documentation walks you through all of the necessary steps, from
downloading BigPerl to editing a few configuration files. BigPerl is quite large
(1.5 megabytes), so be sure you have enough disk space.

In addition to the CGI-DOS files and BigPerl, you will want to download a
library of Perl subroutines called cgi-lib.pl; this library makes CGI form handling very easy. Simply download it from the Web and place it in BigPerl's library
directory (probably \usr\local\lib\perl). You can find cgi-lib.pl at the following URL:

    http://www.bio.cam.ac.uk/cgi-lib/

A good way to try out your CGI interface is to run a sample script. Your server may or may not have included sample scripts in the distribution package, so you may have to find one on the Net or use the simple Perl poem script in Chapter 12 (page 299). Once you successfully run a CGI script from a Web browser, you will know that your environment is correctly configured, and you can start experimenting with additional programs that perform more complex tasks.

8.9 GETTING PROGRAMS FROM THE INTERNET

Once you have your Web server set up, you will want to give it some pizazz by adding pictures, sounds, image maps, CGI scripts, and other nifty features. Fortunately, there are a number of programs already available on the Net that will help you with this task.

As we mentioned in the previous section, you can download and install most Perl CGI scripts and use them with Windows httpd, even if they were not written with Windows in mind. You can also find a few Visual Basic programs, although these are not as common, and you may have to do a little digging to find them.

You won't have to dig, however, for a large number of complete Windows applications that will help you become a fully-connected Internet citizen. You can find huge archives of utilities that will help you create graphics, download files via FTP, read Usenet news, play sounds, and so on. We will describe a number of these programs in the sections that follow.

But first, a bit of explanation: For each program we describe, we have listed the price — most of them are free, although a few require a registration fee — and the URL of a page with more information about the program. (If any of these pages have moved, you should be able to find their new location by using one of the Web search mechanisms such as Lycos or Alta Vista.) This is in no way intended to be a *comprehensive* guide to Net-related Windows applications; these are just the ones that we recommend most highly. Every program listed here is excellent, cheap, or both.

You can also download most of these files by simply looking in the Internet/World Wide Web section of any major software archive that contains Windows software, such as `http://www.winsite.com/`.

Even if you don't need any specific files, you should check your favorite Windows software archive regularly to see if anything new has cropped up. When you get to the directory you're interested in, send a `LIST -lt` command from your FTP program to see a file listing that is sorted by date, so the most recent ones are at the top.

For more information about Internet-related Windows programs — and the most recent prices, version numbers, file locations, etc. — there is a fantastic Web site called the "Consummate Winsock Apps List," written by Forrest Stroud (Fig. 8–16); you can find it at many locations around the world, including these URLs:

- http://cws.wilmington.net/
- http://www.tower.com.au/cws_apps/
- http://www.netppl.fi/consummate

Fig. 8-16 The "Consummate Winsock Apps" page. This is a great resource for finding out about Windows programs that you can use, directly or indirectly, with your server.

A Brief Word About Shareware

Most of the programs available on the Internet are either freeware or shareware. Shareware exists because it's a great way for software authors to have their programs widely distributed without having any marketing overhead. If no one pays for their shareware, there will be no more shareware. Instead, all software will be sold commercially at horrible prices that are inflated, in part, by people who illegally copy software.

We describe a number of shareware programs in this chapter. You are always free to try them out on your computer and see whether you like them — that's another reason shareware is such a wonderful system — but as soon as your trial period is up, you must delete the program if you weren't planning on paying for it.

Obviously, you don't have to pay for freeware programs, but it's nice to send their authors a quick thank-you note via e-mail if you use their program; often, it's the only reward they get. If they say that you don't *have* to send money, but they'd sure like it if you did, you should seriously consider sending five bucks.

The price of shareware isn't always cash; we've seen postcardware, jobware ("if you like this program, hire me"), and even beerware.

Once again, we can't stress enough how important it is to pay for your shareware. So, now that we have that out of the way, keep reading to find out about some great programs that you can download right now and use with your system.

8.10 INTERNET APPLICATIONS

These are programs that allow you to access various Internet services, so they all require a SLIP, PPP, or direct connection to the Internet. Chances are you already have at least a couple of them — or their equivalents — if you have a SLIP or PPP account. If you want to be a fully-connected Internet citizen, it is imperative that you have at least one of each of the following: an FTP program, a Telnet client, a mail reader, and a news reader. There are many applications that fulfill these functions, but the ones listed here are our favorites.

Note that we have not covered Web browsers in this section; that's because we are assuming that by now you already have one! You can get a hold of most or all of these applications at any good Windows FTP archive or via the "Consummate Winsock Apps" list.

WS_FTP

Price: free
URL: http://www.csra.net/junodj/ws_ftp.htm

An FTP client program is essential if you are going to make the most of the Internet, and WS_FTP does everything an FTP client should. The scrolling interface allows you to easily navigate through the file systems of both the host and the client. Transferring files is simply a matter of highlighting the files you want to move from one system to another and clicking on the appropriate direction arrow. The address book is very easy to set up, freeing you from having to remember location names and login differences. All in all, this is a very good program for a complete Net software suite.

EWAN

Price: free
URL: http://www.lysator.liu.se/~zander/ewan.html

Most SLIP/PPP accounts still provide you with a shell account that you can access. Additionally, there are sites on the net that allow outside guest users to log into their system. This is why it's a good idea to have a telnet client available on your system. EWAN ("Emulator Without a Name") is a free telnet client and terminal emulator that supports VT100, VT52, and plain ANSI emulation modes. It has an easy-to-use menu interface that allows you to store information about all of your favorite hosts. You simply point-and-click on the host name and

EWAN makes the connection. Sophisticated users can create their own emulation DLLs for customized connections. This is probably the only telnet program you need.

Pegasus Mail

Price: free
URL: `http://www.cuslm.ca/pegasus/`

If you use mail for anything other than simple notes, Pegasus Mail is probably a good tool for you. The interface is very pleasant to look at and the menus are logically organized. You can compose your messages with its simple, yet efficient text editor that comes with a built-in spell checker, and you can send and receive any type of file as attachments through automatic background encoding/decoding. If connection time is a concern, Pegasus Mail allows you to compose messages off-line and store them in a queue until you are logged into your host. The feature-rich address book is another plus for this wonderfully free product.

Free Agent

Price: free (but commercial users must purchase Agent for $29)
URL: `http://www.forteinc.com/forte/agent/freeagent.htm`

You can use a Web browser to read Usenet news, but many people prefer to use a separate program. Though relatively new to the Net, Free Agent has quickly become the Usenet news reader of choice for many Windows users. Almost every imaginable feature is provided, from automatic threading to on-the-fly, multi-part article decoding. The separate windows for groups, subjects, and articles give you the flexibility you need to maximize the efficiency of your news-reading session. The default configuration was obviously well thought out, and you can learn to use the immense number of more detailed features one-by-one at your own pace.

Commercial users are not allowed to use Free Agent, which is freeware; they must purchase Agent instead. It is essentially the same program as Free Agent, but it has a few more features, and it costs $29. You can get it from the same place that you get Free Agent.

WS_Gopher

Price: free
URL: `ftp://snake.srv.net/pub/windows/archives/`

Another essential piece of software for any Internet user is a Gopher client. While the Web has taken over as the major information retrieval system, Gopher is still a very nice way to get certain information fast and efficiently. If you are currently a Gopher user, you know that its beauty is in its simplicity. That's why WS_Gopher is a pleasant tool. It displays gopher menus and files via a nice, simple interface and provides a very good address book and hotlist facility. There is little else you need in a Gopher client, so you might as well go with this free package.

8.11 HELPER APPLICATIONS

These are applications that you never knew you needed until you started using the Internet applications in section 8.10 to download files. Their purpose is simply to take all kinds of information, created on all kinds of computers, and make it usable on your PC. You might not need *all* of these programs, but at a bare minimum, you should have PKZIP and GraphX Viewer. As always, the files listed in this section are available for downloading from most Windows software archives, as well as from the URLs listed here.

PKZIP

Price: free (individual non-commercial use) or $47 (commercial)
URL: `ftp://ftp.pkware.com/pub/pkware/`

This utility is essential for any IBM-compatible system that is hooked up to the Net. In fact, it is likely that you already have some version of it. Almost all publicly accessible MS-DOS or Windows files on the Internet are stored in ZIP format; you can recognize them by their `.zip` extension. ZIP files are compressed archives. This means that all the files in a package are dumped into a single file, which is then compressed.

Version 2.04G of PKZIP boasts a significant increase in compression ratios over previous releases, and it is *backward compatible*, meaning that all files created with previous releases of PKZIP can be uncompressed as well. PKZIP 2.04G also handles files created with PKZIP clones, such as InfoZip's public domain package. If you don't have PKZIP yet, you need it badly. If you have an older version, upgrade your copy as soon as possible.

GraphX Viewer

Price: free
URL: `http://www.group42.com/graphx.htm`

If you are looking for a quick, free image viewer, this is an excellent package. It handles all of the popular graphics formats and has several "effects" options for creating the images you want. While not particularly feature-rich, it is strong in the area of thumbnail catalog creation and file management. GraphX makes an excellent helper application for viewing files that your Web browser can't handle. This program should be part of every Windows system that is connected to the Internet.

WHAM

Price: free (donations enthusiastically accepted)
URL: `ftp://igc.org/pub/INTERNET/windows/Misc/`

With the increased use of sound associated with Web pages, it's good to have a sound program that simply plays the sound files you access without any work on your part. The latest versions of Netscape for Windows come with the Netscape Audio Player; however, if you don't use Netscape, or if you want to be able to edit sounds as well as play them, you need something like WHAM. This is a simple sound utility that plays all of the common sound formats used on the Net, and allows you to do some simple editing as well. While not a "real-time" player like RealAudio or Xing StreamWorks (see page 252), it meets the sound requirements of the average user, hassle-free.

QuickTime for Windows

Price: free
URL: `http://quicktime.apple.com/winlicense.html`

QuickTime (`.mov`, `.moov`, or `.qt` files) and AVI are quickly becoming the standard formats for movies on the Web. Microsoft Windows comes with software to play AVI files (the Media Player), but you will need Apple's QuickTime for Windows (QTW) program in order to play QuickTime movies on your PC. When properly configured with your Web browser, QTW pops up automatically when you download a file with a suffix or MIME type that designates it as a QuickTime movie. You can optionally run movies in a continuous loop or watch it frame-by-frame. The QTW package also includes a graphics viewer that supports all of the commonly used formats on the Internet.

Mpegplay

Price: free
URL: `http://www.ncsa.uiuc.edu/SDG/Software/WinMosaic/Viewers/mpeg.htm`

This is a nice, simple player for movies in the compressed MPEG format. If you set your Web browser to use Mpegplay as your MPEG movie helper, the program will be automatically launched upon the download of a file with the `.mpeg` or `.mpg` suffix. Because it is a 32-bit application, you need to have `win32s.dll` installed in your `c:\windows\system` directory to use Mpegplay.

8.12 WEB DEVELOPMENT TOOLS

These are applications that you will use to create or modify the files that you place on your site. The programs we are describing here are — once again — all available on the Internet. You may want to return to this section after reading Chapter 10, because that chapter contains some information about Web site creation (especially regarding HTML and image formats) that might be useful to know when you are shopping for Web development tools.

HoTMetaL Free

Price: free
URL: `http://www.sq.com/products/hotmetal/hm-ftp.htm`

HoTMetaL Free is an HTML editor package that ensures you have clean and correct HTML coding. It is great for users who do not want to learn the coding elements in HTML, or users who prefer a graphical interface when editing HTML text files. Graphical tags are shown on the screen to represent the various elements. Inserting and changing elements is done through pop-up menus. These menus are context-sensitive, so only the elements which are legal in that portion of document will be shown on the screen. If you use HoTMetaL Free while your browser is active, you can reload the file after every save and see the results of your work. Many Webmasters who provide support for a number of users insist that an HTML editor such as this one be used. This frees everybody from HTML debugging duties. The only downside is that HoTMetaL Free isn't very friendly to imported HTML files that don't follow HoTMetaL's rules. However, you can save these files from your Web browser as simple ASCII text and then tag them with HoTMetaL Free.

There are many HTML editors on the market right now, with a wide variety of prices and features. We've recommended HoTMetaL because it's free, it does a lot, and it forces you to "be good" with your HTML. But you may find that HoTMetaL's HTML enforcement tactics are not for you, or that it does too much or too little for your needs. Since you will probably spend more time with your HTML editor than any other program in this section, you should shop around and find the one that suits you best. Thanks to the shareware system, you can download and evaluate a dozen different programs if you want. For a list of HTML editors you may want to try, check Forrest Stroud's list (see page 161).

Mapedit

Price: free
URL: `http://www.boutell.com/mapedit`

To use image maps, you must define "hot zones" on the picture that correspond to different links. The zones are regions whose boundaries are written in a map definition file, which can be used with a map serving program such as the `imagemap` program that comes with Windows httpd (see page 159). There are three ways to find the coordinates of the clickable regions: you can guess, you can use a graphics program that will track the coordinates of your cursor (and then jot down the numbers), or you can use a program like Mapedit.

This very useful utility allows you to draw circles, rectangles, and polygons directly onto your graphic (it supports GIF, JPEG, and PNG image formats). The shapes do not stay on the picture; they are just there for your information while creating the map. Mapedit then outputs your shapes' coordinates to the map definition file, along with the appropriate URLs. It is free, and the author issues frequent updates, so you will probably see new features and bug fixes.

WebImage

Price: $39.95

URL: `http://www.group42.com/webimage.htm`

A graphics program like GraphX Viewer (see page 165) allows you to perform some simple operations on image files, but you will probably want to do more. WebImage can create transparent GIFs and interlaced GIFs, and it can convert between any of its supported graphics formats — of which there are many. What's more, WebImage can serve as your image map creation tool; as with Mapedit (see above), you can simply call up a graphics file and highlight different regions of the picture. WebImage then prompts you for a URL and creates the corresponding map definition file. The interface is very logical and pleasing to the eye.

Paint Shop Pro

Price: $69

URL: `http://www.jasc.com/psp.html`

One thing WebImage cannot do is create graphics from scratch. If you are really serious about creating your own stunning graphics or modifying scanned photographs, but you don't have the cash on hand for Adobe Photoshop or a similar commercial program, you should look into Paint Shop Pro ($69). This graphics package is surprisingly rich in features for a shareware product; you can find out more about it, and download a trial version, at the Paint Shop Pro home page (listed above).

8.13 WINDOWS 95 AND WINDOWS NT

With the introduction of Microsoft Windows 95 came the introduction of a number of Web server packages that will run in Windows 95. Most of these server packages will also run in Windows NT in a similar (or identical) manner. Some of them are distributed as shareware, but all of them have a fee associated with them. This book takes the approach that you should first use the Windows httpd package on Windows 3.1 (free for personal use, $99 for commercial use) before you shell out the money for any of the Windows 95/NT commercial packages. This allows you to become familiar with all of the Windows Web serving basics before you make your Windows 95/NT server purchase. Besides, you may find that all of your server requirements are met with the Windows 3.1 set up, negating any need for a 32-bit upgrade.

If you don't have Windows 3.1, or don't want to reinstall it, you can still use the Windows httpd document tree by simply calling it locally from your browser without running the actual server program. For example, instead of calling `http://your.site/`, you simply open the local file `c:\httpd\htdocs`. All of the default files shipped with the server are called relative to this file, so you can easily navigate around the entire server document tree. While this will not give you access to many of the server features, you will still be able to walk through many of the configuration examples described earlier in the chapter.

Server Software Packages

The following server software packages are available as shareware on the Internet, with more arriving every day:

- WebSite: `http://website.ora.com/`
- FolkWeb: `http://www.ilar.com/folkweb.html`
- WebSTAR: `http://www.qdeck.com/qdeck/products/webstar/`
- Cheetah: `http://www.tgv.com/public/cheetah/cheetah_welcome.html`

Netscape also has a few packages available, including their Commerce Server; you can get more information at `http://www.mcom.com/`.

This section uses the WebSite package to give you an idea of how the features you learned about with Windows httpd are incorporated in the feature-rich Windows 95/NT payware.

WebSite

The WebSite package, written by Robert Denny and published by O'Reilly & Associates, is a full-featured, menu-driven server package that runs on Windows 95 and Windows NT. The product comes with three chapters from O'Reilly & Associates' book, *Building Your Own Web Site*, including the chapter called "Installing WebSite." The instructions we provide here should be enough to get your WebSite server running, but you should refer to the instructions shipped with the product for complete details.

WebSite is popular because it is very easy to set up and use. It has a versatile CGI facility that allows you to easily run Visual Basic programs, DOS shell scripts, and Perl scripts with few or no special configuration steps. There is also an easy-to-use image map editor included in the distribution. The WebSite home page is well maintained and contains the latest feature and bug information. It also has a forum for discussion among WebSite users.

Networking Before you can use WebSite, you need to set up your Windows Dial Up Networking facility (if you haven't previously done so). To do this, take the following steps:

1. Install the "TCP/IP" component of the main Windows 95/NT installation. Check your Windows 95/NT documentation for more information on this procedure.

2. In Windows 95, set up your "Dial Up Networking" facility for a connection with your provider. (In Windows NT, this is done through the "Remote Access" feature.) Once again, consult your Windows 95/NT documentation for details. You will probably need some information from your provider as well (at the very least, their telephone number and the IP address of their domain name server).

Downloading   The WebSite software package is available on the Web at http://website.ora.com/. If the 60-day trial offer is still available when you read this book, download the software (which is packaged as a ZIP archive). If you don't have pkzip204g.exe, you can get it from http://www.pkware.com/ (see page 165 for details).

Installation   Once you have unzipped the wsdemo.zip file that you down-loaded from the WebSite location, unzip it in a temporary directory with the following pkunzip syntax:

```
pkunzip -d wsdemo.zip
```

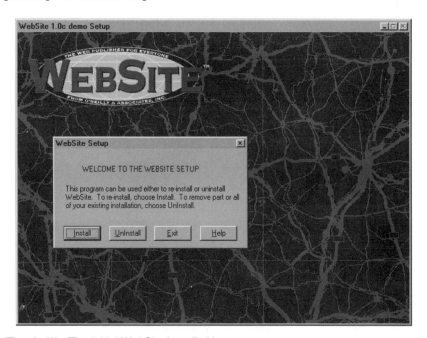

Fig. 8–17   The initial WebSite installation screen.

After you have unzipped the wsdemo.zip file, run the program called setup.exe from within Windows. Select Install when you see the initial instal-lation screen, shown in Figure 8–17. From there, you are prompted for a drive and directory in which to put the WebSite files. Then, you are prompted for the Internet name of your server and the e-mail address of the server administrator, as shown in Figure 8–18. It is important for you put in a fully qualified domain name (FQDN), meaning the one that Internet users will use when getting to your site (such as `parkweb.com`). You also need to provide the e-mail address of the server administrator (probably your own). Finally, you will be prompted for the path that you want to use as the root of your server document tree (same as `DocumentRoot` in Windows httpd; see page 140). Once you have done this, the installation procedure will be finished and you will be able to start your server.

Fig. 8–18   This is where you enter your domain name and e-mail address.

Configuration   To perform a basic configuration of your WebSite server, click on its icon from the program group in which you placed it. If you went through the configuration process with Windows httpd, you will notice that this product uses menus and dialog boxes to configure the same items that you configured by editing the Windows httpd configuration files. Figure 8–19 shows the General Server Admin screen. As you can see, there are eight configured areas that you can go to from this menu: General, Mapping, Indexing, Users, Groups, Access Control, Logging, and CGI. The following list and screen snaps take a quick look of what each one does.

- *General*
  This selection allows you to configure all of the primary information for your server. This is where you change your server path, Webmaster address, server name, and port number. Windows NT users can indicate whether they want the server to run as a Desktop application or a system

Fig. 8–19   This is the window you get when "General" is selected from Server Admin menu. The important stuff here is in the "Network" configuration section.

service. There is also a box that tells you the name of the Windows 95/NT socket program currently configured.

- *Mapping*
  This selection lets you define the directory paths for your server documents and CGI programs (Fig. 8–20). You simply select the item you want to map and enter in the corresponding path and URL. You also use this menu to associate your file types with icon files for server-generated indexes. Additionally, you can set up redirection for any URL on your server.

- *Indexing*
  The indexing menu is where you set up your directory indexing rules. This is a very nice feature that allows you to specify exactly what will and won't be shown in server-generated indexes for any directory. If you want the rules to apply to all directories, just set the rules up for the directory that you configured as your Document root.

- *Users*
  This menu lets you create and update authentication realms, and assign users to them. The password program is automatically called when you go to enter a new user (see the section on User/Password Files, page 174).

- *Groups*
  This menu is similar to the Users menu. It allows you to assign *groups* to authentication realms.

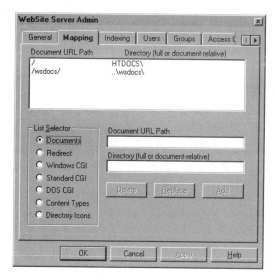

Fig. 8–20 Entering your file mapping information is as easy as clicking buttons and filling in boxes.

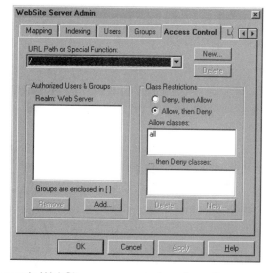

Fig. 8–21 The main WebSite access control configuration screen. This is where you set up security realms.

- *Access Control*

  This menu (Fig. 8–21) lets you set up the access control mechanisms for a given URL on your server. This includes associating a realm with a URL and defining the order in which controls will be enforced (such as "Deny, then Allow").

- *Logging*
  The logging menu is where you give the file names for your `access.log`, `server.log`, and `error.log` files. You also use this menu to define which server events you want to log.

- *CGI*
  This menu lets you change the default information for how CGI requests will be handled by the server. This is an advanced option that should only be used if you really know what you are doing; the defaults are good enough for most users and their programs.

User/Password Files   You only need to create users and passwords if you plan on using the authentication facility. The password program is automatically invoked when you create a new user from the `User` selection on the Server Admin menu. You are given a dialog box where you enter in the user's name and password, as shown in Figure 8–22. As with most password programs, you must enter the password twice to be sure you didn't make any mistakes the first time. Neither of the password entries is shown on the screen.

Fig. 8–22   The WebSite password dialog box; note that the text of the password is hidden.

Unlike in Windows httpd, WebSite's user, group, and password information is stored in the Windows 95/NT system registry. The system registry is only accessible using the registry editor program (`regedit.exe`). Be careful to only use the registry editor to *view* the contents of the registry — do not use it to change the contents, as this could cause irreparable damage to the file. To locate information in the registry, call up the registry editor program and use the `Find` command from the `Edit` menu.

Running Your WebSite Server

Once you have completed this configuration process, you are ready to move your server documents into the configured Documents directory, your programs into the appropriate CGI directory, and your icons into the configured Icon directory. After you have done this, you should test your server using the general information described in section 8.7.

All of the applications described in sections 8.10 through 8.12 should work just fine with Windows 95 and Windows NT. However, you should keep your eyes open for 32-bit versions of these products, which will run faster on your system and may contain snazzy new features. As usual, the "Consummate Winsock Apps" site (page 162) should prove useful.

## CHAPTER 9

Setting Up A
Macintosh Web Server

*I*f you are reading this chapter, you probably already have a Macintosh — or are planning to get one soon — so we don't need to convince you why you should have one. Macintoshes are famous for their ease of use and reliability. Those of us who use them every day can't understand why everyone doesn't have one.

Setting up a World Wide Web server is just as easy as anything else you do on a Mac. There is a common misconception that running a Web site means learning how to program in UNIX, or knowing how to operate $20,000 workstations. In fact, the only prerequisites for running a Macintosh Web server are that you know how to move files around, and you know how to open them in a text editor or word processor!

One reason connecting a Mac to the Web is so easy is that the program you use to do it is so good. MacHTTP, written by Chuck Shotton and sold by StarNine Technologies, is an excellent program that's extremely easy to set up and use, doesn't take up much room, and almost never crashes. What's more, the program is shareware, meaning you can download it *right now* if you want; your Mac could be a Web server in less than ten minutes. (Of course, if you decide to keep MacHTTP, you'll have to pay for it eventually.)

If MacHTTP isn't quite fast enough for you; if your server suddenly quadruples the size of your business; if you want to take full advantage of your new 100 MHz Power Macintosh and ISDN line; or if you just want a bigger, badder machine than your next-door neighbor; then you can upgrade from MacHTTP to WebSTAR. It costs more, but it's faster than MacHTTP and still very easy to set up.

This chapter will walk you through installation and configuration of a Mac server running MacHTTP and will describe a number of free or inexpensive applications that can help you in your endeavor.

9.1 PREREQUISITES

Before you start, there are a few things you need to have. At a minimum, they are: an Internet account, a Macintosh with a modem or direct Internet connection, and either MacHTTP or WebSTAR, which are software packages that allow your Mac to become a Web server.

An Internet Connection

To set up a Web server on a Mac, you will need to have an Internet account that gives your computer a unique IP address that can be accessed from anywhere on the Internet. This can be accomplished by way of a direct connection or SLIP/PPP. If you have used a computer that had its own IP address — possibly at a large company or at a university — it was probably a direct Ethernet connection. From your home or office, however, you probably will be dialing up using a modem, the MacTCP control panel, and SLIP or PPP software (typically MacSLIP, InterSLIP, or MacPPP).

Configuring a SLIP or PPP connection is one of the most difficult parts of hooking up to the Internet, on any platform. We'd love to help, but it seems that every Internet service provider requires a slightly different configuration; your provider will be able to help you with your initial setup.

We cover Internet connections in detail in Chapter 6 and Appendix D, but it is worth a brief review here. When you first start out on the Internet, you will probably have a dynamic IP address; every time you dial into your Internet service provider's system, you are randomly given an IP address from a large pool that is assigned to that provider. This way, thousands of people could share a handful of IP addresses, as long as they did not all try to hook up at once (which they cannot do, since the provider's modem pool is limited).

You *can* run a Web server using a dynamic IP address, but it is not recommended, unless you are still in the testing phase (in which case it doesn't matter, since you are the only one who needs to know your address). But, when you decide the time is right to start a public Web server on your own Macintosh — one that you are going to publicize around the world — you will want to upgrade to a static IP address. When you have a static IP, your SLIP or PPP software always uses the same IP address, which is reserved for you by your provider. You should also register a domain name that always translates to your current IP address (see Chapter 6). This way, even if you switch providers — and therefore IP addresses — people will still be able to locate your server by name. Besides, it is much easier to remember "parkweb.com" than "204.246.64.26"!

If your server really takes off, you will want to get as fast a modem as possible and a dedicated phone line. This way, your server can run 24 hours a day, and it won't interfere with the phone habits of your office or family. Beyond that, you could get a faster digital connection. Talk to your service provider about your available options.

Getting a SLIP/PPP account is not very expensive at all. You should be able to find a provider who will give you nearly unlimited access (around 100 hours) for less than $30 per month. A static IP address is a little more expensive, and a dedicated line (a 24-hour connection) will be much more expensive. If you are setting up a server for a business, and you do it right, it will probably be worth the cost; consider it a part of your advertising expenses. For a hobby server, a non-profit organization, or a business with a small budget, you should still get a static IP address, but the dedicated line might be optional. If you decide not to get one, consider leaving your server on during certain hours each day, and advertise those hours so people know when you are "open."

Macintosh Hardware

You can use almost *any* Macintosh as a Web server. Obviously, a faster machine will work better, especially if you are going to set up CGI applications that can be run by people visiting your site. But the biggest constraint on the speed of your server might be the speed of your modem. If you have a moderately busy server on only a 14.4k bps line, even an old Mac Plus or SE will suffice. (A Mac 512K will *not* work.)

However, in building your Web site, you will probably want to create graphics to adorn your pages; you can't do that on a Mac Plus. So you'll need to have a more powerful Macintosh available; we're assuming that you have one already. (By "more powerful," we mean a Mac with at least a 68030 processor and a color monitor.) You have a couple options here; first, you can set up your server on that Mac, meaning you'll have to share its resources with people all over the world while the server is running. You should at least start out this way. Depending on your computer's processor, memory, etc., you might have no problems at all running the server software in the background while you go about your business. But if you do have problems, and you really need to use your server as your day-to-day Mac, you'll need to go out and spend some money on hardware.

Buying a second computer to use as a dedicated server is really the ideal solution. It's expensive, but you can make it a little easier on the pocketbook by tracking down a second-hand Mac. Look up "Computers–Used" in the yellow pages, read the classified ads in your local paper, or read the Usenet newsgroup `misc.forsale.computers.mac-specific.systems`.

If you decide to get a dedicated server, you should connect the server's hard drive to your other computer(s) via a simple AppleTalk network (you can do this with your existing File Sharing software and an ordinary printer cable). This way, you will be able to manipulate the Web site's file structure without having to disturb the server's computer too much, and you can move files from your other computers to the Web server without having to go through the Internet or walk around with floppy disks.

Whichever computer you decide to use as a Web server, it should have at least the following:

RAM How much RAM is enough? Well, a typical System 7 setup requires about 2 MB of memory just for the system files. MacHTTP needs at least 600 KB, more if you want to allow more than eight simultaneous connections. If you have any CGI applications that will be working with MacHTTP, figure out how much space they will take up if they are all running at once. The bottom line: 4 MB for a plain vanilla server that spits out files and runs one or two CGI scripts; 8 MB if you want to make use of a lot of CGI programs. If you are planning to get really in-depth and write AppleScript programs that take user input and manipulate files in other applications, you may need more.

Disk Space   The MacHTTP application, documentation and tutorial files only take up about 1 MB of hard disk space. You just need to make sure that there is enough remaining room on the hard drive for all the files you want to make available. HTML files don't take up much space at all, but pictures can really add up. And sounds and movies will really eat up your disk space. If you are running a Mac as a dedicated server, disk space requirements will be easier to identify, since you won't have much other software to worry about.

Modem   For a complete discussion of modems and phone line types, refer to Chapter 6. Just remember that a 14.4k modem is the absolute minimum speed that you should purchase, and since prices are coming down every day, you really should think about getting a 28.8k modem, if you are using ordinary phone lines. (Digital lines necessitate faster modems, if you want to get your money's worth.)

On a Macintosh, the internal/external modem debate is not as much of an issue as it is with DOS/Windows machines, because almost all Mac modems are external.

Software

Before you even start thinking about a Web server, you should have the software to run an Internet connection, and you should have a Web browser. You should be able to get the basic software from your service provider, although they may charge you for the convenience of putting it all together for you.

Once you have a Web browser, you can get anything else you want. But before you download anything else, you should have a copy of StuffIt Expander (see page 214), because it will decode and extract any other files that you might download, including MacHTTP. The easiest way to get StuffIt Expander is to copy it from the CD that comes with this book! If for some reason you can't read our CD — or if you want to make sure you have the most recent version — you can get it from the /cmp/ directory at Info-Mac (see "Getting the Server Software" on page 181), or copy it from a friend, or ask your Internet service provider if he or she can give you a copy on a disk.

Once you have StuffIt Expander set up, the next program you may want to download is Anarchie or Fetch (page 211), because those programs make it easier to find and download everything. (In fact, once you have Anarchie or Fetch up and running, you may want to skip ahead to the last part of this chapter and download a number of the applications that we recommend for Macintosh Internet users.) You can also use your Web browser to find helpful information on some of the finer points of server installation. If you are planning to buy another Mac to use as a dedicated server, you can even use your browser to shop for one!

To run MacHTTP, your Mac's system software must be at least System 7.0; it will not run under System 6. If you are running a dedicated server, remove any unnecessary system extensions or control panels that might be taking up valuable memory and processor time. On a dedicated server, you may want to run a screen saver, since it will be on all the time; that's a good idea, but make sure it's a very simple screen saver that does not at all detract from the performance of the system. An easier solution — as well as a cheaper and more ecological one — is simply to turn off the monitor.

Even if you are *not* running a dedicated server, you should toss out the superfluous system extensions. Only keep the really necessary ones (like the Sound Manager and the Thread Manager) and the ones that don't take up much memory and don't interfere with normal operations. A system with just a few necessary extensions is a system that's less likely to crash. In other words, you'll have to live without your hilarious belching-disk-drive extension.

You definitely *should* be running the Thread Manager extension. A Macintosh cannot do true multitasking like a UNIX system can, but with the Thread Manager installed, it can do a pretty good imitation, in programs that support threading. The Thread Manager is built into System 7.5 and later; with earlier versions, you'll have to download it from Apple or find a program that includes the Thread Manager in its distribution package. If you want to get it directly from Apple, here's the very long URL:

```
http://www.info.apple.com/Apple.Support.Area/Apple.Software.Updates/
    US/Macintosh/System/Other_System/
```

9.2 GETTING THE SERVER SOFTWARE

There are thousands of programs available for you to download from the Internet. Some of them are limited-functionality demo versions of commercial programs. Many, like MacHTTP, are *shareware* (see page 184); you are on your honor to pay the authors of the programs that you use. Others are *freeware*, meaning they are copyrighted by the author and freely distributed, but they don't cost anything. A few are in the public domain (uncopyrighted).

All of this downloadable software is stored in enormous archives, which are usually accessible via FTP. For Macintosh software, there are two primary archives: Info-Mac, and the University of Michigan archives (usually called simply "Umich"). Each of these archives is duplicated, or *mirrored*, at numerous sites around the world, because no single server could handle the amount of traffic generated by archives of this magnitude, and because it is more efficient for people to use a mirror site near their home.

In this chapter, we will refer only to the Info-Mac archive, since it is bigger and has more mirror sites, a few of which are listed below. For straight FTP access, try the site nearest your home first; if that's busy, try another. (If you

want a slick Web interface to the archive, use the "HyperArchive" at M.I.T. in
Cambridge, Massachusetts.)

- M.I.T.   `http://hyperarchive.lcs.mit.edu/HyperArchive.html`
- Virginia   `ftp://mirrors.aol.com/pub/info-mac/`
- Missouri   `ftp://wuarchive.wustl.edu/systems/mac/info-mac/`
- Arizona   `ftp://ftp.amug.org/mirrors/info-mac/`
- California   `ftp://mirror.apple.com/mirrors/info-mac/`
- Hawaii   `ftp://ftp.hawaii.edu/pub/mac/info-mac/`
- Canada   `ftp://ftp.agt.net/pub/info-mac/`
- Switzerland   `ftp://ftp.switch.ch/mirror/info-mac/`
- Turkey   `ftp://ftp.bups.bilkent.edu.tr/pub/info-mac/`
- Japan   `ftp://ftp.web.ad.jp/info-mac/`
- Australia   `ftp://archie.au/micros/mac/info-mac/`
- Taiwan   `ftp://nctuccca.edu.tw/Macintosh/info-mac/`

You can get a *complete* list of mirror sites — in HTML format — from Info-
Mac's `/info/` directory. Download the file called `mirror-list.html.txt`, and
view it with your Web browser.

Within those sites, here are some directories that you will find useful in
your quest to build the perfect Web server:

- Internet applications: `/comm/tcp`
- Compression and translation utilities: `/cmp/`
- HTML editors and converters: `/text/html/`
- Graphics utilities: `/gst/grf/`
- Sound utilities: `/gst/snd/`
- Movie utilities: `/gst/mov/`

MacHTTP vs. WebSTAR

Two of the most common Web server packages for the Macintosh are
MacHTTP and WebSTAR. The latter evolved from the former, and they are both
owned by the same company.

You should start out by downloading MacHTTP and trying it out. You have
30 days to use it and decide whether you like it or not. If you want to use it as
your Web server, you must send $95 to StarNine Technologies. (If you are setting
up a server at a school or college, the price is only $65.)

If you suspect that MacHTTP is not going to be enough to meet your site's
needs, or if you are merely curious about this fantastic WebSTAR that they keep
raving about, you can connect to StarNine Technologies' WWW site at
`http://www.starnine.com` and download the latest version of WebSTAR. They

will send you a code that will allow you to use WebSTAR for ten days, after which the software will stop working. If you want to continue to use WebSTAR, you must pay $499 for a license ($295 for educational institutions).

According to StarNine's literature, WebSTAR runs three to four times faster than MacHTTP, and will accept thousands of connections per hour. It also supports other powerful features like remote administration and dynamic Web pages via server push. It is truly an industrial-strength server package, suitable for even the largest companies. (If WebSTAR still isn't enough for you, then you're expecting too much!) But you will probably decide that MacHTTP is all you need for now.

By the way, if you buy MacHTTP, but later decide you want to upgrade to WebSTAR, you can receive a credit for MacHTTP's full purchase price against the price of WebSTAR. So you actually have nothing to lose by starting with MacHTTP, no matter how your needs grow.

This chapter will teach you how to configure MacHTTP, version 2.2 (Star-Nine claims that MacHTTP will no longer be updated, because they are putting all their resources into WebSTAR). If you upgrade to WebSTAR, many of the concepts will be the same, but there will be a few more options to deal with. Consult the WebSTAR documentation for details. The "Applications" sections at the end of the chapter are relevant no matter which server software you use.

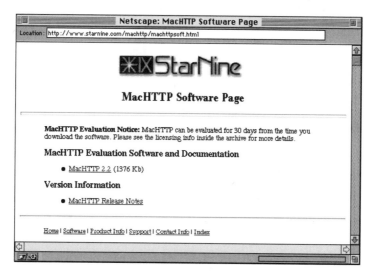

Fig. 9–1 StarNine Technologies' MacHTTP page.

Downloading MacHTTP

You can use any Web browser or FTP client to obtain the MacHTTP software. On the Web, point your favorite browser at StarNine's MacHTTP pages (http://www.starnine.com/machttp/machttp.html) and follow the appropriate links (Fig. 9–1). With FTP, you can connect to ftp.starnine.com and download

machttp.sea.hqx from the /pub/evals/machttp directory, or just get it from the
/comm/tcp/ directory at any Info-Mac mirror site. Use StuffIt Expander to convert the encoded text file into a usable folder.

Paying for MacHTTP

There is a subset of shareware that is sometimes called *crippleware*; these
programs work for a while and then stop working unless you pay up. More common is *nagware*; until you pay for the software, an annoying warning keeps
appearing that reminds you to register the program.

MacHTTP is neither crippleware nor nagware. It works "right out of the
box," and it will keep working indefinitely, without screaming at you. *This is no
excuse not to pay for it!* You *must* pay the shareware fees on any programs that
you continue to use beyond the evaluation period (which is 30 days in the case of
MacHTTP).

Shareware exists because it's a great way for software authors to have their
programs widely distributed without having any marketing overhead. If no one
pays for their shareware, there will be no more shareware. Instead, all software
will be sold commercially at horrible prices that are inflated, in part, by people
who illegally copy software.

In later sections of this chapter, we will recommend a number of shareware
programs. You are always free to try them out on your computer and see whether
you like them — that's another reason shareware is such a wonderful system —
but as soon as your trial period is up, you must delete the program if you weren't
planning on paying for it.

Obviously, you don't have to pay for freeware programs, but it's nice to send
their authors a quick thank-you note via e-mail if you use their program; often,
it's the only reward they get. If they say that you don't *have* to send money, but
they'd sure like it if you did, you should seriously consider sending five bucks.
The price of shareware isn't always cash; we've seen postcardware, jobware ("if
you like this program, hire me"), and even beerware.

Remember, MacHTTP costs $65 for educational users and $95 for commercial entities. Considering what it gives you — the ability to turn your humble
Macintosh into a World Wide Web server, with no technical knowledge
required — this is really a bargain. Send in your payment as soon as possible,
and clear your conscience. You can find StarNine's mailing address in the
Licensing info document that comes with the MacHTTP package, or you can
use their on-line order form:

        http://www.starnine.com/ordering/machttp_order_form.html

9.3 INSTALLING MACHTTP

Okay, we're finally to the good part. You've downloaded MacHTTP, and the folder
is sitting there on your hard drive, waiting to be used. If you're extremely impa-

tient, you could double-click the MacHTTP icon right now. If your Internet connection is properly configured, your Mac will become a Web server in a few seconds. However, the only thing people will be able to see on your server is the MacHTTP documentation!

Most of the basic installation of your Web server software involves nothing more than moving some folders around and performing a few other common Macintosh tasks, like creating aliases and changing memory partitions. Once everything is where it should be, you will be able test your setup to make sure it works.

It is worth noting here that most computer systems organize files into directories; the Macintosh's graphical interface uses folders instead, but they serve exactly the same purpose that directories do in MS-DOS or UNIX. People accessing your server will most likely think of your folders as directories, since they cannot see the cute little folder icons. In this chapter, we will use the two terms interchangeably.

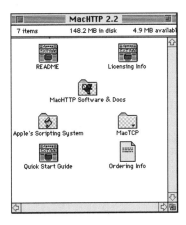

Fig. 9–2 The MacHTTP distribution package. Read the README file.

The MacHTTP Application & Documentation

When you unpack the MacHTTP files using StuffIt Expander, you have one folder with three subfolders and four text documents (Fig. 9–2). Find the MacHTTP Software & Docs folder. Rename it to whatever you want. You could call it simply MacHTTP, WWW, or WebServer; you can even call it Anastasia or Raoul if you want. No one accessing your site will know what you've called it; as far as the Internet is concerned, that folder is just http://yoursite.com/.

Take the Raoul folder — hereafter referred to as "your MacHTTP folder" so as not to offend Anastasia — and put it wherever you want it on your hard drive. While MacHTTP is running, anything you put in this folder is potentially available via the World Wide Web; it is known as your *root directory*. If you want to have access to your MacHTTP folder no matter what you are doing, make a few aliases (using the Make Alias command under the File menu in the Finder) and put them in different folders or hard drives. Be sure to put an alias to your MacHTTP folder in your `Apple Menu Items` folder so that you can access the folder from within any application.

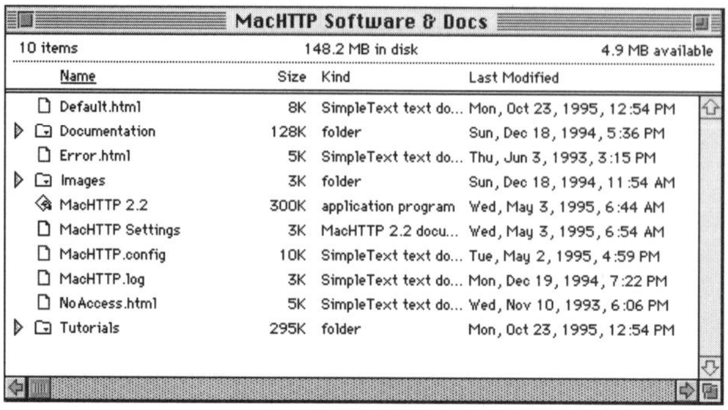

MacHTTP Software & Docs			
10 items	148.2 MB in disk		4.9 MB available
Name	Size	Kind	Last Modified
Default.html	8K	SimpleText text do...	Mon, Oct 23, 1995, 12:54 PM
▷ Documentation	128K	folder	Sun, Dec 18, 1994, 5:36 PM
Error.html	5K	SimpleText text do...	Thu, Jun 3, 1993, 3:15 PM
▷ Images	3K	folder	Sun, Dec 18, 1994, 11:54 AM
MacHTTP 2.2	300K	application program	Wed, May 3, 1995, 6:44 AM
MacHTTP Settings	3K	MacHTTP 2.2 docu...	Wed, May 3, 1995, 6:54 AM
MacHTTP.config	10K	SimpleText text do...	Tue, May 2, 1995, 4:59 PM
MacHTTP.log	3K	SimpleText text do...	Mon, Dec 19, 1994, 7:22 PM
NoAccess.html	5K	SimpleText text do...	Wed, Nov 10, 1993, 6:06 PM
▷ Tutorials	295K	folder	Mon, Oct 23, 1995, 12:54 PM

Fig. 9–3 Your MacHTTP folder, which contains the MacHTTP application. Rename this folder to whatever you want.

As long as you are creating aliases, make an alias of the MacHTTP application itself, which is inside your MacHTTP folder (Fig. 9–3), and place it wherever is most convenient, such as on the desktop. If you are running a dedicated server, put a MacHTTP alias in your `Startup Items` folder.

Don't move anything around inside your MacHTTP folder until you are sure you know what you are doing. All the files in there are exactly where they should be for the documentation pages to work.

Depending on how much RAM your Mac has, you may want to increase MacHTTP's memory partition. The more memory MacHTTP has to work with, the more simultaneous connections it can allow, and the more scripts it can run. So, if you have fast line, or want to do complex things with AppleScript and CGI applications (see section 9.8, "Scripts"), you need to give MacHTTP more memory. For each additional connection you want to allow, you'll need to add about 20K.

Increase MacHTTP's RAM by selecting the MacHTTP application in the Finder, and selecting `Get Info` from the File menu. At the bottom of the Info window is a box that says `Preferred size: 1150K`; increase the number to whatever you think is appropriate.

MacTCP & AppleScript

The MacHTTP package that you download from StarNine includes MacTCP and AppleScript. These are both system extensions from Apple. StarNine has received a license from Apple to distribute them with MacHTTP, so you cannot copy these to any computer that is not running MacHTTP.

You should already have MacTCP in your `Control Panels` folder, if you are on the Internet. But check the version number of your copy of MacTCP and the copy that comes with MacHTTP (using the Finder's Get Info command). If your system has an older version, replace it with the copy you just downloaded.

AppleScript is an extension that makes it easy for different applications on your Mac to "talk" to each other and pass information back and forth. You don't *need* AppleScript to run a simple MacHTTP server, but you will need it if you want to run CGI scripts. If you are so inclined, you can learn how to program in AppleScript and create your own custom scripts to use with MacHTTP. We will say more about this in section 9.8.

To install AppleScript, drag and drop the contents of the For all Extensions folders folder into your System Folder. If you have a PowerPC-based Macintosh, do the same thing with the folder entitled For Power Mac Extensions folder. You will be asked whether you want to place these files into their appropriate homes within the System Folder. Click the OK button, then restart your computer to activate AppleScript.

Your Web Pages

This is the easiest part of installation. Simply take whichever files you want to make available on your server, and copy or move them into your MacHTTP folder. It is a good idea to organize everything into folders first, because you don't want a bunch of loose files floating around with the MacHTTP application and settings files.

Let's say that somewhere on your hard drive, you have a folder full of GIF image files named Photography, and you want to put those pictures on the Web. You may be tempted to make an alias of the Photography folder and put it in your MacHTTP folder, so that you can keep your MacHTTP folder as uncluttered as possible. It's a good idea, but it won't work. MacHTTP will not recognize aliases to folders or disk drives. MacHTTP *will* properly read aliases to files, but any relative links within those files will be interpreted as if they actually lived in the MacHTTP folder. Since image files don't contain any links, you could conceivably fill your MacHTTP folder with aliases to each and every picture in the Photography folder, but there is a much easier solution:

1. Move Photography into your MacHTTP folder.
2. Make an alias of Photography.
3. Move the *alias* back to the original location of the Photography folder.

Now, the Photography folder is effectively in the same place it has always been, but its contents can also be served by MacHTTP.

Many computer systems, such as MS-DOS and UNIX, generally cannot have spaces in their file names. Because the World Wide Web is a universal system, you need to accommodate this fact. The files and folders that you place inside your MacHTTP folder should have no spaces in their names, nor any other "unusual" characters or punctuation. If you use spaces in a file's name, the file *can* be accessed, but it's not pretty. For instance, a file named My Web Page.html in a directory called Personal Files will look like this in a URL:

`/Personal%20Files/My%20Web%20Page.html`. Underscores and hyphens are okay, though, so `My-Web-Page.html` in the `Personal_Files` folder would be fine.

Macintosh files are more difficult to send over the Internet than other platforms' files because they usually have two parts: a *data fork* and a *resource fork*. A file's resource fork generally gets stripped off when you send it. So, if you have a Macintosh-specific file that you want to place in your Web site, you need to do *one or more* of the following:

- Make sure *all* the file's information is in the data fork; this is known as a *flat* file. Most simple documents, such as word processing files and spreadsheets, are already flat. Flat files can be transferred with no problems.
- Convert the file to MacBinary format, using the MacBinary II application that you can find in the `/cmp/` directory at Info-Mac.
- "BinHex" the file; this is an encoded text format that includes all the Macintosh information. You can BinHex a file with most Mac compression programs, or with the BinHex 4.0 application, which you get from the UMich archive at `http://www.umich.edu/~archive/mac/util/compression/`.

Crank It Up!

Once you have placed some subfolders in your MacHTTP folder, it's time to make sure everything works. Hopefully at least one of your files is an HTML document with hypertext links to other files in your site, so you can make sure that the links work. To test the basic functioning of your server, dial into the Net and then go through the following easy steps:

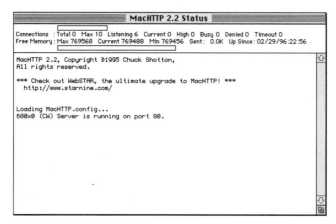

Fig. 9–4   The MacHTTP status window, as it looks when you first load the application.

1. **Double-click the MacHTTP application.** You will see MacHTTP's status window (Fig. 9–4).
2. **Open your favorite Web browser.**

3. Choose `Open Location` or `Open URL` in your browser.

4. Type your IP address or domain name (e.g., `http://yoursite.com`), and click `OK`.

Fig. 9–5 MacHTTP's default home page. You're in business!

5. Voila! You should see the "New MacHTTP Home Page" (Fig. 9–5). If it doesn't work, check and make sure that you typed the URL correctly, and that your connection to the Internet is running as it should be.

6. Enter a URL that includes your site address and a file in your MacHTTP folder, such as `http://yoursite.com/Photography/catalog.html`.

7. Voila again! If you set everything up right, you will see the Web page you just asked for (as in Figure 9–6). Once again, if it doesn't work, check to see that you have entered the correct URL.

8. Go back to MacHTTP. The status window has recorded the "hits" (HTTP requests) on your server (Fig. 9–7).

The MacHTTP default index page is the file called `Default.html`. When you first get MacHTTP, it is configured so that it will try to load a page called `Default.html` if the browser specifies only a directory name (or only a site name, as in step #4 above). If, in this example, we had tried to load the URL `http://yoursite.com/Photography/`, MacHTTP would have sent an error message, since there is no `Default.html` file in the `Photography` folder.

Your Home Page

One of the first pages you will want to create is a replacement for the `Default.html` file that comes with MacHTTP. But keep the old one around, under a different name, because it works as an index for the documentation files

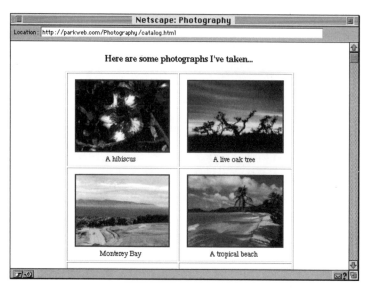

Fig. 9–6 The `/Photography/catalog.html` page in our test server. Every-thing seems to be working just fine.

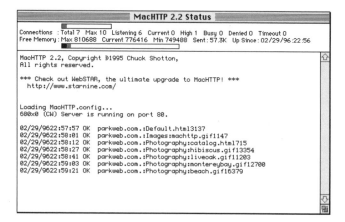

Fig. 9–7 The MacHTTP status window has now recorded seven HTTP requests: two for HTML pages, and five for image files (the MacHTTP icon and the four photographs).

in your MacHTTP folder. You can put anything you want on your new default home page; you might want to start with a catchy graphic (Fig. 9–8).

Many Web servers are set up so that they return a listing of all of a direc-tory's files when no file is specified. The author of MacHTTP could have easily implemented this feature; he chose not to, because he wanted to give you com-plete control over what people can see on your server. If you don't explicitly give them a list of all your files, they don't have it.

Fig. 9–8   Our spiffy replacement for the default home page that came with MacHTTP.

9.4 CONFIGURATION: THE MACHTTP.CONFIG FILE

There is much more you can do to test — and play with — your server, but let's stop for a moment and get everything set up exactly the way you want it. This is mostly done with a series of variables in MacHTTP's configuration file; it's called MacHTTP.config, and it sits right next to MacHTTP in your MacHTTP folder.

MacHTTP.config is a plain text file, so you can edit it with your favorite word processor or with a text editor like TeachText or SimpleText (one of which should have come with your Mac). You may want to poke around in the /text/ directory of the Info-Mac archives and download a shareware text editor like Tex-Edit Plus; most of them have more features than SimpleText but are still much smaller than any word processor (see page 215 for details about Tex-Edit Plus).

Any time you change a setting in MacHTTP.config, you will have to restart the MacHTTP application for the changes to take effect, because the configuration settings are loaded into MacHTTP's memory each time it is opened.

When you first open MacHTTP.config in your text editor or word processor, you may notice that most of the lines start with #. These are all *comment* lines; they have no effect whatsoever on MacHTTP's behavior. If you want to try a couple different settings for any of the variables discussed below, you can write out both of them and then comment the one you *don't* want to use at the moment by putting a # symbol in front of it.

You may also notice that some words are in boldface type. These are the actual variable names. They are only bold for cosmetic reasons, so you can visually pick them out from everything else. If you replace them with plain text, MacHTTP won't care.

Setting the configuration variables isn't the most fun part of setting up a server, but it's very important and you will probably learn something. So grab a cold drink, open up that MacHTTP.config file on your Mac, and we'll walk you through the whole thing, one variable at a time. We are using the MacHTTP.config file that comes with MacHTTP 2.2.

We won't bother to type out possible settings for each and every variable, because the default configuration file already has valid entries for each variable, many of which you won't need to change. You should save a backup copy of the default MacHTTP.config file somewhere on your hard drive, just in case you need it for reference later.

One more note before we begin: each configuration variable should appear only *once* in your MacHTTP.config file, with the exception of the file type mapping statements and the security settings.

Version

The setting of the VERSION variable in your MacHTTP.config file must match the version number in the application itself, so there's no need to ever change this variable.

Default Files

There are a few files that are important to the operation of MacHTTP. When specifying file names in the MacHTTP.config file, you separate segments of a folder/directory path with a colon, as opposed to the slash that you use in URLs. A file name that *starts* with a colon is interpreted to be in the root directory of the MacHTTP server. So, to use our earlier example, the file catalog.html in the Photography folder would be represented in MacHTTP.config as :Photography:catalog.html.

MacHTTP comes with a set of default files. You can use these, you can modify them, or you can toss them out completely and use your own. You could also use scripts or pictures rather than HTML pages, although these will put a heavier load on your server.

DEFAULT   This variable doesn't really have much to do with default *files*, but it is the next variable in your MacHTTP.config file. It defines the default MIME type for files that are not recognized in MacHTTP.config's list of file types and suffixes. The default setting for DEFAULT is TEXT text/html; you might want to change this to TEXT text/plain if you are planning to have a lot of plain text (non-HTML) files in your server. See page 195, "File Type Mapping," for more information about MIME types and such.

INDEX This setting tells MacHTTP the name of the default file that it should look for when only a directory name is specified by an incoming HTTP request. If there is no default file in that directory, an error message will be returned. This should be only a file name, *not* a path name, because each directory will have its own index file: no colons allowed!

When you first get MacHTTP, the INDEX variable will be set to Default.html; although it is strictly a matter of personal preference, we recommend that you set it to index.html, because most World Wide Web servers on other platforms use this as the default. You may as well go with the flow.

ERROR If someone sends your server an improperly formed HTTP request, they will be sent the file or script specified by the ERROR variable. Unlike INDEX, this file name *should* be a path, since you will have only one standard error file in your server.

The default error file is :Error.html. This works just fine, but we actually recommend trying a program called Kelly's Error in place of your default error file. Kelly's Error catches some minor errors caused by improperly formed URLs; see page 207 for details.

NOACCESS This is similar to the ERROR variable; it tells MacHTTP which file or script to send when a browser makes a request that cannot be filled because the browser belongs to an Internet domain that has been banned from using your server (see ALLOW and DENY, page 201).

LOG By default, MacHTTP keeps a record of all its transactions in a file called MacHTTP.log. We can't imagine why you'd want to bother changing this setting, except perhaps to move the log file to a restricted directory (see REALM statements, page 197).

If you *remove* the LOG variable from the MacHTTP.config file (or make it a comment by placing a # in front of it), no log will be kept. You can also turn off logging from within the MacHTTP application.

Connection Settings

These variables control the behavior of MacHTTP's incoming and outgoing network connections. You use them to fine-tune your particular server's performance; there are no universally optimum settings. The best way to determine how best to set these variables is to watch the graphs and numbers at the top of MacHTTP's status window while people are accessing your server, and see how close you come to going over your connection or memory limits.

Since you will not know how your server will perform until you have set up and publicized your site, you will probably want to stick with the defaults for the time being; come back to this section later, once you know what you are up against.

TIMEOUT   If an HTTP connection is open for longer than the time (in seconds) set by the TIMEOUT variable, MacHTTP will sever the connection. The default of 60 is probably reasonable; if your server becomes very busy, you may want to set it a little bit lower to get rid of frozen connections, but only if you have a fast line that can take care of requests promptly.

MAXUSERS   This sets the maximum number of connections that can be open at once. The more connections you allow, the higher you will have to set MacHTTP's memory partition (see page 186).

The default value of 10 is a good place to start, but keep your eye on MacHTTP's status window. If your site contains pages with large numbers of images on them, you will probably need to raise MAXUSERS, because many Web browsers will ask for all the images at once and take up several of your open slots. But if you set it *too* high, MacHTTP and your phone line may not be able to handle all the requests quickly enough, and the connections will time out.

MAXLISTENS   This variable sets how many slots MacHTTP leaves open to "listen" for new connections. Once it "hears" a new request, it places that request in the queue for processing. If you do not have any open listening slots, people requesting files from your server will receive a "cannot connect" message.

The default MacHTTP.config setting for this variable is 6, but 10 is probably a better number, again because of browsers that will send you many requests at once.

PORT   Most Web servers default to run on port 80 of their Internet connection. This is somewhat arbitrary, but there is no point in changing it unless you are running multiple copies of MacHTTP with different port numbers (see section 9.6, "Security Tips," for an explanation of why you might want to do this). If you do change the port setting, you should use a number higher than 1024.

PIG_DELAY   This variable sets how much processor time MacHTTP will "hog" from other applications, in 60ths of a second. You can set this higher on a dedicated server, or lower on a not-too-busy, non-dedicated machine where you need to get a lot of other work done. The default of 30 is a good place to start, but watch your performance and fine-tune accordingly.

DUMP_BUF_SIZE   Read the comments in the MacHTTP.config file about this variable, as they describe it very well: "This is the chunk size that MacHTTP will divide file transfers into." You should probably set this smaller than the default setting of 4096, especially if you have a slow connection; on a 14.4k line, a "chunk" of 4096 bytes will tie up your computer for about three seconds! We recommend setting DUMP_BUF_SIZE to about 1024 bytes.

NO_DNS   In the default MacHTTP.config file, this variable is commented, so NO_DNS is deactivated. The effect of this is that MacHTTP *will* look up the IP addresses of all incoming requests in your local domain name server. The log file then records the names, rather than the IP numbers, of all the hits on your server.

If you don't keep a log, or if you don't mind the cryptic numerical addresses, then you should turn on NO_DNS, because your server's performance will be faster if it doesn't have to look up every incoming address in the name server.

File Type Mapping

When someone requests a document from your MacHTTP server, they don't know what *type* of file they are going to get. When MacHTTP serves a file, it attaches an *HTTP header* that tells the Web browser what's coming so the browser will know what to do with it. In the Internet world, this is accomplished with *MIME types*. (MIME stands for Multipurpose Internet Mail Extensions; the MIME standards were originally developed with e-mail in mind.)

Every file transmitted via HTTP has a MIME type and subtype. The type is a general category such as text, image, or audio, and the subtype is something like html, jpeg, or x-aiff. A list of file type "mappings" in the MacHTTP.config file tells MacHTTP which MIME types and subtypes should be mapped to which files.

First, MacHTTP looks at a file's suffix (the end of the file's name, usually beginning with a period) to determine its type. If it doesn't find a suffix it recognizes, it looks at the Macintosh file type and creator. (For instance, a SimpleText text document has type TEXT and creator ttxt; a standard Microsoft Word 5.1 document has type WDBN and creator MSWD.)

The format of the file type mapping lines in the MacHTTP.config file is as follows:

```
GeneralType  .suffix  MacType  MacCreator  MIMEtype/MIMEsubtype
```

Here are some actual file mapping statements from the MacHTTP.config file (an asterisk means "any"; ToyS is the creator code for AppleScript):

```
TEXT     .HTML  TEXT   *     text/html
BINARY   .GIF   GIFf   *     image/gif
BINARY   .AIFF  *      *     audio/x-aiff
CGI      .CGI   APPL   *     text/html
SCRIPT   *      TEXT   ToyS  text/html
```

There are an infinite number of possible file type mappings. You can look at the default MacHTTP.config file to get an idea of how these look and what some of the types are. You will probably find that you don't need to change the defaults much at all. The list that comes with MacHTTP is pretty comprehensive, and you probably only need to add items if you have binary file types that are not on this list, or if you want to use different suffixes (for example, .mpg instead of .mpeg). Other than this, there is one more thing we suggest adding to the file mapping section of MacHTTP.config, and the best way to explain it is with an example.

Recall the DEFAULT variable from page 192. This sets the transfer type and MIME type that is used if MacHTTP needs to send a file but cannot find *any* suffix, type, or creator matches in MacHTTP.config. As soon as MacHTTP finds any line in the file mapping list that matches even *one* of the file's attributes, it will use that line's MIME type rather than the DEFAULT setting.

Let's say we have a file in our Web site named Table1. This file contains tabular data that is organized with spaces, as if it had been typed on a typewriter. We keep meaning to convert this data to an HTML table, but we haven't gotten around to it yet, so for now it's plain text, created with ClarisWorks (type TEXT, creator BOBO). We have a number of files like this, so we have set the DEFAULT variable to TEXT text/plain (this is the only change we have made to MacHTTP.config). Since it has no suffix, MacHTTP will send Table1 — and all files like it — as plain text, right?

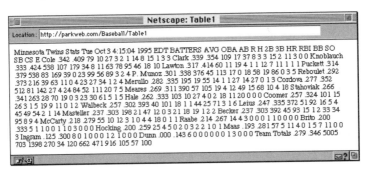

Fig. 9–9 This is what happens when you try to view some plain-text files as HTML. Yuck.

Wrong. Table1's Macintosh file type is TEXT. When MacHTTP receives an HTTP request for the file, it first checks the file mapping list in MacHTTP.config for a matching suffix. Since Table1 doesn't have a suffix, it checks file types and creators and finds type TEXT in the very first line. MacHTTP thinks to itself, "Case closed! Obviously, this is a text/html file. I don't even need to look at the DEFAULT variable!" So MacHTTP cheerfully sends off Table1 as an HTML file, and all the browsers on the other end compress all the formatting spaces down to nothing, and there are no line breaks, and the whole thing is generally a mess (Fig. 9–9).

The solution is to place the following line at the very beginning of the file mappings:

```
TEXT  *  TEXT  *  text/plain
```

This tells MacHTTP to send *any* file with type TEXT as plain text, if it has no recognizable suffix. (The first asterisk pertains to suffixes, the second to creators.) File mappings that include suffixes will override asterisks, so any .html files will still be sent as text/html, but unadorned file names, like Table1, will be text/plain. (Figure 9–10 shows how much better Table1 looks when it's sent as plain text.)

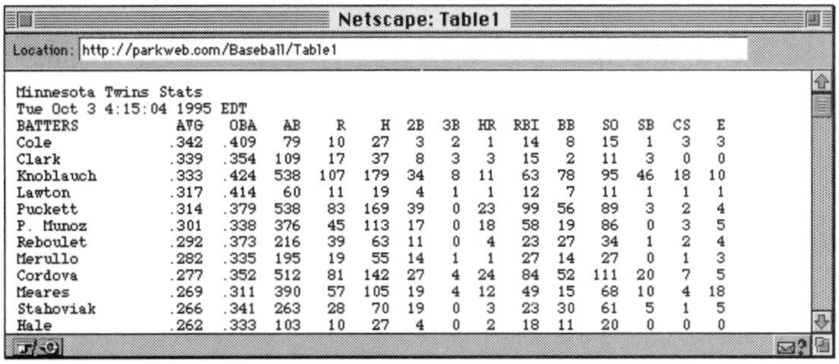

Minnesota Twins Stats
Tue Oct 3 4:15:04 1995 EDT

BATTERS	AVG	OBA	AB	R	H	2B	3B	HR	RBI	BB	SO	SB	CS	E
Cole	.342	.409	79	10	27	3	2	1	14	8	15	1	3	3
Clark	.339	.354	109	17	37	8	3	3	15	2	11	3	0	0
Knoblauch	.333	.424	538	107	179	34	8	11	63	78	95	46	18	10
Lawton	.317	.414	60	11	19	4	1	1	12	7	11	1	1	1
Puckett	.314	.379	538	83	169	39	0	23	99	56	89	3	2	4
P. Munoz	.301	.338	376	45	113	17	0	18	58	19	86	0	3	5
Reboulet	.292	.373	216	39	63	11	0	4	23	27	34	1	2	4
Merullo	.282	.335	195	19	55	14	1	1	27	14	27	0	1	3
Cordova	.277	.352	512	81	142	27	4	24	84	52	111	20	7	5
Meares	.269	.311	390	57	105	19	4	12	49	15	68	10	4	18
Stahoviak	.266	.341	263	28	70	19	0	3	23	30	61	5	1	5
Hale	.262	.333	103	10	27	4	0	2	18	11	20	0	0	0

Fig. 9–10 The suffixless text file is properly sent as plain text after we adjust the file mapping statements in our `MacHTTP.config` file.

In practice, that `DEFAULT` variable rarely has to be used by MacHTTP, since most files will have a recognized suffix, Mac file type, or creator.

Here are a couple of things to keep in mind regarding file type mapping: first, use suffixes whenever possible, so that MacHTTP doesn't have to delve into Mac file types and creators to guess what find of files they are. Second, if you add any new MIME types or subtypes to your `MacHTTP.config` file, use the established standards; don't invent new types like `multimedia/raoul-sings-the-blues`, because no one else's browser will interpret them properly.

Security Settings

Security is a big issue with Web servers, and we will have a little more to say about it, along with some helpful hints, in section 9.6. Here we will just outline the security variables that can be set in the `MacHTTP.config` file. You can have as many `REALM`, `ALLOW`, and `DENY` statements as you want.

REALM A security realm is a particular set of files that can only be accessed by a certain group of people, who gain access to those files by way of a user name and password. A `REALM` setting has two parts: a file name segment and the name of the realm. For example:

```
REALM  my-friends  Friends
```

Whenever MacHTTP receives an HTTP request whose URL includes the string `my-friends`, it knows that the requested file is in the "Friends" security realm. When someone tries to access this file, their browser will prompt them for a name and password. If they do not enter the correct information, MacHTTP will not give them the file. Note that `my-friends` could appear *anywhere* in the URL; in our example, all of these would be in the Friends realm:

```
http://yoursite.com/stuff/my-friends/index.html
http://yoursite.com/miscellaneous/people/my-friends.html
http://yoursite.com/my-friendship-with-ana.txt
```

You can specify as many realms as you want, but make sure your URLs can each belong in only one realm. You may want to pick file name segments that are somewhat unusual, so there is no chance of you accidentally restricting everyone's access to a public file.

The names and passwords for all your realms are set from within the MacHTTP application; see "Realm Passwords" on page 199.

ALLOW Determines which Internet hosts are allowed to access your MacHTTP server. For instance, the statements ALLOW whitehouse.gov. and ALLOW 87.65.43.21. would grant those hosts permission to visit your site. Note that all domain names and specific IP addresses in ALLOW and DENY statements *must* end with a period.

You can use partial addresses in your ALLOW statements. Domain names are read right-to-left, but IPs are read left-to-right. ALLOW d.umn.edu. would allow only those whose domain names *end* with d.umn.edu to visit your site; ALLOW umn.edu. would expand access to any umn.edu address. If you use numeric IP addresses, you use the leftmost numbers to specify a partial address, so ALLOW 76.54.3 would allow people to access your site from 76.54.32.10, but not from 98.76.54.3. Note that *partial* IPs do *not* have to end with a period, but partial domains do.

DENY The syntax of DENY is exactly the same as ALLOW, except any addresses you specify in a DENY statement will, obviously, be *denied* access to your MacHTTP server.

If you put the same address in an ALLOW statement and again in a later DENY statement, the DENY will override the ALLOW simply because it came last. If you contradict yourself *again*, and append yet another ALLOW statement with the same address, the ALLOW statement is now the law of the land. This is a useful feature; let's say you wanted to keep out everyone at xyz.com except your friend, whose machine is named juan.xyz.com. You could accomplish this with the following two statements:

```
DENY xyz.com.
ALLOW juan.zyx.com.
```

As soon as you put *any* ALLOW or DENY statements in your MacHTTP.config file, it is assumed that, in general, you want *no one* to be able to access your server, and only those whom you bless in your MacHTTP.config file will be able to get in. Therefore, you probably shouldn't do anything with ALLOW and DENY statements for the time being, unless you are specifically setting up a private server that you only want a handful of people to have access to.

It's possible, however, that there will be a few select hosts or domains that you want to keep out of your server, while letting most everyone else in. For information on how to do this, see section 9.6.

9.5 CONFIGURATION: MACHTTP MENU ITEMS

If you've been following along with your `MacHTTP.config` file and filling in variable settings, you're through the hard part. Save your work and take a break. There are a few more things you need to set, but they are all in the MacHTTP application itself, and they're easy.

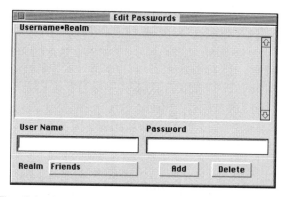

Fig. 9–11   The dialog box where you set passwords and user names for security realms. We have defined a "Friends" realm in `MacHTTP.config`.

Realm Passwords

Open MacHTTP and select the `Passwords...` item from the bottom of the `Edit` menu in MacHTTP (you must be hooked up to the Net or MacHTTP will not load). You will see a dialog box like the one in Figure 9–11. Any security realms that you defined in the `MacHTTP.config` file (page 197) will be items in the pop-up menu at the bottom of the window, next to the word `Realm`.

To add a user name and password to a particular realm, select the name of that realm in the pop-up menu, and type a user name and password in the appropriate text areas. For example, in Figure 9–12, we have defined two realms: "Friends" and "Family." We have already added a couple users to each realm, and we are about to add user "Jeremiah" to the "Friends" realm. His password will be "bullfrog." When we click the `Add` button, `Jeremiah•Friends` will be added to the `Username•Realm` list.

To remove a user, select their name in the list and click the "Delete" button. To change someone's password or realm, you have to delete them from the list and then add them again, with the new information.

The Options Menu

The items under the `Options` menu don't lead anywhere; they are just items that can be checked and unchecked at your whim. These settings are stored in the file called `MacHTTP Settings`, which you should never rename.

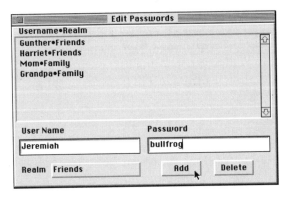

Fig. 9–12   Gunther and Harriet are both in the "Friends" realm already. Mom and Grandpa are in another realm called "Family."

Verbose Messages   When `Verbose Messages` is *un*checked, MacHTTP displays HTTP transactions with a simple, one line synopsis of what happened. With `Verbose Messages` turned on, you get to see an obscene amount of information about everything that goes in and out. This is useful if you are trying to diagnose a problem, but in most situations it's overkill. For day-to-day operations, leave it off.

Suspend Logging   If you have specified a log file in `MacHTTP.config` (using the `LOG` variable), the `Suspend Logging` option will make MacHTTP stop logging and relinquish control of the log file, so you can read or edit it with a text editor or word processor. Or you may just want to check `Suspend Logging` because you've decided that you don't need a log file, and it's easier to select this menu item than go back and edit `MacHTTP.config` again.

Hide Window in Background   If this item is checked, MacHTTP will hide its status window the next time other applications are active in the foreground. It is similar to selecting `Hide MacHTTP` from your Mac's application menu (on the right-hand side of the menu bar), but `Hide Window in Background` will hide the status window *every* time you put MacHTTP in the background, and it has no immediate effect (i.e., when you select the menu item, MacHTTP does not suddenly jump to the background and hide).

Refuse New Connections   This essentially turns off your server, but it allows any currently open connections to finish what they are doing first. Use this option if you are shutting down for the day, or if you want to reorganize your site without quitting the MacHTTP application.

9.6 SECURITY TIPS

We have already briefly discussed all three of the primary ways that you can restrict access to your MacHTTP server. This section will just give some helpful hints about all three methods. Much of this information is also in the "MacHTTP Security" tutorial that comes with MacHTTP (`Security.html`, in the `Tutorials` folder).

ALLOW and DENY

Most likely, you want everyone in the world to be able to visit your Web site. That's easy enough; just don't put *any* `ALLOW` or `DENY` statements in your `MacHTTP.config` file. But remember that as soon as you put one in, there is an "implied `DENY *`" before all your security settings, so everyone is locked out unless you specifically name their host or domain as being allowed.

So, what if you want to keep one particular domain out of your site — let's say you want to keep out people from Belgium, for some reason — while making it accessible to all other domains? You *could* put in an `ALLOW` statement for every Internet domain that exists (except those in Belgium), but that would really be a pain. There is an easier way; just put the following statements in your `MacHTTP.config` file:

```
ALLOW  1
ALLOW  2
ALLOW  3
ALLOW  4
ALLOW  5
ALLOW  6
ALLOW  7
ALLOW  8
ALLOW  9
DENY  .be.
```

All IP addresses begin with a number between 1 and 9. So every IP address in the world is covered by the partial IPs in these `ALLOW` statements. Then the lone `DENY` statement gets rid of Belgium. (By the way, we have nothing against Belgium; we just drew one country's name out of an electronic hat!)

Realms

Setting up realms is pretty straightforward. Even if you don't plan on giving out passwords to certain groups of people, you can use security realms to keep outsiders from seeing certain files in your site.

For instance, you may not want people to see your `MacHTTP.config` file, or any other configuration files you have in your server. (Some CGI applications also create files that end in `.config`.) All you have to do is include the following `REALM` statement in your `MacHTTP.config` file:

```
REALM  .config  Config_Files
```

Any file whose name includes .config is now in the "Config_Files" realm, and you can use the MacHTTP menus to set user names and passwords for this realm. (Since you run the server, you don't really need to set a password for MacHTTP.config; you can just open the file in your text editor!)

You may also not want people snooping in your log file, so you can add this REALM statement as well:

```
REALM  .log  Log_Files
```

If you have a folder full of secret files that only you should see, the safest place for them is actually *outside* your MacHTTP folder! But if you were to put those files *in* your MacHTTP folder, then you could access them even if you traveled halfway around the world, provided your server was running while you were away. What a neat idea! So just set up a realm for yourself, and don't tell anyone the password. (And don't let anyone near your Mac while you're gone!)

Another use of realms might be to set up a directory full of files that you "charge admission" for. This would be like the on-line equivalent of a 900 number. You could place a limited amount of information in public directories in your site, and put even better stuff in the restricted directory. Then, when people send you, say, $5.00, you can send them the password to the restricted area. The security in this scenario wouldn't be airtight, but if you have something on line that you think people are willing to pay for, it might be a way to recoup some of the costs of putting your site together. If you do this, make sure you also have some *free* information, or no one will want to visit!

Running Multiple Servers on Different Ports

Running two MacHTTP servers is somewhat like setting up security realms. But instead of having specific directories that are public or private, you have specific TCP/IP ports.

The details of exactly what constitutes a port are not important here. But the way it works is, a connection to your server with no port number specified (for instance, http://yoursite.com/) defaults to port 80. If you change the PORT setting in the MacHTTP.config file to, say, 8000, then people could only connect to your server by requesting a connection to http://yoursite.com:8000/. If you run two MacHTTP servers on the same Mac, one on port 80 and one on port 8000, then either URL will work, but they will have access to completely different files.

If you wanted the port 8000 server to be your private one, you could adjust that server's MacHTTP.config file so that it denied access to every host except whichever address you were planning on accessing the server from. If you will not always be connecting to your Mac from the same host, you could place all files on the private server into one folder, and define a security realm that includes the name of that folder. For extra security, don't even provide a default file in the root directory; anyone trying to connect to your site will receive an error message unless they know specifically where the files are stored. And if they do manage to guess the file names, they still won't be able to see them, because they won't have the password.

In conclusion, file security in MacHTTP is pretty tight. Any of the methods outlined above should work just fine to keep people from seeing things they shouldn't. You may have heard a lot of talk about *secure transactions* involving credit card numbers and such; that's another matter entirely. If you want more information, you might want to check out StarNine Technologies' home page, since they sell a secure (and quite expensive) version of WebSTAR that you could run on your Macintosh.

9.7 TESTING YOUR SERVER

Now that you have your server set up just the way you want it, try to break it! Construct a page that has a dozen different images on it, and see what happens when you try to load them all at once. Get a bunch of friends with Web browsers together, and have them all try to get into your server at exactly the same time. Now have them all load that picture-laden page at once.

While all this is going on, you should be watching the MacHTTP status window. The statistics at the top of the page can tell you a lot, if you know what to look for. Read the "Performance Tuning" tutorial that comes with MacHTTP (`:Tutorials:Performance.html`).

You should try to hit your server with as many different Web browsers as possible, and make sure they are all seeing the same thing. To make sure the MIME types are being sent correctly, put a large variety of different files in your site and have your friends try to view or download them.

If you have security realms set up, try to access files in each of the realms and make sure MacHTTP lets you in once you enter the password. More importantly, make sure it keeps you out of places you're not supposed to be *without* a password. If you have denied access to all Belgians, ask someone in Belgium to try to access your site, just to be sure they can't! (An easier way to test your DENY statements is to deny access to yourself. If DENY yoursite.com. works, you can assume that DENY .be. probably works as well.)

If you have two MacHTTPs running on different ports, make sure they can both run simultaneously. See what happens if you try to send large files through both ports at the same time.

While you or other people are accessing your server, try to perform other simple tasks on your Mac, like writing a letter or checking your e-mail. If it's difficult because MacHTTP keeps hogging your CPU or your modem, maybe you should think about getting a faster Mac, a faster line, or even another computer to use as a dedicated server.

Once you are convinced that everything is working exactly as it should, and you have tweaked your MacHTTP.config file as best you can, sit back and admire your accomplishments. You are now officially a Macintosh Webmaster! You have created a fully functional World Wide Web site over which you have complete control. You can put anything you want in there, and anyone in the world can connect to your Macintosh and see the fruits of your labor.

Unless, of course, they live in Belgium.

9.8 CGI ON A MACINTOSH

If you want to set up forms, image maps, graphical access counters, and other clever things on your Web site, you need to make use of CGI scripts. CGI stands for Common Gateway Interface; it is a standard method of passing information between external programs and HTTP servers. We will describe it more fully in Chapter 12.

Scripts are the most complicated part of Web sites. Here, we will go over the basics of what you will need if you want to use CGI scripts in your Macintosh server, and we will give you some URLs that you can look up if you want to know more.

There is a wealth of information available on the Web about adding scripts to a MacHTTP server, most notably Jon Wiederspan's excellent "Extending Web-STAR" tutorial. Yes, it says "WebSTAR," but the information is equally applicable to MacHTTP. You can find links to these lessons in the Other_Sites.html file that is included in MacHTTP's distribution (in the Documentation directory), or just go to this URL: http://www.comvista.com/net/www/cgilesson.html. For more information about CGI scripts in general, and AppleScript in particular, Jon's site is a good place to start.

Macintosh CGI Applications

The easiest way to run scripts on your MacHTTP server is to use programs that other people have already compiled into usable applications. You don't need to know anything about how they work. All you have to do is put the proper URLs in your pages; when MacHTTP receives a request for a file whose name ends in .cgi or .acgi, it knows that it should launch a CGI program of some kind. The CGI program knows what MacHTTP needs in order to complete the transaction, and often the CGI program will quit automatically when it is done.

In section 9.9, we recommend a number of useful CGI applications that are available on Web pages or FTP sites, ready for you to download and use with your server. You will definitely want to get at least Mac-ImageMap or MapServe (page 208), since image maps are such a standard part of Web pages nowadays.

AppleScript

As mentioned earlier, AppleScript is a *scripting* language developed by Apple that allows your Macintosh applications to communicate with each other. For our purposes on the Web, AppleScript can be used to write CGI scripts that take information from HTTP requests, process it in some way, and then send something back to MacHTTP, which MacHTTP can send back out again. There is really no limit to what you could do with AppleScript programs.

If you are going to make heavy use of buttons and forms in your Web site, you should learn to program in either AppleScript or Perl. Unfortunately, any programming language takes a while to learn — especially if you have not done any programming before — and computer programming is not for everyone.

If and when you do take the plunge and try to learn AppleScript, you should definitely print out Jon Wiederspan's tutorials (see above) and follow them step by step. Once you've mastered the basics, download some scripts from Web pages or FTP sites and see how they work. Try to customize them to use in your own site. If you want to know even more, we suggest — as does Jon — that you buy or borrow a book about AppleScript. Sometimes it's a lot easier to have all the information there on your shelf than to have to track it down on the Web.

To save AppleScript code as `.cgi` or `.acgi` applications (a more efficient method than making MacHTTP run the code through AppleScript), you will need either Apple's Script Editor or a third-party program such as ScriptWizard. To use any scripts, you should have a few AppleScript extensions — known as OSAXen — that were designed to make Web site scripting easier. Visit the AppleScript FTP archive at `ftp://ftp.scriptweb.com/pub/applescript/` for OSAXen and tons of sample scripts that do all kinds of things, not all of them Internet-related.

Perl

Perl is another scripting language. There are a few advantages to using Perl rather than the AppleScript language. First of all, it is available for all platforms, not just Macintosh, so the fantastic Perl script that your UNIX friend wrote will probably work on your Mac, if you set it up properly. The universality of Perl also means that there are a *lot* of on-line reference materials to help you out.

The second advantage of Perl over AppleScript is that the application you will use to create and run Perl scripts — called MacPerl — is freely available. The biggest disadvantage of using Perl is that it is not integrated into the Macintosh system the way AppleScript is, so there are some things you cannot do with Perl that you *can* do with AppleScript. But for your basic Web site tricks, such as forms, MacPerl will do just fine.

Since this book is about World Wide Web servers in general, not just MacHTTP, we have chosen to focus on Perl, since it can be used with UNIX and Windows as well as Macintosh; our discussion of Perl scripts is platform-independent. Chapter 12 includes a very simple Perl script that will introduce you to the world of CGI scripting; Chapter 13 contains a few more examples of actual Perl scripts that will work with any Perl interpreter; and Appendix C is a Perl quick reference guide.

To use Perl scripts with MacHTTP, you need an extension to MacPerl, called PCGI, which allows MacPerl to save scripts as mini-applications that will work as CGI scripts with MacHTTP, rather than as plain text files. When you do this, be sure to give them a file name that ends in .cgi, so that MacHTTP will know that they should be executed as scripts. If you want to save them with another extension — such as .pl — you need to add the new suffix to the File Type Mapping section of your MacHTTP.config file.

In a nutshell, here are the files you will need to get before moving on to the Perl scripts in Chapters 12 and 13:

MacPerl   We have included both version 4 and version 5 of MacPerl on the CD in the back of this book (in the CGI Stuff folder). You can also find MacPerl in Info-Mac's /dev/ directory, or at ftp://ftp.switch.ch/software/mac/perl/. Once you've downloaded it, you can put the MacPerl application and all its folders anywhere you want, but keep them together.

PCGI   You can get the PCGI extension from the CD or from this URL: ftp://err.ethz.ch/pub/neeri/MacPerl/PCGI.sit.hqx. Once you have downloaded and unstuffed it, put it in the MacPerl Extensions folder that came with MacPerl. Use it by invoking the Save As... menu item in MacPerl and selecting "MacHTTP CGI Script" from the pop-up menu at the bottom of the dialog box.

Cgi-lib.pl   This library of Perl subroutines includes a number of very useful commands that take pieces of information sent from HTML pages and Web browsers, and convert them into a format that is easy to use with Perl. This is not a Mac-specific file; *anyone* who wants to use Perl CGI scripts can use it (see Chapter 12 for more about cross-platform uses of cgi-lib.pl). You can get the latest cgi-lib.pl from http://www.bio.cam.ac.uk/cgi-lib/; it's plain text, and you should save a copy in MacPerl's lib folder in order for your scripts to be able to access it. Technically, you *can* put it someplace else, but you must make sure MacPerl knows to look for it in the new location. You can do this selecting Preferences from the Edit menu; then clicking the Add Path button in the "Libraries" section of MacPerl's preferences. (You will also need to use the Add Path command if any of your folder names change.)

AppleScript Extension   Don't forget to install the AppleScript system extension in your System Folder, or none of your Perl scripts will work at all! This has nothing to do with the AppleScript scripting language; recall that AppleScript lets your various Mac applications — in this case, MacHTTP and your CGI scripts — talk to one another.

In case any of these files have moved around the Internet, you can find their current locations, as well as the URL of the "MacPerl Primer" and other important facts, in the "MacPerl Q & A" document, located at the following URL:

    http://err.ethz.ch/members/neeri/macintosh/perl-qa.html

9.9 RECOMMENDED CGI APPLICATIONS

This section describes a number of CGI scripts that have already been compiled into usable programs and are available from most FTP software archives. All of these will enhance the behavior of your MacHTTP server in some way, without you having to learn anything about AppleScript or Perl. For specific details on configuring and using these applications on your MacHTTP server, be sure to read the documentation that comes with each one.

For each program in this section and the sections that follow, we have listed the price — most of them are freeware, although a few require a registration fee — and the URL of a page with more information about the program. If any of these pages have moved, you should be able to find their new location by using a Web search mechanism such as Lycos or Alta Vista.

You can also download most of these files by simply looking in the Internet/World Wide Web section of any major FTP archive that contains Macintosh software. In the Info-Mac archive, most of the CGI programs are in the `/comm/tcp/web/` directory.

Even if you don't need any specific files, you should check your favorite Info-Mac directories regularly to see if anything new has cropped up. To make your search for new toys easier, aliases to the most recently added files can be found in Info-Mac's `/rec/` ("recent") directory. Send a `LIST -lt` command from your FTP program to see a file listing that is sorted by date so the most recent ones are at the top.

The remainder of this chapter is in no way intended to be a *comprehensive* guide to Net-related Macintosh applications; these are just the ones that we recommend most highly. Every program listed here is either excellent, cheap, or both. (And remember to pay for your shareware!)

Kelly's Error

Price: free
URL: http://www.spub.ksu.edu/other/machttp_tools/error/

This is a must-have for any MacHTTP server; it makes your server a little more forgiving to people trying to connect to your site. If you define your server's default ERROR file to be Kelly's Error — the file name is actually `Error.acgi` — in your `MacHTTP.config` file (see page 193), this program will be run anytime there is an error in a file transfer. If the error was simply that the incoming HTTP request was for a directory, but the request did not include the trailing slash (for example, the browser was looking for `http://yoursite.com/images/hawaii`), Kelly's Error will append a slash to the URL and try the request again (`http://yoursite.com/images/hawaii/`); the person accessing the page will never even know there was a problem.

If appending a slash does not remedy the error, then the directory must not exist; Kelly's Error will then send your original error file if you want it to. Or you can use ResEdit (described on page 223) to define an internal error file, which can include variables such as the referring page. The only real drawback to using

Kelly's Error as your error file is that it takes a little bit longer to load — and thus places more of a burden on your server — than a simple HTML file that says, "Error!"

Kelly only planned for Kelly's Error to work with WebSTAR, but it does work with MacHTTP as well. In MacHTTP, it does exactly what it is supposed to, but the internal log comes up with some cryptic AppleEvent errors that you needn't worry about.

Mac-ImageMap

Price: free

URL: `http://weyl.zib-berlin.de/imagemap/mac-imagemap.html`

MapServe

Price: $20

URL: `http://www.spub.ksu.edu/other/machttp_tools/mapserve/`

Both of these programs allow you to use image maps on your server. First, you will need to create a plain-text map definition file for each image. This can be done by hand or with the help of a program like WebMap (see page 221). In your HTML pages, an image map is defined by placing the `ismap` attribute in an `<IMG>` tag (see Appendix A), and enclosing it in an `<A href>` tag that links to Mac-ImageMap or MapServe, with the name of a map file included in the URL.

MapServe is very easy to configure and works much like the standard UNIX image map programs. Mac-ImageMap's configuration file is a little bit tricky to figure out, but it is free. You'll have to decide whether MapServe's $20 shareware fee is worth the corresponding ease of use.

Count WWWebula

Price: free (individuals and non-profits) or $25 (commercial)

URL: `http://uts.cc.utexas.edu/~grgcombs/htmls/counter.html`

Count WWWebula creates GIF images that are graphical counters of how many people have accessed a particular page at your site. You set it up by creating an `<IMG>` tag whose source is not an actual image file, but rather the CGI program itself. Every time the CGI program is run, a picture is served and Count WWWebula increments the counter for that page (Fig. 9–13); you can put a separate counter on as many pages as you like. You can change the appearance of the counter number by downloading a new set of digits from an archive on the Web or by creating your own. You can also easily prevent other people from hijacking your server's copy of Count WWWebula for their own use.

The numbers generated by Count WWWebula — or *any* graphical access counter, for that matter — are not completely accurate because the image must be sent for the counter to be incremented, and not everyone loads all the images. But it's a fun-looking way to get a rough estimate, or at least a sense of which pages on your server are getting the most hits. For accurate counts, you need something like ServerStat.

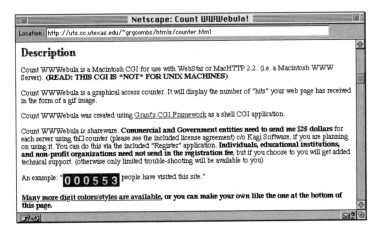

Fig. 9–13 You can use Count WWWebula with your MacHTTP server to create access counters like the "000553" image on this page.

ServerStat

Price: $20 for ServerStat Lite; $30 (educational) or $70 (commercial) for ServerStat

URL: `http://www.kitchen-sink.com/ss.html`

ServerStat is not a CGI program, but we describe it in this section because it works so closely with MacHTTP. ServerStat creates a detailed report that includes all kinds of statistics about your server's log file (it can also read the logs of WebSTAR and Gopher servers). It will break down the number of hits your site has received per day, per week, or per hour. You can also examine which Internet hosts or domains have been visiting your site, and you can see which files have been getting the most requests.

Additional configuration options include the ability to read only the log entries for particular date ranges, exclusion of data from certain sites — meaning, for example, that it won't count when you or your friends access your site — and the option to output the report as plain text or as an HTML file. Not all of ServerStat's features are implemented in the $20 shareware version (ServerStat Lite), but try it out and see if it suits your needs, or if you need to spend the extra $10 or $50 to get the full version.

Annotate

Price: free

URL: `http://snodaq.phy.queensu.ca/phil/phil.html`

This little program lets you set up a page that solicits comments from readers and adds them to that page, where everyone else can see them. They can also delete their comment if they decide they don't like it. Fortunately, the file which holds the comments is a standard HTML file, so you can use your favorite text editor to delete any comments *you* don't like! It's easy to set up and easy for people to use; the only drawback is that it's somewhat slow.

In Chapter 13, we will teach you how to write a "Guest Book" program in Perl that does essentially the same thing Annotate does — albeit without the ability for people to delete their comments — but you can use Annotate right now, without having to learn a single bit of programming.

9.10 INTERNET APPLICATIONS

These programs all allow you to access various Internet services, so they all require MacTCP and a SLIP, PPP, or direct connection to the Internet. Chances are you already have at least a couple of them — or their equivalents — if you have a SLIP or PPP account. If you want to be a fully-connected Internet citizen, it is imperative that you have at least one of each of the following: an FTP program, a Telnet client, a mail reader, and a news reader. There are many applications that fulfill these functions, but these are our favorites.

Note that we have not covered Web browsers in this section; that's because we are assuming that by now you already have one! You can get most or all of these applications from the /comm/tcp directory of Info-Mac.

Internet Config

Price: free
URL: http://www.ese.ogi.edu/peterlewis/programs.html#InternetConfig

When you first set up an Internet application, you often have to give it certain information, such as your e-mail address; the name of the computer that your mail is stored on; the name of the computer that stores the Usenet articles you read; the names of all your helper applications; and so on.

With Internet Config installed on your Mac (it consists of an application and a system extension), you only have to enter this information once, in Internet Config, and many programs will just get the information from there. There are still some preferences you'll need to set in each program, of course, but not nearly as many. You will most appreciate Internet Config if any part of your configuration needs to be changed.

Not all Macintosh Internet-related programs take advantage of Internet Config yet, but many of them do, and more certainly will, as they are updated and revised.

Anarchie

Price: $10
URL: `http://www.ese.ogi.edu/peterlewis/programs.html#Anarchie`

Fetch

Price: free (educational and non-profit) or $25 (commercial)
URL: `http://www.dartmouth.edu/pages/softdev/fetch.html`

Anarchie and Fetch are the most common FTP clients for the Macintosh. Both of them allow you to connect to FTP sites around the world and retrieve files, or copy files from your Mac onto the remote server. (Recall that most FTP connections are *anonymous* FTP; you don't need an account on the machine you're hooking up to. Anarchie and Fetch allow you to connect either anonymously or with an account.) Both programs come with "Bookmark" lists of commonly used sites, and you can add your own favorite sites to your list.

If you have everything properly configured — which is not difficult to do — Anarchie and Fetch will automatically assign the proper Macintosh file type and creator to your files, and it will even *post-process* them if you like. In other words, files that have been compressed or encoded will either be decoded immediately or automatically sent to an application (such as StuffIt Expander; see page 214) that can extract or decode them.

The main advantage of Anarchie over Fetch is that Anarchie allows you to search for file names in Archie databases (hence the name), which are catalogs of the contents of selected FTP sites. While Archie sites do not store the names of every file in the world, they can be very helpful. Fetch cannot do Archie searches, but it has the advantage of being a little bit more user-friendly in terms of allowing you to explore the directories of FTP sites.

If you were running a Web site whose files were stored somewhere on your provider's system, you would use an FTP program to upload all your Web materials. Since you will be running a server using MacHTTP, you probably won't need to do this. However, if your server won't be running 24 hours a day, you may want to see if your provider has an FTP server to store important files for round-the-clock access. You will also probably find an FTP program useful for downloading new shareware programs and other items from public software archives. (You can also do this from within your Web browser, of course, but we much prefer using Fetch or Anarchie.)

NCSA Telnet

Price: free
URL: `http://www.ncsa.uiuc.edu/SDG/Software/MacTelnet/`

NCSA Telnet is a very, very popular telnet client for the Mac. It is in the public domain, so anyone can download it and use it for free. Telnet programs simply hook you up to another computer on the Internet and allow you to log in, if you have an account there. You need a telnet program because your Internet presence will almost certainly include a shell account on your Internet service provider's computer (which is almost always running some flavor of UNIX).

When you initiate a SLIP or PPP connection, your provider's system sees your Mac as a remote site like any other computer in the world, and vice versa. You need telnet to make the connection, whether across the ocean or across the room.

NCSA Telnet also allows you to make FTP connections, but it is like running the `ftp` command in UNIX; you're much better off with Anarchie or Fetch. Many people do not realize this, but NCSA Telnet also lets you effectively turn your Mac into an FTP server, so other people can log in and access files on your Mac. Be very careful with this option; if you make your Mac into an FTP server and don't specify any passwords, anyone in the world can read your entire hard drive!

Eudora Light

Price: free

URL: `http://www.qualcomm.com/ProdTech/quest/light.html`

Eudora is an all-purpose e-mail program for the Macintosh (PC versions are available as well). It is very easy to use, and very problem-free. You can create as many different boxes as you want to store incoming mail; you can even create folders full of related mailboxes. If you like, you can have Eudora check your mail for you at regular intervals while you are on line. If you want to send someone a binary file via e-mail, Eudora can encode it for you; and Eudora can decode incoming messages, as long as they are in a certain format.

There are two versions of Eudora: Eudora Pro and Eudora Light. We recommend that you start with Eudora Light, because it is free and it does everything most people need. If you find that you really need automatic mail filtering and built-in uuencoding and uudecoding (among other things), then you should get Eudora Pro, which costs $89.

NewsWatcher

Price: free

URL: `http://charlotte.acns.nwu.edu/jln/progs.html`

NewsWatcher is a Usenet news reader for the Macintosh. It allows you to define sets of newsgroups to which you "subscribe," follow up to articles, post articles — pretty much anything you would want to do with Usenet. (NewsWatcher does *not* do uudecoding, however. For that you need a helper application like uuUndo; see page 218.)

We actually think it is easier to read Usenet articles from a UNIX shell account —accessed via telnet — using a program like rn or nn. But, if you insist on having that friendly Mac environment in *everything* you do, pick up NewsWatcher. It is very user-friendly, and the author of the program is constantly updating it. There are also "patched" versions of NewsWatcher available that have extra features.

TurboGopher

Price: $25

URL: `ftp://boombox.micro.umn.edu/pub/gopher/Macintosh-TurboGopher`

Even though the World Wide Web has supplanted Gopher as the premier information service on the Internet, there are still a lot of Gopher servers out there, many of which hold information that's not on the Web (yet).

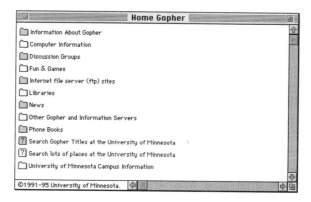

Fig. 9–14   The University of Minnesota's "gopher hole," as viewed with TurboGopher.

TurboGopher is somewhat like NewsWatcher, in that the information being delivered looks pretty much the same whether you are using a Macintosh or an ancient UNIX terminal. However, there is no question in our minds that Turbo-Gopher is easier to use than plain-text UNIX Gopher clients. (If you don't want to bother with a Gopher program like TurboGopher, you may want to simply view Gopher files from within your Web browser.)

The University of Minnesota's Gopher team has recently released a new Gopher client, called TurboGopher VR — yes, that's "virtual reality." It's worth downloading, if only just to see it once for fun. In TurboGopher VR, items are viewed in three-dimensional "Gopherspace" rather than plain old text. Figure 9–14 shows a typical Gopher menu in the "normal" TurboGopher; Figure 9–15 is TurboGopher VR. A word of caution: due to the complexity of the math involved in drawing those 3-D pictures, don't even try running TurboGopher on a Mac without either a floating-point unit (FPU) or a PowerPC processor!

IP Monitor

Price: $5

URL: `http://www.eskimo.com/~ravensys/ipmonitor.html`

You are probably running your Web server with a static IP address, meaning your Mac is assigned the same Internet address every time you hook up. If, however, you don't have a static IP; or you often forget your IP; or you are just in the testing phase and haven't forked over the money for your static IP and

Fig. 9–15 The same gopher hole as in Figure 9–14, this time viewed with Turbo-Gopher VR. We're not sure what the point is, and it's kind of hard to read, but it certainly is impressive.

domain name yet; then you may find IP Monitor very helpful. It displays your current IP address in a very small window, anywhere you want on the screen.

If you type Command-C while IP Monitor is in the foreground, the address will be copied to the clipboard, so you can paste it into other applications. This is very helpful when you want to test your own Web server with a dynamic IP.

9.11 HELPER APPLICATIONS

These are applications that you never knew you needed until you started downloading files off the Internet. Their purpose is simply to take all kinds of information, created on all kinds of computers, and make it usable on your Macintosh. You might not need *all* of these programs, but at a bare minimum, you should have StuffIt Expander, JPEGView, and SoundApp. As always, the files listed in this section are available for downloading from the Info-Mac archives, as well as from the pages listed here.

StuffIt Expander

Price: free
URL: http://www.aladdinsys.com/Aladdin.html#SFP

DropStuff with Expander Enhancer

Price: $30
URL: http://www.aladdinsys.com/Aladdin.html#SFP

Most programs stored on the Internet are compressed to save space. Macintosh files are also usually BinHexed, so that all the binary file information can be safely transferred from one type of system to another without any loss of information. Once you get one of these BinHex files into your machine, you need to change it back to a usable Macintosh file.

StuffIt Expander is *the* decompression/translation program for the Macintosh. It will decode or uncompress BinHex, Compact Pro, StuffIt, and MacBinary files; this covers the vast majority of Mac files found in software archives, so you will probably want to get this program before you download anything else in this chapter!

When programs such as Anarchie, Fetch, Mosaic, or Netscape call up StuffIt Expander to decode a file, it will run in the background so that you don't even notice it. If you are working in the Finder, you can drop archives onto StuffIt Expander — or, better yet, an alias of StuffIt Expander on the desktop — and they will be taken care of. You can even set StuffIt Expander to delete the original encoded files if you like; this saves you a trip to the trash can.

StuffIt Expander is freeware, and we've included a copy of it on the CD in the back of this book for your convenience. If you want to spend the $30 shareware fee, you can get DropStuff with Expander Enhancer. DropStuff allows you to *create* StuffIt archives simply by dropping files onto its icon, and the Expander Enhancer will undo almost every compression scheme ever invented, including UNIX and PC formats.

Tex-Edit Plus

Price: $5

URL: `ftp://members.aol.com/tombb/`

Most plain text files on a Macintosh are SimpleText documents. SimpleText — like its predecessor, TeachText — is a simple text editor that comes with your system software. Most of the time, it works just fine, but it has a couple of drawbacks. One is that it displays all your text in the Geneva font by default. There's nothing wrong with Geneva per se, but many plain text files are formatted such that everything gets out of alignment when you view them in a font where the M's are wider than the I's; dashes, numbers and spaces are unpredictable (Fig. 9–16).

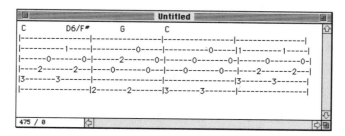

Fig. 9–16 Some guitar music displayed in the Geneva typeface. The vertical lines are *supposed* to line up, but obviously they don't.

Ideally, you will want to view most plain text files in *monospaced* fonts such as Courier or Monaco; all of the characters in these fonts have equal width (Fig. 9–17).

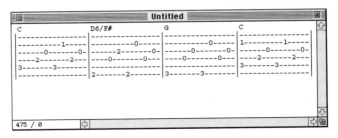

Fig. 9–17   This is the same file as Figure 9–16. The only thing that's changed is the font. It is now displayed in Courier, and everything lines up as it should.

The bigger problem is that TeachText and SimpleText are incapable of opening files that have more than 32,768 characters in them. This "32K limit" is a quirk of the Macintosh operating system; many other applications (e.g., Eudora) have this problem as well. One way to get around this problem is to open text files in your word processor. Unfortunately, word processors tend to use up a lot of memory and can take a while to open.

Our recommended solution is Tex-Edit Plus. It only takes up a couple hundred kilobytes of space on your hard drive and only needs 300K of RAM (minimum; the suggested memory size is 600K). It can open files of any size — *very* large files require more memory, though — and you can set the default font to anything you want, including Courier or Monaco. Unlike many shareware text editors, Tex-Edit also supports styles (bold, italics, etc.), and has other features like find-and-replace.

Some Web browsers require you to specify a text editor for viewing the source HTML of Web pages; Tex-Edit will work very well in this capacity. It is also a useful tool if you like to write HTML documents by hand (rather than using an HTML editor or converter; see page 219). Tex-Edit Plus is well worth the minuscule $5 registration fee.

JPEGView

Price: a colorful postcard
URL: `http://www.med.cornell.edu/jpegview.html`

Jade

Price: free
URL: `http://hyperarchive.lcs.mit.edu/HyperArchive/Abstracts/gst/grf/`
    `HyperArchive.html`

Most World Wide Web browsers can display graphics in GIF and JPEG format. However, you may encounter files that are in some other format, such as the Macintosh PICT or Windows BMP format. Or you might want to view pictures that are already on your computer, without hooking up to the Web. In that case, you need another program, one whose purpose is specifically to display pictures. That's where JPEGView comes in.

JPEGView can view a number of common image formats, and if the pictures are larger than the size of your screen, they will be scaled appropriately. If a picture contains more colors than your monitor can display, JPEG will *dither* the image and display it in however many colors you do have. (Dithering creates a pattern of dots that makes colors appear to blend together.) Frankly, that's about all JPEGView does, but that's really all it needs to do; it's a perfect WWW helper application. And the price is right: if you use JPEGView, you must simply send Aaron Giles a postcard.

Jade is a newer program; it's the first freeware graphics viewer for the Mac that can display progressive JPEG images. It also takes advantage of Apple's Thread Manager, so it's faster than JPEGView, especially when displaying more than one image simultaneously. Jade doesn't have quite as many features as JPEGView, but it's free, so pick up a copy at your local archive.

SoundApp

Price: free
URL: `http://www-cs-students.stanford.edu/~franke/SoundApp`

SoundApp makes an excellent Mosaic or Netscape helper for a number of reasons. Most importantly, it supports a number of different audio formats, so you'll be able to download almost any sound clip you find on the Net. Also, you can set it to automatically quit after playing a sound, so you barely notice it's there. In addition, SoundApp will very easily convert sounds from one format to another. And to top it all off, it's free.

Fast Player

Price: free
URL: `ftp://ftp.wco.com/users/mcmurtri/MySoftware/`

This is a very simple QuickTime movie player. If you set your Web browser to load `.MOV` or `.MOOV` files into Fast Player, this tiny little application will load and the movie can be played. It also has the capability to export QuickTime movies in a "flat" format that all platforms can read (see the "important note" under the description of QuickEditor on page 222 for more information).

There are a few other movie players out there, but this one is the easiest, cheapest, and — at 13K on your hard disk — by far the smallest. If you want more video capabilities, look into the Desktop Movie Trilogy suite of shareware applications, or QuickEditor (described in section 9.12, "Web Development Tools").

Sparkle

Price: free

URL: `http://wwwhost.ots.utexas.edu/mac/pub-mac-graphics.html`

Sparkle's primary purpose is to decode, play, and convert MPEG movie files to QuickTime format (for more about MPEG, see Chapter 10, page 253). Since it can also play QuickTime movies — with a number of options such as looping and half-speed or double-speed — it's a good program to have around. Sparkle can also convert movies from QuickTime to MPEG, so you can use it to create MPEGs for your site if need be.

Unfortunately, Sparkle takes up quite a bit of RAM, and the latest version is only guaranteed to run under System 7.5 or later. If you are using System 7.0 or system 7.1, you will need to make sure you have a few extensions installed, such as the Sound Manager and the Thread Manager. The documentation that comes with Sparkle tells you what you need, but not where to get it, unfortunately.

uuUndo

Price: free

URL: `http://www.med.cornell.edu/~giles/projects.html#uuundo`

Mpack

Price: free

URL: `ftp://ftp.andrew.cmu.edu/pub/mpack/`

These are small programs whose only purpose is to translate binary files that have been converted to plain text. Mpack undoes Base64 encoding, and uuUndo works with files that have been uuencoded. Base64 and uuencoding are commonly used in e-mail and in the Usenet newsgroups, where the medium is strictly text, but people have binary pictures, sounds, movies, or programs that they want to share. Most TCP-based e-mail programs (such as Eudora) also support one or both of these encoding schemes.

Because these applications are free, you might as well add them to your Internet arsenal. You can use them as helper applications with NewsWatcher or with FTP programs (provided the file to be downloaded has a proper suffix, such as `.uu` or `.base64`).

Tar

Price: free

URL: `http://wwwhost.ots.utexas.edu/mac/pub-mac-compression.html`

UNIX systems often create packages of documents called tar files (tar is short for "*t*ape *ar*chives"). Tar files are not compressed, but they are useful because they can take entire directory structures and make them into a single entity.

We are only mentioning Tar for the Macintosh because it is about the only format not supported by StuffIt Expander (with Expander Enhancer). This little program will extract tar files with no frills, at no charge.

ZipIt

Price: $15

URL: `http://www.awa.com/softlock/zipit/`

StuffIt Expander with the Expander Enhancer will extract DOS or UNIX `.zip` files, but it cannot create them. ZipIt will create ZIP archives for you. This is especially useful if you are going to be sharing files with DOS/Windows users, because ZIP is the standard compression format on that platform. ZIP archives created by ZipIt are fully compatible with ZIP programs for DOS and UNIX.

You may want to get ZipIt simply because it is cheaper than Expander Enhancer; just remember that it will only undo ZIP files, not the other UNIX formats such as `.z` and `.gz`.

9.12 WEB DEVELOPMENT TOOLS

These are applications that you will use to create or modify the files that you place on your site. Once again, the programs we are describing here are all available on the Internet.

It might be a good idea to skip ahead to Chapter 10 — especially sections 10.3 and 10.4 — before reading further, because we will be talking quite a bit about image and sound formats here, and it might not make any sense unless you have dealt with these issues before.

HTML Helpers

You don't have to use HTML editors or extensions at all, if you don't want to. A lot of people (for instance, the authors of this book) have created entire Web sites by hand, using nothing but a text editor and raw HTML tags. But this rugged approach isn't for everyone, so there are a *lot* of HTML programs out there, with a variety of features and prices; so many that we won't even pretend to know which one is best for your needs. You can find most of these utilities in the `/text/html/` directory of any Info-Mac archive site. Roughly, they fall into three categories:

Stand-alone Editors   These are programs that function just like word processors; you type in your text and apply styles, which show up as HTML tags. Some of these are *WYSIWYG* ("what you see is what you get"), meaning italicized text actually shows up *in italics* in the editing program. Even if you use one of these, you are probably better off using your favorite word processor to create the verbal raw material for a page, since you can then use spell checking and such. Some examples of stand-alone HTML editors are Arachnid, Bob's HTML Editor, High Tea, HTML.edit, HTML Pro, HTML Web Weaver, and Webtor.

Stand-alone Converters   These programs read a file in some format and spit it out as HTML. Converters of this type exist for RTF (Rich Text Format) files, and for files created in Microsoft Word, PageMaker, and Quark Xpress; check the shareware archives for new ones that might have cropped up in recent months.

Extensions to Other Programs   The idea here is that you create a document in a word processor or text editor just like you normally would. In a word processor, you can save the styled text as HTML without leaving the program. In a plain text editor, you typically use keyboard and menu commands to insert tags without having to type them out.

Extensions are, in our opinion, the best solution, but there are not very many HTML filters out there yet. Moreover, most of them force you to follow rigid rules when you enter your text, and they give you little control over the HTML output. Hopefully, better ones will evolve.

There are add-ins, scripts, filters, or macros for at least the following writing applications: BBEdit, ClarisWorks, Nisus Writer, and WordPerfect. There are also extensions out there to automatically create HTML tables from spreadsheets or databases. (The authors of this book are particularly fond of Ken Sayward's XTML Add-In for Microsoft Excel.)

Graphic Converter

Price: $35
URL: `http://www.goldinc.com/Lemke/gc.html`

Graphic Converter is an application that will read graphics files in almost every format ever created, and it will output files in a number of formats as well, although you probably won't need to deal with anything except PICT, GIF, JPEG, and possibly TIFF.

Graphic Converter also allows you to perform a number of image-editing functions, such as contrast and brightness control, scaling and cropping, sharpening and blurring, and simple rotation. You can also add lines, circles, squares, and text. If you don't have any commercial graphics program (like Photoshop or Freehand) available to you, this might be a very well-spent $35.

Clip2gif

Price: free

URL: `http://iawww.epfl.ch/Staff/Yves.Piguet/clip2gif-home/`

Transparency

Price: free

URL: `http://www.med.cornell.edu/~giles/projects.html#transparency`

Both of these simple little programs allow you to create transparent GIF files from ordinary GIFs (Fig. 10–24, page 248). Clip2gif also allows you to convert from JPEG files, PICT files, or your Macintosh's Clipboard, *and* Clip2gif will create interlaced GIFs (Fig. 10–23, page 247).

Clip2gif's major drawback is that it never even displays the images it is working on. Therefore, if all you need to do is create transparent GIFs, use Transparency, which does show the pictures and is very easy to use. You might as well have both programs, since neither of them costs anything.

WebMap

Price: $25

URL: `http://www.city.net/cnx/software/webmap.html`

The sole purpose of this program is to facilitate the creation of image maps. Without WebMap, you would have to locate the exact X and Y coordinates of all the important points on your picture, and then write up a cryptic file that tells the browser what to do when the image is clicked. With WebMap, you just load your picture (PICT or GIF) into the program, and you draw rectangles, circles, and polygons on it. You type the corresponding links into another part of the window, and WebMap automagically creates the map data file for you. If you plan on making a lot of image maps with irregular shapes, this might be worth the $25 price tag.

SoundEffects

Price: $15

URL: `ftp://ftp.alpcom.it/software/mac/Ricci/html/sfx.html`

This is a surprisingly powerful sound editor, considering its small price. It allows you to record sounds using your Mac's microphone and display them graphically on the screen. Then, you can trim the sound down to size and save it in any sample rate you choose. You can also apply special effects like reverb, flanging, and "robotizing," and creating stereo sounds and mixing is a snap. Unfortunately, SoundEffects will not save in anything other than the standard Mac audio formats, so you will need to use a conversion program like SoundApp if you want your sounds to be usable by anyone other than Mac users.

QuickEditor

Price: $20

URL: `http://www.prism.uvsq.fr/public/wos/multimedia/#quickeditor`

QuickEditor is an excellent QuickTime movie editor. It allows you to do many different types of transitions and fades from one movie clip to another. You can apply video effects such as inversion and chroma key. There are also powerful features for adding soundtracks to movies.

Many of the new "multimedia" Macintoshes have built-in features for recording video straight from televisions or VCRs; you can also create QuickTime movies from sequences of PICT files. QuickEditor will help you take your raw material and turn it into something impressive that you can place in your Web server.

An important note: since most Macintosh files — including QuickTime movies — have resource forks, you should *flatten* your QuickTime movies before making them available to the Internet. When you flatten a QuickTime movie, all the information that was in the resource fork is copied into the data fork; nothing is lost when the resource fork is removed, and people using other platforms can view your movies.

There is a very simple freeware utility in Info-Mac called FlattenMooV whose sole purpose is to flatten QuickTime movies; if you are not sure whether your video editing software flattens movies or not, use FlattenMooV on them anyway, just in case. (Fast Player, which we describe on page 217, also has the ability to flatten movies.)

Progressify

Price: "A kind word" to the author

URL: `http://iagu.on.net/jsam/progressify/`

ProJPEG

Price: $25 (commercial) or $5 (academic)

URL: `http://www.aris.com/boxtop/ProJPEG`

Progressify is a small utility that converts normal JPEG image files into progressive JPEGs (these are JPEGs that "progressively" increase their resolution, much like interlaced GIF files; see Figure 10–23, page 247). ProJPEG is an Adobe Photoshop plug-in; it costs $25, but for Photoshop users, the convenience of having a "Save as progressive JPEG feature" might be worth the cost.

Progressive JPEGs are not supported by all Web browsers yet, but we are betting that they will be soon, because progressive JPEG is really a fantastic image format. Until progressive JPEG is the standard, either don't use it or provide non-progressive alternatives. But once the format becomes widespread, utilities like Progressify and ProJPEG will be very useful, so keep an eye on the Graphics directory at Info-Mac (`/gst/grf/`). You heard it here first.

ResEdit

Price: free

URL: `http://www.info.apple.com/Apple.Support.Area/`
`Developer_Services/Tool_Chest/Developer_Utilities/`

As we mentioned earlier, Macintosh files are more difficult to send over the Internet than other platforms' files because they usually have a data fork as well as a resource fork. This may seem like a pain, but it was actually a stroke of brilliance on the part of whoever invented it. Have you ever noticed that PC and Windows users have to struggle with an awful lot of files for a single program? They have to keep track of things like .DLL's, and .SND, .GRF, and .DAT files. Despite the mess, there's a reason PC programmers create all those separate files: if they want to change something, like a picture, all they have to do is change one of the graphics files, instead of recompiling the whole program.

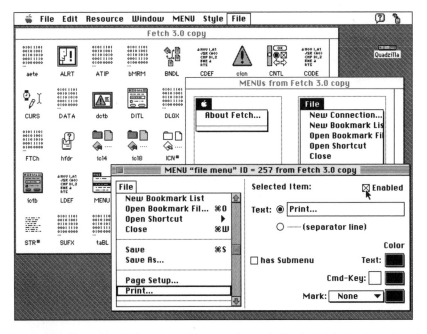

Fig. 9–18 Using ResEdit to futz with menu items in Fetch 3.0 (actually, we're working on a *copy* of Fetch 3.0, just to be safe). The big window in the background shows some of the other resources that you can edit, such as cursors, alert boxes, and icons.

On the Macintosh, these individual elements are all saved as *resources* within a single file. A typical application has a whole pile of resources — separate from the programming code — that define its icons, pictures, menus, windows, dialogs, sounds, version number, text strings, and so on. Changing these resources is easy. So easy, in fact, that *anyone* can do it, if they have a handy utility from Apple called ResEdit (Fig. 9–18). No programming experience required.

We have included a brief discussion of ResEdit here because at some point in your life you will probably download a program (such as Kelly's Error, page 207) that says something like, "if you want to customize the welcome screen, use ResEdit to change PICT resource #129." This may sound a bit intimidating, but it's actually very easy. However, you should *always* make a backup copy of anything you work on with ResEdit, especially when you're new to the game, because ResEdit can completely destroy a program if you are careless. For lots of helpful hints and a few caveats, look up ResEdit Tips and the ResEdit Primer in the `/info/sft/` directory of the Info-Mac archives.

ResEdit is another one on the list of "programs you should have around just in case you need them someday." But if you know what you're doing, ResEdit can be a useful everyday tool. For example, one of the authors of this book was getting sick of accidentally deleting all his old e-mail in Eudora, so he used ResEdit to deactivate the unwanted `Empty Trash` menu item, which had been right next to the very useful `Compact Mailboxes` item.

More importantly, you can use ResEdit to modify a popular freeware screen saver module so that after five minutes of idle time, your Mac flashes random headlines such as *"Pete Palmer And Anne Chenette Abducted By Elvis Impersonators From Pluto — Adam Schneider Has Scars To Prove It!"*

## CHAPTER 10

How To Create
Spiffy Web Pages

*B*y now you've established an Internet presence of some kind, installed your server software, and written a couple of very simple HTML pages to test your setup. Hopefully, you have an idea of what kind of information you'd like to make available. You've surfed the Web enough to have seen a wide range of Web page styles and layouts, and you've probably noticed that you liked some pages much better than others. Some pages made you think, "Hey, this is really helpful; I'll add this site to my Bookmark list and visit it in the future." But then there was that page that made you wonder why you would want to buy computer peripherals from a company that advertised "printers and *modums*" on their home page. This chapter will give some helpful tips on how to create a good-looking Web site that people will want to visit.

We will refer to a number of HTML terms and concepts in this chapter. The purpose of this book is *not* to teach you the HyperText Markup Language. We recommend that you spend some time reading over one or more of the HTML guides available on the Web to familiarize yourself with the most common markup tags and what they do (your browser's home page will have a link to at least one or two good references). You can also look at the source HTML of a few random pages to see what their insides look like. Buying an HTML book at the store is probably not necessary, since there is already such a wealth of material on line that you can access for free and print out if need be. (It wouldn't hurt to check a book out of the library, because that won't cost you anything.) You can learn to write a simple Web page in just a few hours!

We have included an HTML *quick* reference in Appendix A, which lists most of the commonly used tags and their syntax. It should be a helpful resource to you while you are writing your own pages, but it is in no way intended as a replacement for the excellent materials available to you for free. Once you feel confident that you can play the HTML game, turn the page and we'll teach you how to put your newly-acquired skills to use. If you follow the tips we provide in this chapter, you will be on the road to an endeavor that's fulfilling, informative, challenging, and maybe even *fun*!

10.1 PAGE CONTENT

First, you need to decide what sort of information you are going to include on your Web pages. If you have an established base of customers or members, call or e-mail them directly and ask them what kinds of things they would like to see available on line. If you're starting from scratch, the best way to brainstorm some ideas is by surfing the Web for a while. If you can't think of where to start, try the "Random URL" link in Yahoo (Fig. 10–1). This will select a URL at random from the Yahoo database and send you there. If you don't like it, try again. When you see things you like, jot them down in a notepad or add those pages to your browser's Bookmark or Hotlist file.

Fig. 10–1   Some of Yahoo's features, including the "Random URL" link. (We have added the black rectangle for emphasis).

Bigger Is Not Better

Your Web site should contain as much information as you can possibly put on line. The same is *not* true for individual pages. All the information you have made available to the world is probably residing in one directory or folder on your hard drive, but you have probably divided this directory into logical subdirectories. You might have even further subdivisions, so as to keep everything organized. You would never dump all your files into the top-level directory; how would you find anything? Similarly, you shouldn't dump all of your information onto a single page.

Think of your Web site as a book; your home page is like the cover and table of contents, your subdirectories are like chapters, and each page is like a paragraph. Now, remember what they taught you about writing back in elementary school: every paragraph needs a thesis sentence. Every Web page should have a "thesis," or a main focus. Also, you don't want your pages — your "paragraphs" — to be too short or too long. A Web page with only a couple lines of information feels like a wasted hop through cyberspace (especially over long distances), and a really long Web page can take a long time to load.

Very long pages are also a bad idea because nobody wants to read that much. For some reason, you can fool people into reading a lot more text if you break it up into several pieces than if you present as one big chunk. Whatever the "thesis" of any particular page is, it should be visible in the first screen when the page is loaded, or even before the entire page has loaded. Call it laziness if you like, but the fact is, people don't like to have to scroll down to read Web pages. So pick an appropriate heading or title for the page, and don't fill the top of your page with a huge picture or image map, even if it's a really neat one (see Figure 10–2 for an example of what *not* to do).

Fig. 10–2   A poorly designed home page. (We made something up, because it would have been rude to use a real page as an example of a bad layout!) No matter how spectacular the graphics might (or might not) be, many people find it annoying to load such a large picture; in this case, it doesn't even fit on the screen. And of course, people using text-based browsers cannot even use this page.

Big images (including big image maps) are a poor idea for two reasons: first, they might require scrolling down to get to the heart of the page; second, there a lot of people with slow connections who don't automatically load the images on the pages they visit, and a number of people who can't view pictures at all. If a page's content is entirely in the pictures, those people won't be able to see it at all. Many Web sites that are based around image maps or graphical "button bars" present text alternatives at the bottom of the page; if you must use a big image map, we suggest putting the text links at the *top* (as in Figure 10–3).

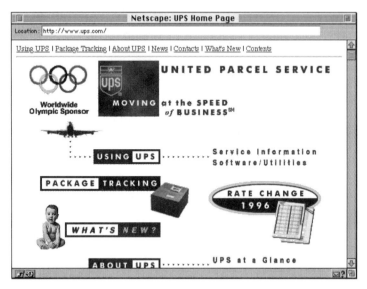

Fig. 10–3 An image map-based page that thoughtfully includes a row of text links at the *top* of the page, for those who use non-graphical browsers or who do not have automatic image loading turned on.

Good Writing Counts

We're sure you realize this already, but it cannot be stressed often enough that your pages should be well-*written*. No matter how great your pictures and layouts are, it looks very bad if you have a big fat typo or an awkward sentence right at the top of your home page.

It's hard to run a normal spelling checker on an HTML document, because your word processor won't recognize HTML tags and Internet addresses as valid English words. What you *can* do, however, is load your pages into your favorite Web browser, save them as text, and spell-check the text files. You'll still run into snags with computerese terms like "cgi-bin" and "www.w3.org," but at least you won't have to worry about the tags this way. If you find mistakes in the output, you can just fix the corresponding source.

To find grammatical mistakes and such, your best bet is simply to view the output in your browser, check it over, and check it again. And have a friend — or many friends — check it as well, to find mistakes that you may have missed. What makes perfect sense to you might be totally incomprehensible to someone else, so it's wise to run your page by a range of people with different levels of expertise in your topic. Remember, you can and should test anything and everything before you make a page available to the world.

Don't Let Your Site Get Stale

If your site changes all the time — and you advertise the fact that it does, possibly by having a "thingamajig of the week/month" page (see Figure 10–4) — people will visit your site more often. They will be much more likely to add your

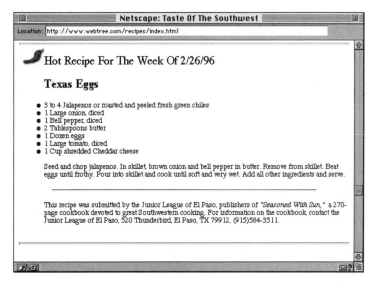

Fig. 10–4 The "Recipe of the Week" from WebTree Internet Services in El Paso, Texas. People who are interested in Tex-Mex cuisine will no doubt visit often to see new recipes.

site to their hot list if they know they'll have a reason to be back. But if you claim that your page is updated weekly, when in fact it sits there for months without changing, it will look bad. We have seen a couple sites that have actually gone over a *year* with no updates! Needless to say, we didn't explore those sites any further.

A good, subtle way to point out that your page is fresh is to use "new" symbols. You can either write in the word "new" after a link to a recently updated item, or you can use a very small image file, like the ones they use in Yahoo (Fig. 10–5).

If you want some pages to be accessible even though they haven't been completely finished yet, you can place what you have on line and let people know that more is coming later. A common way to do this is to have links that point to "This Page Is Under Construction" signs (Fig. 10–6). This is not the best approach, because people get sick of those little yellow and black signs very quickly. If there is nothing to link to yet, just turn the link off and note that it is

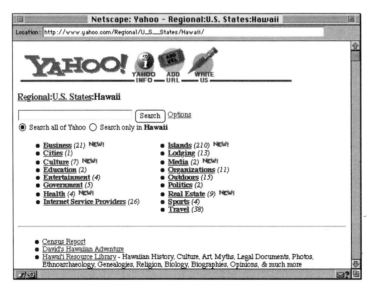

Fig. 10–5 "NEW" icons in Yahoo. The "Business," "Culture," "Health," "Islands," "Media," and "Real Estate" sections contained recently-added links at the time this screen snapshot was taken.

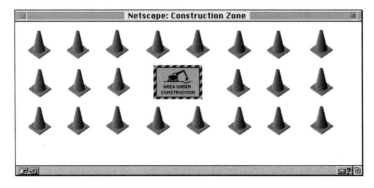

Fig. 10–6 A whole page full of "construction" icons. Use these sparingly, and make sure the "repairs" are done quickly.

"coming soon." Try to get everything finished as quickly as possible, and tell people when you expect it to be done.

If you have "more to come" on your pages, you may even want to include an e-mail link or form interface to let people get on a "mailing list" regarding your site. When major features of your site are completed, you can then easily send a brief note to everyone on the list to let them know. Most of them will probably stop by again to see what's there, because they wouldn't have put themselves on the list if they didn't care about the content of your site.

10.2 PAGE LAYOUT

Some layouts are simply more pleasing to the eye than others. Big companies hire people whose entire jobs are to make sure that their publications — electronic or otherwise — are laid out well. You probably don't need to hire someone, as a little common sense and experience should tell you what looks good and what doesn't.

By the way, this section includes a number of illustrations that we created from scratch, as opposed to simply taking pictures of existing sites. The text in many of these "fake" pages looks like complete gibberish — it's supposed to! The "words" are actually badly corrupted Latin, with some English suffixes throw in. For centuries, publishers and printers have used this collection of verbal garbage — known as "Lorem Ipsum" — to test layouts; the idea is to show how the page will look once the words have been written. Since you don't want to get distracted by the content, you use nonsense instead. There are a few different versions of Lorem Ipsum floating around; if you want to use it in your own design process, just grab a copy off the Internet somewhere. You can find it quite easily by doing a Lycos search at `http://www.lycos.com`; see pages 276-278 for details.

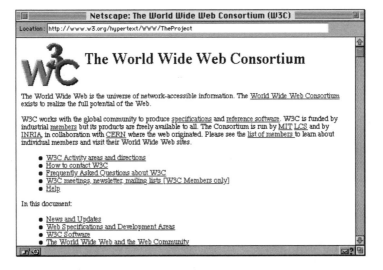

Fig. 10–7 A typical page at the World Wide Web Consortium's site. Its layout is very simple, and it doesn't use any fancy HTML tags. Consequently, it's very easy to read.

Simplicity

Keep your pages simple. Sure, a few people might be impressed by an extraordinarily complicated layout, but you can bet that more people will be turned away because your page looks like garbage on their browser, or even worse, crashes their system (it can happen!). This is especially true of your home page, which is probably the page that people will load when they hook up to your server at `http://www.yoursite.com/`. The folks at the World Wide Web consortium, which includes CERN — the people who *invented* the World Wide Web — have nice, simple pages (Fig. 10–7). And you can be sure that *they* know what they're doing.

We will have more to say about the dangers of heavy image use later, but suffice it to say that you shouldn't fill your page with pictures. They take a long time to load on slower connections, and they will bog down your server. Tables are a nice way to organize multiple items on a page, but not all browsers recognize them (more on this later as well).

Your ideal Web page — especially your ideal home page — will strictly follow HTML specifications and will contain just a few important images and text down the left side of the page, or centered. If you want to use image maps, tables, and other fancy display features, bury them deeper in your site than your home page.

Anchors and Links

Don't overuse links. It is distracting to read a paragraph of text where every other word is discolored and underlined. When you do create hypertext links, make sure the links lead to relevant material. Just because you use the phrase "stock market" in a sentence doesn't mean you need to make it a link that leads to the Dow Jones page. For one thing, if your site is not about stocks, most people will not care about the Dow Jones page. But if they *are* interested in Dow Jones, they might keep following links there and forget about your page. Wait, come back! Too late, you lost them. The moral of the story is: try to keep most of the links in your neighborhood.

You will be best off setting your links apart from your prose. You can add a sentence to the end of a block of text that says something to the effect of, "for more information, click here" or "more information is available." But don't overuse the phrase "click here"; try to find new and creative ways to indicate clickable text, because some people consider the excessive use of click here to be "poor" HTML style.

You can also put all relevant links at the top or bottom of the page in a list of some kind. People are lazy; they don't want to read an entire page of words to find the exact point where they need to click their mouse.

If you have a page that is fairly long but does not lend itself well to being broken up into separate pages, be sure to include anchors to allow navigation within pages. Anchors are `<A href>` tags that specify locations within documents (which defined with `<A name>` tags). A common use of anchors is a table of contents at the beginning of a long document (Fig. 10–8). On a long page, it is also helpful to include a link at the bottom that returns to the top of the page. The link, in this case, would point to an anchor called something like "Top," which is embedded near the beginning of the HTML source.

Finally, a word about relative versus absolute links: you probably want to use relative links as much as possible. A relative link is one that points to a file

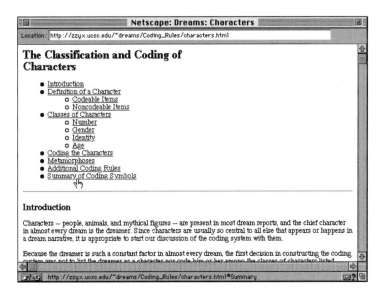

Fig. 10–8 A table of contents at the top of a Web page. Each highlighted phrase in the bulleted list is a link to a hypertext anchor in the text below.

that is on the same system as the referring document; the Internet host name is not necessary, just "directions" from the referring page to the destination. For example, if your personal home page's URL is "`http://yoursite.com/me.html`", and you have a Web page about your softball team that resides in a directory called "fun" — say, "`http://yoursite.com/fun/softball.html`" — then you can link back to your home page from the softball page by referencing simply "`../me.html`", rather than the complete URL. (The double period means "move back one directory.") If you used *absolute* links, they would all become invalid if you changed just about anything about your site. But, with relative links, the path from one file to another will always remain the same, even if you move the whole collection to a different directory, a new server, or another continent — as long as you leave the relative structure intact.

Signatures

It is a good idea to include a "signature" at the bottom of every page in your site (Fig. 10–9). Traditionally, this is set off from the rest of the page with a horizontal rule line, and the text is often formatted with the <ADDRESS> HTML tag (Figure 10–9 does *not* use <ADDRESS>, however). The signature should ideally include a link back to your site's home page, and the e-mail address of a contact person for the Web site (or a contact person for that particular page, if applicable). You can make the e-mail address into a `mailto` link, so that clicking on the address initiates an e-mail message to you (see the source for our example tem-

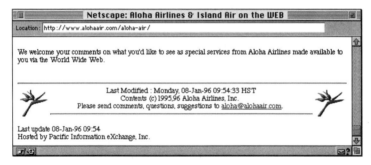

Fig. 10–9   The signature at the bottom of Aloha Airlines' home page. They've included an e-mail address, the date that the page was last updated, and some icons of tropical flowers for decoration.

plate, page 241), or a link to a Web-based e-mail program such as Doug's WWW Mail Gateway (Figure 3–20, page 37).

You may also want your signature to include a note that says when the page was last updated. If you choose to do this, make sure you update your pages frequently, because it will look bad if it appears that you haven't touched your Web site in months, especially if there are mistakes that need correcting!

Headings

Make use of headings wherever possible to break your pages up into logical sections and subsections. This makes it easier for the reader to find what he or she is looking for, and it just plain looks better than a big pile of words.

There are a number of ways to create headings. The easiest way is to simply use the standard HTML heading tags (<H1> through <H6>; see Figure A–2, page 365, for details). These are handy, because it's very easy to picture "level 1 headings," "level 2 headings," and so on — organizing everything using these is a snap. Unfortunately, they take up a lot of space, so they work best in large documents where a little space would actually be helpful. <H1> and its buddies don't work as well for lists or other situations where you need a lot of headings in one place, such as on an index page.

Fortunately, there are a number of other ways to set a few words apart, using boldface type, italics, lists, and line breaks. The source HTML for a few heading styles that we like to use is presented below; Figure 10–10 shows the output. Feel free to experiment and come up with your own designs, but remember to make sure they look good in everyone's browser!

Source HTML for the headings in Figure 10–10:

```
<HTML>

<HEAD><TITLE>Various Clever Headings</TITLE></HEAD>
```

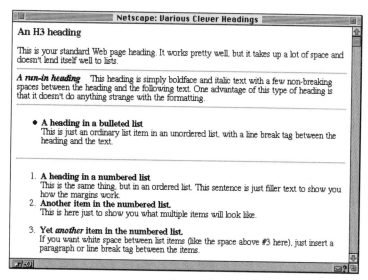

Fig. 10–10   A few different kinds of headings. (The default font size has been slightly increased so you can easily read what we typed.)

```
<BODY>

<H3>An H3 heading</H3>
This is your standard Web page heading. It works pretty well, but
it takes up a lot of space and doesn't lend itself well to lists.

<HR>
<B><I>A run-in heading</B></I>    This heading is
simply boldface and italic text with a few non-breaking spaces
between the heading and the following text.  One advantage of
this type of heading is that it doesn't do anything strange with
the formatting.

<HR>
<UL>
<LI><B>A heading in a bulleted list</B><BR>
This is just an ordinary list item in an unordered list, with a
line break tag between the heading and the text.
</UL>

<HR>
<OL>
<LI><B>A heading in a numbered list</B><BR>
This is the same thing, but in an ordered list.  This sentence is
just filler text to show you how the margins work.

<LI><B>Another item in the numbered list.</B><BR>
This is here just to show you what multiple items will look like.

<P>
```

```
<LI><B>Yet <I>another</I> item in the numbered list.</B><BR>
If you want white space between list items (like the space above
#3 here), just insert a paragraph or line break tag between the
items.
</OL>

</BODY>
</HTML>
```

White Space: The Good, the Bad, and the Ugly

On the Web, white space is blank space that is bounded by text or pictures and the sides of the window. Too much white space makes it look like there are big holes in the page, and it looks terrible. You don't want your Web pages to have big bare patches. Not only do they look bad, they waste precious space, as in Figure 10–11. Remember, you want to get as much relevant information as possible in the first screenful of a page.

Fig. 10–11 Way too much white space.

The `align=left` and `align=right` attributes of the `<IMG>` tag used to be Netscape-specific; browsers such as NCSA Mosaic couldn't interpret them properly. Fortunately for Web publishers everywhere, these attributes have finally made it into the HTML specification, and we wholeheartedly endorse their wanton but educated use. Without the `align=left` and `align=right` attributes, you cannot place more than one line of text next to an image, so your layouts end up looking like Figure 10–11. But if we take that same page and add `align=left` to the `<IMG>` tag in the HTML source, the layout is dramatically improved (Fig. 10–12). A nice feature of these image alignment extensions is that they will not do anything "weird" to browsers that do not recognize them; they will just be

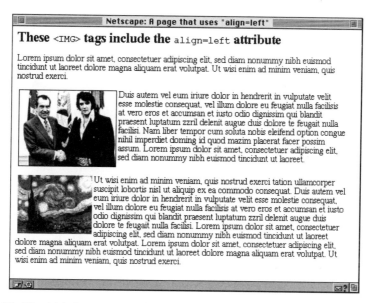

Fig. 10–12 A big improvement in layout. The only difference between this page and Figure 10–11 is that `align=left` was added to the `<IMG>` tags. If Nixon and The King were alive today, they would surely encourage you to use the `align=left` attribute.

ignored. Older browsers will get the boring layout in Figure 10–11, but that's the best you can do until everyone updates their software.

White space isn't always your enemy, of course. It doesn't look good when there are little bits and pieces floating around in it, but it looks fine when it separates large blocks of text or pictures, so you can use it to separate different sections of a page. If you want a more definitive separation, use a horizontal rule line. If you want multiple lines of blank space, you can accomplish this by using the `<BR>` (line break) tag more than once. If you want more horizontal blank space   (something like this),   remember that you cannot simply type a number of spaces; HTML interprets multiple spaces as one. Therefore, you have two choices: you can put in a blank, transparent GIF file to take up space, or you can make use of the non-breaking space, whose HTML code is ` `. Neither of these is a perfect solution, though — the former is messy for browsers and the latter is messy for you — so your best option is to design pages that don't need clever tricks to achieve their layout.

Tables

Version 1.1 of Netscape burst onto the scene in 1995 and allowed people to create tables of almost any size and shape. A lot of people jumped on the tabular bandwagon, and as a result, a lot of people with non-Netscape browsers were left in the dust. Today, most graphical browsers support tables to some extent, but

they do not all support the same features. Since tables are a relative newcomer
to HTML, they should be used cautiously. Anytime you create a table, see how
the output looks in Mosaic as well as Netscape. If you really know what you are
doing, you can even have them look okay in text-based browsers.

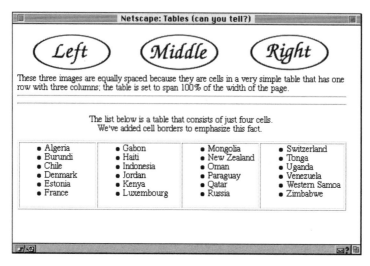

Fig. 10–13   The top of this page uses a simple three-cell table to set the placement of the three images. The bottom of the page uses a table to keep the 24-item
list from scrolling off the screen.

Fig. 10–14   This list has the same source HTML as the bottom half of Figure
10–13. The one-row table looks just fine when viewed with Lynx.

Caveats aside, tables can be a great way to organize parts of your pages.
The simplest — and therefore perhaps the best — use of tables is to place two or
three things side by side on a page. Tables can expand to fill the entire width of a
browser's window, so the table cells will end up evenly spaced across the page (as

in the top of Figure 10–13). In text browsers, the table tags will be ignored and the contents of that table will be placed right next to each other on a line.

Another wonderful use of tables is to organize lists. If you have a very long list of links, consider breaking it up into two or more parts and putting each part into its own table cell (see the bottom half of Figure 10–13). This table should only have *one* row. Text-based browsers reading this HTML document will simply ignore the table tags and append each list segment to the bottom of the one that comes before it (Figure 10–14).

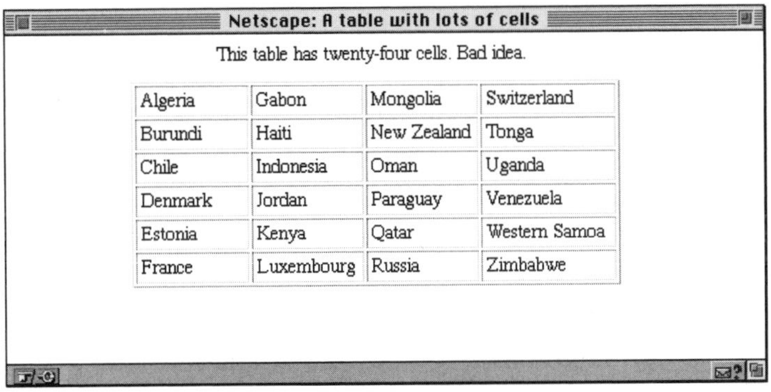

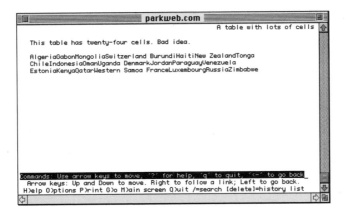

Fig. 10–15 This table contains the same list as Figures 10–13 and 10–14, but here each item has its own cell. Not only will this look horrible in non-graphical browsers, it was also very hard to write the HTML for this page!

Fig. 10–16 This is what happens to Figure 10–15 when it is viewed in Lynx. When the table tags are ignored, everything is read left to right, so the list is no longer in alphabetical order. Not to mention the fact that the formatting is gone, so it looks awful.

Giving each item its own cell is a bad idea. If you were to make a four-column list into a table that gave each list item its own cell, the output would look fine in Netscape (Figure 10–15), but it would be illegible to those without graphical Web browsers (Figure 10–16). If you *must* create tables with many rows and columns, provide non-tabular alternatives if at all possible. In many cases, a spreadsheet program will be able to do this for you automatically.

You can choose whether your tables have borders or not. If you are simply using them to achieve fancy layouts, you should probably skip the borders. For lists or actual tabular data, it's up to you.

Consistency

Your Web site will look more professional and be easier to follow if all the pages have *similar* layouts. Or, use the same layout for all "master index" pages, another layout for the more detailed indexes, and yet another for the individual pages that contain information. It is more important for the "index" pages to have consistent layouts than the individual "end-of-the-line" pages.

One way to stick with consistent layouts is to create a master HTML page, or template, which you start with for all the pages that will use the same layout. Fill the master page with dummy text and pictures, and just "fill in the blanks" when you go to write a page. If you use a word processor to write your HTML pages, just save your master as a template or read-only document. If you use a UNIX text editor, or if your word processor cannot create templates, you can change the permissions on the file to make it read-only. (On UNIX, this means typing "chmod 400 filename".)

A Real Layout Template That You Can Use

Figure 10–17 (page 241) shows an example of a simple layout template that we have created; the HTML source is presented below. Feel free to use this template (or something like this) for your site, if you like the way it looks! (You can either type it in manually, or you can copy it from the CD in the back of this book or from Prentice Hall's Web site: http://www.prenhall.com/template.html.)

Source HTML for our example template:

```
<HTML>

<HEAD>
<TITLE>A Sample Layout Template</TITLE>
</HEAD>

<BODY>

<IMG src="/images/monalisa.gif" align=left height=120 width=91>
<H1>A Blank Web Page</H1>
This section of our World Wide Web site contains information
about lorem ipsum dolor sit amet, consectetuer adipiscing elit,
sed diam nonummy nibh euismod tincidunt ut laoreet dolore magna
aliquam erat volutpat.  Ut wisi enim ad minim veniam, quis
nostrud exerci rulition ullamcorper suscipit lobortis nisl ut
aliquip ex ea commodo consequat.  Vero eros et accumsan et iusto
```

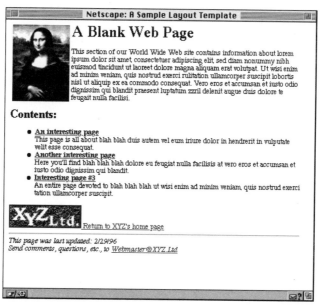

Fig. 10–17   A good-looking, ready-to-use template for a World Wide Web page. To use this as an index page in your own site, all you would need to do is change the text, the pictures, and the hypertext links. See Figures 10–29 through 10–31 (pages 255-256) to see how this page looks in a variety of Web browsers.

```
odio dignissim qui blandit praesent luptatum zzril delenit augue
duis dolore te feugait nulla facilisi.
<BR clear=all>

<H2>Contents:</H2>
<UL>
<LI><B><A href="things.html">An interesting page</A></B><BR>
This page is all about blah blah duis autem vel eum iriure dolor
in hendrerit in vulputate velit esse consequat.
<LI><B><A href="stuff.html">Another interesting page</A></B><BR>
Here you'll find blah blah blah dolore eu feugiat nulla facilisis
at vero eros et accumsan et iusto odio dignissim qui blandit.
<LI><B><A href="misc.html">Interesting page #3</A></B><BR>
An entire page devoted to blah blah blah ut wisi enim ad minim
veniam, quis nostrud exerci tation ullamcorper suscipit.
</UL>

<A href="/"><IMG alt="[XYZ Ltd.]" src="/images/logo.gif">
 Return to XYZ's home page</A>

<HR>

<ADDRESS>
This page was last updated: 2/29/96<BR>
Send comments, questions, etc., to
<A href="mailto:webmaster@xyz.ltd">Webmaster@XYZ.Ltd</A>
</ADDRESS>
```

```
</BODY>
</HTML>
```

A few things to notice about this HTML document:

- The first `<IMG>` tag includes `height` and `width` attributes that aren't supported by all browsers. But that's okay, because they don't cause any harm either.
- The `<A href>` tag for "XYZ's home page" points to "/". This simply leads to the default page at the very top of the server (`http://yoursite.com/`); in other words, the *server root*.
- Note that the `<IMG>` tag for the logo (near the bottom of the page) includes `alt="[XYZ Ltd.]"`. This ensures that people using text-based browsers, or who don't habitually load images, will see a text version of the logo, so they will know how to reach the site's home page.
- We have assumed here that all the site's pictures are stored in a directory called `images`, which is at the root level of the server; hence the file names `/images/monalisa.gif` and `/images/logo.gif`. If you use this template, be sure to have those tags point to the real locations of *your* images.
- "`Webmaster@xyz.ltd`" is obviously not a real e-mail address, because "`ltd`" is not even a valid domain name! We used it because we didn't want to risk using a real address that might exist now or in the future.

10.3 IMAGES

Multimedia items such as pictures and sounds have become such an important part of most Web sites that they deserve their own sections in this chapter. It's *possible* to create a Web site full of perfectly good pages without using a single piece of graphics. But, like they say, a picture is worth a thousand words, and the strategic placement of images within your document can greatly improve your pages. Of course, there are a few things you need to consider: how many images is too many? How big should they be? What format should you use?

Number and Size of Images

Use graphics to *enhance* your text, not replace it. You should never write a page that consists of a huge image map and nothing else (see pages 227 and 258 for tips on how to avoid this). Nor should you use an image in lieu of words in a sentence. For instance, if you want to say that something is exciting, you may be tempted to create a colorful image file of the word "exciting" with confetti, fireworks, etc. Resist the temptation. It *might* look great on graphical browsers that are automatically loading images, and it might even look okay in Lynx if you give the HTML image tag an appropriate `alt` (alternate text) attribute, but to everyone else it will look awkward, with a big picture in the middle of your paragraph, forcing the lines apart (Fig. 10–18).

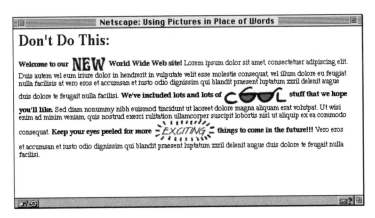

Fig. 10–18 An example of what *not* to do, if you want to give emphasis to particular words. You're better off with simple *italics* or **boldface** type.

There is no rule of thumb for how many different images to put on a page, since every page is different, but if you have more than about ten, you should think about revising your design. Not only is it annoying for the viewer to wait for images to load (especially in browsers that refuse to display anything until all images are complete), but each image loaded means another hit on your server, which can slow things down or even prevent others from using your server. If you want to use a "bullet" such as a 3-D circle or stars to delineate many items in a list (see Figure 10–19), that's fine, since the browser only has to load the image once, even if it's displayed 100 times.

Along with the issue of number is the question of size, in bytes. To Web users with a relatively slow modem connection (a significant proportion), many small images are preferable to a few big ones. Keep in mind that those with a 14.4k connection can download between 80K and 90K of data per minute; if viewing your page requires downloading a 150K image file, they're going to have to sit and wait for more than a minute and a half before it's done loading. Many people don't have that kind of patience; they may even become annoyed with your organization for creating such a time-intensive Web site. Fortunately, there's an easy way to solve this problem while still letting people see your large, high-quality images: thumbnails.

Thumbnails

For pictures that are important files by themselves (and not just colorful decorations to enhance your layout), a good way to get around the image size problem is to create *thumbnails* of your pictures. A thumbnail is a much smaller version of the original picture that should give the viewer a general idea of the content of the picture without forcing him or her to download the whole thing. Usually, the thumbnail is a simple hypertext link to the larger file, and the size of the larger file is commonly listed next to the thumbnail, so people know how

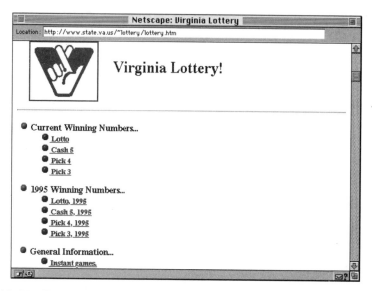

Fig. 10–19   These lists tastefully use small graphics rather than HTML bullets to mark individual items.

long they will have to wait if they choose to load it. See Figure 10–20 for an example of a page that makes good use of thumbnails.

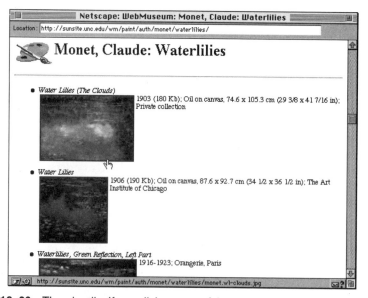

Fig. 10–20   Thumbnails. If you click on one of these small images, you will get to see a larger, high-quality picture. The small ones let you decide whether you want to bother downloading the big version.

To create thumbnails, all you need is a graphics program that will scale images down; there are shareware or freeware utilities available for every major platform. Save the smaller images as GIF files with slightly different file names than the large images. In your HTML source, enclose each thumbnail's `<IMG>` tag in an `<A href>` tag that points to the larger file.

Height and Width Attributes

In some browsers, you can set the exact amount of space that an image will take up on the screen. If an image has not loaded yet, a blank rectangle will be placed on the page; the rectangle's size — in pixels — is the same as the image about to be loaded (see the top half of Figure 10–21 for an example). If the `height` and `width` attributes are not the same as the actual size of the picture, it will be scaled up or down. However, scaling the picture down does not reduce the file size or transfer time; so if you want it smaller, shrink it with your graphics program, not with everyone else's Web browser. You should also never allow a picture to be scaled *up*, simply because it looks terrible.

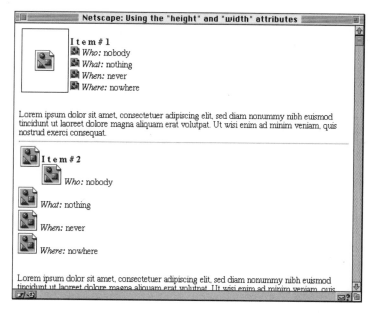

Fig. 10–21 The top half of this page makes use of `height` and `width` attributes in the `<IMG>` tags; the bottom half doesn't. You can see the results for yourself.

We encourage you to make use of `height` and `width`, for a couple reasons. For one thing, it will give people without automatic image loading an idea of exactly how large an image is, so they will know, roughly, how long it will take to load that particular picture. More importantly for you, setting the `height` and `width` attributes to the proper size means that — at least in those browsers that

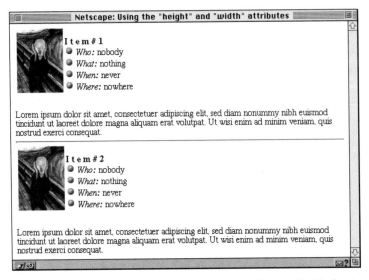

Fig. 10–22   Once the images have been loaded into Figure 10–21, the two halves look identical. In other words, the height and width attributes can only help you; they rarely create problems.

support this feature — your layout will not be affected by whether the images have been loaded or not. Figure 10–21 shows a sample Web page whose images have not been loaded yet. On the top half of the page, `height` and `width` attributes have been added to the `<IMG>` tags, but on the bottom, the tags were left "as is." You can see that the top half looks much better. (Of course, once the images load, as in Figure 10–22, the top and bottom will look exactly the same.) The only difference in the source HTML between the two halves is that the top half's `<IMG>` tags includes the following: `height=100 width=76` for the big image, and `height=14 width=14` for the small ones.

This example illustrates that setting the `height` and `width` is just as helpful for small images as for large ones, because it causes the placeholder graphic to shrink, meaning it takes up less space and preserves your layout. Unfortunately, this trick doesn't work very well with the `alt` attribute, so decide which one is more important in each case.

HTML for the pictures in the top *half of Figures 10–21 and 10–22:*

```
<IMG align=left width=76 height=100 src="scream.gif">
<IMG height=14 width=14 src="ball.gif">
```

HTML for the pictures in the bottom *half of Figures 10–21 and 10–22:*

```
<IMG align=left src="scream.gif">
<IMG src="ball.gif">
```

File Formats

There are many possible formats for image files in a computer. For your purposes in composing a Web site, there are really only two, because almost all graphical browsing programs recognize them and can view them internally: GIF and JPEG. Each format has its advantages and disadvantages.

GIF The Graphic Interchange Format, developed by CompuServe, takes a 256-color (8-bit) image file and compresses it. When a viewing program reads the GIF files (whose names usually end in .gif), all the original information is retained; it is "lossless." Files that have large areas of perfectly homogenous color or blank space are compressed very well by the GIF algorithm. A GIF file can be *transparent*, meaning that the background color is hidden when it is displayed, and it can also be *interlaced*, meaning that the image information is stored in such a way that its resolution appears to improve as it loads (Fig. 10–23) — at least in browsers that can display images while they are in the process of loading.

Fig. 10–23 Interlaced vs. non-interlaced GIFs. All three pictures will end up looking identical to the one on the left, which has been completely downloaded already. The center (non-interlaced) and right (interlaced) images have both been loading for exactly the same amount of time. The one on the right is blocky at first, but at least you can see immediately what the entire picture will look like. Notice how the top of the right-hand image is clearer than the bottom; this is how interlaced GIF files work.

JPEG This format (usually denoted by .jpg at the end of a file name) is named after the Joint Photographic Experts Group — the committee that "invented" it — and it also compresses files, often to a much greater degree than GIF. And where a GIF file can have only 256 colors, JPEG can handle 16 million colors (24 bits). However, it is "lossy," meaning that some information is lost in the compression. You can tell heavily compressed JPEG files because any sharp edges in the pictures will appear to have distorted "halos" around them. Fortunately, when you create a JPEG file, you can control the amount of compression, and a lightly compressed (and therefore high quality) JPEG image is still often smaller than the same file compressed as a GIF. Unfortunately, while they are often smaller, JPEG files may take longer to decode than GIFs, at least on older, slower computers.

You set the format and specific characteristics (compression, transparency, etc.) of your image files with the program that you use to create or edit the pictures. There are a number of freeware or shareware programs available for every platform to help you do this.

So which format should you use? The answer is: both. For smaller images (icons, buttons, bullets, etc.), always use GIF. Small pictures usually do not require more than 256 colors (and grayscale images *never* need more than 256), and if you use GIFs, you can make them interlaced and transparent. In fact, we recommend that you make sure *all* your GIFs are interlaced files, because people with slower connections will appreciate that they can at least see *something* of the picture while it is being sent. In fact, image maps in Netscape can be clicked before they have even finished loading. So, if someone can see enough of the picture to know where to click, they can save some time, provided they can see what they are doing.

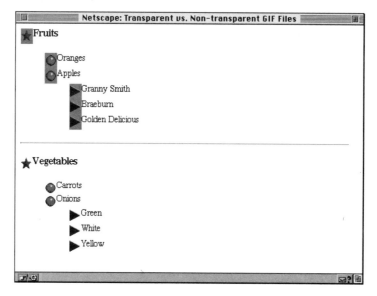

Fig. 10–24 Transparent vs. non-transparent GIFs. The bullets under "Fruits" are non-transparent; the "Vegetables" bullets are transparent, and will look good with any background color.

For images such as bullets and logos, where you want people to be able to see the "background" of the page through the GIF, don't forget to also make use of transparency. If you don't, the image will be surrounded by a big ugly rectangle in browsers that have different background colors than the one you had in mind when you designed the picture. Figure 10–24 shows a page with two sets of GIF files; the ones on the top half of the page are transparent, and the ones on the bottom are not. They were created in a graphics program using a light gray background, but this page has a white background.

If you have larger pictures, such as scanned photographs of people or products, use JPEG. You will want your pictures to be as clear as possible, and there is a big difference between 8-bit and 24-bit color. Don't worry about the fact that most people only have 8-bit video capability; their browsers will reduce the number of colors and allow them to see it no matter what. You want to give them as much information as possible to work with. If you are concerned about losing something in the translation, use less severe compression; try saving a picture with a few different compression ratios and see which one gives you the best compromise between image size and quality.

The latest browsers support an image format known as "progressive JPEG." The compression is by way of JPEG, but the idea is similar to that of interlaced GIFs; you can see a lower-quality "rough draft" as soon as the image begins loading, and it gets progressively better as it loads. We think this is an exciting development, but only time will tell whether the Internet community at large embraces the progressive JPEG format.

The various pros and cons of GIF and JPEG are presented in Table 10–1.

Table 10–1 GIF vs. JPEG

Use GIF when...	Use JPEG when...
The original file has 256 colors or less, or is grayscale.	The original has thousands or millions of colors, and you need to keep them in the compressed file.
The picture has many sharp edges (e.g., cartoons) and/or a lot of blank space (e.g., scanned handwriting).	The picture has soft gradients from one color to another (e.g., scanned photographs).
You want the viewer to have a vague idea about the contents of the entire image as it loads.	The viewer needs to see the whole picture anyway, so it doesn't matter if it fills in from top to bottom.
You need to make the background transparent (e.g., a bullet or title banner containing a logo or other drawing).	The original is very large, and compressing the file down to a manageable size is more important than preserving every last detail.
You want to create thumbnails.	(The larger files that the thumbnails are linked to will often be JPEGs.)

Organizing Your Images

As your site grows, you will probably accumulate more and more image files. They can become a real mess if you're not careful, especially if several pages use the same images — this is likely to happen with bullets, logos, icons, and other small files. Poorly organized files do not affect the outward appearance of your pages, but if you take a little time and plan ahead, you will save *yourself* some headaches in the future.

The best way to explain the image location issue is with an example. Let's say you have a directory called `/funstuff`. In this directory is a page called `parks.html`, and this page contains a picture called `redball.gif`, which also resides in the `/funstuff` directory. Now let's say you have another file — called `bunnies.html` — in the `animals` directory, and it also uses `redball.gif`. The `<IMG>` tag on the Bunnies page can reference the red ball as `"../redball.gif"`. Simple enough. But if the Bunnies page moves to a new location, its reference to `redball.gif` may suddenly have an invalid path.

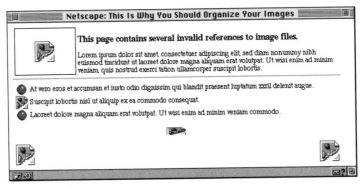

Fig. 10–25 If a page contains references to images that the server cannot find, Netscape will display these "broken" icons where the pictures would be. These icons are a sign of a careless Webmaster, so keep them off your site!

One solution is to place your *shared* images in directories that can always be accessed using absolute file names, rather than relative paths. Simply make a directory at the top level of your server space called `images` (or `pictures`, or `Hubert`, or whatever you want). Now, every image in your site can be referenced with a path name like `"/images/redball.gif"`. There are no relative double periods here, so there's no way to get lost; `/images` is `/images`, no matter how you slice it. (Note that in Web parlance, `"/images"` is a *relative link*, since it does not specify a server name, but as a *file name*, it is absolute.)

If you have (or plan to have) more image files than would be practical to dump into a single directory, you can make subdirectories in `/images`: `/images/bullets`, `/images/cartoons`, etc. Another approach is to divide your Web files into several major sections, then give each section its own `/images` directory (for instance, you could have `/business/images`, `/personal/images`, and `/travel/images`).

Of course, you can always put the images wherever is most convenient at the time, but don't blame us when you move one file and end up with a site full of "broken" picture icons (Fig. 10–25)!

10.4 SOUNDS AND MOVIES

We said that you should never replace text with images. This is even more true in the case of sounds. Perhaps you would like to provide an audio clip of your own friendly voice welcoming people to your site, in order to give it a more "human" touch. That's a nice idea, but it shouldn't be the focus of your page, because there are a lot of people whose computers are not capable of playing sounds, or whose computers are in locations where it would be inappropriate to play sounds (for instance, a school's computer lab or a corporate office). Of course, if you are a musician or a record label, sounds should indeed be a main focus of your site; you just need to warn people that they are about to download a sound that might jump out of their speakers and startle their classmates or co-workers.

Sound Formats

There are three widely used "normal" sound formats: AU (a.k.a. SND), AIFF, and WAV. They are primarily used on Sun, Macintosh, and Windows systems, respectively, but in these days of cross-platform compatibility, there are programs for each platform that can play all three. Macintosh users should beware of AIFF-C (compressed AIFF) format; it's a great way to compress sounds on a Mac, but some audio players only recognize "normal" AIFF. In choosing between the "big three" formats, record sounds in whichever format is easiest for you; if you have the time, inclination, and disk space, you may even want to provide your sounds in more than one format. And to *really* ensure that everyone will be able to hear them, you may want to include a page of links to audio players for various platforms (see Figure 10–26 for an example).

The most highly compressed (and therefore not so "normal") audio file format is MPEG-2; it crams an incredible amount of CD-quality sound into a comparatively small amount of disk space (and therefore it will download quickly), but it takes a very long time to decode, and on most systems the uncompressed, playable file will be just as large as if it had been an AIFF or WAV file originally. Someday, MPEG-2 may become the standard, but for now many PCs simply don't have the horsepower to handle it. If you want to use MPEG-2, be absolutely sure to provide a low-fidelity alternative for those with lesser CPUs. We won't mention names (or URLs), but at least one record label lost a potential sale to an author of this book because they provided no alternative to the MPEG-2 samples of their songs, and it would have taken literally *hours* to decode those files!

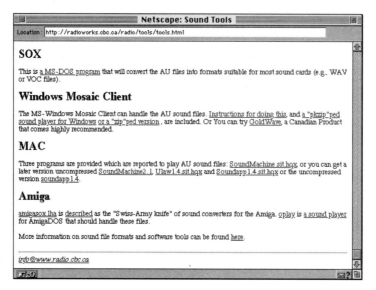

Fig. 10–26   The Canadian Broadcasting Company has AU format sound files available for downloading at their site, so they have provided this page to ensure that anyone can access the sounds.

Sampling Rates

How long should your sounds be? Well, an audio CD has a "sampling rate" of about 44 kHz; this means that every second of sound is defined by more than 44,000 pieces of information. On a computer, this means that every second takes up more than 44 kilobytes of disk space or RAM; one minute of sound would take up more than 2.5 megabytes! Most desktop computers with sound capabilities are capable of playing and recording sounds at 22 kHz, which sounds pretty good, although you do notice a slight lack of treble. Even 11 kHz sounds okay, and for recordings of spoken words, 7.4 kHz should suffice. There will always be a trade-off between quality and disk space, so keep this in mind and decide for yourself which rate you want to use. If your server can spare the room, you may even want to provide your sounds in two or three different sampling rates, so that people can decide for themselves, based on the speed of their connection, whether they want a quick and dirty 7.4 kHz sample or a relatively hi-fi 22 kHz one. Whether you provide alternative sizes or not, be courteous and list the sound's size and format (e.g., "11 kHz AIFF file, 247K") on the page that includes the link.

RealAudio and Xing StreamWorks

There is relatively new technology available that allows you to serve sounds in *real time*; Web surfers can hear sounds as they are downloaded. If they have a fast connection, they will hear higher-quality sound, so the Webmaster is freed from having to decide which sample rate to use. Radio stations have used this method to broadcast concerts or on-air programming directly onto the Web (Fig. 10–27). Sound too good to be true? Well, it's true, but it's expensive. To use this technology, you need to purchase a special server that allows you to serve real-time audio files; the price tag may be in the thousands of dollars. If this sounds really intriguing (and within your budget), you can get more information from these URLs:

- `http://www.realaudio.com/`
- `http://www.xingtech.com/streams/`

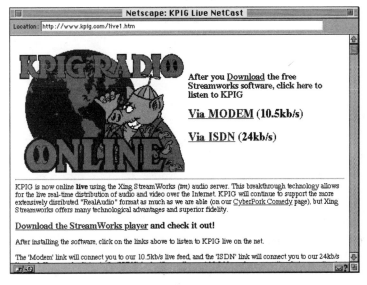

Fig. 10–27 With the help of Xing Technologies, KPIG (107-"oink"-5 FM) broadcasts live over the Internet from Freedom, California.

Movies

Movies on Web pages are less common than sounds, but they are becoming more frequent as more and more people buy "multimedia" computers (Fig. 10–28). As with anything that is complex and takes a long time to download, you should try to provide the information in non-movie form as well as you can. There are three common movie formats out there currently: MPEG, QuickTime, and AVI. All of them use some form of "lossy" compression, but you can control how much compression and therefore how much loss.

MPEG does an incredible job of compressing information, but it usually cannot include audio information, and it takes some time to decode. So you could use it to show, say, a 3-D rotating schematic view of some gizmo, but not a rock

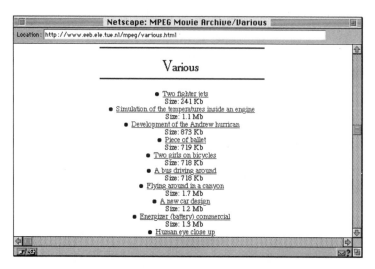

Fig. 10–28   This site is home to a large repository of MPEG movies. This page shows you some of the types of movies that you can download.

video. (By the way, MPEG video is much more user-friendly and widespread than its big, bad audio cousin, MPEG-2.)

QuickTime was developed by Apple and is used on many platforms. AVI is primarily a Windows format, but AVI decoders also exist for other platforms. Both QuickTime and AVI files can include sound, and they are less CPU-intensive than MPEG because they are not compressed as much.

If you want to record a movie without audio, use MPEG, but if you need sound, you should probably use QuickTime, since it seems to be the preferred format out there in Webland. As with sounds, be sure to list the movie file's format and size so that people know what they are getting into and whether they have the software to view it.

10.5 COMPATIBILITY

The issue of compatibility cannot be stressed enough. If you create pages that can only be viewed by people using one particular platform, you *will lose* potential customers (or members, or dates, or whoever it is you're trying to reach). In order to make sure your pages look good on all platforms, you should round up as many different browsing programs as you can get your hands on (including Lynx, which should be available through your shell account), and try out your pages using all of them. Don't forget about America Online, CompuServe, Prodigy, and other national service providers; they all use their own World Wide Web software. (Many of these services offer a free one-month membership; you can sign up, and then use that free month to try out their software so you know how your Web pages will look to their millions of subscribers.) You should also test your

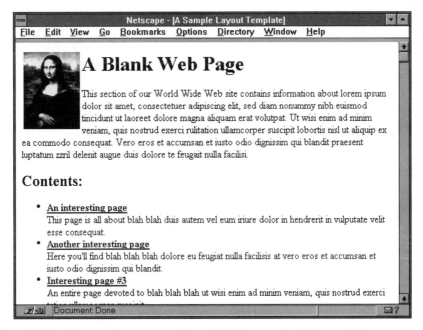

Fig. 10–29   Remember our layout template? Figure 10–17 (page 241) was a snapshot of Netscape running on a Macintosh. This illustration shows Netscape for Microsoft Windows.

pages using both Windows and Macintosh browsers (Fig. 10–29 and Fig. 10–30), and even X Windows (UNIX) if possible. If you don't personally have access to any of these operating systems, find a friend or colleague who is willing to "beta-test" your site for you.

General Web Compatibility Issues

First of all, remember that even if two people are using the same browser on the same operating system, they might have slightly different equipment, such as abnormally large or small monitors. Hardware concerns aside, they might have set their browsers' default fonts to different sizes or even different typefaces. And then there are the variations between operating systems. For example, Netscape on a Macintosh with a 14-inch monitor defaults to open in a window that takes up about two-thirds of the horizontal width of the screen; the default font is Times 12. Netscape for Windows, using the same monitor, opens in a window which fills the entire screen; the font is still Times 12 (actually Times New Roman, but who's checking?), but because Windows uses a screen measurement of 96 dots per inch compared to the Mac's 72 dpi, the letters show up much bigger on the screen.

You can see that, given all these variables, you'll never know exactly how many words on a line or lines on a screen any particular person will see. There-

Fig. 10–30   Here's the template again, this time viewed with NCSA Mosaic for Macintosh.

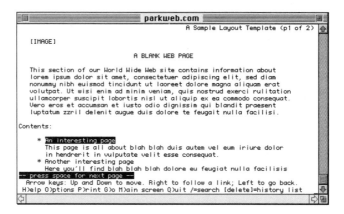

Fig. 10–31   And this is the Lynx browser, running on UNIX. (The program pictured here is NCSA Telnet for Macintosh; the UNIX system is being accessed via a shell account.)

fore, if you want a line to break in a certain place, you need to make sure you use a `<BR>` (line break) or `<P>` (new paragraph) tag. If you want a certain amount of material to show up on the first screenful that they see when they open your page (before scrolling down), find a browser and a platform with the biggest fonts and smallest window — probably a 24-row by 80-column UNIX terminal or terminal emulation program (Fig. 10–31 and Fig. 10–32) — and use that as your testing ground.

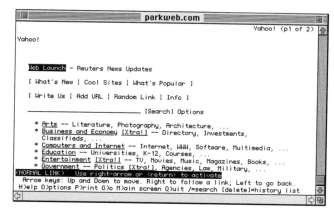

Fig. 10–32 The Yahoo database, viewed in Lynx. Compare the amount of information on this screen with Figure 11–12 (page 278), which shows Yahoo viewed in Netscape.

In summary, do not assume that your browser is going to look like *anyone* else's. Remember, the whole point of HTTP is that the server sends only vague instructions, and the client (the browser) is expected to handle the details of displaying the content; HTML was never really intended as a page-layout language, even if everyone is using it that way these days. Design your site with the least common denominator in mind; you don't necessarily have to "dumb down" your pages to work with the simpler browsing programs, but you do need to accommodate them, so that your potential audience is as large as possible.

Graphical vs. Non-graphical Browsers

At least four out of five Web surfers use graphical browsers (Netscape, Mosaic, etc.) that run on Windows, Macintosh, or X Windows; the remaining 20% are using text-based programs like Lynx. You don't want to lose that 20%, so be sure your pages are accessible to everyone. This section offers some tips on how to do that.

Alternate text in <IMG> tags One of the attributes of the `<IMG>` tag — to which we have made many references up to this point — is `alt="..."`. Use it liberally. A non-graphical browser displays the text of the `alt` attribute in lieu of the image itself. If the top of your page is a banner with your company's name and logo, put `alt="Wizbang Widgets, Inc."` in the `<IMG>` tag so Lynx users will know just what on earth they are looking at (or, more precisely, what they're *not* looking at). Using alternate text is also beneficial to people who use graphical browsers but have turned off automatic image loading; often, a one-word descrip-

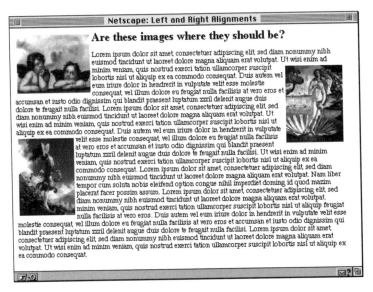

Fig. 10–33   This page uses `align=left` and `align=right` attributes to create a very interesting layout, at least in Netscape.

tion of an image (which appears as part of the image's placeholder) is enough to help them decide whether to take the time to download the picture or not.

Placement of images   Be careful where you put your pictures, especially if you use the more complicated layout attributes such as `align=left` and `align=right`. Image alignment tags have no effect on the output of text-based browsers; the placeholders for the images take up much less space than you sometimes think they will, and they end up in weird places (compare Figure 10–33 with Figure 10–34). Put simply, there is no way to achieve really clever layouts on programs like Lynx; the best you can do is make sure that your pages are *clearly legible*, no matter who is reading them.

Image maps   Image maps are one of the most frequently *abused* features of HTML. They can be pleasing to look at and quite ingenious in their use, but they are completely unusable to users of text-based browsing programs. We have seen a number of home pages that consist of a single, enormous image map and nothing else (see Figure 10–2 for a horrible — but fortunately fictional — example). This is a very bad idea. If you must base the "front door" of your site around a big image map, make sure to do one of the following: provide a single text link that says, "if you can't use image maps, click here," and which leads to a completely text-based home page; or provide a list of text links that encompasses all the same choices that the image map does. Alternatively, if your image map is really a "button bar," forget the map, make each "button" a separate image, and use the `alt` attribute for each one.

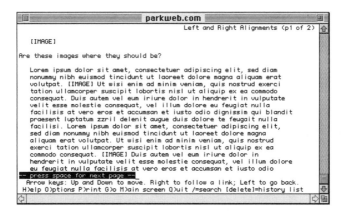

Fig. 10–34 This page has the same source HTML as Figure 10–33, but because Lynx does not recognize image alignment tags, the [IMAGE] placeholders are interspersed throughout the text, and it looks bad. This could be remedied by adding alt=" " to the <IMG> tags; then, Lynx users wouldn't be aware of the images at all.

Netscape

Of all those people using graphical browsers, the vast majority of them are using Netscape. But keep in mind that some of them are *not*, for whatever reason. Netscape is available for free only to certain users (such as those at educational institutions), so some people may not want to spend the extra money when they can use NCSA Mosaic for free. Many people who use the Web from their place of employment cannot use Netscape because their company has not purchased a license. We are detailing some of these reasons so that we can point out that it is therefore quite rude to include a line on your Web pages that says, in essence, "We made these pages with Netscape in mind; if you're not using Netscape, you're scum of the earth unless you get it immediately."

That said, Netscape understands a number of useful HTML tags and attributes that other browsers do not understand. We list some of the more common Netscape extensions and their details in Appendix A; in section 10.2, we offered tips on why you should or shouldn't use a couple of these extensions. Here, we will just give some general tips about which Netscape extensions you can use "safely."

Centering   Go for it. Use it as much as you want. Browsers that do not understand centering will just align text on the left as if the centering tags weren't even there. In Netscape 1.1, centering was accomplished via the <CENTER> tag, but it is being incorporated into the HTML standard in a different form: centered or right-aligned text will be enclosed in <DIV> tags or <P> tags with an align attribute. The new versions of Netscape support these new centering methods, so the <CENTER> tag may become obsolete.

Font Size, Font Colors, Word Breaks, Blinking   As far as compatibility goes, these features are also "harmless," in the sense that, as with centering, browsers that do not understand the tags or attributes will simply ignore them. But be careful: if you try to make something really stand out by using the biggest font possible and making it blink, people using non-Netscape browsers won't even notice. CAPITAL LETTERS are the only sure way to really get *everyone's* attention.

Image Alignment   As we have pointed out before — with glee — Netscape's `align=left` and `align=right` attributes have been incorporated into the current version of HTML. Netscape also supports a few other arguments to the `align` attribute, such as `absmiddle` and `texttop`. Use the many flavors of the `align` tag with our blessing, but make sure your pages don't look ridiculous in graphical browsers that don't support them; is the relative placement of text and images still correct? (This is especially an important issue when you come up with a great layout serendipitously!)

Fig. 10–35   Don't be this arrogant. All these <HR> tags just waste space.

Horizontal Rule Lines   The Netscape extensions let you fool around with the width, thickness, and positioning of horizontal rule lines (the <HR> tag). Sometimes people like to make patterns with multiple rule lines of various lengths (Fig. 10–35), but this looks pretty weird in Lynx (Fig. 10–36). You're probably best off using one <HR> at a time, or two if you *really* want to mark a division between different sections of a page.

Dynamic Pages   Netscape supports "dynamic" HTML documents, meaning they change, reload, or relocate without any input from the user. There are two ways this can be accomplished. First, the server can leave the HTTP connection open and continue sending data; this is called "server push." Second, the

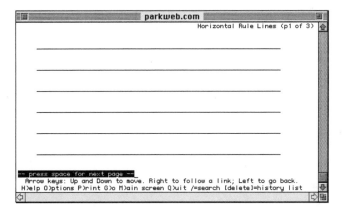

Fig. 10–36 See? In Lynx, the rule lines take up so much room that the obnoxious message isn't even visible on the first page. (Okay, so maybe that's a good thing!)

browser program can be given instructions to open a new HTTP connection after a given amount of time; this is "client pull."

Server push involves writing complicated programs that work with the server software, and not every server even supports it. Client pull, on the other hand, is achieved by way of a single HTML tag at the beginning of a document, and it is actually quite easy to implement. Nevertheless, we recommend that you *not* create dynamic documents. Many people get confused when their browser starts loading new data all by itself, especially when they haven't even finished reading the previous page! This is especially true for people with slow connections.

There are only two cases where we *fully* endorse automatic reloading. One is when you have moved files from one location to another. When people click on the old URL, you can have their HTTP request automatically rerouted to the new location. For those whose browsers do not support client pull, you can simply give them a link to click for the new address.

Client pull lets you perform another neat trick. Let's say you have two different versions of the same page: one is optimized for fancy graphical browsers like Netscape, with tables and animations and client pull and who knows what else, and the other is a simple, plain text page for those whose browsers do not support all your HTML tricks. Now, put an instruction at the beginning of the simple page that immediately redirects browsers to the complex page. The Netscape people will barely notice that they skipped over the simple page, and people without dynamic document support (who are, in large part, the same people whose browsers do not support complicated layouts) will simply *stop* at the simple page, and everybody's happy.

Whether you decide to take advantage of dynamic documents or not, it is worth reading about. There is not much documentation available on the Web yet, but here is the URL of Netscape's page on the topic:

http://www.netscape.com/assist/net_sites/pushpull.html

Newer Netscape Extensions   Netscape 2.0 (and later versions) adds an entirely new set of extensions that allow you to do really wild things with pages. For instance, you can use "frames" to divide a Web page into a number of smaller areas, each of which contains another page, complete with scroll bars (Fig. 10–37). An HTML page that uses frames usually has an entire section — enclosed by

Fig. 10–37   Frames in Netscape 2.0. Each rectangle on this page is defined by its own HTML document; the page we are looking at just ties them all together. But, if we view this page with an earlier version of Netscape, or with another browser, we will see an alternate layout that may be completely different from what we see here.

<NOFRAME> tags — that contains whatever will be displayed on browsers incapable of handling frames; it's much like the alt attribute of the <IMG> tag. As long as you consistently include <NOFRAME> sections, there is no reason you shouldn't explore the use of frames in your pages.

We mentioned Netscape's new progressive JPEG images earlier; while these are an exciting trend for the future, they are not well-supported yet; current browsers (and even graphics programs) that can normally display JPEGs will choke on progressive JPEGs. So, unless you want to use *both* formats (with thumbnails or text links for the progressive JPEGs), it's best to stick with interlaced GIFs and normal JPEGs until some point in the future when you are certain that *everyone* can see your nifty progressive JPEGs.

The other Netscape 2.0 extensions mostly fall into the "harmless" category: font colors, some new align attributes, superscripting and subscripting, and right text alignment can be used safely as long as they do not interfere too badly with layouts in other browsers. And most of these will probably be included in the next revision of HTML anyway. As always, test and test again to make sure it all works, for all browsers.

See Appendix A, page 373, for more information about Netscape's newest features.

Your Site and the Future of HTML

As the Web evolves, the HyperText Markup Language will grow, and the number of file formats for images, sounds, and movies will grow. The Netscape folks may continue to make up their own rules, or they may decide to go along with standard HTML; certainly, the HTML specification will end up absorbing some of Netscape's best features. Perhaps a new browser will rise up to challenge Netscape's supremacy. The important thing for you to remember, as a Web site designer, is that no matter which program or operating system is the "best" or most widespread, there will always remain a significant number of people who, for whatever reason, are not going along with the crowd. You need to consider this minority when writing your pages and making files available. Stick with the established standards, whatever they become. By having a universally legible Web site, you gain an instant advantage over those who latch on to the latest trend and choose glitz over accessibility.

10.6 DOING BUSINESS ON THE WEB

If you are setting up a Web site for a small business, a successful Web site might translate directly to increased profits. Your Web site will in many ways be just like any other part of your advertising budget, but has the distinct advantage of being dynamic and far more interesting. It's also much easier to design your own Web page than your own print ad, since there are already certain constraints on what you can and cannot do. You might not trust yourself to put together your tri-fold brochure, but there's no reason you — yes, *you* — can't build your entire Web site from scratch. Along with everything else in this chapter, this section presents a few more things to keep in mind when you're trying to decide how to design your business' pages.

Give Something Back

A good Web site is one that gives something back to the on-line community. Most sites accomplish this simply by giving information. A nursery might provide tips on when to plant your spring bulbs; an investment firm might give out a few "hot tips." A Web site set up by a night club will get more visitors if they include a calendar of *all* upcoming local attractions, not just the ones on their stage.

You can also give away more tangible things. In Chapter 3, we showed you a graphic design company that gave out a free "font of the month" and a mortgage

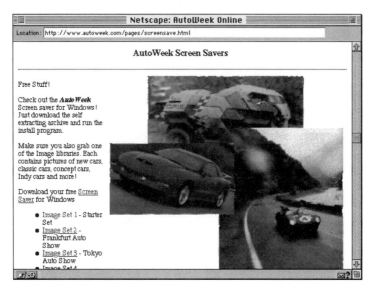

Fig. 10–38 AutoWeek gets people to visit their site by offering a free screen saver that you can download.

company that gave out customized financial analysis tools (pages 33-35). Here's another example: AutoWeek magazine has a screen saver program that you can download and use with Microsoft Windows, just for fun (Fig. 10–38).

If you really can't think of any information or software related to your site that you can give away on the Web, then why not give away something that has *nothing* to do with your site? Put up schedules of local sports teams, or the recipe for your grandma's gingerbread cookies! Anything that gets people to visit your site is a good thing, and the more stuff you can provide, the better. Brainstorm, and be creative!

Selling Merchandise on the Web

Most people don't like to actually purchase things via the Internet, because they are afraid that their VISA card numbers might be intercepted by unscrupulous hackers who will use their credit cards to buy X-rated CD-ROMs. This fear is mostly unfounded, because one of the hottest topics on the Web today is security. (Strangely enough, most people have no qualms about ordering over the phone, where security issues are not much different.) Netscape claims to have developed a virtually uncrackable security scheme, and the browser can warn people if they are entering non-secure Web space.

Credit cards are not the only way to spend money on the net. "Virtual banks" have sprung up here and there. This is somewhat like an on-line checking account. You send them money, and various Web sites will withdraw money from your virtual account when you buy things from them. Needless to say, people who don't like giving out their credit card numbers don't like this idea either. (For more information about security, see Chapter 14.)

Regardless of how safe any on-line payment method might be, you need to take people's concerns into account. In other words, you should include as much information as possible regarding *non*-Internet transactions. If your company has a toll-free number for ordering, make sure it is prominently displayed on your site, possibly even in a signature at the bottom of every page. Even if you don't have a toll-free number, be sure to give phone numbers, e-mail addresses, and postal addresses. Somewhere in your site, you should list your hours of operation, and all of your shipping and return policies. In other words, provide as much basic information as possible.

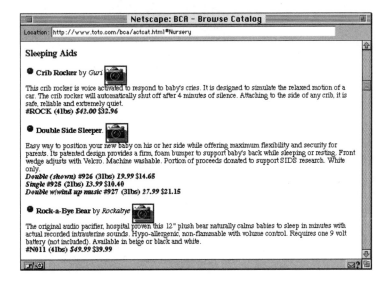

Fig. 10–39   A very well done on-line catalog of baby products. They have provided product descriptions, prices, catalog numbers, and pictures of the items. (The pictures are viewed by clicking on the camera icons.)

Catalogs

If it is at all feasible, create an on-line catalog (Fig. 10–39). If you sell any kind of merchandise, you should try to include a picture of every item that is available for purchase. (If you are going to have a lot of pictures, a flatbed color scanner might be a wise investment, so you don't have to pay anyone to use theirs.) Make bulleted lists of features; include comments from customers.

If you sell services, your catalog should be as verbally detailed as possible, without looking dry and boring. If you can think of a way that a picture would be helpful, do it. Again, well-organized lists and samples of customer feedback might be useful.

No matter what you are selling, include exact prices, and say whether those prices include sales tax. You may even want to offer discounted "Web specials" to get people interested in on-line shopping. If something happens to be out of stock, let them know when you expect it in. The bottom line is, you want your customers to have *all* the information they need to decide whether they want to buy or not. They should have available to them everything they would have if you printed a glossy catalog and sent it through the mail.

The Worldwide Market

By setting up a Web site for your business, you are suddenly opening up your potential customer base to the entire world. Think about this while designing your site. Do you want to accept orders from other countries? If you accept credit cards, payment is not a problem, but shipping might be, so come up with different rate charts for international customers. On a more basic level, do you want your site to be exclusively in English? Many sites, especially those with large numbers of Japanese or French visitors, provide information in more than one language.

10.7 SUMMARY

It is very important to keep in mind all the page layout and page content concepts that we have talked about in this chapter when building your Web site. And remember that on a for-profit server, good page design isn't just a good idea, it can also mean money. Here are a few of the more important points that we've discussed in this chapter:

- Put as much as possible in your site, but keep the individual pages down to a reasonable size.
- Keep your site fresh. A "whatchamacallit of the week/month" is a good way to generate repeat visits.
- On a related note, stay on top of things. If you provide an e-mail address or form for feedback, make sure you check it regularly and respond promptly.
- Use images wherever they can enhance the appearance or content of a page, but don't put too many on a single document. Use thumbnails for large images, and alternative text for anything important.
- If you must include sounds, movies, or other complex media, provide them in a universally readable format, or in many formats — and indicate exactly what those formats are.
- Keep your layouts simple and consistent, yet interesting. Don't waste space, especially in that first screenful.
- Test your site to make sure that every Web browser on the planet can view your site as it was meant to be viewed. Don't overuse the newest HTML extensions, and don't assume that everyone uses Netscape.

## CHAPTER 11

Publicizing Your
World Wide Web Site

*B*y this point you should have at least a home page set up on your server. You might even have a few "major" pages all put together, or maybe you've got a complete Web site, with all the trimmings. You've tested it to make sure everything works the way it's supposed to. You've asked all your friends to test it to work out a few more bugs. Now, it's time to unleash your information on the unsuspecting world. This chapter will tell you how to get along with your new electronic neighbors, and what you can do to let them know you've moved in. Think of this chapter as your "housewarming party."

11.1 NETIQUETTE

The users of the Internet form a community unlike any other on Earth. They are neighbors in the space of ideas, rather than the space of real estate. Friendships and even bitter enmities may grow between people who have never met. And, unlike your real next-door neighbors, who are likely to share your cultural, educational, or economic background, neighbors on the Net may have nothing in common other than their species. And sometimes not even that (Fig. 11–1)!

Despite the apparent strangeness of the on-line community, it does offer some parallels with our own towns and neighborhoods. In particular, a common sense of respect and good behavior has developed, not by fiat but by shared experience.

If you were a big company looking to expand its business into a foreign country, you would want to know something about that country before you even got started. You would want to be familiar with the local laws and customs, and you would probably want to learn at least a few words in the language. If you didn't take the time to do this, you would be resented and ignored, or even run straight out of town.

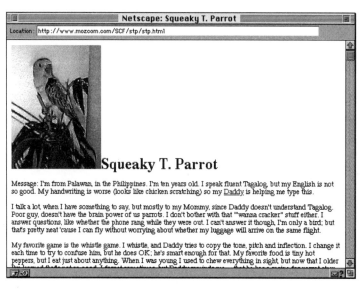

Fig. 11–1   Not everyone with a home page lives in North America, and not everyone walks on two legs!

The Internet is no different than our hypothetical foreign country. While there is no central government and therefore no code of laws, there is definitely a set of cultural norms, collectively known as "netiquette." If you violate netiquette, you will be quickly reminded of its various fine points. Beyond the conventions of good behavior and polite language, there are collective ideas of what is in good or poor taste. If you create a really lousy Web site, few people will actually express their disgust to you, but they certainly won't recommend your site to their friends. Internet old-timers have grumbled about the huge influx of Internet newcomers due to nationwide services like America Online and Prodigy. As more of the newcomers have caught on to the rules, the tension has eased somewhat, but be careful, regardless. The last thing you want is to be branded a "clueless newbie."

So, what's the best way to find out all about netiquette? Spend some time on line. The Usenet newsgroups are the most turbulent Internet environment, because they feature constant interactions between people. More specifically, interactions between their opinions, in which there is somewhat more potential for disaster. In any single newsgroup, some people gain reputations as "upstanding citizens," and some are looked upon as netiquette-ignoring, immature rabble-rousers (many of whom take twisted pride in the designation). If you can survive (and tolerate) the chaotic and contentious world of Usenet, you can probably make it anywhere.

If you're impatient, and want to plunge in immediately, take a little time to read a few Web pages dealing with netiquette. The "classic" document is "Emily Postnews." It is a tongue-in-cheek guide to Internet etiquette (mostly Usenet), written in the style of "Miss Manners" (Fig. 11–2). For general Internet and

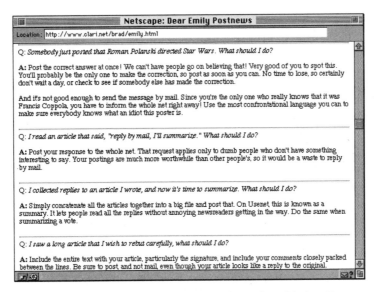

Fig. 11–2 Emily Postnews answers your questions about Netiquette.

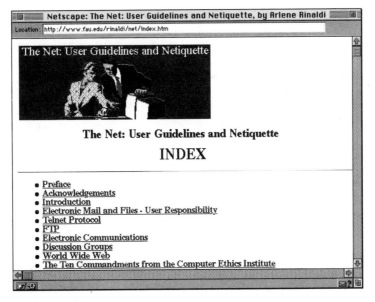

Fig. 11–3 Arlene Rinaldi's Web site, dedicated to helping you make a good impression on the Internet.

WWW decorum tips, another good place to visit is Arlene Rinaldi's "User Guidelines and Netiquette" site (Fig. 11–3).

Whatever you decide to do to educate yourself, keep in mind that ignorance of the norms is no excuse, nor is ignorance bliss. Getting off on the right foot is very important. And if you have employees or colleagues using your system, make sure that they are "in the know" as well.

11.2 ADVERTISING OUTSIDE THE WEB

Once you have your site up and running, you will want to tell the world about it. It is very important to understand that there is a right way and a wrong way to do this. Whatever you have learned about netiquette, from us or from other sources on the Web, it is imperative that you apply it when you plan your on-line marketing strategy.

E-mail

Don't rely on e-mail to advertise your site. Some supposedly clever entrepreneurs have gotten hold of large lists of e-mail addresses, possibly by grabbing the names off Usenet articles, and sent their advertisements to every name on the list. This is a very bad idea. Everyone expects to receive junk mail in their mailbox out on the curb, but for some reason they really hate it in their e-mailbox. Not only is it annoying to sift through the unwanted mail, but some people actually pay per message received, and many people pay for time spent on line. Sending unsolicited commercial e-mail is just plain rude, and very bad P.R. for you and your site.

E-mail will still be an important part of your Internet presence, though, since it will be the primary way that visitors to your Web site will give you feedback. Be sure to respond politely and promptly to whatever mail you might receive from potential customers. If you want to send form letters thanking people for their feedback, you can, but keep in mind that form letters via e-mail can seem just as impersonal as regular form letters. (On the other hand, you can get away with form letters a little more easily on the Net, since everything is electronic anyway; you don't have to worry about the grainy appearance of a photocopied signature!)

Usenet

The Usenet newsgroups are a great way to publicize your Web pages — and anything else you want to spread the word about — but only within certain guidelines. You can think of all Usenet newsgroups as falling roughly into three categories: newsgroups intended for commercial and announcement postings; groups directly related to the product, service, or organization that your site deals with; and groups that have little or nothing to do with your site.

Commercial and "For Sale" Newsgroups   The `biz` hierarchy of newsgroups was created specifically to provide a place for businesses to post advertisements for their products or services. Unfortunately, it is not very heavily used, mostly because people don't really want to subscribe to a group that contains nothing but ads! (Would you?)

Consequently, many businesses end up posting their ads in groups that were originally intended for private-party "for sale" and "wanted" ads. An example of this kind of group would be `rec.music.makers.marketplace`, where people buy and sell musical instruments. These newsgroups function exactly the same as the classified ads in the newspaper, except they cover the entire world rather than your city or state. You can post ads for your business here if you like, but unless you have something specific to sell, you will probably receive some criticism from Usenet purists who object to *any* commercial content in the newsgroups.

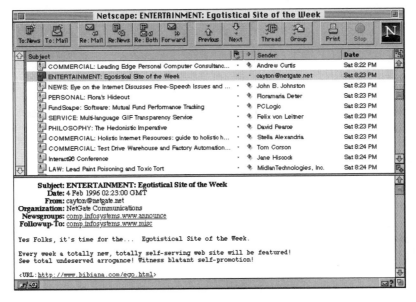

Fig. 11–4 The Usenet newsgroup `comp.infosystems.www.announce`. This list represents less than *one day's* worth of article subjects.

There is also a group called `comp.infosystems.www.announce` that was created expressly for announcements of new World Wide Web sites (Fig. 11–4). You have nothing to lose by announcing the birth of your site here, but this newsgroup suffers somewhat from the same problem that afflicts the `biz` hierarchy: no one wants to read a bunch of advertisements. (To be fair, though, `comp.infosystems.www.announce` includes announcements of some interesting personal and non-profit pages as well.)

Relevant Newsgroups If you own a company that, say, manufactures kayaks, you might be tempted to post messages advertising your site to the `rec.boats.paddle` newsgroup (Fig. 11–5). You can do this if you want, but once again, you may have to endure a storm of criticism from the Usenet community. In the on-line world, a vocal minority can have a large impact; even if only one

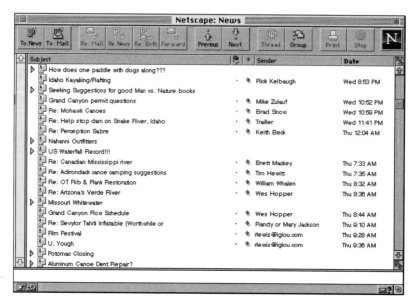

Fig. 11–5 `Rec.boats.paddle`. This illustration is provided to give you an idea of the kinds of articles you can expect in a typical, topical newsgroup.

person gets ticked off by your marketing approach, they can make a lot of noise that can potentially be seen by millions of people.

Instead, you should "infiltrate" the newsgroup. This sounds much slimier than it really is; we just mean you should try to become a part of the `rec.boats.paddle` community. Since you make kayaks, this probably won't be too painful for you; you probably enjoy talking about kayaking and offering your otherwise unbiased opinions about technique, paddles, etc. If you don't, maybe you have an employee or partner who does.

Read the newsgroup for a few days to acclimate yourself, then start posting messages that have nothing to do with your business. But create a nice-looking "signature" file. This is a short text file (no more than five or six lines) that gets appended to every Usenet article or e-mail message that you send. So, when someone in the newsgroup asks about kayaking on the Kettle River, you can tell them about your trip there last fall, and at the end of the article it will say, "Visit MegaKayak's home page at `http://www.megakayak.com/`." The more you post, the more people will see your signature file; eventually, many of them will be intrigued enough to check it out for themselves.

If you really become accepted as a valuable asset to the `rec.boats.paddle` community, you might finally want to try posting a short article describing your site. But you probably won't have to. WWW pages are popping up like mushrooms, and everyone knows this. Everyone wants to know if their favorite hobby or avocation has a home page. Thus, almost every newsgroup gets articles whose subject lines are something along the lines of, "Is there a Web site about ___?" When someone asks the question, "Is there a Web site about kayaks," *this* is your opportunity to jump in and say, "why yes, there is." Of course, if you have built a really great site, you may not even have to answer, because other people may answer on your behalf!

And this is your ultimate goal. You want your site to be generally known by kayakers as a great Web site where they can go to find fun and valuable information. Many of those "fans" will add links to your site on their home page, and they will mention your site in Usenet articles. Your site may be mentioned in the kayaking FAQ (Frequently Asked Questions list). Ideally, every kayaker who uses the Internet will at least visit your site once.

Irrelevant Newsgroups   The only way you should ever mention your Web site in a newsgroup that does not relate to your site in any way is in your signature file. If you enjoy Beatles music and read `rec.music.beatles` regularly, you can go ahead and leave your ad for `www.megakayak.com` in your signature when you post Beatles-related articles; kayaking Beatles fans may see it and visit your Web site. But in a newsgroup that has nothing at all to do with the material in your pages, you should never, ever post a message that does nothing but talk about your site.

Spam and EMPs   *Spam* is the name given to a Usenet article that is posted to as many groups as possible, most of which, of course, fall under the label "irrelevant newsgroups"; *to spam* is also a verb. EMP stands for "excessive multiple posting," and it means essentially the same thing. After our discussion on the *proper* use of Usenet as an advertising medium, it should be obvious to you that spamming is at least as bad as sending bulk e-mail. It's the electronic equivalent of those annoying flyers that people slip under your car's windshield at the mall parking lot.

In other words, *do not spam!* Nothing gets the Usenet community more riled up than seeing the same useless message in every group they read. Whatever advantage you might have gained by sending your message to millions of people in thousands of newsgroups will be more than canceled out by the ire that will be directed toward you. Not only that, you could have your account revoked by your service provider, and your articles will probably be canceled en masse anyway.

11.3 ADVERTISING ON THE WEB

Having read this far, you might be a little bit discouraged about your prospects for advertising on the Internet. It seems those billboards along the clichéd information superhighway have an awful lot of zoning regulations and land-use permits attached to them! Well, don't despair. This book is about the World Wide Web, so now we're going to tell you that — you guessed it — the Web is an absolutely *perfect* electronic advertising medium.

One reason the Web works so well for advertising in the quirky on-line world is that Web pages are completely passive. You will never, ever see a Web page unless you actually choose to go there. When someone posts an ad on Usenet, it gets in the way of the other articles. When someone sends you commercial e-mail, it takes up room in your "in" box. But on the Web, the reader has complete control over how much they see. This fits very well with the freedom-loving philosophy of most Net users; if you don't like it, don't look at it.

The best way to publicize a World Wide Web site is on the Web itself. We are now going to list a few of the most common ways to ensure that your Web site is noticed by as many people as possible. You should follow *every one* of these suggestions, plus any more schemes that you think of. Each one takes very little time, and no money. You have nothing to lose.

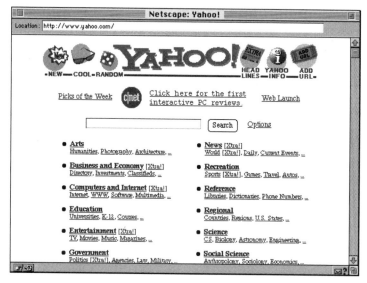

Fig. 11–6   Yahoo!

Yahoo

Yahoo (`http://www.yahoo.com`) is a vast database that lists thousands upon thousands of World Wide Web sites, organized into hierarchical categories (Fig. 11–6). This is the jumping-off point into the Web for a very large number of people. Let's say we've called up Yahoo, and we are looking for information about rock climbing. First, we would select the "Recreation" category from Yahoo's top level. From there, we click on the "Outdoors" subcategory, and finally on "Climbing." That takes us to a list of Web pages or sites devoted to rock climbing (Fig. 11–7). Even the Climbing page has a few more subdivisions at the top of the list. Anyone with a rock climbing-related Web page, be they a climbing club, a manufacturer of rock-climbing equipment, or just an individual who's a big fan of carabiners and ropes, should get themselves listed on this Yahoo page.

Yahoo doesn't pretend to be the most comprehensive listing of Web pages, just the best organized. And since it's so intuitive, many people use Yahoo as

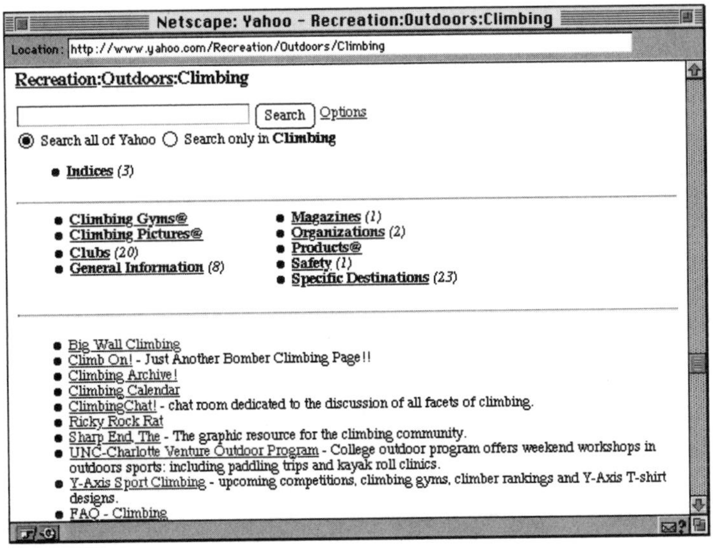

Fig. 11–7 This is the "Recreation:Outdoors:Climbing" page in Yahoo. The bold-face items between the horizontal lines are further subdivisions within Yahoo; the links at the bottom are individual pages.

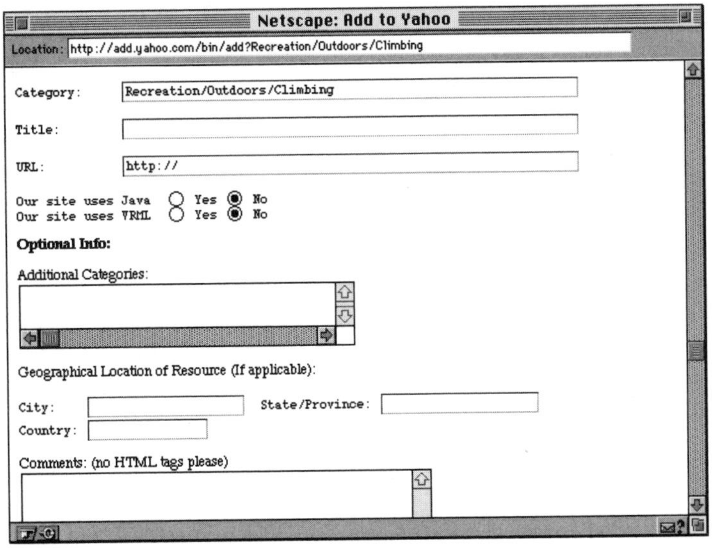

Fig. 11–8 Yahoo's "Add URL" form. Pretty straightforward.

their default home page (the page that is loaded when they first turn on their Web browser). If Joe Shmoe — amateur Web surfer extraordinaire — wants to find something, there's a good chance he'll look for it first in Yahoo.

Adding your pages to Yahoo couldn't be easier. Just click the "Add URL" button in the banner at the top of the page, and you are given a form to fill out with information about your site (Fig. 11–8). Within a few days, the Yahoo folks will check to make sure your site actually exists, and it will be added to the database. Since Yahoo includes a nice search interface (see Figure 11–6; note the blank text box with the "Search" button), you should include a decent description of your site when you fill out the form. Work in as many words as possible that pertain directly to your pages; our hypothetical kayak manufacturer from section 11.2 would want to make sure they used the words "kayak," "whitewater," "boat," "canoe," "paddle," "water sports," etc. This way, the page will be found by more keyword searches than if the description said simply, "We make kayaks."

Fig. 11–9   Yahoo's "Web Launch" page. The companies advertised here paid a handsome sum of money for the privilege of showing up on your screen.

Yahoo also offers a service called "Web Launch," whereby they announce new sites on a special page that includes illustrations and links to those sites (Fig. 11–9). They charge quite a bit for this service; as with advertising in any medium, you'll have to decide for yourself whether it's worth it or not. See `http://www.yahoo.com/weblaunch.html` for more details.

Lycos

Lycos (`http://www.lycos.com/`) is another World Wide Web database (Fig. 11–10). It is not organized into menus the way Yahoo is, but what it lacks in style it makes up for in size. Lycos *claims* to have catalogued over 90% of the Web, which translates to *millions* of pages.

Whereas Yahoo has a search mechanism that is helpful when you can't find something right away, you *have* to use the search function to find anything in

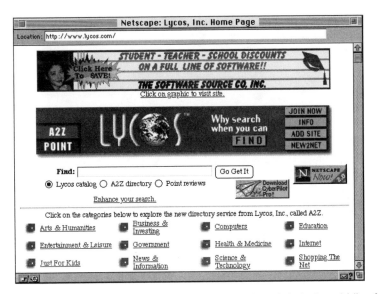

Fig. 11-10 Lycos. The important part is the "Find:" box right in the middle of the page; you might also want to "Enhance your search."

(© 1996 Lycos. Inc.; Lycos™ "Catalog of the Internet" © 1994, 1995, 1996 Carnegie Mellon University.)

Lycos. If we want information about vegetable gardening, we just type those two words into a text box, click the button, and wait a few seconds.

Uh-oh. Because of the phenomenal size of the Lycos database, it found 9,491 URLs that it thinks *might* be relevant to the keywords "vegetable" and "gardening" (Fig. 11-11)! Fortunately, Lycos automatically gives a "score" to each page that it finds; this score is a rough indicator of how relevant that site is to the keywords that you entered (higher scores are given when, for example, the keywords are adjacent in the page, or when they are in the title or header of the HTML document). The URLs with the highest scores are listed first. So, even though you get a list of over 9,000 URLs, the "good" ones are likely to be near the top. And Lycos often provides you with an abstract of the page, making your search even easier.

Aside from simply choosing to view pages with the highest scores, the other way to limit the search results is simply to add another keyword. So, just to see what would happen, we tried searching for "vegetable gardening lettuce" instead of just "vegetable gardening" — after all, you can't really make a decent salad without lettuce — and the list was pared down considerably: Lycos only found 12 documents this time, a few of which even reside on the same Web server. It probably wouldn't be too hard to look into *all* of the "lettuce" URLs that Lycos found for us.

Lycos builds its catalog in two ways: first, you can add your own URLs using a form similar to Yahoo's — although it's even easier, since you don't have to fill out a description (Fig. 11-12); second, Lycos runs programs called "spiders" (the name "Lycos" is related to a genus of spider) that search the Web automati-

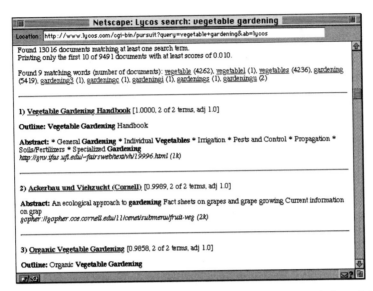

Fig. 11–11   The results of a simple Lycos search for the keywords "vegetable gardening." Lycos tries to list the supposedly more relevant pages first.

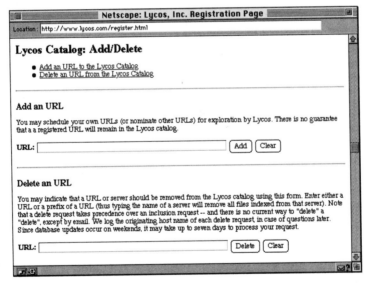

Fig. 11–12   The form that you use to submit your site's URL to Lycos. Within a couple of days (or weeks), Lycos will explore your site and add the pages to its database.

cally, jumping from one link to another and jotting down everything they see along the way. Because these spiders are prowling around every day, you might

find that your pages are already in the Lycos database! But if they're not, get
them in as soon as possible.

Like many free WWW services, Lycos now accepts advertising on its pages
(note the "Software Source" picture at the top of Figure 11–10) to defray their
costs; this is very similar to Yahoo's "Web Launch" concept. And once again,
you'll have to decide whether you want to pay for the extra exposure or just live
with what the spiders can do for you.

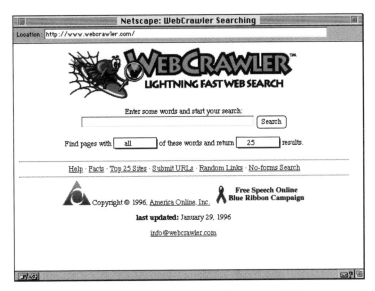

Fig. 11–13 WebCrawler's home page. As with Lycos and Yahoo, you can initiate
a search right here on the intro page.

WebCrawler

More arachnids here: WebCrawler even puts one in their logo (Fig. 11–13).
This is essentially the same kind of service as Lycos. Its database is significantly
smaller than Lycos', but some people prefer its no-nonsense approach; search
results are returned as a simple list, presented in order of relevance, and you're
unlikely to be faced with 5,000 URLs about vegetables. WebCrawler only found
95 pages — a much more manageable number —when we asked it about "vegetable gardening" (Fig. 11–14), and the first one on the list is a good site ("Internet
Gardening" was also near the top of Lycos' list). You may have noticed that Web-
Crawler is peppered with advertisements as well (like the "HomeArts" banner at
the top of Figure 11–14). The Internet community as a whole was initially
resentful of all these ads, but remember that they keep you from having to pay
for this stuff!

WebCrawler's "Submit URLs" form is very similar to Lycos' as well. In fact,
WebCrawler's is better, because you can send in a whole pile of URLs at once
(Fig. 11–15). Supposedly, their little spider/robot will explore your whole site if

Fig. 11–14   Results of a WebCrawler search for "vegetable gardening." Compare this with Lycos' results in Figure 11–11. Lycos found more documents, but WebCrawler's list is easier to read.

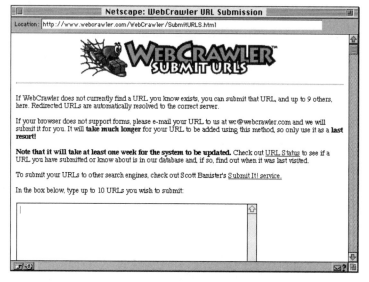

Fig. 11–15   WebCrawler's "Submit URLs" page. Note that you use the scrolling text box to enter many URLs at once.

you just tell it about the top level, but you may as well list *all* your substantial pages, just in case.

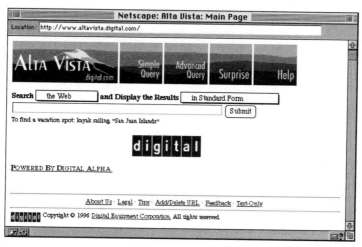

Fig. 11–16 Digital's Alta Vista search engine.

Alta Vista

Alta Vista (Fig. 11–16) came onto the scene after Lycos and Webcrawler, but even on its first day, it indexed about 50 percent more URLs than Lycos did at the time. If it's on the Web, Alta Vista will find it. In fact, Alta Vista will even find it on Usenet, if it was posted in the last month or so. Unfortunately, Alta Vista doesn't prioritize its output as nicely as Lycos does, so simple searches are often quite overwhelming. Look what happened when we looked for "vegetable gardening" in Alta Vista: about 20,000 matches (Fig. 11–17)!

Because Alta Vista has a tendency to find *too much*, you shouldn't rely on it as an advertising mechanism. However, you will find it to be very handy as a searching tool, especially if you need to find really obscure information on the Web. (The "Advanced Query" function is better than anything found in the other major indexes.) Even though it won't serve as your primary "billboard," you should add your site to its database anyway, if Alta Vista's very efficient spiders haven't found you already.

Submit It

Submit It is a great service that allows you to submit your page's URL and description to over a dozen Web indexes and directories, including Yahoo, Lycos, WebCrawler, Alta Vista, and many others (Fig. 11–18). If you go through Submit It, you don't even need to go through the steps we outlined earlier! But we described them anyway, because it's quite educational to do it step by step, and you should be familiar with the workings of those famous databases. Use Submit It to take care of all the rest of the indexes. Remember, you might as well get listed everywhere, especially when it's this easy.

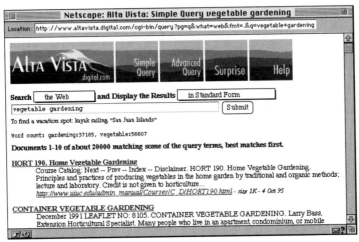

Fig. 11–17 The results of an Alta Vista search for the keywords "vegetable gardening." Clearly, this is more than we wanted to find!

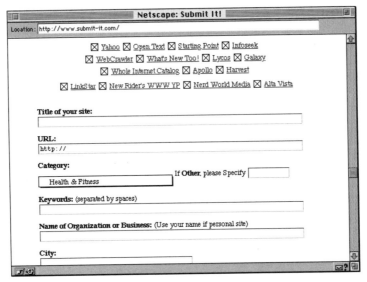

Fig. 11–18 The Submit It home page. The check boxes at the top of the window represent all the different places you can register your page just by using this one form.

"What's New" Pages: Mosaic and Netscape

Netscape and NCSA Mosaic both maintain pages of new Web sites (Figure 11–19 shows Mosaic's) that are directly accessible from these browsers' respec-

Fig. 11–19 NCSA Mosaic's "What's New" page.

tive home pages. (Some other sites also have "What's New" pages, but Mosaic's and Netscape's are very heavily used.) Because there are so many new Web sites popping up every day, both NCSA and Netscape screen the incoming entries so as to keep the number of new sites manageable. Mosaic has a few categories of pages that they refuse to publish in "What's New" (e.g., adult bookstores or make-your-own assault weapons) and Netscape has only a few that they *will* publish; Netscape says that they want to present those sites that "are not only new to the Net but that use or advance the technology of the Net in new ways." You may as well try to get in there anyway; the better your site is, the better chance you'll have of being "accepted."

ALIWEB

ALIWEB (Fig. 11–20) is a slightly different kind of database. When you submit information about your site to ALIWEB, you must create a file — called `site.idx` — with a particular format, and place it on your site. This file can include an awful lot of information (Fig. 11–21). ALIWEB is not nearly as large as some of the monsters like Lycos and Yahoo, but it's nice that someone is collecting this level of detail, and their search interface is well done. Even though their submission format may look like a pain, be sure to sign up with them, because they're doing a great job, and it seems to be a slightly "higher class" kind of operation than the riff-raff you may find elsewhere.

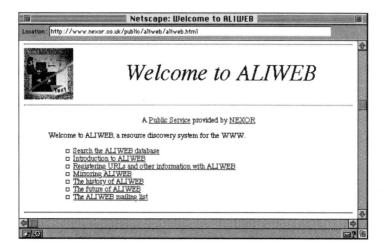

Fig. 11–20   ALIWEB. When you click on the "Search" link, you will be given the opportunity to search using a server close to your home, since ALIWEB is based in Great Britain.

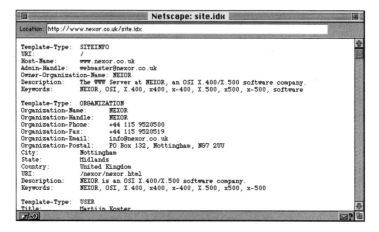

Fig. 11–21   A sample `site.idx` file. For the ALIWEB database to include your site, you need to create a file like this and place it on your server. The file in this illustration is actually ALIWEB's own information.

Point's "Top 5%" Awards

Point Communications (`http://www.pointcom.com/`), a "subsidiary" of Lycos, reviews WWW sites (Fig. 11–22). If they think a site is worthy, they declare it to be in the "Top 5%," quality-wise, of all sites. It's sort of like a "Good Housekeeping" seal for the World Wide Web. If they so honor your site, you can

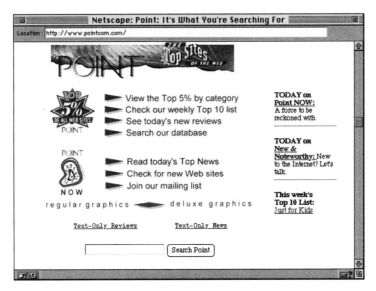

Fig. 11–22   Point Communications' home page. If Point decides that your site is in the 95th percentile of all the sites out there, you will be allowed to put the "Top 5%" badge (the image on the upper left) on your pages. If people see this badge on your home page, they will know they have found a good site, and they will likely explore further.

put a little badge on your pages to brag about your achievement. (And of course, Point maintains a list of all the sites that they have blessed.) This is never a bad thing, so once you think you're really in that top 5%, you can submit your site for review and hope for the best. But be sure to keep your site fresh and interesting, because Point claims that they can and will revoke the anointed status of sites that decline in quality or get stale.

Other Indexes and Lists

You can find a whole list of Web indexes (and indexes of indexes) in Yahoo; see Figure 11–23 for the exact location. Some of these catalogs will take anything, but other cover specific topics; you can look through Yahoo's list for yourself and decide which ones would be appropriate for your site. If you think there's a chance your site might be appropriate, send it in!

There are a number of sites on the Web whose sole purpose is to gather a comprehensive list of links devoted to a particular topic. Let's go back to our earlier example, and say that you run the Web site for MegaKayak, Inc. You should seek out pages like the one shown in Figure 11–24 — the page itself doesn't contain much concrete information, just a huge collection of interesting and informative canoe and kayak links. Make sure that your site is included in this collection, along with any other similar collections about kayaks, boats, or the

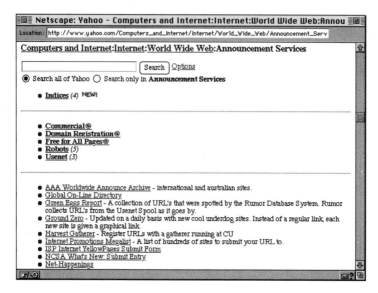

Fig. 11–23   Yahoo's list of World Wide Web indexes and "announcement services." Go through the list and use as many as possible.

outdoors in general; check those pages for information on how to get added. Basically, you want to ensure that if someone surfing the Web is looking for pages about kayak manufacturers, they *will* find your site.

Fig. 11–24   An entire page of rafting, canoeing, and kayaking resources. Anyone with a page even remotely connected to these topics should be sure to get a link to their site on this page.

Many Web catalogs are simply organized by geography, and you should look into these as well. Most local Internet service providers — and many FreeNets, universities, and businesses — maintain a page full of local links (Fig. 11–25).

Fig. 11–25 A page that lists Web sites in and around Portland, Oregon. Most large cities have at least one or two sites like this.

Even though there is something exciting about being able to browse the wares of a corner store in Istanbul, when it comes right down to it most people would rather deal with someone in their real, geographical neighborhood. Everyone likes that hometown touch. And of course, if your site is devoted to a club or organization that has meetings or organized activities in a particular location, this is even more true.

Other People's Pages

The most grass-roots way to spread the word about your site is through other sites just like yours. As we have stressed over and over in this book, you have really arrived as a Web site when you start getting added to other people's pages. Hopefully, your site is good enough that people will add it on their own, and if you're really lucky, their site is somehow related to yours. But, if you run across a site that offers to include a link to your site (e.g., "To get added to my 'hot links' page, <u>click here</u>"), do it. The only real danger is that your link on their page might get sandwiched between "Spike's Smut Shack" and "The Salmonella Page"!

If you are feeling assertive, go ahead and *ask* if people are willing to add your link to their site, if it looks like your page is up their alley. You will have a much better chance of getting a "yes" if you tell them you've already added *their* site to *your* list! You are also better off asking people who already *have* a List-o'-Links; not everyone does.

11.4 KEEPING TRACK OF YOUR SUCCESS

Now that you've done your best to tell the world about your Web pages, you probably want to know whether your publicity efforts are paying off. Has anybody even been to your site? Which part of your site is the most popular? Which part of the world are they coming from? During what time of day are they most likely to visit? There are a couple of different ways to record this information.

Graphical Counters

A graphical counter is simply a picture of a number (Fig. 11–26). The image is generated by a program at your server; every time someone requests its URL, it increments the counter by one and sends a GIF file. Programs like this are available for just about every platform; search for "Access Counts" in Yahoo for a list.

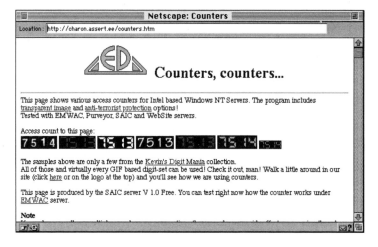

Fig. 11–26   You can use many different styles of digits for use in graphical access counters. This site — in Estonia! — maintains a graphical counter for Windows NT servers.

Note that the number doesn't show how many people have visited that page; it really shows how many times *that image* has been sent. To get a more accurate count, you can politely ask your site's visitors to load your counter's image.

Graphical counters are probably the easiest way to record how many "hits" (HTTP requests) a page has received, and they're kind of fun. Moreover, since the picture is sitting right there on the page, everyone can see how busy your site is (or isn't). Unfortunately, all the calculations on the part of the counter program — not to mention the image files — place a load on your server. They're also pretty inaccurate. Some people can't view images at all, and some people just don't want to. We figured out that somewhere around *half* of all the people visiting one of our pages were actually loading the counter.

The Server Log

Most Web servers keep a log of everything that they do. That log file records when people were in the site, which pages they looked at, and where on the Internet they were. Some servers will also record which browsers are being used to access the site, and from which pages they were referred.

Since you are probably running your own Web server, you have access to any and all log files that your server produces. You could look through the log files by hand — and there are actually times when this is useful, for trouble-shooting purposes — but more likely you will want to get a program that analyzes the log files for you. You can find a list of these under "Log Analysis Tools" in Yahoo.

There are two main kinds of log analysis programs. One kind looks at the server log, finds the information you tell it to look for, and adds a simple number (as plain text) to the appropriate page. The other kind analyzes the log file on your command and produces a detailed report in either text or HTML format (Fig. 11–27). You can make this report available for others to see, or you can keep it to yourself.

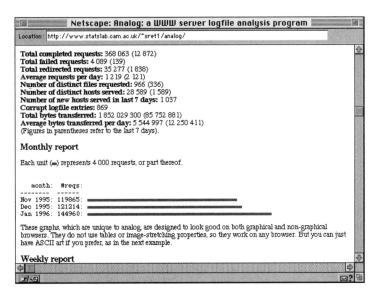

Fig. 11–27 Analog is a program for UNIX or MS-DOS that produces HTML pages that summarize your server's activity. This illustration is actually Analog's demo page; follow this URL to find out more about the program.

Graphical counters and log analysis programs are not mutually exclusive. You could install a numerical image for the benefit of other people who might be curious about your popularity, and then analyze the server log for yourself. You could even analyze the log and then manually add a statement to your pages that says, "1600 people visit this site every day!" Do whatever works best for you and your site.

Feedback

If you don't want to take the trouble to install counters or analyze your log files, you don't have to. But no matter what you do, you should definitely solicit feedback from those who visit your site. A simple `mailto:` link (see page 368) will do the trick, but you may want to try something more complicated, like a comments form or a survey (people like filling out surveys).

Few people will write to you to say they hate your Web site, but if they do, maybe there's really a problem. Similarly, most people won't bother contacting you if they think that your pages are just "okay," so when you get positive e-mail, it's a very good sign. Keep up the good work!

Running CGI Programs
On Your Web Server

*T*his section describes the World Wide Web's powerful programming interface known as the Common Gateway Interface (CGI). This system allows programs to be run on your server with the press of a button. CGI programs (sometimes called *scripts* or *gateway scripts*) allow you to provide customized and up-to-the-minute information to the users of your Web server. These programs also allow you to gather input from users and process it in one way or another.

You can think of CGI as the bridge between your Web server and your application programs. The idea behind this interface is quite simple: a user provides some input data, which is then passed to a program that knows how to use it. The program does its work and gives the result back to the user through the server.

The previous chapters have shown you how to get your Web server running as a simple file server. This is fine for many situations where no interaction with the server is required. Now, you probably want your server to do more, even if it is to just count the number of visitors your server is getting or to allow users to sign a guest book. You may have even greater expectations of your server — you will probably want to run various application programs that perform some specific operation on behalf of your users.

12.1 WHAT YOU CAN DO WITH CGI

You can do almost anything you want with CGI programs. Here are just a few suggestions:

- Display the number of visitors ("hits") to your Web Pages.
- Collect visitors' names and comments in an Internet "guest book."
- Produce a random joke, quote, image, or product.
- Search a database based on detailed queries.

- Play an interactive game (hangman, "mad libs," crossword puzzles, etc.).
- Produce a customized page based on people's input (using HTML forms). A few interesting uses of forms include horoscopes, personality analysis, excuse generators, foreign-language dictionaries, and computer speech of user-selected phrases.

12.2 OVERVIEW OF CGI

CGI is built into your server. When the server receives information (in the form of a URL) from an established connection on the port it is listening to, it first evaluates the contents of the information. If it determines that the requested URL is intended to activate a program residing on the server's machine — because the URL points to the `cgi-bin` directory or to a file that ends in the `.cgi` suffix — it sends the request to the CGI portion of the server software.

How a "Normal" URL Is Processed

When someone sends a request for one of your "normal" URLs to your server, the following actions take place:

1. The browsing program sends the URL to your HTTP server.
2. The HTTP server finds the specified file on your server and sends it to the user's computer without altering the data.
3. The user's computer displays the file in the appropriate format (text, image, sound, movie, etc.).

How a CGI URL Is Processed

When a user asks for a CGI URL from your server, the intermediate steps are a little bit more complicated:

1. A browsing program sends the URL to your HTTP server.
2. Your HTTP server finds a specified CGI program on your system and executes it on *your* machine (an important point).
3. The program that was called in the URL sends the output back to your HTTP server, which passes it on to the browser along with some system environment variables. (The CGI program — *not* your server software — is responsible for preparing the output for display.)
4. The user's Web browser displays this output in the appropriate format.

The "Web-Tender" — an on-line reference for making alcoholic and non-alcoholic drinks — is a good example of using a Web interface to search a database. The search function in the database is a CGI program. Figures 12–1 and 12–2 show the setup and results of searching for all drinks whose names contain the keyword "cider."

Fig. 12–1   The Web-Tender's search page.

Fig. 12–2   The results of a search in the Web-Tender. The name of the search program is `wtnamesrc`; the argument sent to the program was "cider."

The important thing to note is that the result of this database search is not the display of an existing page. As useful as it may seem, there is no file called `cider.html` on this server, because it would need constant updating; not only that, there would have to be a search results page for *every keyword* in the database! The CGI search program "built" this page specifically for this search, by combining the output of the database search with additional text and some basic HTML coding so that the page displays nicely. It is this capability of CGI scripts, when combined with the power of HTML, that makes the Web such a fun and interesting place.

Understanding a CGI URL

Since a URL can point to a program just as well as to a file, you can skip some intermediate steps if you know exactly what you want to search for and how to do it. The following example shows a URL to the Web-Tender that doesn't just go to the Web-Tender's home page; this link actually searches for the keyword phrase "shirley temple."

```
http://www.pvv.unit.no/pallobin/wtnamesrc?shirley+temple
```

Fig. 12–3 Search results for the keyword phrase "shirley temple." Note that the spaces are represented by plus signs; sometimes they are shown as %20, or some other code, but they are *never* displayed as spaces.

As you can see, the URL for this CGI program starts with the site name (www.pvv.unit.no). The next part, /pallobin/, says that the file or program we are looking for is in the pallobin directory at www.pvv.unit.no (the fact that the directory name ends in bin is a clue that we are dealing with CGI here). The name of the CGI program is wtnamesrc. Everything after the question mark — shirley+temple — is the *argument* being sent to this program, using the ISINDEX method of form data submission (we will not cover ISINDEX in this book, because there are newer, better ways to submit queries). The plus sign takes the place of the space character in this example. Figure 12–3 shows the page that this URL points to; we could type this URL in directly without stopping by the original search page that we saw in Figure 12–1.

You will often see URLs that end in pairs of words joined by equal signs (=) and separated by ampersands (&). For instance, Figure 12–4 was created by a form in a site that creates maps on demand (in GIF format) from raw cartographic data, and the various parameters for creating the map are visible at the end of the URL. When you can see the arguments in the URL like this, you know that either the method of form submission was set to GET, or no method was specified (see page 303 for details).

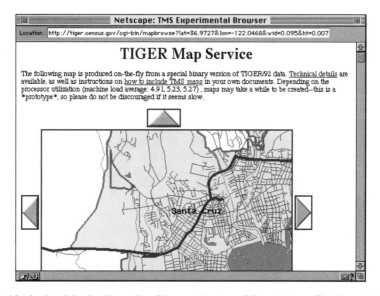

Fig. 12–4 Look in the "Location:" box at the top of the window. The form that created this page passed a number of arguments (such as latitude, longitude, and the width and height of the map) as part of the URL.

The drink database program on www.pvv.unit.no uses its arguments as input for a search; the TIGER Mapping Service uses them to generate maps on the fly. Both programs parse and interpret the submitted data as necessary, create an output file that includes HTML tags, then send the newly created page to the browser for display. You could include a link to either of these CGI programs, complete with arguments, in one of your Web pages just by including an <A HREF> tag with the URL and all of its arguments; we will do something similar to this on page 297.

When a CGI program uses the POST method of form data submission (again, see page 303 for details about HTML form syntax), the arguments are not shown as part of the URL; only the software knows what's being sent. This can be useful if you want to keep things secret or if you don't want to confuse anyone with your cryptic variable names.

CGI Programming Languages

You may be wondering what type of program can be a CGI program. It can be any program that runs on your computer! This can include programs in any of the following languages, or others:

- Perl
- UNIX shell scripts (such as sh, csh, and ksh)
- C and C++
- Pascal
- Fortran
- Visual Basic
- AppleScript
- Python
- TCL

One of the most popular programming languages for CGI programs is Perl. This is due in large part to the fact that Perl is written with lines of ASCII text that can be used by any system. Because so many people use Perl, there are many examples of Perl-based CGI programs available on the Web. To use Perl with your server, all you need is a Perl interpreter and a way for that interpreter to communicate with your server. See the chapter that's specific to your system for more information on getting Perl to work with your server software.

12.3 USING CGI PROGRAMS

Before we discuss the details of writing CGI programs from scratch, let's take a look at how you make existing CGI programs work on your system. This will allow you to become familiar with basic CGI concepts and techniques before starting the more complex task of writing your own programs.

Executing Other People's Programs

As long as you know the URL of a CGI program on another server, you can execute this CGI program from the comfort of your own computer. You don't need any special compilers or interpreters; the other system is responsible for that.

Let's examine how to do this with the Yahoo search tool. To search Yahoo, you usually access Yahoo's Home Page (http://www.yahoo.com/), then enter a keyword in the text box next to the Search button. However, you can bypass this first page by including a link to Yahoo's CGI program, which is named, appropriately enough, search.

The URL of the Yahoo database's search engine is as follows: http://search.yahoo.com/bin/search. You can specify a simple search string by including a value for the argument p. For example, you can search for "chocolate" with the URL http://search.yahoo.com/bin/search?p=chocolate (the question mark starts the argument that is passed to the search program).

To execute this CGI program from your page, you merely add this modified URL to the HTML source. Figure 12–5 shows a simple Web page that includes a link that searches for Yahoo's most recent collection of chocolate links; the HTML source for Figure 12–5 is listed below, and the results of the search are shown in Figure 12–6.

```
<HTML>
<TITLE>More Chocolate Links</TITLE>
<BODY>

<H2>More good chocolate links:</H2>

<UL>
<LI>
<A HREF="http://sobe.com/sobe/market/leonidas/index.html">
Leonidas - Belgian Chocolate</A>
<LI>
<A HREF="http://www.giftex.com/belgian/">
The Belgian Chocolate Shop (Toronto)</A>
<LI>
<A HREF="http://search.yahoo.com/bin/search?p=chocolate">
Search Yahoo for even more chocolate pages</A>
</UL>

</BODY>
</HTML>
```

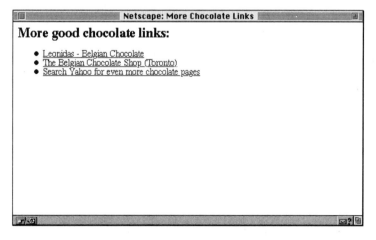

Fig. 12–5 The Web page created by the HTML source above. The third link executes a Yahoo search command.

Finding CGI Programs

The concept of executing CGI programs from a Web page is relatively simple. But how do you find programs that you can use in your *own* server? Easy — you ask people, you search the Net, or you write your own.

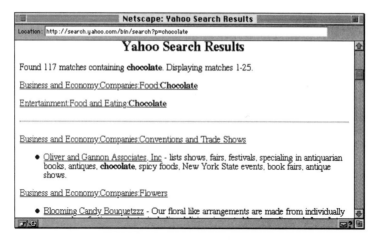

Fig. 12–6 The results of clicking on the third link in Figure 12–5. Note that Netscape's "Location:" box shows the complete URL for this search, including the arguments.

There are thousands of CGI programs and routines all over the Net. Many are available for your use; others are available for you to examine and learn from. To find sample Perl CGI programs and libraries of routines, use an Internet search tool (such as Yahoo or Lycos) to find the latest libraries, or check out the following URLs:

- Index of Perl/HTML archives:
  http://homepage.seas.upenn.edu/~mengwong/perlhtml.html
- Matt's script archive:
  http://www.worldwidemart.com/scripts/
- Jeffrey's Perl stuff:
  http://www.wg.omron.co.jp/~jfriedl/perl/
- Perl WWW development libraries:
  http://www.oac.uci.edu/indiv/ehood/perlWWW/dev/index.html

Installing CGI Programs on Your System

If you find a freeware CGI program that interests you, you can save a copy of it on your system with your browser's "save" or "download to disk" function. If you have a graphical interface, you can even cut-and-paste the text from your browser's screen into your word processor.

To use CGI programs with your Web server, the server must be able to tell which files are programs to be executed and which are simply documents to be served. Many CGI scripts are plain text files; how does the server know whether that's a database search engine or your grocery list?

In UNIX and Windows httpd servers, the distinction is usually accomplished by way of a special directory, usually named cgi-bin. Anything in that directory — and that directory *only* — will be treated as a CGI script. (On multi-user systems, users can have a `cgi-bin` subdirectory off of their home directories, as long as this feature has been preset in the server configuration. This can create administration problems; see page 311 for details.)

On a Macintosh server running MacHTTP, CGI programs can live anywhere in your server space, but they must have a suffix or Macintosh file type that indicates that they are scripts rather than ordinary documents (see Chapter 9 for details). The most commonly used suffix for this purpose is `.cgi`.

UNIX servers can also use a `.cgi` suffix to designate scripts anywhere in the server file space, but only if you add the following line to your server resource map file (`httpd/conf/srm.conf` in UNIX):

```
AddType  application/x-httpd-cgi  .cgi
```

If you are using a UNIX system, you also need to worry about file permissions; your scripts must be readable and executable by everyone. Type the following line at your command prompt if you're not sure how your permissions are currently set:

```
chmod 755 file_name.cgi
```

See Appendix B for more information on UNIX file permissions.

12.4 CREATING CGI PROGRAMS

Even though there are a lot of CGI programs available on the Internet, you may find that you need to write one of your own to handle a specific function. This book doesn't teach you everything about writing CGI programs; you'll probably need a language-specific reference or tutorial for that, plus some basic knowledge of programming principles. Here we will show the start-to-finish process for writing, testing, and using a very simple Perl script that you could use as a CGI program. In Chapter 13, we'll provide some more complex examples.

A Simple Example: A Personalized Poem

This Perl script does very little; it merely asks for the user's name, then prints a poem accompanied by a personalized greeting.

Figure 12–7 shows the Web page that contains the link to the CGI program; it requests the user's name and provides a "click here" button that activates the Perl script. The source HTML for Figure 12–7 is presented below; refer to section 12.5 for more information on creating your own forms.

```
<HTML>
<TITLE>Clickable Poetry</TITLE>
<BODY>

<H2>Poem of the Week</H2>

<FORM method="POST"
```

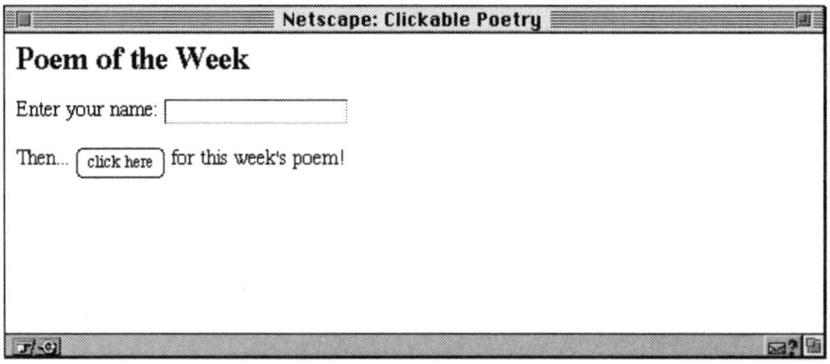

Fig. 12–7   An HTML form. Clicking on the "click here" button will run a program that reads whatever is typed into the text box as input.

```
     action="http://parkweb.com/cgi-bin/poem.cgi">
Enter your name:
<INPUT TYPE="text" NAME="yourname">
<P>
Then...
<INPUT TYPE="submit" VALUE="click here"> for this week's poem!
</FORM>

</BODY>
</HTML>
```

When someone named "Sven" enters his name in the box and clicks the button, a program is run on parkweb.com's server, and Sven receives a page that looks like Figure 12–8. Here is the HTML for that page:

```
<HTML>
<BODY>
<H2>This Week's Poem</H2>
Here's your poem, Sven:
<P>
Thirty days have September, April, June, and November.<BR>
All the rest have peanut butter,<BR>
Except for Grandma; she rides a bicycle.
</HTML>
</BODY>
```

Notice that Sven's name is actually part of the source HTML for that page, because this batch of HTML was created especially for Sven. The actual Perl script that generated the customized Web page is presented below:

```
#!perl
# This script displays a personalized poem in HTML.

# We'll need have the "cgi-lib.pl" file installed in order to
# use this script:
require "cgi-lib.pl";

# This is one of the routines in "cgi-lib.pl"; it converts the
```

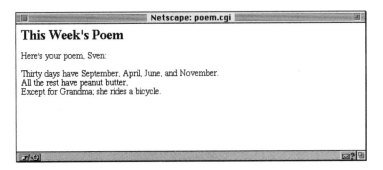

Fig. 12–8   Sven's personalized poem page.

```
# form data into something Perl can understand:
&ReadParse;

# Print the HTTP header, followed by an empty line:
print "Content-type: text/html\n\n";

# Print the HTML source:
print <<ENDOFTEXT;

<HTML>
<BODY>
<H2>This Week's Poem</H2>
Here's your poem, $in{'yourname'}:
<P>
Thirty days have September, April, June, and November.<BR>
All the rest have peanut butter,<BR>
Except for Grandma; she rides a bicycle.
</HTML>
</BODY>

ENDOFTEXT
```

Take a close look at this Perl script. There are a few things you can see without knowing anything about programming:

- The first line of the script is `#!perl`. If you were to use this script with your server, you would need to adjust this to indicate the location of the Perl interpreter on your system; for example, `#!/usr/local/bin/perl` .
- We needed to include the statement `require "cgi-lib.pl";`. This gives the script access to the programming subroutines in the file `cgi-lib.pl`, which we have installed in our Perl interpreter's "library" directory (see Chapter 7, 8, or 9 for information on how to do this in your system). Without `cgi-lib.pl`, form data is very difficult to process in Perl.
- A script that sends output back to the Web must produce an *HTTP header*, which tells a Web browser what kind of file it is about to receive. In this case, the header is `Content-type: text/html`, followed by a mandatory

empty line. (The \n character sequence sends a line break, so two \n sequences produce a complete blank line.)

- There is only one unusual element in the rest of the script: instead of "Sven," our Perl code says `$in{'yourname'}`; when you use `cgi-lib.pl` to read form data, all your variables will be in the form `$in{'variable'}`. (Note that this variable name matches the name we used in the <FORM> definition: `NAME="yourname"`.)

If you read Chapter 13 and Appendix C, this will all make perfect sense, and you'll be able to create Perl scripts far more complicated than this one. It's really not very hard!

12.5 HTML FORMS: AN OVERVIEW

Forms are just HTML files (or portions thereof) enclosed within the <FORM> tag. They are used to collect input from people browsing the Web, and they are very useful for passing several arguments at once to a CGI program.

Like everything else displayed on a Web page, you use HTML tags to construct a form; tag attributes specify variable names and default values that are then passed to the CGI program for processing. There are several types of form input, such as text entry fields, individual- and multiple-select menus, checkboxes and radio buttons, and submit and clear buttons. Each of these input devices works differently, and you have to decide which is the best to use for your input information.

Appendix A of this book is a general HTML quick reference guide, but we did not include forms there because they must be used with a CGI interface, and you need to read this chapter to find out how to do that. Therefore, our forms reference guide is located right here in Chapter 12. For even more detailed coverage of forms and their associated CGI programs, you can also find a number of excellent resources on the Web. Here are a few URLs to look into:

- Carlos' Forms Tutorial:
  `http://robot0.ge.uiuc.edu/~carlosp/cs317/cft.html`
- CGI for the Non-Programmer:
  `http://www.catt.ncsu.edu/~bex/tutor/index.html`
- Brian's Home Page Creation Information:
  `http://www.mindport.net/~b_ruth/htmlstuff.html`
- NCSA's Fill-Out Form Support:
  `http://www.ncsa.uiuc.edu/SDG/Software/Mosaic/Docs/fill-out-forms`

In addition, there are a few lists of forms-related links in Yahoo. From Yahoo's "Computers and Internet" section, go to "Internet: World Wide Web: Programming: Forms," or "Software: Data Formats: HTML."

The <FORM> Tag

Form markup tags begin with <FORM> and end with </FORM>. The basic syntax for the <FORM> tag is:

```
<FORM method="{GET or POST}" action="URL">
-- Form definition goes here --
</FORM>
```

All your form input elements (buttons, text areas, etc.) will go inside the <FORM> tag; so will any text that you include to describe the input elements. In fact, the only thing you can *not* include inside a form is another form.

If you have more than one form on a single page, be aware each one will have its own "submit" button, and that button doesn't care what's in all the other forms.

Method   The method attribute of the <FORM> tag tells a Web browser how it should send data back to the server. POST is, according to the HTML gurus, the "preferred" method; it sends the data as a separate, mostly invisible chunk of information with its own HTTP header. GET sends the variables as part of a URL. If you do not specify a method, the default is GET.

The GET method is handy if you want to let people pass particular arguments to your CGI programs from anywhere in the world, but some servers impose a limit on the size of a URL. POST is nice because it "hides" the inner workings of your programs from the world, and there is no limit on how much information can be passed; you can send entire pages as form data if you want.

Action   This attribute specifies where to send the information in the form. The URL usually points to a CGI program, which decodes the form's input data. On most servers, if you are referencing a script on the same server as the form, you don't need to include the full URL — just the relative path.

Some server packages require that all CGI programs reside in a directory called cgi-bin, or a directory that has cgi-bin as an alias. Other servers require that all CGI programs end in the .cgi suffix. In our examples, we will do both.

If you do not specify a value for the action attribute, the form will execute *itself*. This can be useful when the <FORM> tags have been generated by search scripts or other programs that are often run repeatedly (for example, see our search program on page 345 of Chapter 13), but you must never leave the action attribute blank on a plain HTML page, because plain old Web pages can't take CGI arguments!

The <INPUT> Tag

<INPUT> tags are used within forms to create simple form input devices, such as text fields and buttons. The syntax of <INPUT> is similar to the <IMG> tag (see page 367 in Appendix A), in that it can include a number of attributes and

does not require a closing tag. Here is a sample `<INPUT>` tag, followed by descriptions of all the possible attributes:

```
<INPUT type="text" name="variable1" value="Hello!">
```

Type="*type*"   The `type` attribute is not strictly *required*; if you leave it out, you will get a one-line text box. (Even if that's what you wanted, you should include a `type` attribute anyway, if only so you can keep track of your own markup tags.) The `type` attribute defines which *type* of input device is created by the `<INPUT>` tag. So far, there are eight different types, which are described below. Figure 12–9 shows six of the types (we can't *show* you the `hidden` type!), along with the HTML tags used to create them; if you get confused while reading this section, the illustration should help.

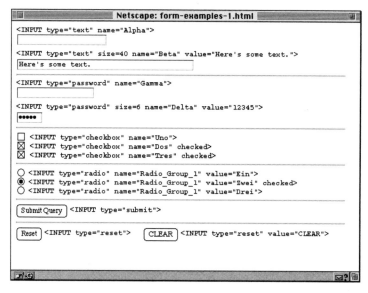

Fig. 12–9   Some of the various types of input devices, and the HTML tags used to create them. Note that the two buttons at the bottom of the window are *both* `reset` buttons, but the second one has a `value` attribute set to `"CLEAR"`.

Text   If for some reason you do not specify a type of input, `text` will be the default. It is a simple, one-line text entry box.

Password   This is just like `text`, except characters that are typed into the box show up as bullets or asterisks, so other people cannot see what is being typed. It is useful for password information (hence the name, `password`).

Checkbox   This is a small square that can be checked or unchecked by someone viewing your page. A CGI program will read a checked box as `on`; unchecked boxes are ignored.

Radio   Typically, radio buttons are used in groups in which every radio button has exactly the same `name` attribute (see below). When one button in the group is checked, all others are automatically *un*checked. Each radio button *must* have a unique `value` attribute (again, see below), or the server won't know which button was checked.

Submit   This creates a button whose purpose is to send all the data in the current form to the program specified in the `<FORM action>` attribute. You can use the `value` attribute to specify what the button looks like.

Reset   This creates a button that, when selected, returns *all* form elements to their default values. This is often used as a "Clear" button, if the defaults are empty fields.

Hidden   If you include a hidden input element on a page, data will be sent to the CGI program without any input from the person accessing the page. This can be useful if you have a long string of forms that need to keep track of the same data; by putting the data in hidden variables, it need not be typed in repeatedly.

Image   This is a poorly documented but very interesting input type. An `image` input device works essentially like a standard image map, and the tag can contain attributes normally found in the `<IMG>` tag, such as `height`, `width`, and `align`. A `src` attribute — which defines the picture that will be used in the map — is *required*. The advantage of using form-based maps over "normal" image maps is that you can process the input however you like. The disadvantage is that you do have to write a program; you can't use a pre-configured "image-map" program. Note that clicking on a form-based map has the effect of submitting the entire form, so any other input fields must be filled in *before* clicking. One more caveat: not all browsers support form-based maps yet.

Name="*name*"   The `name` attribute specifies the name of a variable that will be sent to the CGI program named in the `<FORM action>` attribute. CGI programs generally take input in the form of *name/value pairs* — each variable has a name assigned to it, and a value which that name represents. If there is no name assigned to an input element, no value can be sent. `Reset` buttons are the only input types that never have names (and therefore cannot send values).

A set of radio buttons (a group of buttons of which only *one* can be selected) must all have the same name. If a set of checkboxes all have the same name, then more than one value will be sent under that name. This is acceptable, but it makes it a little harder to write the corresponding CGI program.

In the case of form-based image maps (`type="image"`), *two* name/value pairs are sent: *name*.x and *name*.y, corresponding to the X and Y coordinates of a click on the picture.

Value="*value*"   For text and password entry fields, the `value` attribute specifies the default text that appears in the box when the form is first called up. If the person looking at the page does not change the defaults, then the CGI program receives whatever was included in `value`; if they make any changes, the name/value pair will include the new input instead.

For checkboxes, radio buttons, submit buttons, and hidden variables, `value` sets the value of the variable that is sent to the CGI program as part of a name/value pair. Radio buttons and checkboxes send *no* value if they are *not* checked. Checkboxes default to sending the value "on" if no `value` attribute is present; but for radio buttons and hidden variables, a `value` attribute must be used or they will not accomplish anything.

For `submit` and `reset` buttons, the `value` attribute is mostly used to tell a browsing program what to write on the button; if a `submit` button also has a `name` attribute, the writing on the button is sent as part of a name/value pair.

Checked This attribute is only used with checkboxes and radio buttons. When present, it indicates that the button or box will be selected by default when the page is first loaded. See Figure 12–9 for examples.

Size=*n* This attribute is only used with text and password fields. It represents the size, in characters, of the box. Since every browser sets its own default font, the actual size — in inches or pixels — will vary somewhat.

Maxlength=*n* The `maxlength` attribute lets you limit how many characters can be typed in a text or password box. (The `size` attribute sets the on-screen size of a text or password input element, but it does not prevent people from typing more text than will visibly fit.)

The <SELECT> Tag

<SELECT> serves much the same purpose as the <INPUT> tag, but it defines different devices and has a different syntax. <SELECT> needs an opening and closing tag, and it must contain one or more <OPTION> tags.

A <SELECT> tag creates one of two kinds of selectable lists: either a pop-up menu — a list of items of which only one is visible until you click on it with your mouse — or a rectangular list box that includes scroll bars if there are more items than can fit in the box. Figure 12–10 illustrates two selectable lists, along with their source HTML.

Name="*name*" This `name` attribute is required; it is the name of the variable that will be sent to the CGI program along with the value of whichever list item was selected. (If it is a multiple-select list — see below — there can be more than one value associated with this name.)

Size=*n* If the `size` attribute is present, the <SELECT> tag will create a scrolling list box rather than a pop-up menu. The `size` attribute does *not* define how many items are in the list, just how many of them are visible at once.

If `size` is not specified, the list will be a pop-up menu, unless it is defined as a multiple-select list. A multiple-select list will *always* be a scrolling box, and its size will be set to the total number of items in the list if none is given.

Multiple If this attribute is present in the <SELECT> tag (it needs no value), more than one item can be selected from the list. As was the case with identically-named checkboxes, this makes the CGI processing a little bit more

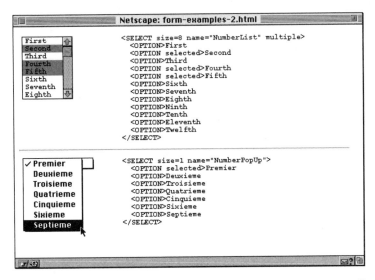

Fig. 12–10 Selectable lists. The top half of the window illustrates a scrolling list box; the bottom half is a pop-up menu. We have clicked on the pop-up menu and are about to select "Septieme"; "Premier" was originally selected by default.

difficult, because you will have more than one value associated with a given variable name.

<OPTION> Tags   The names of the items in a pop-up menu or scrolling list are set by placing one or more <OPTION> tags between the open and close of a selectable list tag. (Note that within a <SELECT> tag is the *only* place that you can use <OPTION> tags!)

Value="value"   The <OPTION> tag may contain a value attribute. If it does, value defines which value will be submitted when that option is selected. If there is no value attribute, the actual text of the list item will be sent as the value. It is a good idea to use value, because you'd rather have your CGI program deal with variable names like "links" than "My Fantastic Collection of Web Links."

Selected   The <OPTION> tag can take one more attribute: selected. When present, this causes a list item to be selected by default when the page is first loaded. See Figure 12–10 for examples.

The <TEXTAREA> Tag

A <TEXTAREA> is a multi-line text entry box. Its syntax is similar to the <SELECT> tag in that it needs to be opened and closed. However, since this is not a list, there are no <OPTION> tags.

<TEXTAREA> has no value attribute; its *plain text* default contents are defined by everything between the opening and closing tags, *including the line*

breaks. If you include HTML markup tags in the default contents, they will show up just as you type them, brackets and all. See Figure 12–11 for a couple examples of multi-line text areas.

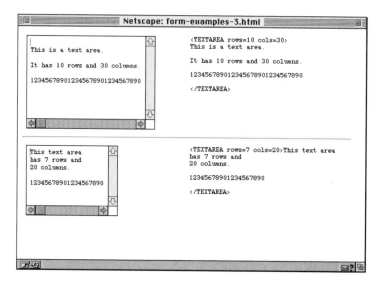

Fig. 12–11   Two multi-line text areas. Note that *all* of the line breaks between the opening and closing <TEXTAREA> tags are included as default text, even the one right after the opening tag; this is why the contents of the first box begin with a blank line.

Name="*name*"   This is just like the `name` attribute for all the other form input devices; it defines the name of the variable that will be sent to the CGI program as part of a name/value pair. (Text areas have the capacity to send very large values!)

Rows=*n*   Cols=*n*   These attributes set the number of rows and columns, in characters, that will visibly fit in the text area. Like the `size` attribute of one-line text fields and password fields, they do *not* limit how much text can be typed into the box.

The best way to learn more about forms is to create some. First, figure out how your HTML markup tags affect the on-screen appearance of the various input devices, then pay attention to what happens to your name/value pairs as you type in different text, click different buttons, or change attributes in the source. To find out what data your form is submitting (that is, what your name/value pairs look like), just set the `action` attribute in your <FORM> tag to point to the `post-query` program at the following location:

```
http://hoohoo.ncsa.uiuc.edu/cgi-bin/post-query
```

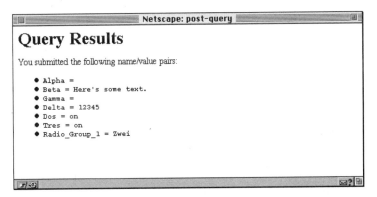

Fig. 12–12 This is what was sent back by NCSA's `post-query` program when we clicked the "Submit Query" button in Figure 12–9. (Refer to 12–9 to see exactly where these name/value pairs came from.) Note that the blank text entry fields show up here as empty variables, but unchecked radio buttons and checkboxes do not show up at all.

This is a program that does nothing more than read your form's input and spit it back out at you, with the variable names and their values clearly marked (Fig. 12–12). If you are going to be using Perl, you can get a Perl script for your own server that does everything the aforementioned `post-query` does, and more. It's called `generic.pl`, and you can find it at this URL:

```
http://homepage.seas.upenn.edu/~mengwong/forms/
```

Don't forget to fix up `generic.pl` so that your server can use it! UNIX users need to set file permissions, check the `perl` path in the first line, and make sure that it's either in a `cgi-bin` directory or has an appropriate suffix; Windows users must place it in the appropriate directory; Macintosh users must use MacPerl to save it as a Perl CGI script with the proper suffix.

12.6 TESTING YOUR CGI SCRIPTS

Once you have created some HTML forms and CGI scripts that run on your server, you should test them before allowing access by others. There is a lot going on within the server when CGI is activated, so there are a number of potential problems. To complicate matters, the input you provide to your programs comes from your server, so command-line testing may not always give you accurate information.

Check Your Setup

While it is impossible to predict the errors that you may encounter, the first thing you should do is make sure you have your environment set up correctly.

Check to see that there is enough free memory available for everything to function properly, and that any system environment variables have the right settings. UNIX users need to make sure that file permissions are as they should be. If your programs require the use of other files (such as `cgi-lib.pl`), be sure those files are in a place that can be accessed by the compiler or interpreter.

Check Your Forms

Start your testing by viewing the page from which the CGI script is called. You can do this off-line by calling up the HTML page with an "open local file" selection in your Web browser. Be sure that everything appears on the screen exactly as you designed it. This includes input boxes, radio buttons, tables, and so on. You should also enter in the information and make the selections you would expect the user to make. You may need to be on-line when you go to submit your form, as some servers require a TCP/IP connection to function correctly. Besides, you always want to be simulating the actual events that will be occurring on your system.

Run Programs Locally

If your form is working correctly, or if you have a program that is called directly from a URL without user input, you should test it by running it locally on your system. If your program is a Perl script — and you are using a system that allows command line options (UNIX or DOS) — use Perl's debugging option (`-d`) and see if you are given any errors or warnings. (If your program was written in a compiled language such as C, you probably would have seen any critical errors during the compiling and linking process.) Simply type the following command at your DOS or UNIX prompt:

```
perl -d filename
```

Mac users cannot use the `-d` command line option, but MacPerl does provide some useful debugging information in the window entitled "MacPerl."

Even if your system thinks the program runs flawlessly, you still need to make sure it does what *you* want it to do. If you are running the program locally, you may want to insert a few bogus lines of codes that assign different values to the variables within the program. Or get on line and fill out the input form with bizarre stuff and see what happens.

Check the HTTP Header

Your script must print an HTTP header (the `Content-type` line followed by a blank line) as the first line of output from your script. If you forget, your script might look fine when you run it locally, but won't look right when you call it from your HTML file — the output of the script will probably appear as a text file instead of HTML.

12.7 CGI SECURITY

CGI programs and scripts are potentially dangerous, because they *run* on your system rather than simply *residing* on it. The potential damage they can cause is limitless. A malicious Perl script could delete every file that it has access to with a single line of code. This is not meant to scare you away from having safe, solid, and useful programs available on your system, but there are a few things you should be aware of.

As we said in the previous section, test all your scripts thoroughly before making them available to the world. Make sure they don't have unintended side effects, such as clogging your entire hard drive with bloated output files. If possible, set up your server so that CGI programs can only be called from pages on your site. You don't want people halfway across the world using your image map program with their pages.

Remember that your scripts have access to your entire system, not just your server space. Theoretically, if you prompt a user for a file name in an HTML input form, they could conceivably enter a file name such as `../../../secret`. Depending on what your script does, it might be possible for people to view or change the contents of a file that you did not intend to make public. Therefore, you should be very careful with file operations in your CGI scripts; if file names are to be entered, present a list or menu rather than allowing free-form input.

Multi-user systems present a unique challenge. If you just have a few trust-worthy and competent programmers, it is not unreasonable to allow them to set up their own `cgi-bin` directories that outsiders can access. If you have a lot of users, or users that you don't know very well, be sure to have only a single `cgi-bin` directory that only you can write to. You should play librarian by having users e-mail you scripts (or paths to programs) that they want in the `cgi-bin` directory. This way, you can test and evaluate the scripts before making them available to other users.

12.8 JAVA AND JAVASCRIPT

Java and JavaScript —languages that allow people to create client-side Web applications — are quickly becoming very popular. These are two distinct products that work in very different ways, as explained below. Java is a product of Sun Microsystems, and JavaScript comes from Netscape. Both are supported by Netscape 2.0, but most other browsers will likely support them in the very near future.

Java Java is a full-fledged object-oriented programming language, similar in design to C++. With Java, you can create stand-alone programs or programs that can be run by a supporting Web browser. You can get the particulars of the Java programming language and the Java Development Kit at Sun's Java Web site: `http://java.sun.com/` (Fig. 12–13).

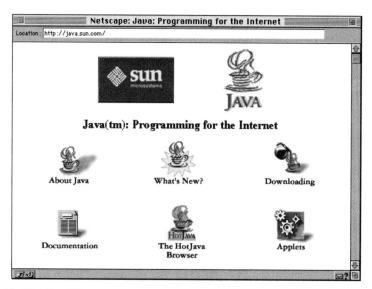

Fig. 12–13   Sun Microsystems' Java home page.

The executable program that Java creates — called an *applet* — is sent from an HTTP server to the calling browser, which then executes it locally. Java is often used to create applets whose appearance in the browser's window is defined by an HTML tag. The following line of HTML code requests an applet called dance from the server:

```
<APPLET code="dance" width=100 height=100> </APPLET>
```

The dance applet, which could be something like a short movie of dancing coffee beans, is executed in an area that is 100 pixels high by 100 pixels wide. The HTTP server only sends the dance program to the Java-supported browser, which then executes it on its own. This is the opposite of the way CGI works; CGI programs are executed on the HTTP server, and only the results are sent back to the calling browser.

JavaScript   JavaScript should not be confused with the Java programming language. While some of the syntax may be similar, it is fundamentally different. JavaScript consists of instructions written in ASCII text and placed into HTML files (between the <SCRIPT> and </SCRIPT> tags). These instructions are interpreted by the client's browser (once again, the opposite of the way CGI programs work). You can find complete documentation for JavaScript at the following URL:

```
http://www.netscape.com/eng/mozilla/Gold/handbook/javascript/
```

You can also find some interesting uses of both Java and JavaScript at this location:

```
http://www.gamelan.com/
```

Security Because the programs from each of these languages execute on the browser side, there is the potential for security problems. However, browser developers have placed huge restrictions on what these programs can do on the browser's home system. A lot of holes were discovered in the beta releases of Netscape 2.0 and were corrected with subsequent releases. You can keep abreast of developments in Java and JavaScript security by regularly reading Lincoln Stein's wonderful World Wide Web Security FAQ:

```
http://www-genome.wi.mit.edu/WWW/faqs/www-security-faq.html
```

12.9 CONCLUSION

Now that you've tried out a few examples, and you're confident about the security of your server, you're more than ready to fill your Web server with all kinds of Perl scripts so that you can do more than simply serve up files. Remember, the Web is an interactive medium; you should try to make visits to your site as enjoyable as possible, so that people will come back again and again.

If you are like most Webmasters, you will want to do much more than give people personalized poetry! So, move on to the next chapter, where we'll teach you how to really have some fun with Perl and CGI.

A Bunch Of Perl Scripts

*I*f you want to know everything there is to know about programming in Perl, you should probably buy a book about it. If you want to know all the basics, read this chapter and Appendix C. If you just want a couple of scripts that you can run on your system, and you don't really care how or why they work, then you can stick with this chapter.

The goal here is to make you familiar with the Perl programming environment by creating a couple of fun, useless programs and a few very useful ones. You are encouraged to modify these Perl scripts as much as you like, in order to get them to do what *you* want them to do.

There are a few different ways you can use this chapter. You could just sit down and read it, and try to follow along. That may be helpful, but it won't be much fun. If you're really a glutton for punishment, you could type all of these scripts into your computer by yourself. But we recommend copying them off the CD that comes with this book, or downloading them from our Web site at `http://www.prenhall.com/~palmer/scripts/`. Then you can try them out with your own server, and you won't have to expend much energy to do it! (See Appendix E for more details about the CD and the Web site.)

13.1 AN HTML MAD LIB

Remember "mad libs"? You ask someone for goofy words of a certain type, and then plug their answers into the blank spaces of a little story. So if you ask for a present-tense verb, a road, an adjective, an animal, and a person's name, you might end up with sentences like "One day, I was *swimming* down *the New Jersey Turnpike* when a *chilly centipede* named *Amanda* attacked me." We will show you how to create a Perl script that will generate a mad lib using words entered on an HTML form. What could possibly be the purpose of having mad libs in your

Web site? Frankly, there's no purpose at all. But it might be good for a couple gig-gles, and you'll learn about writing Perl scripts.

By now, you should have tried out – or at least read – the "personalized poem" script in Chapter 12. The poem script introduced you to the following con-cepts: use of `ReadParse` (from `cgi-lib.pl`), HTTP headers, printing text, and using a variable that was passed from a form. The mad lib will serve as a review of those concepts, and it will introduce you to the use of multiple variables in a single form.

Here's the mad lib template we will be working with:

Health Bulletin

Two [adjective] studies in the current issue of the *[country] Journal of Medi-cine* [adverb] prove that prolonged exposure to [plural noun] causes bizarre mutations of the [body part] in 9 out of 10 [animals] studied in the laboratory.

Dr. [person's name], a spokesperson for the University of [country], which sponsored the study, had this to say: "We think it's very important that the public be made aware of this [adjective] hazard. At least [number] people have [past participle of a verb] already!"

First, build the form that will collect the input for the mad lib (Fig. 13–1). If you want, you can spruce this up and make it into a fancy layout with images and headings and so forth, but we'll just stick with the basics for now. (If you try out this script, make sure you replace the URL in the `action` attribute of the `<FORM>` tag with the name of the script on your server!).

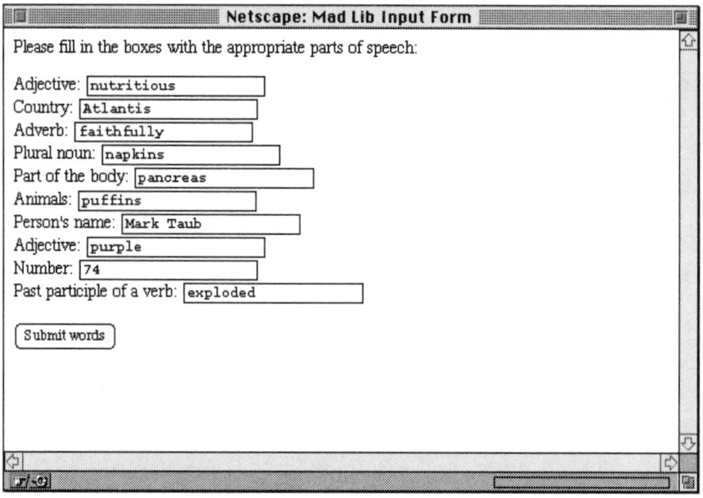

Fig. 13–1   The form that will collect words for the mad lib. The boxes will be empty by default, but in this illustration, we've typed in some words.

```
<HTML>
<HEAD><TITLE>Mad Lib Input Form</TITLE></HEAD>
<BODY>

<FORM method="POST"
    action="http://yoursite.com/cgi-bin/madlib.cgi">

Please fill in the boxes with the appropriate parts of speech:
<P>
Adjective:          <INPUT type="text" name="adjective1"> <BR>
Country:            <INPUT type="text" name="country"> <BR>
Adverb:             <INPUT type="text" name="adverb"> <BR>
Plural noun:        <INPUT type="text" name="nouns"> <BR>
Part of the body:   <INPUT type="text" name="bodypart"> <BR>
Animals:            <INPUT type="text" name="animals"> <BR>
Person's name:      <INPUT type="text" name="person"> <BR>
Adjective:          <INPUT type="text" name="adjective2"> <BR>
Number:             <INPUT type="text" name="number"> <BR>
Past participle of a verb:  <INPUT type="text" name="verbed">
<P>

<INPUT type="submit" value="Submit words">

</FORM>

</BODY>
</HTML>
```

For more information on constructing forms, see Chapter 12, pages 302–309. Now you need to write a Perl program to take the input from the HTML page and synthesize it with the mad lib. Let's go through the program one step at a time.

1. Tell the server where the Perl interpreter is located. On our LINUX system, it's in the /usr/bin directory.

   ```
   #!/usr/bin/perl
   ```

   (If you are using a Macintosh or Windows server, this step is not crucial; #!perl will suffice.)

2. Allow this script to use subroutines from cgi-lib.pl. This file must be in Perl's lib (libraries) directory. Note that this statement and all the following statements must end in a semicolon.

   ```
   require "cgi-lib.pl";
   ```

3. Call the ReadParse subroutine from cgi-lib.pl. This converts all form data into a single, easy-to-use, associative array (which is called %in).

   ```
   &ReadParse;
   ```

4. Start building the HTML page that will be created. The first part – which is absolutely mandatory – is an HTTP header, followed by a blank line. If you do not start your script's output with a proper HTTP header, you are violating HTTP standards, and there will be an error every time. In this case, the header will be `Content-type: text/html`, because the output is an HTML page. If the output was going to be plain text, the header would be `Content-type: text/plain`.

You can output any text you want by using Perl's `print` function. Within the `print` statement's quotes, special characters are indicated by using a backslash. All you need to know for now is that a backslash followed by n is a line break, so `\n\n` creates a blank line.

Here's the Perl code for the HTTP header:

```
print "Content-type: text/html\n\n";
```

5. Print out the actual HTML source for the output page. You could do this by typing a Perl `print` statement for every line of HTML code, but there's a clever trick you can use to make life much easier: `print<<ENDOFTEXT;`. This says, in English, "print out everything from the end of this line all the way up to the ENDOFTEXT marker." (ENDOFTEXT is an arbitrary marker; you could just as well use *any* unusual character sequence.) This way, you can type in your HTML code exactly the way you want it to look. If you are using a graphical interface, you can even paste the HTML source from another document directly into your Perl script.

There's a slight catch, of course. You don't want to give exactly the same HTML to everyone; you need to include their mad lib words. So every time there's a blank space in the mad lib, type a variable instead. All the variables will be of the form `$in{'variablename'}`, where *variablename* is the value of the `name` attribute of the associated `<INPUT>` tag from the form that was used to collect the data. For example, the first form input box asked for an adjective, and the HTML tag included the attribute `name="adjective1"`, so your Perl script thinks of that noun as `$in{'adjective1'}`.

Rather than list step 5 by itself and then again as part of a complete script, we'll show the entire script now. The output of the script, using the words that were entered into Figure 13–1, are shown in Figure 13–2.

```
#!/usr/bin/perl

require "cgi-lib.pl";

&ReadParse;

print "Content-type: text/html\n\n";

print<<ENDOFTEXT;
```

```
<HTML>
<HEAD><TITLE>A World Wide Web Mad Lib </TITLE></HEAD>
<BODY>

<H4>Here's the mad lib you created. Boy, you're weird.</H4>
<P>
<BR>

<H3>Health Bulletin</H3>
Two $in{'adjective1'} studies in the current issue of the
<I>$in{'country'} Journal of Medicine</I> $in{'adverb'} prove
that prolonged exposure to $in{'nouns'} causes bizarre
mutations of the $in{'bodypart'} in 9 out of 10 $in{'animals'}
studied in the laboratory.
<P>
Dr. $in{'person'}, a spokesperson for the University of
$in{'country'}, which sponsored the study, had this to say:
"We think it's very important that the public be made aware
of this $in{'adjective2'} hazard. At least $in{'number'}
people have $in{'verbed'} already!"

</BODY>
</HTML>

ENDOFTEXT
```

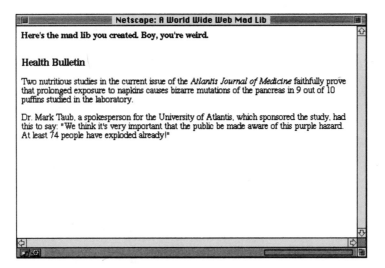

Fig. 13–2 The output of the mad lib script, using the words that were entered
into the text boxes in Figure 13–1.

Once you've typed in the script, don't forget to take the steps necessary to
ensure that the script can be run as a CGI program. We covered this in Chapter
12, but here it is again to refresh your memory: on UNIX, check your file permis-

sions; on Windows and UNIX, put the file in the right place and give it the proper
`.pl` or `.cgi` suffix; on a Macintosh, save the script as a Perl CGI script and give it
the `.cgi` suffix. These instructions apply to all the examples we'll be showing you
in this chapter.

13.2 A POP-UP MENU

This example won't teach you much about Perl, but it will show you how to use
hidden CGI variables and how to point browsers to new locations (rather than
simply feeding them HTML). Unlike the mad lib script, this example will actually give you a useful tool that you can apply to your own Web pages. We will
show you how to create a simple pop-up menu that people can use to access different directories, files, or programs in your site.

First, make a list of the files to which you want to provide access via a
menu. For instance:

1. Guitar information (`/guitar/`)
2. Photographs (`/photos/`)
3. My résumé (`/personal_files/resume.html`)
4. Twin Cities restaurant guide (`/food/index.html`)
5. On-line mad lib! (`/fun_stuff/madlib.html`)
6. A program for searching this Web site (`/cgi-bin/search.cgi`)

Then, create an HTML form to format this list as an HTML pop-up menu.
You will use a series of `<OPTION>` tags within a `<SELECT>` tag to build the pop-up
menu. (The select tag must *not* contain a `size` attribute, unless you want a
scrolling list box rather than a pop-up menu.) The text following each `<OPTION>`
tag will be the text that appears on the browser's screen (Fig. 13–3). The text
assigned to each `<OPTION>` tag's `value` attribute will be the value of the variable
passed to the CGI script; in this case, this should be the name of the file.

Your form should also include a *hidden* variable that contains the name of
your site; the Perl script will use this hidden variable with the file name in the
`<OPTION>` tag to figure out where to go when the submit button is clicked. A hidden variable is sent via an `<INPUT>` tag with the `type="hidden"` attribute. (Note
that it is not *completely* hidden; anyone can see it by simply viewing the source
HTML of the form.)

```
<HTML>
<HEAD><TITLE>A Simple Pop-Up Menu</TITLE></HEAD>
<BODY>

<FORM method="POST"
  action="http://yoursite.com/cgi-bin/menu.cgi">

Select the file or directory that you would like to view:
```

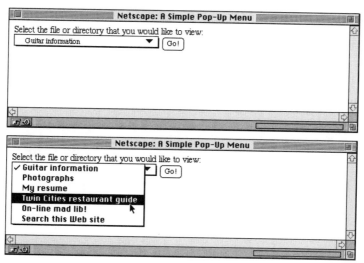

Fig. 13–3 Two views of the same pop-up menu. The top picture shows the menu as it first appears on the screen. The bottom picture shows what happens when someone clicks on the menu with their mouse and "pulls it down."

```
<SELECT name="file">
  <OPTION value="/guitar/">Guitar information
  <OPTION value="/photos/">Photographs
  <OPTION value="/personal_files/resume.html">My resume
  <OPTION value="/food/index.html">Twin Cities restaurant guide
  <OPTION value="/fun_stuff/madlib.html">On-line mad lib!
  <OPTION value="/cgi-bin/search.cgi">Search this Web site
</SELECT>

<INPUT type="submit" value="Go!">
<INPUT type="hidden" name="site" value="http://yoursite.com">

</FORM>

</BODY>
</HTML>
```

Note that the hidden `site` variable does not end with a slash, because all the file names *begin* with slashes. You could also do it the other way around; the important thing is that the two pieces fit together to form a valid URL. And don't forget to change all of the `<OPTION>` tags so that they point to real files in your site!

Now you write the Perl script. This will be very easy, since you don't even need to send any HTML code. All you need to do is to send a new location; if someone selects "Twin Cities restaurant guide" from the pop-up menu, they should be sent to the URL `http://yoursite.com/food/index.html`.

1. The first three lines of the script will be identical to the mad lib script. In fact, every Perl CGI script that you write will probably start with these same three lines.

```
#!/usr/bin/perl

require "cgi-lib.pl";

&ReadParse;
```

2. The first part of the HTML output is, as always, the HTTP header. But in this simple script, the header will also be the last part! Instead of a `Content-type`, the header will consist of the word `Location:`, followed by a URL. (A valid header might be `Location: http://www.lycos.com/`.)

   The input form that we created used two variable names: `site` and `file`. The `ReadParse` subroutine lets us refer to those variables as `$in{'site'}` and `$in{'file'}`. So this Perl script constructs an HTTP header like so:

```
print "Location: $in{'site'}$in{'file'}\n\n";
```

That's it! When a Web browser sees that `Location` header, it immediately jumps to a new location, so it would be fruitless to add anything else to the script. So, to recap, here's the entire script – all four lines! The most difficult part of this example turned out to be constructing the form.

```
#!/usr/bin/perl

require "cgi-lib.pl";

&ReadParse;

print "Location: $in{'site'}$in{'file'}\n\n";
```

This script is very easy to customize. One thing you might want to do is make the hidden site variable have no value (give the `<INPUT>` tag the following attribute: `value=""`). Then you must give full URLs for the `file` variable, but your menu items will be able to point to files anywhere on the Web, not just on your site.

13.3 MORE MAD LIBS

Now that we've done something useful (the pop-up menu), let's go back to the useless mad lib for a little while. We're simply going to take the original mad lib input page, and add a set of three radio buttons. You may be asking yourself, why would I possibly dignify that silly CGI script with *another* type of input device and a bunch of extra code? It's because we're going to show you how to use conditional (`if`) statements and subroutines in Perl (yes, this is almost real program-

ming now!); you'll also use both `Location` and `Content-type` headers in the same
script.

As always, start by constructing the form (Fig. 13–4). It will be exactly the
same as the form in section 13.1, but you will be adding three radio buttons at
the bottom of the input boxes, right above the submit button.

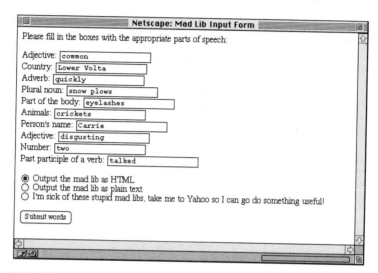

Fig. 13–4 This form is identical to Figure 13–1, except for the three radio buttons at the bottom. (We've also typed in different words!)

```
<HTML>
<HEAD><TITLE>Mad Lib Input Form</TITLE></HEAD>
<BODY>

<FORM method="POST"
    action="http://yoursite.com/cgi-bin/madlib2.cgi">

Please fill in the boxes with the appropriate parts of speech:
<P>
Adjective:          <INPUT type="text" name="adjective1"> <BR>
Country:            <INPUT type="text" name="country"> <BR>
Adverb:             <INPUT type="text" name="adverb"> <BR>
Plural noun:        <INPUT type="text" name="nouns"> <BR>
Part of the body:   <INPUT type="text" name="bodypart"> <BR>
Animals:            <INPUT type="text" name="animals"> <BR>
Person's name:      <INPUT type="text" name="person"> <BR>
Adjective:          <INPUT type="text" name="adjective2"> <BR>
Number:             <INPUT type="text" name="number"> <BR>
Past participle of a verb:  <INPUT type="text" name="verbed">
<P>
```

```
<INPUT type="radio" name="output_type" value="html" checked>
Output the mad lib as HTML <BR>

<INPUT type="radio" name="output_type" value="plaintext">
Output the mad lib as plain text <BR>

<INPUT type="radio" name="output_type" value="vamoose">
I'm sick of these stupid mad libs, take me to Yahoo so I can
go do something useful!

<P>
<INPUT type="submit" value="Submit words">

</FORM>

</BODY>
</HTML>
```

Note that the radio buttons must all have the same value for the `name` attribute, so that only one button can be checked at a time. This name (which we have arbitrarily called `output_type`) will either have `html`, `plaintext`, or `vamoose` for its value. The presence of the `checked` attribute in the first button's HTML tag indicated that it will be checked by default when the page is first loaded (see Figure 13–4); if the person viewing the form leaves the buttons alone, `output_type` will be `html`.

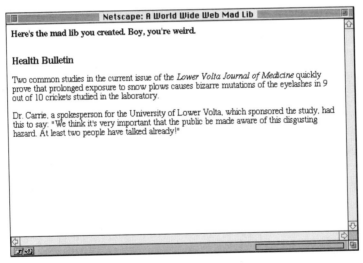

Fig. 13–5   If the first button in Figure 13–4 is checked, this HTML page will be the output of the new script. Except for the values of the variables, it is identical to Figure 13–2.

There are three possible outcomes of this script – an HTML page (Fig. 13–5), a plain text file (Fig. 13–6), or a new location. The first two are a little bit messy, so to keep your script clean, you should put them in *subroutines*. A subroutine is like a mini-program within a script; it serves a specific function, and it has a name. Perl subroutines are usually placed after the code for the main program, and they are called with statements such as &MySubroutine;. (You already have experience calling the ReadParse subroutine from cgi-lib.pl; this time, you'll be creating your own.)

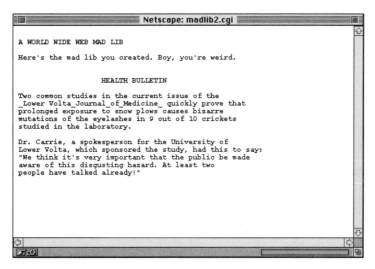

Fig. 13–6 If the second button in Figure 13–4 is checked, this plain-text page will be returned by the script.

Okay, it's script-building time. In addition to the programming concepts we promised to teach you in this section, we will also introduce you to the use of *comments*. Comments are lines in a program that don't do anything; you use them to write notes in the script that explain what each part does. In Perl and many other languages, any line that begins with a number sign (#) is a comment.

1. The first step should be getting very familiar by now. This time we've added a few comments.

```
#!/usr/bin/perl

# The following lines are included in all the scripts we write.
# They make it much easier to process HTML form in Perl.

require "cgi-lib.pl";
&ReadParse;
```

2. From here on out, the output of the script depends completely upon which of the form's radio buttons was checked. That information is passed to your Perl script via the $in{'output_type'} variable. You need to set up some if statements that evaluate this variable and execute the proper command or subroutine.

An `if` statement consists of a logical expression to be evaluated (in parentheses), then a logical operator, and then the commands to be executed if the expression is true {in curly brackets}. Note that the curly brackets need not be on the same line as the statements they enclose; in fact, many programmers like to give each bracket its own line.

The logical operator you will be using in this example is `eq`, which is used to compare the values of two text strings. If we wanted to compare numerical values, you would use a double equal sign (`==`). Do *not* use a single equal sign (`=`) in an `if` statement, because it just won't work. Only use equal signs to assign values to variables; for instance, if for some reason you wanted to override the form input data and assign the value "Xanzabar Hoosfoos" to the `$in{'person'}` variable, you could include the following statement near the beginning of your script: `$in{'person'} = "Xanzabar Hoosfoos";`. But enough about operators for now; on with the script!

```
# If the first radio button was checked, call the subroutine
# (OutputHTML) which creates an HTML version of the mad lib.

if ($in{'output_type'} eq "html")  {
   &OutputHTML;
}

# If the second radio button was checked, call the subroutine
# (OutputText) which creates a plain-text version of the mad lib.

if ($in{'output_type'} eq "plaintext")  {
   &OutputText;
}

# If the third radio button was checked, go directly to Yahoo.

if ($in{'output_type'} eq "vamoose")  {
   print "Location: http://www.yahoo.com/\n\n";
}
```

3. Write the subroutines. A subroutine begins with a statement like `sub MySubroutine`, and all the statements that make up the subroutine are placed between a pair of curly brackets. The only Perl statements you'll be including in these subroutines are `print` statements.

```
# ------------------------------------------------------------
# The "OutputHTML" subroutine sends an HTTP header with the
# text/html MIME type, and a complete HTML page, using the
# input from the mad lib form.

sub OutputHTML  {
print "Content-type: text/html\n\n";
print<<ENDOFTEXT;
<HTML>
<HEAD><TITLE>A World Wide Web Mad Lib </TITLE></HEAD>
```

```
<BODY>

<H4>Here's the mad lib you created. Boy, you're weird.</H4>
<P>
<BR>
<H3>Health Bulletin</H3>
Two $in{'adjective1'} studies in the current issue of the
<I>$in{'country'} Journal of Medicine</I> $in{'adverb'} prove
that prolonged exposure to $in{'nouns'} causes bizarre
mutations of the $in{'bodypart'} in 9 out of 10 $in{'animals'}
studied in the laboratory.
<P>
Dr. $in{'person'}, a spokesperson for the University of
$in{'country'}, which sponsored the study, had this to say:
"We think it's very important that the public be made aware
of this $in{'adjective2'} hazard. At least $in{'number'}
people have $in{'verbed'} already!"

</BODY>
</HTML>
ENDOFTEXT
}

# ------------------------------------------------------------
# The "OutputText" subroutine sends an HTTP header with the
# text/plain MIME type, and a text file with the filled-in
# mad lib, using the input from the mad lib form.

sub OutputText  {
print "Content-type: text/plain\n\n";
print<<ENDOFTEXT;

A WORLD WIDE WEB MAD LIB

Here's the mad lib you created. Boy, you're weird.


                    HEALTH BULLETIN

Two $in{'adjective1'} studies in the current issue of the
_$in{'country'}_Journal_of_Medicine_ $in{'adverb'} prove that
prolonged exposure to $in{'nouns'} causes bizarre
mutations of the $in{'bodypart'} in 9 out of 10 $in{'animals'}
studied in the laboratory.

Dr. $in{'person'}, a spokesperson for the University of
$in{'country'}, which sponsored the study, had this to say:
"We think it's very important that the public be made
aware of this $in{'adjective2'} hazard. At least $in{'number'}
people have $in{'verbed'} already!"

ENDOFTEXT
}
```

For the sake of saving space, we'll leave it to you to put the pieces of this script together. (You can also get a complete copy from the CD included with this book, or from `http://www.prenhall.com/~palmer/scripts/`.) Your completed script should contain the beginning `#!perl`, `cgi-lib`, and `ReadParse` lines, then the three `if` statements, then the two subroutines, plus some comments.

13.4 A Perl Guest Book

In this section, we'll show you how to set up a "Guest Book" on your server. People visiting your site will be able to leave comments for others to see. The comments will be stored in an ordinary HTML file on your server, so you can delete — or even alter — them as you please, if you don't like what they said! In our example, new comments will be placed at the top of the list, but adjusting the Guest Book so that the new comments are placed at the bottom is a very simple matter, and we'll tell you how to do it. (Inspiration and part of the code for this script came from Matt Wright, who has made a number of handy Perl scripts freely available on his Web site: `http://www.worldwidemart.com/scripts/`.)

Of course, you're going to need to use some new Perl commands. And even if you don't completely understand everything we do in this script, you should be able to follow along enough to apply these concepts to similar projects of your own. You will learn about a new logical operator, `unless`; you'll learn how to open and write to a file; you will write a `foreach` loop; and you will use a number of `if` statements in new and creative ways. And, as an added bonus, you'll learn how to make a Perl script generate the current time and date in a legible format.

As always, the first step is going to be to create an HTML form that takes the input for the script (see Figure 13–7). You're probably quite the forms expert by now, so feel free to use a different layout if you want. But keep the variable names the same, unless you want to change all of them in the Perl script as well. And name it `guestadd.html` so that the references all match up. (DOS/Windows users will have to change all the `.html` suffixes to `.htm`.) Your input page, the Guest Book, and the Perl script should all be in the same directory.

```
<HTML>
<HEAD>
<TITLE>Add Your Comments to our Guest Book</TITLE>
</HEAD>
<BODY>

Fill in the blanks below to add your comments to our
Guest Book. The only fields that you <I>have</I> to fill in
are your name and the comments. Thanks!
<HR>

<FORM method="POST" action="guestbk.cgi">
Your Name: <INPUT type="text" name="name" size=30>
<BR>
E-Mail: <INPUT type="text" name="email" size=40>
<BR>
```

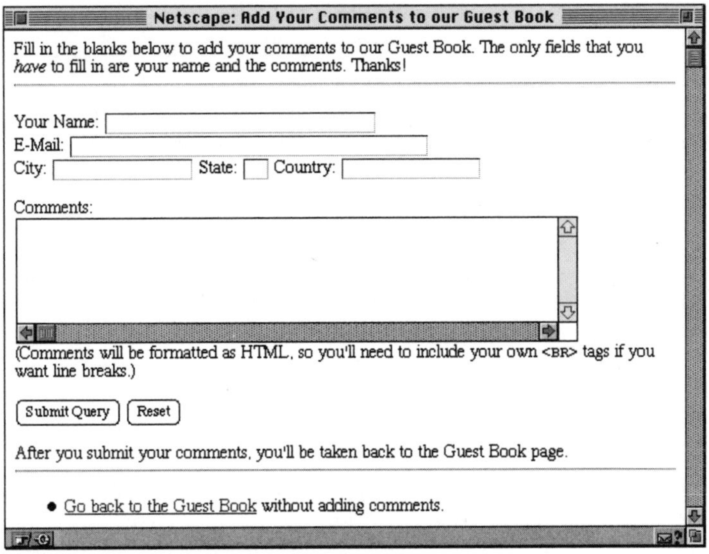

Fig. 13–7 This is the form that will collect comments for the Guest Book. This file should be named `guestadd.html`.

```
City: <INPUT type="text" name="city" size=15>
State: <INPUT type="text" name="state" size=2>
Country: <INPUT type="text" name="country" size=15>
<P>
Comments:<BR>
<TEXTAREA name="comments" cols=60 rows=6></TEXTAREA><BR>
(Comments will be formatted as HTML, so you'll need to
include your own <TT>&lt;BR&gt;</TT> tags if you want
line breaks.)
<P>
<INPUT type="submit"> <INPUT type="reset">
</FORM>

<P>
After you submit your comments, you'll be taken back to
the Guest Book page.

<HR>

<UL>
<LI><A href="guests.html">Go back to the Guest Book</A>
without adding comments.
</UL>

</BODY>
</HTML>
```

You also need to create a Guest Book file that doesn't have any comments in it yet. This file can take on any shape you want, but it should ideally have a link back to the entry form, and it *must* have a line that says `<!--begin-->` and nothing else. In HTML, a line that begins with `<!--` and ends with `-->` is a comment, similar to Perl lines that begin with `#`. So the word "begin" will not show up in the output. That line is simply used to tell the Perl script where to insert new comments.

You should name your Guest Book file `guests.html` to match the references in the Perl script and the "add your comments" form. Since the Perl script will actually be using input from the Web to modify this file, UNIX users need to make sure that the file is publicly writable (`chmod 666 guests.html`). Here is the source HTML for our blank Guest Book:

```
<HTML>
<HEAD><TITLE>Guest Book</TITLE></HEAD>
<BODY>

<B><A href="guestadd.html">Click here</A> to add <I>your</I>
comments to the Guest Book.</B>
<P>
(If you already added your comments, but you don't see them
here, you may need to have your Web browser reload this page.)
<HR>

<!--begin-->

</BODY>
</HTML>
```

After someone enters a comment, the page will look like Figure 13–8, and the source HTML for the last part of the page will have been modified to look something like this:

```
<!--begin-->
6/10/96, 4:07 PM:<BR>
There's no place like your home page!<BR>
- <I>Frank Baum (toto@oz.org), Emerald City, KS</I><BR>
<HR>
```

Neat, huh? Now we'll tell you how it works. In the previous three sections, we explained the Perl script step by step and gave it to you in pieces. This time, we're going to give you the entire script all at once. Don't worry, we'll still explain everything! But the explanation will be in the form of detailed comments within the script. When you put this script on your server, you can take out the comments if you want to save space, or you can leave them in if you think they'll help you understand it later.

The Perl script should be named `guestbk.cgi`; as always, make sure it can be run as a script.

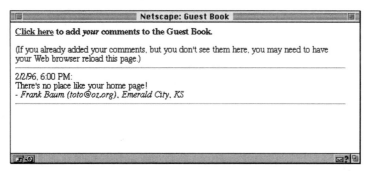

Fig. 13–8   This is what the Guest Book (`guests.html`) looks like after one person has filled out the form. As more people add their comments, this entry will get shoved down to the bottom.

```perl
#!/usr/bin/perl

# Remember to change the above line if it's different on
# your system.

#############################################################
# THIS SECTION OF THE SCRIPT CONTAINS VARIABLES THAT YOU    #
# *MUST* CUSTOMIZE FOR YOUR OWN SITE!                       #
#                                                           #
# This variable is the *full* URL of the guest book file:   #
$guest_book_url = "http://YOURSITE.COM/CGI-BIN/guests.html";

# This one tells the script which file to modify; since all #
# the files are in the same directory, a simple file name   #
# will suffice.  If you want to put the Guest Book elsewhere, #
# you'll need a relative or absolute path:                  #
$guest_book_file = "guests.html";

# This is the name of the current script.  You need to define #
# it here so that the script can generate a new form that    #
# refers to $guest_book_script.                             #
$guest_book_script = "guestbk.cgi";

#                                                           #
#############################################################

# Convert the form input to a usable form, using the
# 'ReadParse' subroutine from "cgi-lib.pl":
require "cgi-lib.pl";
&ReadParse;

# Run the 'CurrentTime' subroutine, which formats the current
# date and time and puts them into the $datetime variable:
&CurrentTime;
```

```
# Let them know if they forgot to enter their name or comments.
# In English, the first line says, "run the 'Missing' sub-
# routine unless the $in{'comments'} variable exists."  The
# second line says the same thing for the $in{'name'} variable.
# If both variables are there, 'Missing' is not called at all.
&Missing  unless  $in{'comments'};
&Missing  unless  $in{'name'};


# This is the trickiest part of this script; we'll take it one
# piece at a time.  First, open a new *filehandle* named FILE,
# and fill it with the contents of the file named by the
# $guest_book_file variable.  A filehandle is like a nickname
# for a pile of data.  It's similar to an ordinary file name,
# but it only exists within the program.
open (FILE,"$guest_book_file");

# Create an array called @LINES (arrays start with a @ symbol),
# and set it equal to FILE.  When you dump a filehandle into
# an array like this, each element in the array is one complete
# *line* of the filehandle.  At this point, @LINES now holds
# the complete contents of the Guest Book file.
@LINES = <FILE>;

# Close the FILE filehandle.  Since you've read all of its
# data into the @LINES array, you don't need it anymore.
close(FILE);

# Open a new filehandle called GUESTBOOK.  Rather than read
# another file *into* this filehandle, you're going to
# redirect everything that comes into GUESTBOOK into the file
# named $guest_book_file, replacing the old contents of the
# $guest_book_file.  This is done by placing a 'greater than'
# sign (>) in front of the file name.
open (GUESTBOOK,">$guest_book_file");

# Start a 'foreach' loop.  A foreach loop says, in English,
# "repeat everything within my curly brackets as long as there
# continues to be input." In this case, it will go through the
# entire @LINES array and stop after it has evaluated the last
# line in the array.
foreach ( @LINES ) {

  # Now you're within the 'foreach' loop.  If the current
  # input (one line of the GUESTBOOK file, read as an element
  # of the @LINES array) contains <!--begin-->, execute the
  # statements between the curly brackets. (The first few lines
  # of the file will *not* contain <!--begin-->, so nothing in
  # the 'if' statement will take place; the program will skip
  # to the 'else' down below.)
  if (/<!--begin-->/)  {
```

```
        # If the program has made it here, inside the 'if'
        # statement's curly brackets, it must have found the
        # "begin" marker.  It will spit out a new <!--begin-->
        # line, and then the new guest book entry.  Because you
        # are outputting to a filehandle rather than to the
        # "standard" output, the 'print' statements all begin
        # with 'print GUESTBOOK' rather than just 'print'.
        print GUESTBOOK "<!--begin-->\n";
        print GUESTBOOK "$datetime:<BR>\n";
        print GUESTBOOK "$in{'comments'}<BR>\n";
        print GUESTBOOK "- <I>$in{'name'}";

        # Everything up to this point was straightforward: the
        # "begin" marker, the $datetime variable, the comments,
        # and the person's name, with some line breaks and HTML
        # tags thrown in.
        # But we didn't *require* them to write down their e-mail
        # address, city, state, or country, so we have to create
        # 'if' statements to decide whether to print them.  This
        # is easy.  Look at the first one: "if the $in{'email'}
        # variable exists, then output it to GUESTBOOK, with some
        # parentheses around it."  The rest are all very similar.
        #
        # The last line in this section simply finishes up the
        # new entry with a line break and a horizontal rule line,
        # and the curly bracket closes off the 'if' statement that
        # looked for the "begin" marker.
        if ( $in{'email'} )
          { print GUESTBOOK " ($in{'email'})";        }
        if ( $in{'city'} )
          { print GUESTBOOK ", $in{'city'}";          }
        if ( $in{'state'} )
          { print GUESTBOOK ", $in{'state'}";         }
        if ( $in{'country'} )
          { print GUESTBOOK ", $in{'country'}";       }
        print GUESTBOOK "</I><BR>\n<HR>\n";
      }

    # If the current line does NOT contain <!--begin-->, print
    # out the current input ($_) again, unchanged.  ($_ is a
    # special, predefined variable.)  This ensures that whatever
    # was in the Guest Book before will still be there:
    else { print GUESTBOOK "$_"; }

  # This bracket simply finishes off the 'foreach' loop:
  }

# Close the Guest Book filehandle, thus ending any output
# to the file named by $guest_book_file:
close (GUESTBOOK);

# Send the user to the Guest Book HTML file so they can see
# what they wrote.  This is just a simple HTTP header, which
# you should know all about by now:
print "Location: $guest_book_url\n\n";
```

```
# [END OF MAIN PROGRAM]

# Earlier, we promised that we'd tell you how to make the
# new entries show up at the bottom of the list rather than
# the top.  Here's how: in the 'print GUESTBOOK' statements
# where the new entry is placed into the Guest Book, move the
# 'print GUESTBOOK "<!--begin-->\n"' statement to the *end*
# of the output -- right before the curly bracket that finishes
# the 'if (/<!--begin-->/)' statement) -- rather than at the
# beginning.  It's as simple as that!


#################################################################
# The "Missing" subroutine takes care of situations where the
# user leaves either the Name or Comments field blank.
sub Missing {

# Print the HTTP header and the start of a new form that
# tells people to supply whichever information was missing.
# These will be ordinary print statements, as opposed to the
# ones in the main program that sent output to a filehandle:
print "Content-type: text/html\n\n";
print "<HTML>\n";
print "<HEAD><TITLE>Need more information</TITLE></HEAD>\n";
print "<BODY>\n";

# You need to figure whether it was the Name or Comments field
# that was left blank.  By default, you will say that the
# missing information was BOTH fields; if information is found
# in either one of those, the $missing_info variable will be
# changed later.
$missing_info = "both the Name AND the Comments fields!";

# But if the Name field exists, then it was only the Comments
# which were left blank.  Nothing is output at this stage; you
# are just filling in variables.
if ( $in{'name'} )
   { $missing_info = "the Comments field."; }

# If there are Comments, then the Name must be missing.
if ( $in{'comments'} )
   { $missing_info = "the Name field."; }

# Now you simply tell them which information they forgot to
# to write, using the $missing_info variable:
print "You forgot to fill in $missing_info";

# Now you just have to give them a new form to fill in.  It
# will look much like the original Guest Book entry form, but
# the original information will be placed into the form boxes
# by using the 'value' attribute of the <INPUT> tags.  You can
# use the good old 'ENDOFTEXT' trick.
print<<ENDOFTEXT;
```

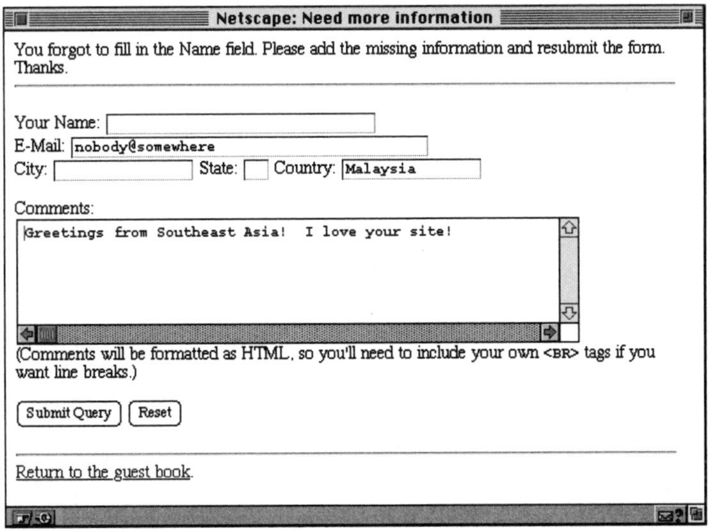

Fig. 13–9   This is what will be returned to a guest if they forget to enter their name when they sign the Guest Book.

```
Please add the missing information and resubmit the form.
Thanks.
<HR>

<FORM method="POST" action="$guest_book_script">
Your Name:
   <INPUT type="text" name="name"
   value="$in{'name'}" size=30> <BR>
E-Mail:
   <INPUT type="text" name="email" size=40
   value="$in{'email'}"> <BR>
City:
   <INPUT type="text" name="city" size=15
   value="$in{'city'}">
State:
   <INPUT type="text" name="state" size=2
   value="$in{'state'}">
Country:
   <INPUT type="text" name="country" size=15
   value="$in{'country'}">
<P>
Comments: <BR>
   <TEXTAREA name="comments"
   cols=60 rows=6>$in{'comments'}
   </TEXTAREA> <BR>
(Comments will be formatted as HTML, so you'll need to
include your own <TT>&lt;BR&gt;</TT> tags if you want
line breaks.)
```

```
<P>
<INPUT type=submit> <INPUT type=reset>
</FORM>

<HR>
<A href="$guest_book_url">Return to the guest book</A>.
</BODY>
</HTML>

ENDOFTEXT

# The 'exit' statement makes the script stop right here in the
# subroutine, rather than returning to the main program.  The
# curly bracket officially finishes off the subroutine.
exit;
}


#################################################################
# The "CurrentTime" subroutine converts Perl's localtime(time)
# variable to a more readable format.
sub CurrentTime {

# Perl's 'time' function counts the number of seconds since
# a certain date in the past.  The 'localtime' function
# converts this number to a list of nine elements. You can
# dump this list into nine meaningful scalar variables with
# the following statement ($isdst tells whether it's Daylight
# Saving Time or not):
($sec,$min,$hour,$mday,$month,$year,$wday,$yday,$isdst) =
    localtime(time);

# 'Localtime(time)' thinks January is 0 and December is 11, so
# you need to add 1 to the $month variable.  Also, set a new
# variable called $ampm to "AM" by default.
$month = $month + 1;
$ampm = "AM";

# The hour will be in 24-hour time, so 0 is really 12.  Also,
# hours greater than 12 will be reduced by 12, and the $ampm
# variable will become "PM".  Finally, minutes less than 10
# need to have a leading zero added.
if ($hour == 0) { $hour = 12; }
if ($hour > 12) { $hour = $hour - 12; $ampm = "PM" }
if ($min < 10) { $min = "0$min"; }

# This statement just strings all the date & time pieces
# together and puts them in a variable called $datetime.  This
# subroutine does *not* have an 'exit' statement, because it
# *should* return to the main program when it's done.
$datetime = "$month/$mday/$year, $hour:$min $ampm";

}
```

13.5 AN ORDER ENTRY SYSTEM

At this point, you should have all of the basic information you need for writing your own scripts, or tailoring existing scripts to meet your specific needs. The order entry form and script presented in this section can easily be used "as-is" or modified to meet the requirements of your site.

This form contains all of the basic fields necessary for recording customers' information so that you can process an order using the Web. The required information includes their name, address, product code, and credit card number. This information is processed by the script and then recorded in a delimited text file. This file can then be used by almost any database or spreadsheet program. If you are truly adventurous, you can forget about a commercial database program and write your own Perl scripts that use this information to create work orders for your business, order-status reports, inventory control reports, and so on.

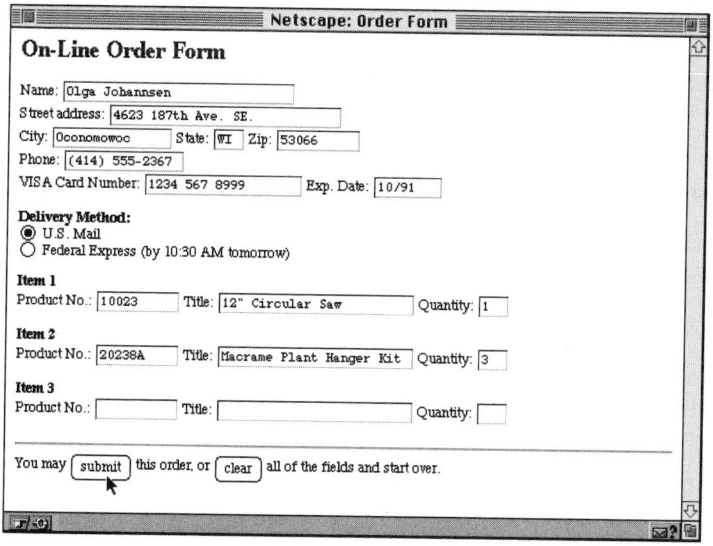

Fig. 13–10   The form for the on-line order entry system.

Let's start with the HTML form that accepts the information that will be used by the script (Fig. 13–10). We start with the usual header information, which defines the form's title and subject. Easy enough. We then move to defining the `method`, which is our old friend `"POST"`. The `action` is the relative path to the `order.cgi` script. From there, the form fields for the customer's information are listed and given input names so that the script knows which information is which. Then, we use a couple of radio buttons so customers can designate how they want their merchandise delivered (in this case, regular mail or Federal Express). Finally, we have input boxes for the items to be ordered, as well as an option for the customer to clear the form and start over before submitting the information.

```
<HTML>
<HEAD><TITLE>Order Form</TITLE></HEAD>
<BODY>
<H2>On-Line Order Form</H2>

<FORM method="POST" action="/YOUR-CGI-PATH/order.cgi">

Name:    <INPUT name="NAME" size=30> <BR>
Street address: <INPUT name="ADDRESS" size=30> <BR>
City:    <INPUT name="CITY" size=15>
State:   <INPUT name="STATE" size=3>
Zip:     <INPUT name="ZIP" size=10> <BR>
Phone:   <INPUT name="PHONE" size=15> <BR>
VISA Card Number: <input name="ACCOUNT" size=20>
Exp. Date: <input name="EXPDATE" size=8>


<P>
<B>Delivery Method:</B><BR>
<INPUT type="radio" name="DELIVERY" value="Standard" CHECKED>
    U.S. Mail<br>
<INPUT type="radio" name="DELIVERY" value="FedEx">
    Federal Express (by 10:30 AM tomorrow)


<P>
<B>Item 1</B><BR>
Product No.: <INPUT name="CODE1" size="10">
Title: <INPUT name="ITEM1" size="25">
Quantity: <INPUT name="QUANTITY1" size="3">
<P>
<B>Item 2</B><BR>
Product No.: <INPUT name="CODE2" size="10">
Title: <INPUT name="ITEM2" size="25">
Quantity: <INPUT name="QUANTITY2" size="3">
<P>
<B>Item 3</B><BR>
Product No.: <INPUT name="CODE3" size="10">
Title: <INPUT name="ITEM3" size="25">
Quantity: <INPUT name="QUANTITY3" size="3">
<P>


<HR>
You may <INPUT type="submit" value="submit"> this order, or
<INPUT type="reset" value="clear"> all of the fields and
start over.

</FORM>

</BODY>
</HTML>
```

The Perl script for the order entry form works much like the Guest Book; as in that program, the first significant chunk of code validates user input. The Missing subroutine that was introduced in the Guest Book script is included, but the conditions for its use are slightly more complicated. The reason for this is that is that the customer's personal information is absolutely required, but they can order different numbers of items, leaving the potential for some fields to be legitimately left blank. (A page generated by the `Missing` subroutine is shown in Figure 13–12.)

Identifying which fields need to be completed is done using conditional OR operators (`||`) and "negation" symbols (`!`). This means that the `Missing` subroutine will be executed if there is neither a name, *nor* an address, *nor* a city, etc. In the second potential call to `Missing`, the script checks to see if *all* of the "Quantity" fields are left blank by using the AND operator (`&&`). This means that the `Missing` subroutine will be executed only if *all* of the Quantity boxes are left empty.

The next step in the order entry script (if the input data is acceptable) is to print out an HTML page that shows a customer exactly what they ordered, and to whom it will be sent (Fig. 13–11).

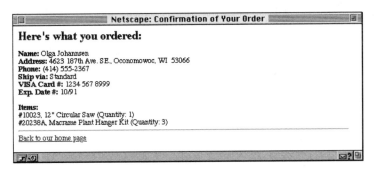

Fig. 13–11   When the data in Figure 13–10 is submitted, this page will be sent back to the customer, and the order database will be updated as well; the database is *not* accessible from the Web.

Immediately after printing this "receipt" page, the new information is added to the order database. The Guest Book inserted a comment in the middle of a preexisting file, but the order entry system only has to append a new line to the *end* of the file; this is *much* easier to accomplish, because the contents of the old file do not have to be read in and then spit out again.

Before you run this program, you *must* adjust the `$order_file`, `$order_script`, and `$home_page` variables in the first section, so that everything will work on your system. The value of the `$order_file` variable is actually a very important detail. It tells the script where the database entries will be stored. In the Guest Book program, the Guest Book file was simply in the same directory as the Perl script, which made referencing the file very easy. With your order entry system, however, that would be a serious security risk, because you *don't* want the whole world to be able to see what others have written!

The best solution is to put the database file *outside* the server's file space, where the Perl interpreter can reach it, but HTTP transfers can't. Therefore, you should define `$order_file` with a statement like the following (note that this is an absolute path defined relative to your *entire hard drive or file system*, not just the server space):

```
$database_file = "/business/data/database.txt";
```

Macintosh users can do the same thing, but the syntax is slightly different. You need to start absolute path names with the name of your hard disk, then separate folders with colons instead of slashes, like so:

```
$database_file = "Your Hard Disk:Business ƒ:Data:database.txt";
```

(If you want to use *relative* path names on a Mac, a single colon indicates the current folder, :: means go back one folder, ::: means go back two folders, and so on.)

The rest of the program contains minor variations on themes previously introduced in this section. Most of the picky details of how it works are included in comments within the script (feel free to remove the comments from the parts that you understand already). Go ahead and try it out on your server. If you don't have any products to sell right now, create a cyber-garage sale!

```
#!/usr/bin/perl

# Remember to change the above line if it's different on
# your system.

##############################################################
# THIS SECTION OF THE SCRIPT CONTAINS VARIABLES THAT YOU     #
# *MUST* CUSTOMIZE FOR YOUR OWN SITE!                        #
#                                                            #
# This variable defines exactly where the orders will end up.#
# It should be a complete path to a file OUTSIDE your server #
# space.  (See the text in Chapter 13 for details.)          #
$order_file = "COMPLETE-PATH-TO-ORDER-FILE";

# This is the name of the current script.  You need to define #
# it here so that the script can generate a new form that    #
# refers to $order_script.                                   #
$order_script = "order.cgi";

# This is the URL of your home page, or whichever page you    #
# want to return them to after they order:                   #
$home_page = "http://YOUR-SITE";

# The $t variable defines what will be used to separate      #
# fields in your order file.  We have set it to the tab      #
# character ("\t")by default; this should work well if you   #
# are going to be accessing the orders via a spreadsheet or  #
# database application.  You could also use semicolons,      #
# pipes, asterisks, etc.  DON'T use spaces.                  #
$t = "\t";

#                                                            #
##############################################################
```

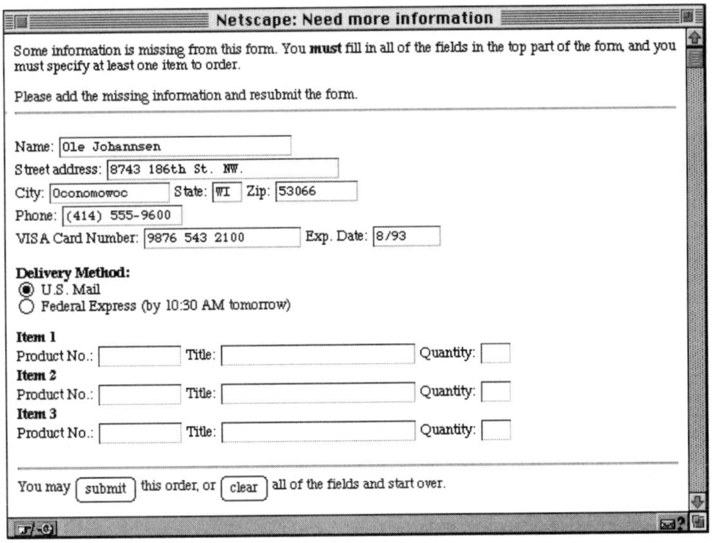

Fig. 13–12 This "Need more information" page is created by the `Missing` subroutine if some of the required data is not supplied. Ole forgot to tell us which products he wants to order.

```perl
# Convert the form input to a usable form, using the
# 'ReadParse' subroutine from "cgi-lib.pl":
require "cgi-lib.pl";
&ReadParse;

# First, you need to check to see that they entered all the
# required data.  If they didn't, send them to the "Missing"
# subroutine, which will prompt them again.
# The first 'if' statement (actually a 'do-if' statement,
# because the action that might be taken comes *before* the
# logical expressions) has a number of expressions of the
# form '!$x'; those say, "if $x does NOT exist."  These
# expressions are separated by || markers; this means that
# "Missing" will be executed if ANY of those do not exist.
# (The || is a logical OR operator.)
&Missing  if ( !$in{'NAME'}     || !$in{'ADDRESS'} ||
               !$in{'CITY'}     || !$in{'STATE'}   ||
               !$in{'ZIP'}      || !$in{'PHONE'}   ||
               !$in{'ACCOUNT'}  || !$in{'EXPDATE'}    );

# The second 'if' statement has && markers between the
# expressions; this means that "Missing" will be executed
# only if ALL "Quantity" fields do not exist.  (The && is a
# logical AND operator.)
&Missing  if ( !$in{'QUANTITY1'} &&
               !$in{'QUANTITY2'} &&
               !$in{'QUANTITY3'}    );
```

```
# Print the HTTP header and a new page that
# shows people what they entered.
print "Content-type: text/html\n\n";

print<<ENDOFTEXT;
<HTML>
<HEAD><TITLE>Confirmation of Your Order</TITLE></HEAD>
<BODY>
<H2>Here's what you ordered:</H2>
<P>
<B>Name:</B> $in{'NAME'} <BR>
<B>Address:</B> $in{'ADDRESS'}, $in{'CITY'},
      $in{'STATE'}  $in{'ZIP'} <BR>
<B>Phone:</B>          $in{'PHONE'}     <BR>
<B>Ship via:</B>       $in{'DELIVERY'} <BR>
<B>VISA Card #:</B>    $in{'ACCOUNT'}   <BR>
<B>Exp. Date #:</B>    $in{'EXPDATE'}   <BR>
<P>
<B>Items:</B><BR>
ENDOFTEXT

# If they only ordered one item, there's no need to print out
# blank entries.  You can use three 'if' statements that are
# only executed if their respective entries exist.
if ( $in{'QUANTITY1'} )
   { print "#$in{'CODE1'}, $in{'ITEM1'} ";
     print "(Quantity: $in{'QUANTITY1'})<BR>";   }
if ( $in{'QUANTITY2'} )
   { print "#$in{'CODE2'}, $in{'ITEM2'} ";
     print "(Quantity: $in{'QUANTITY2'})<BR>";   }
if ( $in{'QUANTITY3'} )
   { print "#$in{'CODE3'}, $in{'ITEM3'} ";
     print "(Quantity: $in{'QUANTITY3'})<BR>";   }

# Finish up the confirmation page by giving a link back to
# your home page:
print<<ENDOFTEXT;
<HR>
<A href="$home_page">Back to our home page</A>
</BODY>
</HTML>
ENDOFTEXT

# Open a filehandle called ORDERS, and have the contents of
# ORDERS *appended* to the end of the file specified with the
# $order_file variable.  This is done with a >> symbol before
# the file name (a *single* > would completely *replace* the
# order file).
open ( ORDERS, ">>$order_file" );
```

```
# Dump all the order information into the order file, represented
# by the ORDERS filehandle.  Every piece of information will be
# separated by the field separator, which is defined by $t.
# At the end of the data, a new line character ("\n") is sent.
# (You can reorganize these if you like; you could also use the
# "CurrentTime" subroutine from the Guest Book script and
# include its output as a field.)  Note that as we have written
# it here, it it simply one 'print' statement with lots of
# arguments.
print ORDERS "$in{'NAME'}$t",
             "$in{'PHONE'}$t",
             "$in{'ADDRESS'}$t",
             "$in{'CITY'}$t",
             "$in{'STATE'}$t",
             "$in{'ZIP'}$t",
             "$in{'ACCOUNT'}$t",
             "$in{'EXPDATE'}$t",
             "$in{'DELIVERY'}$t",
             "$in{'CODE1'}$t",
             "$in{'ITEM1'}$t",
             "$in{'QUANTITY1'}$t",
             "$in{'CODE2'}$t",
             "$in{'ITEM2'}$t",
             "$in{'QUANTITY2'}$t",
             "$in{'CODE3'}$t",
             "$in{'ITEM3'}$t",
             "$in{'QUANTITY3'}$t",
             "\n";

# Close the ORDERS filehandle.
close (ORDERS);


#############################################################
# The "Missing" subroutine takes care of situations where the
# some of the required fields are left blank.
sub Missing {

# Print the HTTP header and a new form that tells people to
# supply whichever information was missing.  This output will
# essentially be the same as the original order form, but
# with values inserted where they DID provide information the
# first time around, by way of 'value' attributes in the
# <INPUT> tags.
print "Content-type: text/html\n\n";

print<<ENDOFTEXT;
<HTML>
<HEAD><TITLE>Need more information</TITLE></HEAD>
<BODY>
Some information is missing from this form. You <B>must</B>
fill in all of the fields in the top part of the form, and
you must specify at least one item to order.
```

```
<P>
Please add the missing information and resubmit the form.
<HR>
<FORM method="POST" action="$order_script">
Name:    <INPUT name="NAME" size=30
         value="$in{'NAME'}"> <BR>
Street address: <INPUT name="ADDRESS" size=30
         value="$in{'ADDRESS'}"> <BR>
City:    <INPUT name="CITY" size=15
         value="$in{'CITY'}">
State:   <INPUT name="STATE" size=3
         value="$in{'STATE'}">
Zip:     <INPUT name="ZIP" size=10
         value="$in{'ZIP'}"> <BR>
Phone:   <INPUT name="PHONE" size=15
         value="$in{'PHONE'}"> <BR>
VISA Card Number: <input name="ACCOUNT" size=20
         value="$in{'ACCOUNT'}">
Exp. Date: <input name="EXPDATE" size=8
         value="$in{'EXPDATE'}">
<P>
<B>Delivery Method:</B><BR>
<INPUT type="radio" name="DELIVERY" value="Standard" CHECKED>
    U.S. Mail<br>
<INPUT type="radio" name="DELIVERY" value="FedEx">
    Federal Express (by 10:30 AM tomorrow)
<P>
<B>Item 1</B><BR>
Product No.: <INPUT name="CODE1" size="10"
         value="$in{'CODE1'}">
Title: <INPUT name="ITEM1" size="25"
         value="$in{'ITEM1'}">
Quantity: <INPUT name="QUANTITY1" size="3"
         value="$in{'QUANTITY1'}">
<BR>
<B>Item 2</B><BR>
Product No.: <INPUT name="CODE2" size="10"
         value="$in{'CODE2'}">
Title: <INPUT name="ITEM2" size="25"
         value="$in{'ITEM2'}">
Quantity: <INPUT name="QUANTITY2" size="3"
         value="$in{'QUANTITY2'}">
<BR>
<B>Item 3</B><BR>
Product No.: <INPUT name="CODE3" size="10"
         value="$in{'CODE3'}">
Title: <INPUT name="ITEM3" size="25"
         value="$in{'ITEM3'}">
Quantity: <INPUT name="QUANTITY3" size="3"
         value="$in{'QUANTITY3'}">
<P>
<HR>
```

```
You may <INPUT type="submit" value="submit"> this order, or
<INPUT type="reset" value="clear"> all of the fields and
start over.
</FORM>
</HTML>
</BODY>

ENDOFTEXT

# The 'exit' statement makes the script stop right here in the
# subroutine, rather than returning to the main program.  The
# curly bracket officially finishes off the subroutine.

exit;
}
```

13.6 A SEARCHABLE INDEX

The last script we're going to show you is one that will allow people to perform a simple search for pages within your Web site. This script won't introduce many new concepts, but we hope you'll find it to be a useful addition to your Perl collection.

This searching mechanism requires an index file, which you must create. This index file lists the URL, the title, and key phrases for every page you want to be included in the search process. Each line in your index file will have this format:

```
URL;Page Title;key1 key2 key3 key4 ...
```

It is important that the URL and the title be separated by semicolons, because this is how the script knows which part is which. In fact, you could also separate the list of key words with semicolons, but this is not necessary. The URLs in your index need not start with http:// and a site name, because they are only used to create links in the list of search results.

When you create your index file, you can name it whatever you want, but it will be easier if you put it in the same directory as the script, because then the script will not have to worry about directory paths. We created a sample index file and named it database.txt. In our example, the URLs start with / so that no matter where in the site they are referenced from, the path name will always be evaluated relative to the top of the server space.

```
/index.html;Home Page;home main welcome top
/images/;Images Directory;images pictures bullets icons GIF JPEG
/stats.html;Server Statistics;stats log analysis hits traffic
/otherlinks.html;Links to Other Sites;bookmarks hotlist external
/animals/inverteb.html;Creepy Crawlies;bugs worms sponges crabs
/animals/verteb.html;Vertebrates;mammals birds reptiles fish
/animals/mammals.html;Mammals;bunnies tigers blue whales humans
/animals/birds.html;Feathered Friends;blue jays eagles puffins
```

If we were to use our search script to look for the key word "birds" in this site, the script would show us links to `birds.html` and `verteb.html`. Searching for "blue" would give us `mammals.html` and `birds.html`, because one contains "blue whales" and the other has "blue jays." If we search for "amoeba," the script won't find anything.

Here's how the script works:

1. If no arguments are passed to the script, it outputs a new form in which a search query can be entered (Fig. 13–13).

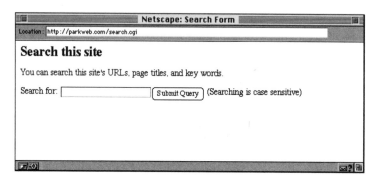

Fig. 13–13   This is the page that is output by the script if it is called with no arguments.

2. Once the query has been submitted, the script reads the index file. If there is any kind of problem opening the index file, an error message is returned (Fig. 13–14). The subroutine that creates this error page (`FileError`) can be easily ported into other scripts that open files.

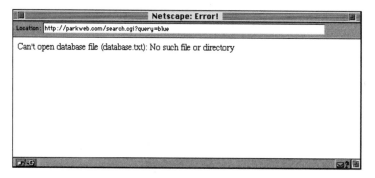

Fig. 13–14   This error page is created by the `FileError` subroutine. It comes up when there is a problem opening the index file.

3. If a query *is* passed, the script searches for a match in the index. Matching is case sensitive, so for simplicity's sake, the key phrases in our sample index file are all lowercase.

4. If matches are found, every matched page is displayed in the form of an unnumbered list of links, and a new search form is given (Fig. 13–15), which allows another search without backing up to the initial form.

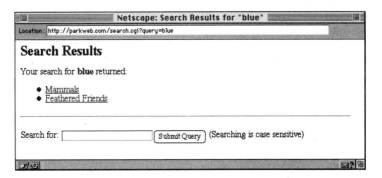

Fig. 13–15 Searching for the word "blue" in our sample index file yields two matches. Note that the URL for this page includes `query=blue`.

5. If no matches are found, the script says this and gives a new search form (Fig. 13–16).

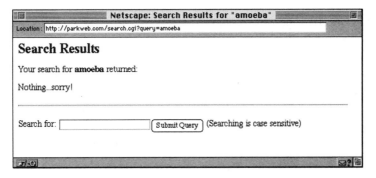

Fig. 13–16 Searching for "amoeba" yields *no* matches, so the resulting page has no links on it.

Every other script we've showed you so far was called from an HTML page that was independent of the script. This one is different; to call up the search form, a browser looks for a file named `search.cgi` (or whatever you name the script). The script then generates its own page on the fly. Later, when a search query is passed to the script, it activates itself with new parameters. This will make more sense once you try it out.

This script is also different from the previous examples because it does not specify `method="POST"` in the `<FORM>` tag. Therefore, all arguments (only one in this case) are sent as part of the URL for the new page (see Figures 13–15 and 13–16, where the URLs end with `?query=blue` and `?query=amoeba`). You could execute a search for a particular key word just by typing in a new URL or including that URL in an <A href> tag on another page.

Without too much work, you should be able to modify this script to search an order entry database or any other kind of text file. You may want to use a delimiter other than semicolons, or you might experiment with checkboxes or radio buttons that modify the search process or the output. Be creative, and have fun!

```perl
#!/usr/bin/perl

# The first statement in this script is, as usual, the one that
# requires cgi-lib.pl.  But we are NOT calling the 'ReadParse'
# subroutine immediately, because it will be used later, in an
# 'if' statement.
require "cgi-lib.pl";

# The $data_file variable is the name of the file that stores
# the URLs, page titles, and key words for your site.  It can
# be a relative or absolute path, but it's easiest to put the
# data file in the same directory as this script, so that you
# need only list the file's name.
$data_file = "database.txt";

# No matter what happens, the script will be returning an HTML
# file as output, so print an HTTP header:
print "Content-type: text/html\n\n";

# Call the 'ReadParse' subroutine (from cgi-lib.pl).  If nothing
# is returned ("!&ReadParse" means "NOT &ReadParse"), call the
# 'NoQuery' subroutine (at the end of this script).  This is, of
# course, what happens the first time the script is called, with
# no query.
if ( !&ReadParse )
  { &NoQuery; }

# Everything from this point on is executed if 'ReadParse'
# *does* return something; i.e., a query WAS passed to the
# script.  Note that 'ReadParse' was called from the 'if'
# statement, so our form data (if there was any) has been
# dumped into the %in array.
else
  {

  # Open the database file into a filehandle called DATABASE;
  # if that doesn't work, call the 'FileError' subroutine.  The
  # || operator (logical OR) is being used for flow control.
  open ( DATABASE , $data_file ) || &FileError;

  # Read the contents of DATABASE into the @data_lines array.
  @data_lines = <DATABASE>;

  # Go through the contents of @data_lines one line at a time.
  foreach ( @data_lines )
    {
```

```
            # Split the current line ($_) at the semicolons, and put
            # all of the pieces into an array named @phrases.  Note that
            # this array will change each time a new line is read from
            # the @data_lines array.
            @phrases = split ( /;/ , $_ );

            # This 'if' statement looks for the search key in the
            # @phrases array. @phrases need not be mentioned by name
            # here, because it is the current input ($_), which is the
            # default pattern search space.
                if ( /$in{'query'}/ )

              # If the key was found, then add a line to the variable
              # called $found.  The period is a text operator that
              # simply concatenates two text strings.   $phrases[0] is
              # the first piece of a database line (which is a URL), and
              # $phrases[1] is the second piece (a page's title).  If
              # the search key is found in any more lines in the
              # @data_lines array (on future passes through the
              # 'foreach' loop), they will be added to the end of
              # $found, so it will end up as a list of one or more HTML
              # links preceded by <LI> tags.
              { $found = $found .
                " <LI><A href=\"$phrases[0]\">$phrases[1]</A><BR>\n"; }

            # This curly bracket ends the 'foreach(@data_lines)' loop.
            }

    # Print out the results of the search.  Whether something was
    # found or not, the top of the output page will be the same.
    # The search query is included in the title of the page.
    # (By the way, these lines are not indented because everything
    # between the ENDOFTEXT markers is taken literally, and we
    # don't want those extra spaces.)
print <<ENDOFTEXT;
<HTML>
<HEAD><TITLE>Search Results for "$in{'query'}"</TITLE></HEAD>
<BODY>
<H2>Search Results</H2>
Your search for <B>$in{'query'}</B> returned:
<P>
ENDOFTEXT

    # If the search key matched any items in the database, then
    # the $found variable will exist, so print out its contents,
    # enclosed in a <UL> tag (because $found is a series of <LI>
    # list items).
    if ( $found )
      { print "<UL>\n$found</UL>\n<HR>\n"; }

    # If nothing was found, say exactly that:
    else
      { print "Nothing...sorry!\n<P>\n<HR>\n"; }
```

```
    # And this bracket finally closes off the else statement that
    # was started when 'ReadParse' was called and was not empty:
    }

# Finish off the HTML page.  Every page will end with the
# search input box, whether anything was found or not.
print <<ENDOFTEXT;
<FORM>
Search for: <INPUT name="query"><INPUT type="submit">
(Searching is case sensitive)
</FORM>
</BODY>
</HTML>
ENDOFTEXT


###################################################################
# The 'FileError' subroutine is called when the script has a
# problem opening the data file (either the file was not
# found or it was not readable).  The $! predefined variable
# is the current error message.  After printing out a page with
# the error message, the script immediately exits.

sub FileError {
print <<ENDOFTEXT;
<HTML>
<HEAD><TITLE>Error!</TITLE></HEAD>
<BODY>
Can't open database file ($data_file): $!
</BODY>
</HTML>
ENDOFTEXT

exit;
}


###################################################################
# The 'NoQuery' subroutine is called when no arguments are
# passed through 'ReadParse', either because a blank form was
# submitted or because the script is being called for the first
# time, and there has been no opportunity to enter a query.
# All this subroutine does is print out the top of a new
# search form; the actual input box is in the main program,
# because that will always be printed, regardless of what
# happened with 'ReadParse'.

sub NoQuery {
print <<ENDOFTEXT;
<HTML>
<HEAD><TITLE>Search Form</TITLE></HEAD>
<BODY>
<H2>Search this site</H2>
You can search this site's URLs, page titles, and key words.
<P>
ENDOFTEXT
}
```

## CHAPTER 14

Web Server Security
And Maintenance

When the term "computer security" is mentioned these days, it is usually perceived as meaning "protecting your computer against unwanted, malicious intruders." While this is certainly a major concern for any computer user or network administrator, it is only part of the equation. When you think about securing your Web server, you need to first define your overall goal. In the most general sense, this goal could be defined as follows: the server hardware and system software must be operational at all times, and the integrity of programs and files on this server can never be compromised.

Is this goal achievable? Probably not all of the time in this imperfect world, with imperfect people using imperfect hardware and software. Keep in mind that even ultra-secure government systems (the ones that might say, "I'm sorry Mr. President, but I can't give you a login") are still at the mercy of the abilities and character of the system operator. However, there are things you can do to minimize your potential problems. This chapter describes some of the steps you can take to meet this goal, from routinely backing up your system to creating a network firewall.

For the most complete and up-to-date information on some of the topics we cover here, check out Lincoln Stein's answers to frequently asked questions about WWW security:

```
http://www-genome.wi.mit.edu/WWW/faqs/www-security-faq.html
```

14.1 KEEPING YOUR SERVER RUNNING

There is no magic involved in keeping your server running at all times. You just need to keep Murphy's Law in mind — if something can go wrong, it will. Therefore, you need to have a solid hardware and software setup and a plan that will allow you to react to any failure and get your system up and running again as soon as possible. This section describes some of the things you can do to make your server as reliable as possible.

Buy a Reliable System

If your goal is to have the most reliable system possible, you might start by purchasing a system that has a proven track record for reliability. To find the right hardware, go to the library or bookstore and read current issues of the trade publications for your specific platform. You can usually find reviews of the latest offerings from the popular vendors. The independent tests that are performed are very extensive and should give you some idea of the systems' overall quality.

You should also be prepared to spend money on sturdy cables, phone cords, and connectors. Let's say you trip on your modem's cheap phone cord and sever it at, say, 7 p.m. on a Sunday evening. Unless you can scrounge up an extra one somewhere on the premises, the odds are good that you will be off the air until the following morning; definitely not a desirable situation! A good way to determine what you need to worry about is to simply remember the things that have caused you problems in the past. For example, there is a certain brand of discount modems that gave us such grief that we would never consider purchasing another one, especially if the availability of our server depended on it.

Be Familiar with Your System

Being a proficient user of any platform is not enough. You really have to know how your system works in order to quickly react to a failure. This means that if you run a Windows 3.1 site, you should know MS-DOS as well as the Windows program itself. If you are a PC user who installed LINUX for a dedicated server, you are well advised to learn how UNIX works. The fact that you managed to get your server software running is not enough, especially if you want to provide a layer of system security. Even Macintosh Webmasters should understand as much as possible about the guts of their system.

Backup, Backup, Backup

Back up everything, and do it often. Removable storage media, like tapes and diskettes, are very cheap. You will have to decide on the frequency of backups for your system, which will depend on the amount of activity you have. Even if you don't regularly update your server files, you still may want to keep daily backups of your access logs. If possible, you should keep a copy of your backup media off-site. This protects you in cases of natural disaster or theft.

Have a Substitute Server Available

If your server goes down with a serious problem, it's a good idea to have a backup server available. This doesn't necessarily mean that you need to have an identical system laying around waiting for a break down. If you have a dedicated server and another system that you do your computer work on, you can keep a copy of your server space on that system. Even though it probably will not have the performance of your dedicated server, you will still have your site available to the world. The last thing you want is for your server to appear to no longer be on the Web.

You can also keep a current copy of your files on another Web site (for instance, one belonging to a friend). Then, if you can recover your own system just to the point where it can handle a few simple HTTP requests, you can redirect requests to the alternative site while you restore the rest of your system. If it looks like you will be down for days or weeks, you can ask your provider if they can temporarily redirect all requests to this alternative site.

Have a Reliable and Supportive Provider

This is a very crucial point. Your server is nothing but a link in a chain. If your provider is unable to move packets to and from your site, you have problems. Folks accessing your site won't know (or care) why it is they can't access your system. It can very difficult to evaluate the reliability of a provider and the support they provide without actually using their services, so you may have to test the waters by signing up with a provider with the understanding that you may have to switch sometime in the future. While it won't tell you how reliable or friendly the various ISPs are, "The List" (`http://www.thelist.com`) will give you useful information about some of the technical details of thousands of providers around the world.

Keep Your Software Updated

As a rule of thumb, the most recent version of a given software package is usually the best and most stable (unless, of course, it's an "alpha" or "beta" version). Therefore, it's in your best interest to install the very latest versions of all your software — including your server package — as soon as they are released to the public.

Not only does having the latest software help you create a more crash-proof server, but new programs are often faster, making your site easier for people to visit. And, since security — especially in terms of on-line commerce — is such a hot topic on the Internet, security features are always being added. (For example, in late 1995, Netscape did a major re-release of their browsing software when a small security glitch was uncovered.) To find out which versions of your programs are the most current, check your favorite software archive periodically, or visit the home pages of the individual programs.

Read the Web Newsgroups for Your Platform

A few minutes each day reading these discussions can be time well spent. There is a wealth of information from Webmasters just like you who are encountering problems that you may have to deal with, or should be aware of. You can also become a valuable member of the Web server community by participating in these discussions and possibly lending a helping hand to someone else with problems. The actual names of these newsgroups are listed below:

- UNIX: `comp.infosystems.www.servers.unix`
- Windows: `comp.infosystems.www.servers.ms-windows`
- Macintosh: `comp.infosystems.www.servers.mac`
- General discussion: `comp.infosystems.www.servers.misc`
- Internet/Web security: `comp.security.announce`

You can also subscribe to a mailing list dedicated to Web server security by sending e-mail to `www-security-request@nsmx.rutgers.edu` with the following text in the message body:

```
subscribe www-security you@your.address
```

Beware of Viruses

No matter what you are using your computer for, you should be aware of the potential damage caused by viruses and Trojan horse programs. This is especially true when you are adding publicly distributed software from the Net or BBSs (though commercial software is not immune from this problem). You should take reasonable precautions to prevent your system from being infected. There are a number of software packages — many of them available for free — for every platform that can detect, identify, and remove viruses. You should get one of these packages and run it on a regular basis. Your best defense is to have the virus detector program run automatically every time you start your system.

To find virus protection software for your computer, check any of the major Internet software archives for your platform.

14.2 MANAGING USERS

If you allow people other than yourself to provide information on your server, you need to have a plan to limit what they can and cannot do. Even if you totally trust all of your users, they can make mistakes that could prove disastrous to your system.

This control is easier to enforce on single-user systems than on multi-user systems, because you can simply limit who has physical access to your computer. You can have people put their files (and changes to their files) on a diskette and do the copying yourself. You can also have them e-mail you the files for their server space. This way, you only have your own mistakes to worry about.

Multi-user systems have much more to worry about because numerous users have access to a common computer or network, usually from another location — be it down the hall or around the world. You probably already have a security policy set up at your site, but you should always be aware of a few things:

- Limit file and directory access. You need to let your users *execute* commands, but you certainly don't want people to be able to change them or delete them.
- On UNIX systems, alias dangerous commands, such as `rm *` and `rm -r *`, so that a user can't accidently wipe out everything in a directory tree.
- If your server software supports it, only allow users to set up Web file space off of their home directories, and not in the main server space. By allowing them access only to their own file space, any mistakes will only affect them and not other users.
- Set up some rules for your users about what they can put on their Web space. For example, you could limit their use to personal home pages that have content specific to their work or hobbies. The last thing you want is for one of your users to contract out as Webmaster for a Fortune 500 company on your server, thus saturating all your resources. And it's not just commercial activity that you should be worried about. If you want to see how quickly your server can get jammed with requests, simply allow one of your users to set up The Nude Supermodel Home Page!

Network Firewalls and Proxies

If you are installing a server on a network that is protected by a firewall, you have to decide where you are going to place your server. A firewall is usually a computer (or special router) that sits in front of your network, through which all information outside of your network comes in, and all information leaving your network goes out. The firewall rejects all packets that do not have the address of the network gate as the message originator or destination. However, the firewall can permit certain services to go through, such as e-mail and finger requests.

If you set up your firewall to permit HTTP transactions (or FTP, or Gopher, etc.), you are giving outsiders some of the access you deliberately set out to prevent. Therefore, it is probably best to put your Web server outside of the firewall. This, of course, means that the security you enjoy inside your network is not in effect on the server, but that is better than compromising every computer on your internal network.

You can also install a piece of software on your firewall machine called a *proxy*. When the proxy program is running, all HTTP requests for your network are automatically sent only to your Web server, which then returns all information back through the proxy and on to the requester. This is very useful for allowing users on a firewall-protected network to set up their Web pages without surrendering much of the security provided by the firewall. There is a wonderful site for proxy information and software located at `http://ftp.tis.com/`.

14.3 SELECTING A SERVER PACKAGE

Perhaps the most critical decision you make about server security is deciding which server package to install on your system. Windows 3.1 and Macintosh users have a limited number of choices, but Windows NT, Windows 95, and UNIX have a wide variety of server options available to them (and the list grows every day!). The best way to figure which server software best matches your needs is to make out a list of your requirements, and then read Paul Hoffman's WebCompare page, which you can find at `http://www.webcompare.com/`. This site reviews and evaluates all of the major features of virtually every known server package. This tip alone may be worth the time you spend reading this chapter!

14.4 PROTECTING YOUR DATA

Protecting your server from unwanted intruders is, perhaps, the most difficult security issue you will have to deal with as a Webmaster. The best way to prevent anyone from breaking into your server is to simply disconnect it from the Internet or your local network. Of course, this would defeat the purpose of having a Web server, so we need to examine some of things you can do to prevent unauthorized access. PC and Mac users are not as vulnerable as UNIX systems, but they certainly need to be aware that there are ways in which their systems can be broken into by remote users.

Once you have your server program installed, you need to worry about your configuration, and who has access to program and configuration files. It is very important to set it up right the first time. Once your server is up and running, it is very difficult to make major setup changes (like reorganizing your server file tree or disallowing user-owned Web directories).

File Space

The first thing you need to do is correctly configure your server's file space so that only that portion of your file system is accessible from HTTP calls. Once you are certain that only the files and programs that you *want* to be accessed are the only ones that *can* be accessed, you have solved many of your potential security headaches. You also need to carefully think out your server's file permissions. You should totally restrict access to critical server files.

CGI

Programs that run on your Web server make your site more interesting, but they also create a large number of potential security problems. For instance, a clever Web user might be able to submit form data that executes a command on a UNIX system, and a poorly designed script could accidentally take over an entire hard drive. See the end of Chapter 12 for details on CGI security.

Server-Generated Indexes

Server-generated indexes are very nice, and very safe if you define them correctly in your configuration. However, it is very easy to *not* set them up safely. One slip, and outsiders can potentially navigate throughout your entire file system!

Symbolic Links

Some servers allow the server space to include symbolic links (a.k.a. aliases) to directories in other areas of the file system. Once again, if the permissions are correctly set, this should not present a problem. Now, back to reality: if the permissions are open to everyone, any user can (potentially) see any file on your file system that your internal users can see. It's probably not a good idea to allow symbolic links to directories in your server's file tree; links to individual files are not nearly as much of a problem.

Port Numbers

The default software port for HTTP is port 80. However, all Web server packages allow you to set this port number to something else (as long as the number is greater than 1024). If you set your port number to 5002, all HTTP requests must include this number in their URLs. Remember, the real syntax of a URL is `http://web.server.site:port_#/filename`. If the port number is not included in the URL, port 80 is assumed. So, unless 5002 is included in the requestor's URL, the request is rejected by the server. While having a strange port number makes it harder for intruders to find you, it also makes it more difficult for the people you *want* to have access. You may want to set up two servers, with public files on port 80 and more sensitive documents on 7394, or some such random number.

UNIX Server Processes

UNIX servers should be careful to not have the effective user ID of server processes set to `root` (though you should be certain to *launch* your server as root-only). To do this, have the server program *owned* by `root` with exclusive `root` executable permissions set. But, set the user ID to a fictional, ordinary user named WWW (or JoBlo) in the main configuration file. This way, any attacker will be limited to doing only what WWW or JoBlo is allowed to do.

User Authentication

If you plan on limiting access to some files — or your entire server — to a defined set of users, you should use the authentication mechanisms described in the chapter that applies specifically to your platform (see Chapters 7 through 9). You can either allow and deny access to specific hosts, or you can require a password for access to your server. Every common server package that we have seen provides allow/deny and authentication facilities that are quite secure.

Other Internet Services

On multi-user systems, you need to worry about unauthorized access to your server from a variety of access points, not just your HTTP software. The fact that users can log into your system from a remote location leaves your entire computer at risk. The list of vulnerable spots on your computer includes (but is not limited to):

- Telnet hosts
- FTP servers
- NFS
- rlogin
- Gopher servers
- UUCP
- E-mail handlers
- Usenet news managers

All of these have particular security issues associated with them because they serve as individual access points to your system. Additionally, having interpreters and compilers available on your server is dangerous. Hackers that gain entry to your system are like kids in a candy store with these tools at their disposal. These issues are outside of the realm of this book; consult the software's documentation for specific security solutions.

You should also be aware that many of these services — and their associated security headaches — were once exclusive to the UNIX world. This is no longer the case, as all of them have been ported to other platforms in one way or another. For example, you can NFS-mount a DOS file system onto a UNIX system; you can set up UUCP and Gopher servers on PCs and Macintoshes; some seemingly harmless telnet utilities have the ability to turn your home computer's entire hard drive into a public FTP archive; and you can install an SMTP e-mail handler on any platform. A very good book that addresses many of these issues is *Practical UNIX Security,* by Simson Garfinkel and Gene Spafford, published by O'Reilly & Associates, Inc.

Message Encryption

Most Web documents on your server probably contain some sort of e-mail address so that people accessing your server can send e-mail to the page's author. If you want this e-mail to be protected, you should encourage both internal and external users to use message encryption. What's the best way to do this? Well, there is an emerging standard in Internet message encryption known as Pretty Good Privacy (PGP), developed by Philip Zimmermann. It requires software that you can get from links on `http://world.std.com/~franl/pgp/`. This URL also explains all of the gory details about how PGP works. However, the concept is relatively easy to understand.

When you encrypt a file, you scramble its contents into something unreadable or unusable. The contents of the scrambled file depend upon a key that was used in the scrambling procedure. So, a file with the key `abc` will be totally different from a file scrambled with the key `xyz`. The person receiving the file needs to know the key to decrypt the message. You could e-mail the receiver the key in a subsequent e-mail, but that would defeat the purpose because the interceptor could grab that message as well.

PGP solves this problem by providing a system that requires the recipient of a message or a file to create a public key (for encryption) and a private key (for decryption). Perhaps you have seen 128 characters of gibberish at the bottom of some e-mail messages or news postings. This is the compressed public key of the sender. If you want to send protected mail, you would use this key to encrypt a message with the PGP software. The software creates a garbled file that can only be decrypted with the recipient's private key. The actual implementation is a bit more complicated, but the software is easy to use.

14.5 RECOVERING FROM A BREAK-IN

In the event that a break-in has occurred on your system, you need to act quickly, especially if the break-in has been a malicious one. The first thing you need to do is to prevent it from happening again. In order to do this you should consider disconnecting your server from the outside world while you figure out what has happened. If files were altered or destroyed by the attacker, you should take this time to restore the files using your most recent backups.

To discover how the break-in happened, examine some of your server's log files. On Macintoshes and PCs, you will probably only have your HTTP server log files to review, unless you have other services (like FTP and Gopher) running on your system.

On a UNIX system with accounting turned on (which you should always have configured), you have a few more log files at your disposal. The `acct`, `utmp`, `wtmp`, `transferlog`, and `lastlog` files contain information about login and user activity. If your UNIX system has the `syslog` feature enabled, you have yet another resource for doing your detective work. The idea is to find the origin of the break-in and to see exactly which commands the intruder executed. This is just a starting point. If you can't trace the attack you should consult a book on computer security or one of the many security FAQs on the Net.

An intruder can come in from your local network, the Internet, or through a dial-up modem. A local network intruder may be the easiest to track down simply because the possible origination points are limited. It could easily be that some user forgot to log off, leaving it free for anyone walking by to do their thing. In this case, the remedy is to stress to all users the importance of logging off, and to implement some way to automatically log off idle users.

If the attack came from the Internet, you should contact the administrator of the originating site and see if they can solve the mystery. To locate an authority at the site, finger `root`, `webmaster`, or `postmaster` at that site. When you get a good contact name, send them e-mail describing the problem. This won't always be a solution, because the intruder could easily have come in through a chain of systems before getting to yours, but at least you've started the detective work.

If the attacker came in through a dial-up modem, it will be difficult to find where they called from unless you have some sort of caller identification system at your end. You should contact your phone company for details on this service and how to use it with your particular server platform.

If you do manage to find out who broke into your system and what they did, you need to determine if the activity warrants criminal prosecution. This is, again, far beyond the scope of this book, but your Internet service provider will probably be able to help you choose your course of action.

14.6 COMMERCIAL ACTIVITY

There is no universally accepted method for ensuring the security of commercial business on the Web, but there are plenty of products competing for this potentially lucrative market. The products and services from the following companies provide the means for secure commercial transactions over the Internet. However, they are usually proprietary commercial-ware in nature, and are not stand-alone, "off-the-shelf" products that can be appropriately described in this book. Read the information at these URLs and see if any of them has the transaction system that meets the requirements of your business.

- Digicash: `http://www.digicash.nl/`
- Cybercash: `http://www.cybercash.com/`
- VeriFone: `http://www.verifone.com/products/commerce/`
- First Virtual: `http://www.fv.com/`
- Netscape: `http://www.netscape.com/comprod/netscape_commerce.html`

HTML Quick
Reference Guide

*T*his appendix is, as its name implies, a *quick* reference guide to the most common HTML commands. The purpose of our book is to help you set up the hardware and software to build a functional World Wide Web server, and you will need to know some basic HTML tags to accomplish this. But we do not have enough room for a complete discussion of all the ins and outs of HTML. (One thing not covered in this Appendix is HTML forms, because we go through those in detail in Chapter 12.)

If you are interested in learning more, there are many excellent books on writing HTML; there are also many Web sites with *complete* HTML reference guides or tips on writing "good" HTML. Here are a few URLs you might want to check out:

- A Beginner's Guide to HTML:
  `http://www.ncsa.uiuc.edu/General/Internet/WWW/HTMLPrimer.html`
- The WWW Consortium's HTML Specification page:
  `http://www.w3.org/pub/WWW/MarkUp/html-spec/html-spec_toc.html`
- A list of various HTML guides:
  `http://union.ncsa.uiuc.edu/HyperNews/get/www/html/guides.html`
- Netscape's HTML reference materials:
  `http://www.netscape.com/assist/net_sites/`

NOTE: It makes no difference at all whether your HTML tags are uppercase or lowercase. In this book, we have generally followed the pattern of writing the names of tags in capital letters (e.g., `<IMG>`, `<BR>`) and the attributes of these tags in lowercase (e.g., `align=left`, `clear=all`). When writing your own HTML, you'll find that uppercase is nice because it stands out, but lowercase is easier to type. Use whichever you feel comfortable with, and don't be surprised when you view the HTML source for other people's pages and find that they use all uppercase, all lowercase, or a random mix of both!

A.1 STRUCTURAL TAGS

<HTML>...</HTML>

These tags enclose the entire HTML document, and tell the browser that everything in between should be read as HTML. In practice, some browsers don't care whether these tags are actually present or not, but that's no excuse for leaving them out.

<HEAD>...</HEAD>

Encloses the header of the HTML document. Usually, the header includes only the title of the document.

<TITLE>...</TITLE>

The title of the document is always in the header. It defines what shows up at the top of the browser's window. In a browser such as Netscape or Mosaic, this is also the default text that gets inserted into a Web surfer's bookmark file or hotlist. Ideally, someone should be able to glance at the title and know exactly what the page is about.

<ISINDEX>

This tag is usually placed in the header, although it can go anywhere. It indicates that the document includes an interface to a database retrieval program; the browser then adds its own default search form to the page.

<BODY>...</BODY>

These tags should enclose everything after the header, except for the final </HTML> tag.

A.2 TEXT STYLES

Most of the tags in this section change the appearance of individual letters, so they have little effect in text-based Web browsers such as Lynx. Furthermore, the exact appearance of most of these text styles is determined by the browser, so keep it simple.

The <EM>, <STRONG>, <CODE>, and <ADDRESS> tags are called "logical" styles; they represent *concepts* of text formatting, and it is left to the browser to decide exactly what the output will be. <B>, <I>, and <TT> (bold, italics, and typewriter) are "physical" styles. They do exactly what their names imply.

Technically, it is preferable to use logical styles to provide emphasis and other character formatting, but the output of logical and physical tags is usually identical, so in the end it is up to you. You may prefer to use `<B>` and `<I>` simply because the tags take up less space, and they make your HTML source a little easier to read.

Figure A–1 presents a list of most of the HTML text styles, along with samples of how they are displayed in Netscape.

Netscape: HTML Text Styles

HTML tag	Output in Netscape
`<I>`	*Italics*
`<B>`	**Bold face**
`<TT>`	`Typewriter text`
`<EM>`	*Emphasis*
`<STRONG>`	**Strong**
`<CODE>`	`Code`
`<ADDRESS>`	*Address*

Fig. A–1   HTML character tags and their output in Netscape.

`<EM>`...`</EM>`

Emphasis. Most browsers interpret this as *italics*.

`<STRONG>`...`</STRONG>`

Supposedly, this is "stronger" emphasis than the `<EM>` tag. It is usually displayed in **boldface**. If you want even more emphasis, you can use `<EM>` and `<STRONG>` together.

Tip: if you want a block of text to begin with a "heading" that sits on the same line as the rest of the words, `<STRONG>` or `<B>` is probably your best bet, since it does not cause a line break like the heading tags do. (A further hint: to have a really nice run-in heading, add three or four non-breaking spaces — ` ` — between the heading and the text; see Fig. 10–10 on page 235 to see what this looks like).

`<CODE>`...`</CODE>`

Causes any enclosed text to be displayed in a `monospaced` (equal-width) font such as Courier or Monaco. The `<CODE>` tag is often used to format e-mail addresses or URLs. It is named "code" because it was originally intended for displaying computer programming code.

<ADDRESS>...</ADDRESS>

This is supposed to be used for information (phone, e-mail, etc.) about the author of a page, or disclaimers, copyrights, etc. It is usually displayed in *italics*, and usually goes at the bottom of the page.

<I>...</I>

Italics. This physical style usually has exactly the same effect as the <EM> (emphasis) tag.

<B>...</B>

Boldface type. Corresponds to the <STRONG> tag.

<TT>...</TT>

"Computer" text (although the "TT" abbreviation actually comes from "teletype"). This tag has essentially the same effect as <CODE>.

<PRE>...</PRE>

This tag encloses preformatted text. Anything between the <PRE> tags is displayed *as is* with regard to horizontal spacing and line breaks. (Other HTML tags will still work, however.) Use <PRE> when you have tabular data in plain text format.

<H1>...</H1>, <H2>...</H2>, etc.

There are six levels of headings; H1 is huge, and H5 and H6 are usually smaller than body text (and consequently quite hard to read!). When you end a heading, you automatically start a new paragraph. Figure A–2 shows the appearance of all six levels of headings in the Netscape browser.

A.3 Page Layout

The following tags are used to indicate line breaks, white space, indentation, rule lines, and other layout elements. They are usually implemented in text-based as well as graphical Web browsers, in some form or another. (Of course, the exact spacing, margins, etc., will vary from one program to another.)

<P>

The <P> tag separates paragraphs, with a line of white space between them. In earlier HTML specifications, <P> had to be finished off with </P>; the closing

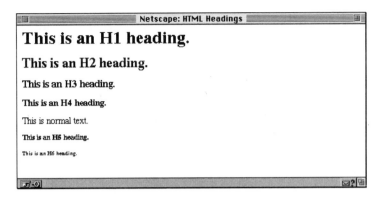

Fig. A–2   The six levels of HTML headings, as displayed in Netscape.

tag is now optional, although some HTML editing programs may complain if you omit it. Adding many consecutive <P> tags does *not* add more white space; for that you need to use <BR>. The latest versions of the HTML specification also allow you to add an align attribute to the <P> tag; see page 374, "Divisions and Aligned Paragraphs," for details.

Inserts a line break. It differs from the <P> tag in that it does *not* add a blank line, it just moves the next line of text back to the left margin. *Multiple*
 tags, however, can be used to insert large amounts of white space.

<BR clear={left,right,all}>

The clear attribute of the <BR> tag is only used with the align=left and align=right attributes of the <IMG> tag (see section A.5 below), so don't worry about it on pages that contain no images! Clear=left inserts a line break, then moves down past any images to the first place with a clear left margin. Clear=right does the same thing on the right side, and clear=all resets both margins.

<HR>

A horizontal rule line. Includes a little bit of blank space on either side. In graphical browsers, it has a shaded, 3-D appearance.

<BLOCKQUOTE>...</BLOCKQUOTE>

Encloses a block of text that is slightly indented from both the left and right margins.

> In publishing, of course, a block quote is used for large blocks of material quoted from another source, like this. (Except, this isn't quoted material, it's just an example of what a block quote looks like.)

A.4 LISTS

There are three types of lists: unordered, ordered (numbered), and definition. Any of the list types can be used within each other or within themselves. The browser program will distinguish the increasingly deeper levels of list items with indentation and/or different bullets. Don't forget to close off your list tags, or everything from that point on will remained indented or bulleted!

You can make use of HTML lists to create some nice-looking headings; refer to pages 234-236 in Chapter 10 for details and an illustration (Fig. 10–10).

<UL>...</UL>

An unordered list. List items are typically indented and preceded by a bullet or asterisk.

<OL>...</OL>

An ordered list. The list items are indented and automatically numbered, starting with 1.

<LI>

This tag goes at the beginning of each item in unordered or ordered lists (*not* definition lists), and places a bullet or number there.

<DL>...</DL>

A definition list. It is so named because it is intended to be used for a list of definitions or glossary terms. Of course, you don't have to use it that way; sometimes <DL> can be useful for indenting some text or pictures in a particular way. The items in the list are defined by the <DT> and <DD> tags.

<DT>

The key term to be defined, in a definition list. It will be placed along the left margin of the page.

<DD>

The definition part of a definition list, usually containing more text than the <DT> item. All lines following <DD> will be indented a few spaces over from the left margin.

A.5 IMAGES

The basic image tag is <IMG>, but the attributes included within the brackets control everything about it, so we will list them in detail:

Src="*filename or URL*"

This is the "source" attribute, and it is the only one that *must* be present in an <IMG> tag. It defines which picture is to be displayed, and it can be either a relative file name (e.g., `"../../images/photo1.gif"`) or a complete URL to a picture or a program that outputs a picture.

Alt="*alternate text*"

Text-based browsers cannot display images, so you can specify some alternate text that will show up instead of the default `[IMAGE]` placeholder. Also, some graphical browsers will display the alternate text if automatic image loading is turned off.

Align=*{top,middle,bottom,left,right}*

If you set the alignment to `top`, any text before and after the image (on the same line) will be aligned with the top edge of the image. The `align=middle` and `align=bottom` attributes follow the same pattern.

`Align=left` and `align=right` are slightly more complicated. If you give an image `left` alignment, the image will go on the left side of the screen, and any subsequent text will be placed along the right side of the image, even if there are many lines of text. Once the text reaches the bottom of the picture, it will return to the left margin of the page; in other words, the text flows *around* the picture. `Right` alignment does the same thing, but the image is placed along the right margin. Use the `clear` attribute of the <BR> tag (page 365) to move down past an image and return to the margin.

Figure A–3 shows simple examples of all of the standard <IMG> alignments.

Ismap

If the <IMG> tag includes the `ismap` attribute, the image will be interpreted by browsers as a clickable image map, and clicking on the image sends a pair of

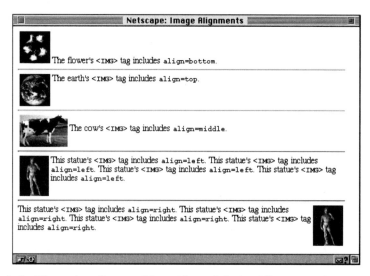

Fig. A–3 The various flavors of the `align` attribute of the `<IMG>` tag.

coordinates back to the server. Text-based browsers such as Lynx cannot use image maps at all.

To put it all together, here is a sample `<IMG>` tag that incorporates three of the commonly used attributes:

```
<IMG align=bottom alt=" :) " src="/images/smiley.gif">
```

A.6 LINKS AND ANCHORS

`<A href="filename or URL">...</A>`

This is your basic link tag. Like the "source" (`src`) attribute of the `<IMG>` tag, the quotes can contain an absolute file name on your own system, a relative file name, or a full URL. Everything (text and/or images) between the beginning and closing tags will be highlighted by browsers, and clicking on the highlighted area will call up the file located within the `href` attribute.

Besides pointers to files and programs, there are two other common uses of `<A href>` tags: newsgroups and e-mail. `Href="news:sci.med"` will lead to the `sci.med` newsgroup, and `href="mailto:bob@yoursite.com"` will initiate an e-mail message to Bob, at your site.

`<A name="nametext">...</A>`

Use this tag to set "anchors" within documents. The `<A name>` tag does not affect the appearance of the documents, just specifies the location of the anchor.

An anchor is a specific *point* within a document that can be referenced with a URL or file name that ends with a # symbol and the name of the anchor. Here is an example of an `<A href>` tag that references an anchor in another file, which was defined with `<A name="shells">`.

```
<A href="http://www.ostrich.org/Eggs.html#shells">
```

If you were to follow this link, your browser would load the HTML document named `Eggs.html`, but you would be shown the section of the page marked with the `shells` anchor, rather than the top of the page.

A.7 SPECIAL CHARACTERS

HTML allows you to use a number of characters that are not standard on most computer keyboards. To display these characters (such as accented letters or mathematical symbols), you must use a special code instead. Even if your computer *can* type these characters, you should use the HTML character codes, because browsers may not recognize your system's encoding of these symbols. The following list presents some of our favorites, along with the codes used to display them. Each symbol has both a named code and a numeric code; you can use either one, but more browsers understand the numeric codes.

	` `	` `	Non-breaking space
<	`&#60;`	`&lt;`	Less-than sign
>	`&#61;`	`&gt;`	Greater-than sign
¢	`&#162;`	`&cent;`	American cent
£	`&#163;`	`&pound;`	British pound
¥	`&#165;`	`&yen;`	Japanese yen
©	`&#169;`	`&copy;`	Copyright
®	`&#174;`	`&reg;`	Registered trademark
±	`&#177;`	`&plusmn;`	Plus or minus
÷	`&#247;`	`&divide;`	Division sign (obelus)
°	`&#176;`	`&deg;`	Degree sign
é	`&#233;`	`&eacute;`	Lowercase E with acute accent
ñ	`&#241;`	`&ntilde;`	N with tilde
ö	`&#246;`	`&ouml;`	O with umlaut

Two caveats: first, these *are* case sensitive, unlike everything else in HTML; second, the Internet community has not come to any sort of agreement about which codes should be included in the official HTML specification, nor what the named codes should be. So if you want to use some the more obscure characters — ¿the inverted question mark, for example? — use the numeric code rather than the named one.

For a *complete* list of the special characters and their codes, see the following URL:

`http://www.uni-passau.de/~ramsch/iso8859-1.html`

A.8 NETSCAPE 1.1 EXTENSIONS TO HTML

Netscape 1.1 supports a number of nifty tags and attributes that other browsers do not. (Netscape 2.0 supports even more; those are covered in the next section.) The majority of people use Netscape as their primary Web browser, but keep in mind that many do not. We recommend using many of the Netscape extensions, since they allow you to create some pretty cool page layouts, but — and this is a very important "but" — *make sure* that your pages look okay in the other browsers, especially text-based ones.

Keep in mind that many of the Netscape extensions will eventually be incorporated into the standard HTML specification (especially the good ones!). Many of them may even have been included by the time you read this. Since HTML is constantly changing, it is wise to keep abreast of the latest developments on the Net. For information on the current standards, visit the WWW Consortium's HTML page: `http://www.w3.org/pub/WWW/MarkUp/`.

Tables

Many people still refer to HTML tables as "Netscape 1.1 tables," because Netscape 1.1 was the first widely released browser to support them. Tables are no longer exclusive to Netscape, although Netscape supports a number of table tags that other graphical browsers do not. We will not cover the specific syntax involved in creating tables here, because they are somewhat complicated, and the best way to see how they work is to look at various real-life examples on the Web. Therefore, we will refer you to some excellent on-line documents that will teach you everything you need to know about Netscape tables.

- Netscape's document that lists all table tags and their syntax:
  `http://www.netscape.com/assist/net_sites/tables.html`
- Netscape's very straightforward examples of all kinds of table layouts:
  `http://www.netscape.com/assist/net_sites/table_sample.html`

<CENTER>...</CENTER>

This tag does exactly what it sounds like it does: text is centered horizontally on the page. Be sure to also read about the `<P align=center>` and `<DIV>` tags on page 374; they accomplish the same thing as `<CENTER>`, but they're newer and will be an official part of HTML.

<BLINK>...</BLINK>

The infamous blink tag. It produces text that blinks on and off. *A lot of people hate it,* and Netscape for Windows doesn't implement it very well, so use it only if you really, really, really need to get someone's attention.

<BASEFONT size=*n*>

If you include this tag in your document, you can change the default size of the text (the range is 1 to 7, and the default is 3). The `<FONT size>` tag can adjust this size for individual letters, words, or paragraphs.

<FONT size=*{n,+n,-n}*>...</FONT>

Use this tag to specify the exact size of your text, from 1 to 7. If you use a relative number (e.g., +2 or -1), it will make the text larger or smaller than the `basefont` size. Don't forget to close the tag with `</FONT>`!

Rather than `<FONT size>`, HTML gurus would rather you used the `<BIG>` and `<SMALL>` tags, which will definitely be incorporated into the HTML specification; see page 374.

<NOBR>...</NOBR>

"No break." Any text encompassed by this tag will *not* wrap around to the next line. Use it for long sequences of characters that include spaces but which must not be broken up. If you just have one or two words that must stay together, it is easier to simply insert one or two non-breaking spaces — ` ` — than to mess around with `<NOBR>`.

<WBR>

We love the "word break" tag. It allows you to specify that a sequence of characters *can* break at a certain point. For instance, if you want to write "male/female", and you want to let it break between the slash and the "f" (if that happens to be where the edge of the page falls), you can write the HTML like this: `male/<WBR>female`. This tag is also useful for writing long names of Usenet newsgroups, like `rec.music.makers.songwriting`.

<HR size=*n*>

Specifies how thick, in pixels, a horizontal rule line should be. The default is 2, and it can range from 0 to 100, although `size=0` and `size=1` just produce thin black lines, and anything thicker than about 8 looks more like an empty rectangle than a rule line.

The `size` attribute, along with the other three `<HR>` modifications that follow, has no effect on non-Netscape-compatible browsers. The horizontal rule lines will show up as if they had no special attributes.

<HR width={n,n%}>

Sets the horizontal width (length) of a rule line; the default is 100%. If the argument is a plain number, it is interpreted as a width in pixels — most screens are about 640 pixels across, but it can vary widely. Therefore, a better solution is to specify a percentage, which is a percentage of the full width of the Netscape window.

<HR align={left,right,center}>

Sets a rule line's left-to-right position on the page. If you don't specify anything, it will be centered. (Note that this only affects lines whose width is less than 100% of the screen, since full-screen lines don't have any room to move!)

<HR noshade>

Removes the 3-D appearance of a rule line; instead, it shows up as a plain black line of whatever thickness you define with the `size` attribute.

<IMG align={texttop, absbottom, absmiddle, baseline}>

Netscape was the first program to make use of the `align=left` and `align=right` attributes. Other browsers recognize these tags now, but Netscape still has a few other alignments that you can use, and a few other extensions to the `<IMG>` tag as well.

Texttop   Since Netscape allows you to change the size of the text, this `align` attribute was created to align an image with the top of the *tallest* text in a given line.

Absbottom   Aligns the image with the *absolute* bottom of the current line (surprisingly, this is *not* what the standard `align=bottom` attribute does).

Absmiddle   Aligns the image with the *absolute* middle of the current line of text (again, `align=middle` doesn't quite accomplish this).

Baseline   Exactly the same as the standard `bottom`, but the Netscape folks think this is "a better name."

<IMG width=*{n,n%}*>, <IMG height=*{n,n%}*>

These attributes simply set the size of the rectangle in which an image is displayed (*not* the size of the image file itself). If *n* is a plain number, it is a measurement in pixels. If *n* is a percentage, it is a percentage of the height or width of the current browser window, *not* of the image itself.

<IMG border=*n*>

The `border` attribute places a solid border of thickness *n* (in pixels) around the image (the default is 2 for linked images and 0 for non-linked images; the range is 0-127). For images enclosed in the `<A href>` tag, this border is colored the same as all other links on the page; otherwise, it is the color of the plain text. Setting `border=0` in a linked image can be useful in certain circumstances, but keep in mind that it makes it hard to tell if an image is "clickable." Giving any image a border thicker than about 10 pixels usually looks ridiculous.

<IMG hspace=*n*>, <IMG vspace=*n*>

These attributes create an *invisible* border around an image (default: 0; range: from 0 to 127). They are usually used to keep text from butting right up against a picture. (Note: some versions of Netscape *automatically* put a small "buffer zone" — equivalent to `hspace=3` — next to images formatted with the `align=left` and `align=right` attributes.)

A.9 NETSCAPE 2.0 EXTENSIONS TO HTML

With the release of Netscape 2.0, the world's most popular Web browser added even more features to its already expanded HTML (dubbed "NHTML" by some). Most of the new Netscape 2.0 tags were included in the *proposed* specification for HTML 3.0, and Netscape claims to have implemented those features that they felt would probably be approved in the final draft. They also added a few things that were not in the proposed spec at the time, but which they were planning to add to the proposal, and which would probably be eventually approved because so many people use Netscape.

We're not going to cover *all* of the Netscape 2.0 extensions, but there are a few new things we think you should be aware of. All of the Netscape 2.0 features that we are describing here are ones that *were* in the HTML 3.0 draft when Netscape introduced them, so we are confident that they will be incorporated into HTML. By the time you read this, they may have already been included, or at least supported by other browsers such as Mosaic.

For a *complete* discussion of Netscape 2.0's new features, check out the following documents:

```
http://www.netscape.com/eng/mozilla/2.0/relnotes/
```

```
http://www.netscape.com/assist/net_sites/html_extensions_3.html
```

Superscripts and Subscripts

Netscape 2.0 allows you to create superscripted and subscripted text by using the ^{and _{tags, respectively. They are logical styles that work just like <EM>, <STRONG>, etc. Don't forget to close off your superscripting or subscripting with} or}.

<BIG> and <SMALL>

More logical styles. These accomplish pretty much the same thing as Netscape's <FONT size> feature, but you can only choose between "big" and "small," not sizes 1 through 7. The good news is that all browsers will support <BIG> and <SMALL> at some point in the future, whereas <FONT size> might remain exclusive to Netscape.

Divisions and Aligned Paragraphs

The <DIV> tag is used to define sections of a page that should be centered, aligned along the left margin, or aligned along the right margin. The syntax is as follows:

```
<DIV align={center,left,right}> Text goes here </DIV>
```

Divisions are an official part of HTML 3.0, and as such are a universally accepted replacement for Netscape's <CENTER> tag, because <DIV align=center> will accomplish exactly the same thing. But until everyone is using browsers capable of understanding HTML 3.0 or NHTML 2.0, you'd better stick with <CENTER> if you want things in the middle of the page.

Both Netscape 2.0 and HTML 3.0 also support the use of the align attribute in the <P> tag. This works exactly like the <DIV> tag. If you use <P align={left,right,center}>, be careful to close your centered or right-aligned sections with </P>; without an align attribute, <P> does not require a closing tag, so it's easy to forget.

Figure A–4 illustrates all of the Netscape 2.0 extensions that we have covered so far: superscripts, subscripts, big text, small text, and aligned paragraphs.

Frames

Frames are a way to compile several Web pages into a single screen. We mentioned them in our discussion of compatibility in Chapter 10; see page 262. We will not explain how to create frames in this quick reference guide, but we will point you to Netscape's official documentation:

```
http://www.netscape.com/assist/net_sites/frames.html
```

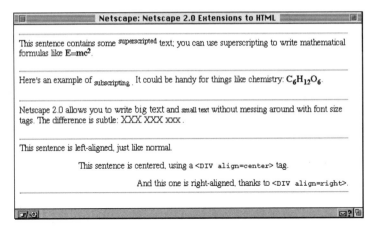

Fig. A–4   Some of the Netscape 2.0 extensions to HTML.

As we said in Chapter 10, don't forget to include <NOFRAME> tags for the benefit of those who are not using Netscape 2.0. As with any new features, you are free to use frames as much as you want, if you keep your pages backward-compatible with older browsers.

Client-Side Image Maps

Yet another nifty feature whose exact syntax is too complicated to explain here. With normal (server-side) image maps (<IMG> tags that include the ismap attribute), there must be a map serving program on the Web server that reads a special map definition file, which declares what the various "hot zones" on the map mean.

In a client-side image map, the coordinates of the hot zones and their associated URLs are included in <MAP> and <AREA> tags in the HTML source for the page upon which the map resides, and the browsing program decides what to do. This is much faster and more efficient than server-side image maps. What's more, the <MAP> tag allows for alternate text links that can be read by non-graphical browsers — hallelujah!

Whoever dreamed up client-side image maps was really thinking when they put it together. Not only will the <MAP> and <AREA> tags be safely ignored by browsers that don't support them, but you can also set up a picture so that it can be used as both a client- *and* server-side map. For details, check out the following URLs:

```
http://www.netscape.com/assist/net_sites/html_extensions_3.html

http://www.spyglass.com/techspec/img_maps.html
```

UNIX Quick Reference Guide

*K*nowing some UNIX is valuable for a Webmaster; it is likely that you will either be running a UNIX server or connecting to one to transfer files. At the very least, your arrangement with your Internet service provider will probably include a UNIX shell account that you can log into. Therefore, it helps to understand UNIX basics like file naming conventions, file permissions, file compression, and a few other things.

This quick reference presents the basic UNIX concepts and commands that will let you be productive on a UNIX system without having to invest a lot of time learning all the details. If you want more in-depth information, refer to one of the many UNIX books on the market today, or check out one of these very useful Web sites:

- UNIX Reference Desk at Northwestern University:
  `http://www.eecs.nwu.edu/unix.html`
- CERN UNIX User Guide:
  `http://wsspinfo.cern.ch/file/doc/unixguide/unixguide.html`
- UNIX Help for Users:
  `http://unixhelp.ed.ac.uk/index.html`

There are several versions of UNIX available, including UNIX System V, originally from AT&T; BSD UNIX, from the University of California at Berkeley; AIX, for the IBM world; ULTRIX, for DEC systems; and LINUX, for IBM-compatible PCs. Although there is much similarity between all these versions of UNIX, there are some differences in commands and system behavior.

The commands in this quick reference are available on virtually every implementation of UNIX. The examples shown are from a LINUX system.

B.1 GETTING STARTED

Here are the basics for getting logged in, ensuring that the system recognizes your terminal or PC, typing characters, and logging out.

Logging In

Because UNIX is a multi-user system, you have to log in to start your session, and log off to end your session. Here is what the login process looks like on a machine running LINUX:

```
Linux 1.2.13 (parkweb) (ttyp0)

parkweb login: bob
Password:
Last login: Thu Feb 29 19:57:58 from dialup-15-c.gw.u

%
```

Enter your user ID — also called your login name — and password when prompted (for security reasons, the password will not show up on the screen as you type).

Once you have logged onto a UNIX system, you are connected to the shell (command interpreter), which gives you a system prompt. The appearance of this prompt varies by system and by shell. Common prompts are a dollar sign ($), a percent sign (%), the system name, or a string of characters indicating your current directory (e.g., /usr/joe).

No matter what the prompt looks like, you should have a cursor on that line waiting for you to type in a command. MS-DOS users should be very familiar with this concept; in fact, many of the basic commands have identical or similar command line syntax.

You always start out in your home directory; see section B.2 for more information on what this means.

Changing Your Password

For security reasons, you should change your initial password (the one first assigned with your new account). You should also change your password occasionally, to discourage others from guessing it.

Use the passwd command to change your password. You will be asked for your old password, for verification, and then for the new password, twice. Most systems require that your password have between 6 and 8 characters; at least two characters must be alphabetic, and at least one must be non-alphabetic (numbers or punctuation). It also cannot be too similar to your login name or your previous password.

This sounds obvious, but remember your password; if you forget it, the system administrator can't tell what your current password is (no one can), but he or she can give you a new one if you ask nicely.

Setting Your Terminal Type

UNIX supports many different terminal types, and it handles the display and keyboard definitions appropriately. If you want full-screen displays and editors such as `vi` to behave correctly, you or the system administrator must set your account up to handle your terminal or PC.

If your terminal doesn't seem to be handling the display correctly, you can reset the terminal type with the following commands. Here is an example for the C shell (`csh`) and the VT-100 terminal type:

```
% setenv TERM vt100

% unsetenv TERMCAP
```

For the Bourne shell (`sh`) and Korn shell (`ksh`), the following commands should work:

```
$ TERM=vt100
$ export TERM
$ TERMCAP=""
```

Characters: Backspace, Special Characters, etc.

There are several special keys and characters defined for UNIX systems. These definitions can be customized by system, by terminal type, and by user, so the actual keys can vary. However, the following definitions are common. (The ^ designation means hold down the "control" key while pressing the following key.)

Backspace/character erase: Usually the "Backspace" or "Del" (delete) key

Line kill/line erase: Usually ^U or ^X

Line redraw: Usually ^R

Stop/abort command: ^C

Exit from command or shell: ^D

Suspend: ^Z   (restart with "`fg`" or "`bg`")

Log out (exit from shell): ^D   (some shells block this character)

Determining Your Shell

A "shell" is a command processor that interprets your commands and passes them to the operating system for execution. It is often helpful to know which shell you are running. Among other things, the shell can determine your system prompt and which command repetition and command editing functions you have available.

There are many different shells available; some of the more common ones are explained in the following list:

- The Bourne Shell (sh): The "original" shell on AT&T UNIX systems; offers basic programming functionality.
- The C Shell (csh): The original shell on BSD UNIX systems; allows job control and repetition of commands.
- The Korn Shell (ksh): Combines the best of sh and csh, and adds file name completion and command line editing.
- Tom's C Shell (tcsh): Enhanced C shell with file name completion and command line editing.
- Tcl Shell (tclsh): Simple shell containing a Tcl interpreter.

When your account is created, the system administrator determines your default shell (what you get automatically when you log in). Chances are, any shell is just fine for occasional use. More frequent UNIX users may find it useful to research the different shells (by asking experienced users which they use and why) and select one with the most appealing features.

Use the command finger *username* to display that user's current shell; to find out what your shell is, finger yourself (now stop laughing). The following example shows that user bob is running the C Shell (/bin/csh):

```
% finger bob
Login: bob                               Name: Uncle Bob
Directory: /home/bob                     Shell: csh
Last login Mon Mar 18 16:49 (CST) on ttyp2 from parkweb.com
Mail last read Mar 16 22:34:10 1996

%
```

You can try out a different shell by typing the name of the shell (for example, tcsh) as a command at a system prompt; type exit or ^D to exit the new shell and return to your original shell.

Logging Out

You must log out to cleanly end your UNIX session. One of the following commands will probably work:

logout

exit

^D (control-D)

B.2 NAVIGATING AROUND A UNIX SYSTEM

UNIX File Systems

Files in UNIX are stored in a hierarchical tree of directories much in the same way as MS-DOS. This means that individual files reside in directories created by the user in an existing directory. The directory tree looks something like a pyramid, starting with the root directory (Fig. B–1):

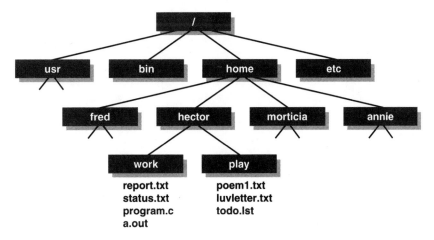

Fig. B–1 A typical directory tree in UNIX.

UNIX Path Names

To move to or access a directory, you can specify the path to the directory in two ways: as a full path name or a relative path name. A full path name specifies the path to the file starting at the root directory; as shown in the following example, a full path name always starts with the slash (/) character:

```
/usr/spool/mail/barney
```

A relative path name specifies the path to the file starting from the current directory (the one you are in); a relative path name never starts with the slash (/) character. Two periods (..) mean "go back one level in the directory structure"; a single period (.) means "stay in this directory." Relative path names look something like this:

```
music

./work/files/secret/recipes

../fred/letters/taxes/1995

../../../this/that
```

Listing the Contents of a Directory

Use the ls command to show the contents of a directory, as in the following example:

```
% ls
filesys       pathnames    tar.gzip
finger        perms        yellow
man           shells       zap
mymail        stuck
```

If you want to get fancy, you can use the ls command's -F option to display the type of the file. With -F, directory names are followed by a / character, and executable files (commands) are followed by a * character. The following example shows that man and stuck are directories, and yellow is an executable file:

```
% ls -F
filesys       pathnames    tar.gzip
finger        perms        yellow*
man/          shells       zap
mymail        stuck/
```

ls has many other useful options as well. You can find out about them by typing man ls at your command prompt; man displays the "man" page about any standard command (see section B.7 for details).

Changing Directories

The cd and chdir commands are used to change directories when navigating. These commands are essentially interchangeable, except that, on some UNIX systems, chdir is only available for C Shell users.

The following example shows how to use the cd command to change to the /usr/spool/mail/bigbird directory, using an absolute path name:

```
% cd /usr/spool/mail/bigbird
```

If you were already in /usr/spool, you would just type this shorter relative path name:

```
% cd mail/bigbird
```

Finally, if you were in the /usr/spool/mail/snuffy directory, you could get to /usr/spool/mail/bigbird like so:

```
% cd ../bigbird
```

Finding the Current Directory

Use the pwd command to display the name of the directory you are in, as in the following example:

```
% pwd
/usr/spool/mail/bigbird
```

Finding Your Home Directory

When you log in to a UNIX system, you always start out in your home directory. No matter where you roam, you can always quickly jump back to your home directory with the cd or chdir command. (If you don't specify a directory name after the command, you return to your home directory.)

Simply type the cd or chdir command with no directory name:

```
% cd
```

Creating Directories

The mkdir command creates directories.

To create a directory, you must be in a directory that allows you to add and delete files; for example, in your home directory or in /tmp. (Chances are that you will not be allowed to use mkdir in a system directory, unless *you* are the system administrator.)

The following example shows the creation of a new subdirectory called zygote within the current directory:

```
% ls -F
filesys       pathnames     tar.gzip
finger        perms         yellow*
man/          shells        zap
mymail        stuck/

% mkdir zygote

% ls -F
filesys       pathnames     tar.gzip
finger        perms         yellow*
man/          shells        zap
mymail        stuck/        zygote/

%
```

When you create a directory, you need to verify the directory's access permissions. See the "File Permissions" section on page 386 for information on this topic.

Removing Directories

The rmdir command removes directories.

The following example shows the use of rmdir to remove the newly-created directory zygote:

```
% rmdir zygote

% ls -F
filesys       pathnames    tar.gzip
finger        perms        yellow*
man/          shells       zap
mymail        stuck/

%
```

A directory must be empty before you can delete it; you must remove all its files first (see "Deleting Files," page 385). If there had been files in the `zygote` directory, an error message like this would be displayed:

```
rmdir:  zygote:  Directory not empty
```

Sometimes, you may think a directory is empty when it really isn't. "Dot" files may be the culprits. These are files whose names begin with a dot (`.`); you can see them by using `ls -a` or `ls -Fa` (the "a" stands for "all"). In fact, you might want to *always* use "a" in your `ls` commands.

B.3 FUN WITH FILES

Now that you know how to move around a UNIX file system, it's time to learn how to use certain commands to create, change, move, and delete files, as well as set UNIX file permissions.

In UNIX, a file can contain "anything" — text, binary information, graphics, application-specific information, you name it. Even a directory or a disk drive is represented as a file on a UNIX system. For the purposes of this quick reference, we will discuss only text files.

Creating Files

In general, you can create a file by moving or copying another file, saving news or e-mail messages, redirecting output from a command (not discussed in this guide), or opening a new file in an editor.

One of the simplest ways of creating a file is with `cat`. After you type a `cat` command, anything you type goes into a new file, until you end the command (and close the file) with the `^D` command. After this, you will again see the system prompt.

The following example shows the use of the `cat` command to create a short text file called `songs`:

```
% cat > songs
I Love Trash
Put Down The Ducky
Beginning, Middle, End
It's Not Easy Being Green
Somebody Come and Play Rubber Ducky
^D

%         .
```

For information on using the vi editor to create files, which allows you to correct typing errors and move to previous lines while creating the file, see section B.6.

Moving and Renaming Files

Use the mv command to rename a file or to move it to a different directory. The following example renames the file willow to willow.new:

```
% mv willow willow.new
```

Copying Files

Use the cp command to create a copy of a file. The following example *copies* the file willow to willow.new, so we are left with two identical files:

```
% cp willow willow.new
```

Deleting Files

Use the rm command to delete a file, as in the following example:

```
% rm dead.letter
```

Once you delete a file with rm, it's gone forever! Depending on your system backup policy and when you last changed the file, a current or previous version may be backed up, but there's no guarantee you can get it back. Be extremely careful when using rm. Make sure you know which directory you are really in, and which files you are really going to remove.

Consider always using the rm -i option, which requests confirmation before actually removing the file (which gives you a little time to reflect on your intended action). The following example shows this process:

```
% rm -i dead.letter
rm: Remove dead.letter (y/n)? y
```

If you answer y (for yes), the file is removed; if you answer n (for no), the file remains.

Changing Files

Although there are several ways to change a UNIX file, the easiest is with an editor. See section B.6, "Editing Text Files With The vi Editor."

File Permissions

All UNIX files (including directories) have associated owner, group, and access permissions, which control access to the file.

To view the permissions for a file or directory, use the ls -l ("long") option, as in the following example:

```
total 24
-rw-r--r--    1 bob         users       6058 Mar 23 15:29 filesys
drwxr-xr-x    1 bob         users        550 Mar 23 15:53 man
-rw-------    1 bob         users       1334 Mar 23 15:36 mymail
drwxr-x---    1 bob         users        469 Mar 23 16:21 stuck
-rwxr-xr-x    1 bob         users      15301 Mar 26 00:48 yellow
```

The ls -l command shows the file permissions (-rw-r--r--), owner (bob), group (users), and the size of the file in bytes, as well as the last modification time and the name of the file. The d at the beginning of the lines for man and stuck indicate that they are directories.

File access can be limited to the owner, extended to the owner and other members of the same group, or extended to all users of the system. The available permission codes are as follows:

Read access (r): The file can be examined or copied; if the file is a directory, its contents can be listed.

Write access (w): The file can be changed (but *not* deleted; for that, you need execute access).

Execute access (x): If a command, the file can be executed; if a directory, the directory may be entered or traveled through (using cd) and files may be added or deleted.

All the files you create are owned by you, and are in your group (the group is defined by the system administrator). The permissions are set by default; you can change them as you see fit. For example, it is usually a good idea to allow yourself read, write, and execute permission to all your files and directories, but if you do not want others to change them, you should deny write access for others.

The chmod command changes the permissions of a file. The permissions may be specified as absolute (with numbers) or symbolic (with letters); only absolute mode is discussed here.

The absolute mode consists of a three-digit number; each digit can be in the range 0-7. The first digit controls permissions for the owner of the file. The middle digit controls permissions for all members of the group. The last digit controls permissions for all other users.

The digits themselves have the following meanings:

0 No permission
1 Execute permission
2 Write permission
3 Execute and write permission
4 Read permission
5 Read and execute permission
6 Read and write permission
7 Read, write, and execute permission

Basically, **4**=read, **2**=write, and **1**=execute. Add any combination of these together and you'll get a number between 1 and 7.

Use the chmod command to change file and directory permissions. After the command name, specify the absolute permissions (the three-digit number), and then the file name. (And remember that directories must have execute permission in order for the cd command to work.) For example, to allow yourself to change a file, but allow others to only look at it, use the following command:

```
% chmod 644 look-at-this
```

To set permissions for a directory that you want others to be able to look at, but in which only you can add and delete files, use the following command:

```
% chmod 755 see-my-directory
```

If you don't want anyone else to be able see the contents of a file or directory, use the following permissions for the chmod command:

```
% chmod 600 secret-file
```

```
% chmod 700 secret-directory
```

If you want to set the most liberal file or directory permissions possible, so that anyone can change or delete a file — or add files to a directory — use the following commands:

```
% chmod 666 anybodys-file
```

```
% chmod 777 public-directory
```

Note that the only permission required to delete a file is *write* permission on the *directory* in which that file exists. This means that anyone with write permission to a directory can delete any or all of the files in that directory, regardless of the permissions on the individual files.

File Compression

It's a rare system that has room for unlimited file storage. In your travels around the Internet, sooner or later you will come across a file that has been compressed to take up less space. Or you may find that you need to compress your own files so that you can free up more space.

There are several compression programs available on UNIX systems, including compress, pack, zip, and gzip. Each has a corresponding "uncompression" command to be run on the compressed file (like uncompress, unpack, unzip, and gunzip).

The newest compression command is usually the best (in other words, it compresses the file the most). At the time of writing, the gzip command provides the best freely available compression of standard text files. This command is shown in the following example, which also uses the ls -s ("size") command to display the size of the file before and after compression.

```
% ls -s
320 my-file

% gzip my-file

% ls -s
64 my-file.gz

%
```

Decreasing the file from 320 blocks to 64 blocks is quite a savings! Note that the compressed file is marked with the .gz extension. Use the gunzip command to restore the file to its original form, as in this example:

```
% gunzip my-file.gz

% ls -s
320 my-file

%
```

The gzip compression method seems to work best on text files and tar ("tape archive") files.

B.4 NETWORK COMMANDS

We assume that you are using UNIX in a networked environment — otherwise, you wouldn't be on the Web! The most basic network commands are ftp, telnet, and rlogin.

FTP

FTP is the Internet standard File Transfer Protocol. The ftp command allows you to transfer files to and from another site on the network. Generally, you must have an account and password on the other system. However, some sites allow "anonymous FTP" connections, which permit any user to connect with the user ID `anonymous` or `ftp` (no password is required for anonymous FTP, but you are requested to type your e-mail address in the password field).

When connected to a remote site via FTP, you are in a "restricted" environment; you can perform only a few operations, and you cannot explore the entire system.

To initiate an FTP connection to another system, type `ftp` and the desired site name on the command line. Enter your user ID (if different from your current one) and password when prompted. The following example shows the use of `ftp` to connect to the site `parkweb.com`:

```
% ftp parkweb.com
Connected to parkweb.com.
220 parkweb FTP server (Version wu-2.4(1)) ready.
Name (parkweb.com:stinky): bob
331 Password required for bob.
Password:
230 User bob logged in.

ftp>
```

Once connected to the other system, you can perform several tasks, such as a directory listing (`ls`), changing directories (`cd`), copying a file from the remote system (`get`), or putting a file from your system onto the remote system (`put`).

`ftp` is a command interpreter; when `ftp` is waiting for a command from the user, it displays the prompt `ftp>`.

While you are at the `ftp>` prompt, typing a `?` (question mark) will display a list of available `ftp` commands. (For more complex ftp operations, consult the `ftp` "man" page (see page 397) or a detailed UNIX guide.)

The `cd` command changes to a different directory, and behaves much like the UNIX `cd` command. The following example shows the use of this command:

```
ftp> cd stuff/things
250 CWD command successful.

ftp>
```

To display the contents of the current directory, use the `ls` command:

```
ftp> ls
200 PORT command successful.
150 Opening ASCII mode data connection for file list.
finger
man
perms
shells
stuck
tar.gzip
yellow
yourfile
zap
```

```
226 Transfer complete.
195 bytes received in 0.039 seconds (5.2 Kbytes/s)

ftp>
```

To copy a file from another system onto your system, use the `get` command as follows:

```
ftp> get yourfile
200 PORT command successful.
150 Opening ASCII mode data connection for yourfile (998 bytes).
226 Transfer complete.
local: yourfile remote: yourfile
1054 bytes received in 0.75 seconds (1.4 Kbytes/s)

ftp>
```

To copy a file from your system onto the remote system, use the `put` command as follows:

```
ftp> put .alias
200 PORT command successful.
150 Opening ASCII mode data connection for myfile.
226 Transfer complete.
local: myfile remote: myfile
1565 bytes sent in 0.0055 seconds (2.8e+02 Kbytes/s)

ftp>
```

To exit the FTP command interpreter and go back to your shell, use the `quit` command:

```
ftp> quit
221 Goodbye.

%
```

Telnet

Telnet is another system connection protocol; it allows you to log into another system anywhere on the Internet, as long as you have an account on that system.

To connect to another system, type `telnet` and the remote system's name on the command line, and enter your user ID and password when prompted, as in the following example:

```
% telnet parkweb.com

Trying 204.246.64.26 ...
Connected to parkweb.com.
Escape character is '^]'.

Linux 1.2.13 (parkweb) (ttyp0)

parkweb login: bob
Password:
Last login: Thu Feb 29 21:04:35 from dialup-34-a.gw.u

parkweb%
```

Once connected to the other system, you can perform any operation that you could perform as a directly-connected user.

To terminate the connection, log out as usual (with exit, logout, or ^D).

In addition, you can communicate with the telnet program by entering the telnet escape character, then entering telnet-specific commands. The default telnet escape character is ^] (telnet nicely shows you its escape character when you log in, as in the previous example).

Specific telnet commands allow you to debug a flaky connection (an advanced topic not covered here). However, the telnet quit command is useful for everyone; if the remote system hangs, enter the escape character followed by the quit command to terminate the connection and return to your original system.

Rlogin

The rlogin command is essentially the same as telnet; it allows you to remotely log in to another system, as long as you have an account (user ID and password) on that system. Once connected, you can use the rcp (remote copy) command to transfer files back and forth, as long as the two systems are configured correctly (this is an advanced topic; ask a system administrator or consult a UNIX book for more information).

Connecting to another system with rlogin is much like using telnet. Just type rlogin and the name of the remote system:

```
% rlogin parkweb.com
Password:
Last login: Fri Mar  1 20:01:53 from maroon.tc.umn.ed
Linux 1.2.13.

parkweb%
```

To terminate the connection, log out as usual (with exit, logout, or ^D).

B.5 SHARING FILES

Part of the fun of using networks is sharing information. In addition to copying files with `ftp`, `telnet`, and `rlogin`, you can send and receive text files by e-mail. Because e-mail is poor at handling binary files and collections of many files, you need to use utilities like `uuencode` and `tar` to prepare these types of data for sharing.

Sending and Receiving E-Mail

All UNIX systems have a command called `mail`. You can use this command to send e-mail to other users on the system, or to someone on another system, if networks are in place.

Most UNIX systems have other, fancier e-mail utilities, such as `elm`, `mailtool`, `xmailtool`, and MH (`mhmail`, `exmh`, `xmh`). But the default `mail` command can handle your basic e-mail needs.

To send mail, you need to know the e-mail address of your recipient. Then, you just enter the `mail` command with the desired e-mail address. You may be prompted for a subject line for the message, after which anything you type is put in the body of the message. To terminate the message, enter ^D or a period on a line by itself.

The following example shows how to send e-mail to someone whose address is `beulah@aol.com`.

```
% mail beulah@aol.com
Subject: Interesting information

Hi Beulah,
Remember to buy tickets for the show tomorrow.
We all want to sit in the balcony.

Thanks,
Bob
.

%
```

If you make a mistake on the line you're typing, you can back up with the backspace or line kill characters, but if you notice a problem in a previous line, you're out of luck. However, you can edit the entire e-mail message before you send it by entering the command ~v. This command invokes the editor (often `vi`, but not always) so you can make changes. To send the message, write your changes and quit the editor, then type a period or ^D. (See section B.6 for more information on using `vi`.)

To read your e-mail messages, enter the `mail` command alone on a line:

```
% mail
```

The behavior of the `mail` program varies from system to system, but usually, you will see either a list of messages (subject, sender, and date) or the content of each message, one after the other, or the message, "No mail for *you*." The following commands tend to be available in most versions of mail:

next: Displays the next message

print (or type): Displays the specified message

delete (or d): Deletes the specified message

undelete (or u): Restores the specified deleted message.

hold (or preserve): Holds the specified message in the incoming mail

reply (or r): Reply to the authors (only) of the message

Reply (or R): Reply to the authors AND recipients of the message. (But be careful: the meanings of reply and Reply are often backwards, so check carefully before you send your email!)

save (or s): Saves the specified message to a file

quit: Exits the mail program, with updates

x: Exits the mail program without updating the mailbox

Uuencoding

You can mail binary files by preparing them first with the uuencode command, which converts them into a text format that can be sent anywhere. In this example, we have taken the binary file apple.gif and saved it as the uuencoded text file apple.uue; when the file is uu*de*coded, it will be called applepic.gif. (The syntax is: uudecode currentname newname > uufile .)

```
% uuencode apple.gif applepic.gif > apple.uue
```

If someone e-mails you a uuencoded file, just save the message as a separate file and decode it using the uudecode command. Here's what you would type to decode the apple.uue file that we just created with uuencode; a file named applepic.gif will magically appear.

```
% uudecode apple.uue
```

Tar

The tar command creates an archive (a collection of small files and directories) that can be written to another file, to disk, or to tape. This archive is called a "tar file." You can prepare large text files, or collections of many files, in this manner.

If you need to transfer several files, or a directory and the files it contains (such as the source code and documentation for a software package), tar is a convenient way to package all these files as one "logical" file for storage and transmission purposes.

If you use shareware, you will often see tar files being used to hold the software being distributed. A tar file usually has the extension .tar appended to the file name.

Once you have a tar file on your system, you must "un-archive," or extract, its contents so that they can be viewed, edited, compiled, or whatever. Use the following form of the tar command to do this:

```
% tar xvf filename.tar
```

To create a new tar file, gather all the desired components into a directory, then run the tar command as in the following example:

```
% tar cvf filename.tar myfile1 myfile2
```

The resulting file is named filename.tar, which contains the files myfile1 and myfile2. You can verify this with the tf options of the tar command, which display the contents of the archive:

```
% tar tf filename.tar
myfile1
myfile2

%
```

Once you have created your tar file, you can uuencode it and include it in your e-mail. You may want to compress your tar file (using zip, compress, or gzip) before uuencoding; this will make for shorter file transfer times and less disk space.

B.6 EDITING TEXT FILES WITH THE VI EDITOR

Almost without exception, there is a version of the vi text editor on every implementation of UNIX. Programmers and UNIX users who grew up using vi love it for its enormous number of features. Unfortunately, if you grew up using a menu-driven, WYSIWYG (what-you-see-is-what-you-get) editor, or one with pre-programmed hot keys, you are probably going to be uncomfortable with the vi editor, at least at first. The good news is that the most basic operations are easy to learn (and remember).

In this section, we present only a basic subset of vi commands. There are many more commands, as well as shortcuts for series of commands. If you are interested in learning more, see the vi "man" page or a UNIX book with a discussion of vi.

Invoking The VI Editor

To edit a file with vi, specify the file name after the vi command. This can be an existing file or a new file (vi will create the new file after the first save/write command). The following example shows the use of the vi command:

```
% vi filename
```

In the following descriptions, CR stands for carriage return and ESC stands for the Escape key.

Modes

The most significant difference between vi and most WYSIWYG word processors is that there are three modes in vi: command mode, input mode, and "last line" mode.

Command mode   The initial and "normal" mode, which allows you to execute commands but not enter text. Other modes return to command mode upon completion (usually by way of a CR or ESC key). The ESC key is used to cancel a partial command.

Input mode   Entered by setting one of the insert, append, or change commands (such as a, i, o, O, or c). Almost any text may then be entered. Input mode is terminated with an ESC character, or ^C.

Last line mode   So called because commands appear on the last line of the screen; entered by using the :, /, ?, or ! commands. Used for reading input for these commands. This mode is terminated by typing a carriage return; an interrupt cancels the termination.

Moving Around a File

The following commands allow you to move around a file by changing the position of the cursor. Note that in addition to the letter commands (h, j, k, and l), you can also use the arrow keys.

h	Move the cursor one character to the left
l	Move the cursor one character to the right
k	Move up one line
j	Move down one line
^	Move to the beginning of the line (shift-6, not Control)
$	Move to the end of the line
w	Move forward one word

b	Move back one word
^U	Scroll up a half-screen
^D	Scroll down a half-screen
1G	Go to the first line of the file
23G	Go to the 23rd line of the file
G	Go to the last line of the file
/text	Find the next occurrence of the specified text
?text	Find the previous occurrence of the specified text

Inserting and Appending Text

a	Append text after the cursor; end with ESC
i	Insert text just before the cursor; end with ESC
A	Append text to the end of the current line; end with ESC
o	Insert (open) line before current line; end with ESC
O	Append (open) line after current line; end with ESC

Deleting Text

x	Delete the current character (at the cursor)
dw	Delete the current word (from the cursor forward)
dd	Delete the current line
d5d	Delete five lines
D	Delete the rest of the current line (from cursor position)

Changing Text

cw	Change the current word to new text; end with ESC
cc	Clear and change the current line to new text; end with ESC
C	Clear and change the rest of the current line (from cursor position); end with ESC
rx	Replace the current character with x
R	Replace from the cursor until you type ESC

Undoing Changes

| u | Undo the last change |
| U | Undo all changes to current line (since last line change) |

Importing Text

To import the contents of a text file, use the following command:

```
:r filename
```

To import the output of a UNIX command, use the `:r!` command. The following example shows how to read the output of the `ls` command into the file being edited:

```
:r !ls
```

Saving Text

To save your changes, use the write command:

```
:w
```

You can save your changes to a different file than the one you are currently editing by specifying a file name after the `:w` command, as follows:

```
:w myfile.new
```

Getting Out of the VI Editor

To exit the `vi` editor, write your changes, then quit:

```
:w
```

```
:q
```

You can combine these commands into one, as follows:

```
:wq
```

And you can accomplish the same thing by typing `ZZ` (capital letters) while in command mode (no colon).

If you use the `:q` command before writing your changes, `vi` usually warns you that there are unsaved changes. However, if you want to exit a file without saving your changes, you can use the "forced quit" command:

```
:q!
```

Note: when you use the `:q!` command, you are given no warning that your changes have been discarded.

B.7 GETTING MORE INFORMATION: THE "MAN" COMMAND

All UNIX systems have a command called `man`, which searches for a specific topic in the on-line reference manual, or "man pages." The `man` command displays either complete man pages that you select by name, or one-line summaries selected by keyword (`man -k`), or by the name of an associated file (`man -f`). You can also find BSDI's searchable collection of man pages on the Web:

```
http://www.bsdi.com/bsdi-man/
```

Man pages are notorious for telling you everything except what you want to know. However, if you understand how they are organized and what to expect, you will have an easier time finding the information you need.

First, note that man pages describe a command, routine, or file, not a task or procedure. They usually document "what," not "how."

It also helps to know that the average man page follows a standard template. It starts with a one-line description, then gives the command syntax (available options and arguments), followed by a detailed description that usually explains each option. Further down, you may find a section labeled EXAMPLES, which can provide useful "how-to" information. Finally, most pages end with a SEE ALSO section, which provides pointers to related man pages.

If your system has an index of man pages (creating one is an additional step for the system administrator), the `man -k` command can be an extremely useful tool in your quest for knowledge. This command searches through the index for the keyword you specify, and displays all the man pages that match this keyword, along with the associated one-line description of each command.

For example, if you want to find out what mail commands are on your system, you can use `man -k` to find them, as shown here:

```
% man -k mail
Mail            mailx (1)         - interactive message processing system
addresses       aliases (4)       - addresses and aliases for sendmail
biff            biff (1b)         - give notice of incoming mail messages
elm             elm (1)           - an interactive mail system
fastmail        fastmail (1)      - quick batch mail interface to a single address
forward         aliases (4)       - addresses and aliases for sendmail
mail            mail (1)          - read mail or send mail to users
mailto          mailto (1)        - Simple multimedia mail sending program
mailx           mailx (1)         - interactive message processing system
rmail           mail (1)          - read mail or send mail to users
sendmail        sendmail (1m)     - send mail over the internet
tarmail         untarmail (1)     - encode/decode binary to printable ASCII
vacation        vacation (1)      - reply to mail automatically
wnewmail        newmail (1)       - programs to asynchronously notify of new mail
xbiff           xbiff (n)         - mailbox flag for X
```

You can then call up the man page for any of the commands listed by specifying the name from the left or middle column with the `man` command:

```
% man elm
```

Some UNIX systems also have a `man -f` command, which looks for a man page that exactly matches the specified text. For example, the following command displays all the man pages called "intro":

```
% man -f intro
intro              Intro (1)  - introduction to commands and application programs
intro              Intro (1m) - introduction to maintenance commands and
                               application programs
intro              Intro (2)  - introduction to system calls and error numbers
intro              Intro (3)  - introduction to functions and libraries
intro              Intro (4)  - introduction to file formats
intro              Intro (5)  - introduction to miscellany
intro              Intro (6)  - introduction to games and demos
intro              Intro (7)  - introduction to special files
intro              Intro (9)  - introduction to device driver interfaces
intro              Intro (9e) - introduction to device driver entry points
intro              Intro (9f) - introduction to DDI/DKI functions
intro              Intro (9s) - introduction to kernel data structures
```

With a little perseverance, you can use the man pages to help answer your questions and increase your knowledge of UNIX.

Perl Quick
Reference Guide

*T*his appendix is included in this book for those who really want to get into programming. It provides a short guide to the Perl programming language. We'll cover the more common (and easy to explain) commands, functions, and data structures, along with an overview of Perl basics. Perl's creator says that the Perl slogan is, "there's more than one way to do it." That's certainly true, but in the interest of brevity, we can show only a couple of ways to do it, with an emphasis on getting you started in Web programming: HTML form processing, text processing, and file manipulation. You can find more complete (albeit sometimes cryptic) information on the Internet and in the official Perl documentation (for which this appendix is *not* a substitute).

If you tried the CGI script examples in Chapters 10 and 13, you've already had a whirlwind tour of Perl, and you should be able to write many new scripts on your own. This section will be a little more systematic than Chapter 13, starting with the very basics and moving on to more complicated concepts. Unfortunately, in discussing any language — whether you're talking about Perl or Swahili — it is difficult to be *completely* systematic. So if some of our examples use concepts that have not been introduced yet, don't worry; it'll all come together once you've read this entire appendix.

We have found that the best way to learn Perl — or any computer language — is to read a little bit, then copy and modify an existing public-domain program to try out what we have read. It is usually easier to start by modifying a program rather than by immediately writing your own.

Although much of the Perl documentation assumes knowledge of the C language and the awk and sed programming environments, this guide does not. But we do assume that you know the fundamentals of programming concepts and techniques.

C.1 INTRODUCTION TO PERL

Perl stands for Practical Extraction and Report Language; it was written by
Larry Wall (and is still maintained by him) to provide support for UNIX system
management tasks. It is particularly good at text manipulation and file processing, making it quite popular among Web users. However, Perl is quite complex, in
part because it is based on (and borrows many elements from) existing UNIX
tools (such as `awk`, `grep`, and `sed`), UNIX shells, and the C programming language.

Because Perl is faster and more powerful than shell scripts, simpler and
more secure than C language programs, and freely available on *many* platforms
(which makes Perl programs portable between systems), we feel it is definitely
worth learning.

Perl Release Status

The most current version of Perl is version 5. However, many sites are still
using Perl 4, and several books and many Web documents describe Perl 4. The
good news is that programs written for Perl 4 should continue to work with
Perl 5.

If you don't have a copy of Perl yet, we recommend getting Perl 5. However,
if you have Perl 4, you can continue using it unless you want the improvements
of the latest version, which include:

- Many usability enhancements
- Modularity and reusability (sharable modules)
- Better regular expressions and pattern matching
- Built-in security checks ("taint checking")

For more details on Perl 5.0, see the following URLs:

- Perl 5 general information:
  `http://www.metronet.com/perlinfo/perl5.html`
- Changes from Perl 4 to Perl 5:
  `http://www.metronet.com/perlinfo/perl5/Changes`
- Perl 5 man page:
  `http://icg.stwing.upenn.edu/perl5/`

Obtaining Perl and Its Documentation

Perl is freely available software that runs on nearly all major architectures
and operating systems, including UNIX, MS-DOS, and Macintosh. UNIX systems generally have Perl installed already. If you are using DOS/Windows or
Macintosh, consult Chapter 8 or Chapter 9 for information on installing Perl on
your system.

On UNIX systems, the Perl software comes with a man page, which should be installed with the other local man pages. The DOS and Macintosh versions of Perl have on-line help that is mostly taken straight from the UNIX man page. The man page is also available as a searchable collection of HTML documents at the following URL:

```
http://www.cs.cmu.edu/htbin/perl-man/
```

There are several books available on Perl. *Learning Perl*, by Randal Schwartz (published by O'Reilly & Associates), provides a tutorial-style introduction to Perl. For experienced programmers, the definitive Perl reference is *Programming Perl*, by Larry Wall and Randal Schwartz (also from O'Reilly & Associates). Wall and Schwartz's book is often called "the camel book" because it has a picture of a camel on the cover. It comes with the *Perl Quick Reference Guide* by Johan Vromans, which is a useful summary of Perl for the frequent user. Note that the camel book is a *complete* reference that we do not recommend for beginners.

You can find Perl FAQs (answers to Frequently Asked Questions) and information files at the following URL:

```
http://www.khoros.unm.edu/staff/neilb/perl/metaFAQ/
```

Finally, there is a Usenet newsgroup for discussing Perl-related issues: `comp.lang.perl`. Be sure to thoroughly read the FAQs before posting a question on the newsgroup.

C.2 PERL BASICS

This section contains basic information for creating Perl programs (also called *scripts*). It tells you how to run programs, what the file name and file format conventions are in Perl, and how to document your programs.

How to Run Perl Programs

Perl is an *interpreted* programming language, so you don't need to compile a program before running it. On UNIX and DOS systems, simply use the `perl` command to run a Perl program (make sure the `perl` executable is in your path):

```
perl [options] [filename]
```

See the Perl man page for a description of the available options (also called *command-line switches*). The beginning Perl programmer doesn't need to use most of Perl's options. The exceptions are the checking and debugging options (`-c`, `-d`, and `-w`); see section C.10, "Debugging," for more information.

On UNIX systems, you can also run Perl programs by simply making the script executable using the `chmod` command (see Appendix B, page 386).

On MS-DOS systems, you can only execute files that end with a `.com`, `.exe`, or `.bat` extension, so if you want a Perl program to run by itself, it needs to be contained in a `.bat` file. For example, if you want to run a script called `run-me.pl`, you need to create a text file called `run-me.bat` with text looking something like this:

```
cd \usr\bin
perl run-me.pl
```

To run a Perl program on a Macintosh, just open the MacPerl application and select `Run Script…` from the `Script` menu. You will be given a standard Open dialog. (If you have an open script already, use the `Run "YourFileName"` command.) The output of the script will show up in a new window entitled "MacPerl." Unfortunately, there is no easy way to enter command-line options in MacPerl.

File Naming Conventions

By convention, Perl files end in the extension `.pl`. This extension is not required, but it can be useful, especially if you plan to share archives of Perl files with other Perl aficionados. However, you may want or need to use the `.cgi` extension to mark Internet-related Perl files as CGI programs. Perl has no problem with this, as long as you mark the file as a Perl program on the first line of the file. See "Required First Line" (below) for more information.

Program Format

Perl is a "free-format" programming language. Variables and other data structures don't need to be declared at the beginning of the program. You don't need "begin" or "end" statements (although they are allowed in Perl 5.0). There is no official "main" declaration for your main program routines, and subroutines can be declared and defined almost anywhere in your program.

There is one major rule to be aware of: each statement must end with the `;` (semicolon) character. (For the last statement in a block — that is, the last statement before the closing curly bracket — a final semicolon is optional.) A block is a group of statements that are {enclosed in curly brackets}, usually because they are in a loop of some kind. Blocks can span several lines or can be contained on a single line.

Comments are marked with the number sign character (`#`). When this character is encountered, Perl ignores the rest of the physical line (up to the next line break). Here are some examples of valid comments:

```
# An entire line that is treated as a comment

$SamIAm = 0;    # A comment included on a line of code

############# a separator ###########
```

Required First Line

The first line of a Perl program is always a number sign (#), followed by an exclamation point (a "bang" in programming terminology), followed by the location of the Perl interpreter on your system. This is the only place where a line beginning with a number sign means anything.

UNIX On many UNIX systems, the `perl` command has been installed in the `/usr/bin` or `/usr/local/bin` directory, so the first line would look like one of the following:

```
#!/usr/bin/perl
```

```
#!/usr/local/bin/perl
```

Macintosh and MS-DOS On DOS/Windows and Macintosh systems, this first line is not actually required, but you should include it anyway in case you share scripts with friends who use UNIX. You can use this simple statement for the first line:

```
#!perl
```

C.3 VARIABLES

Perl variables are called "data types" in the official documentation. There are three basic types of variables in Perl: simple variables (*scalars*), normal arrays, and associative arrays.

Simple Variables (Scalars)

Simple Perl variables hold numerical or character values. A simple variable is marked with the $ character; sample variable names are $var, $Fred, $my_data, $num1, and so on.

Use the = operator to assign singular values to scalar variables, as in these examples:

```
$brillig = 494;             # integer
$SLIthy = 3.127;            # real
$TOVES4 = 7e42;             # scientific
$gyre = 0767;               # octal
$gim_ble = 0x3f9            # hexadecimal
$WABE = "sword";            # string
$mimsy = 'Alice and me';    # another string
$Borogoves = `pwd`;         # string input from "backticks"
```

Numbers Numeric variables can have any of the following types of values:

- Integer (0, 1, -55, etc.)
- Floating point, or real, number (such as 3.22579)
- Scientific notation (for example, 4e12)
- Octal number (base 8)
- Hexadecimal number (base 16)

Any number starting with 0 is assumed to be an octal number. For example, when Perl sees the number 027, it decides that it is really two 8's and seven 1's; in other words, twenty-three. So be extremely cautious about numbers starting with 0.

In addition, any number starting with 0x is assumed to be a hexadecimal number. Hexadecimal numbers can also include the letters a, b, c, d, e, and f, standing in for 10 through 15. (For example, hexadecimal 0x4a is decimal 74).

Strings A variable is assumed to be a string when it is defined as a series of alphanumeric characters between a pair of quote characters ("double" or 'single'), or when it is the output of a command enclosed in `backticks`. (Backticks are mostly a UNIX feature; consult your documentation to see what, if anything, you can use them for.) An additional method of quoting multi-line strings, called "here" documents, is described on page 415.

You can use either single and double quotes to enclose a string; they have identical meanings, except that using single quotes protects the string from *variable interpolation*. This means that you can use the $ character inside a single-quoted string and it is left alone (not treated as the start of a variable name). Conversely, you can use a variable inside of a double-quoted string, and the value is substituted (interpolated) in the string when it is processed. The comments in this example show the difference:

```
$honey = "Winnie the Pooh";
print 'I love $honey';      # Output:  I love $honey
print "I love $honey";      # Output:  I love Winnie the Pooh
```

Perl converts between numerical and string values whenever appropriate; for example, you can give the string value "1" to a variable, then add it to a numeric variable, as in this example program (which prints the answer as 101):

```
$dalmations = 100;
$pongo = "1";
print $dalmations + $pongo;
```

The default value of a simple variable, if it has not been assigned a value, is null (0 or ' ', depending on the context). Remember to always use the $ prefix when typing a variable name, or you will end up with unexpected results!

Normal Arrays

Normal arrays hold numbers or strings and are indexed by integers (0, 1, 2, etc.). Arrays in Perl are one-dimensional and are dynamic — the size increases as needed. A normal array is marked with the @ character.

By default, array indexes start at 0, so array elements are $array[0], $array[1], $array[2], etc. An element in the array is a simple variable and is therefore marked with the $ character; for example, the first position in an array named @grinch is assigned by this type of statement:

```
$grinch[0] = 9;     # Remember, arrays start with entry 0
```

Here are some examples of assigning values to an entire array. We will use the list capability of Perl (a list is a group of comma-separated values within parentheses), as well as the .. range designator:

```
@friends = ("Huck", "Tom", "Becky");
@yertle = (1,2,3,4,5);
@tidwick = (6..10);          # sets the array to 6,7,8,9,10
```

To clear an array (set its value to null), use the null list () in an assignment statement, like this:

```
@sneeches = ();
```

The predefined variable $#array_name is the length of the associated array. However, because array indexes start at zero, you need to add one to get the "real" length; for example, with the @lorax array:

```
$length = $#lorax + 1;
```

Two Perl functions that are useful with arrays are shift and sort. The shift function grabs the first entry from the array and shifts all other entries up one space, thus shortening the array. The following code can be used to print all entries in an array; note that the scalar value of an array is 1, or "true," if it has *any* entries, so it can be used as the expression in a complex statement, in this case while:

```
while (@piglet)
  { $entry = shift(@piglet);     # This erases the entry, too
    print $entry; }
```

The sort function sorts the contents of an array or list alphabetically. For example, the following code prints a sorted list of the contents of @eeyore.

```
@eeyore = ( "Milne","Winnie","Christopher","Robin","Piglet" );
print ( sort(@eeyore) );
# outputs "Christopher Milne Piglet Robin Winnie"
```

If you try sorting numerical values with the sort function, the numbers are treated as strings and are sorted alphabetically; this means that "10" comes before "3", for example. If you want to sort an array or list numerically, you must

supply a short subroutine to handle the numerical portion, as in this example
adapted from Wall and Schwartz's *Programming Perl*:

```
sub numerically { $a <=> $b; }   # This is the subroutine

@mydata = (10,2,314,44,5,61);
@sorted_data = (sort numerically @mydata);
foreach (@sorted_data) { print "$_ "; }
```

This mysterious code — in which the name of the subroutine is used as if it
were an English adverb! — really works. Take it on faith, or, better yet, try it for
yourself. (Some of this code will become less mysterious if you read on; we will
explain $_ and foreach on pages 413 and 416, respectively.)

Associative Arrays

Associative arrays hold pairs of values — called *key-value pairs* — which
are indexed by arbitrary strings. They're called associative arrays because they
allow you to effectively associate, or link, pairs of strings. An associative array is
marked with the % character. Here's an example of assigning values to an entire
associative array with three key-value pairs:

```
%pooh = ('roo','springy', 'tigger','fierce', 'owl','wise');
```

Entries in the array are indexed by the first value of the pair (the key). An
element in the array is a simple variable and is therefore marked with the $
character. For example, the entries in the %pooh array are as follows:

```
Entry key                Value
================         ===========
$pooh{'roo'}             'springy'
$pooh{'tigger'}          'fierce'
$pooh{'owl'}             'wise'
```

Note that associative arrays use {curly brackets} to mark indexes (also
called *subscripts*), unlike the [square brackets] used for normal arrays. Also note
that the "value" portion of associative arrays can hold either numbers or strings
(or both in the same array).

The predefined variable %ENV is an associative array containing all the environment variables of the calling process. (On Macintosh and DOS systems, the
%ENV array is quite limited; it was designed for UNIX systems.) For example, in
UNIX, $ENV{'HOME'} contains the home directory, $ENV{'user'} is the user ID
(login name), and $ENV{'SHELL'} is the calling shell.

Three Perl functions that are useful with associative arrays are each, keys,
and delete. The each function returns a normal array containing the next key-
value pair from an associative array, then moves the remaining key-value pairs
up one entry in the array (that is, the retrieved key-value pair is removed from
the array). This is similar to the shift function, which returns (and removes) the
next entry from a *normal* array.

The following each example uses the %pooh array defined above:

```
# Loops through each key-value pair in array %pooh
# and exits when no more pairs are available
while ( @nextpair = each %pooh )
  { print "$nextpair[0] is $nextpair[1]\n"; }
```

The above `while` loop prints out the following output (although not necessarily in this order):

```
owl is wise
tigger is fierce
roo is springy
```

This example, using the `keys` function instead of `each`, also prints the values of the %pooh array:

```
# Foreach loops through all entries in array %pooh
# and exits the loop when no more entries are available
foreach ( keys %pooh )
  { print "$_ is $pooh{$_}\n"; }
```

The output is the same as in the demonstration of the `each` function. Note that `$_` is a predefined variable that represents the current argument; in this code example, it is the string returned from the `keys` function (i.e., the string indexing the array %pooh). Page 413 contains a more detailed description of the `$_` predefined variable.

The `delete` function deletes a key-value pair from an associative array. For example, the following code deletes owl's entry from the %pooh array:

```
delete ( $pooh{'owl'} );
```

Remember to use the `%` prefix when referring to an entire associative array; use the `$` prefix and `{}` index characters for an element in the array.

C.4 OPERATORS

The operators in Perl can be divided into several categories: arithmetic, relational, file test, and miscellaneous. Perl has more operators than we list in this section (for example, the bit-wise operators >> and <<), but this subset should be enough to get you started.

True and False in Perl

Perl has a well defined concept of "truth" (something most philosophers have struggled with for centuries). When a Perl operation is evaluated, it returns either the value true (usually represented by the value 1) or false (the value 0 or ''). This value is returned in *addition* to any other operation performed by the statement.

A value is true if it is *not* 0 or the null string (''). Specifically, a number is "true" if it is not equal to 0, and a string is "true" if it is not the null string or the string `"0"`. An array is "true" if it has entries. An undefined variable is always false. In general, functions and subroutines return true if they execute, and false if they do not.

This concept of truth means that you can use virtually any Perl statement in the conditional portion of an `if` or `while` statement. The following example shows how you can test the contents, or lack thereof, of an array as a test in an `if` statement:

```
if ( @moonintroll )
    { print "There's something in that array!"; }
```

If the array named `@moonintroll` has any elements, then the expression (`@moomintroll`) is true, and the `print` statement is executed.

Arithmetic Operators

The following operators are used to perform arithmetic operations. These operators take two arguments.

+   Addition

–   Subtraction

*   Multiplication

/   Division

%   Modulo division (computes the *remainder* of integer division)

**   Exponentiation

Each of these operators can be combined with the assignment operator (=) to create arithmetic-assignment operators, such as +=, which performs addition as it assigns a value. For example, both of the following pairs of statements give `$snork` the value 15:

```
$snork = 10;   $snork = $snork + 5;

$snork = 10;   $snork += 5;
```

Relational Operators

Relational operators are used to test the equality or inequality of variables. These operators take two arguments. Perl differentiates between string relational operators and numeric relational operators. (When strings are compared in terms of "less than" and "greater than," their relative positions in an alphabetic list are what is being compared.) Conveniently enough, the string operators are letters and the numeric operators are symbols!

Numeric relational operators

==   Numeric equality

!=	Inequality
<	Less than
>	Greater than
<=	Less than or equal to
>=	Greater than or equal to
<=>	Compare; returns -1 if less than, 0 if equal, and 1 if greater than

```
if ( $you < $me )
  { print "I am better than you.\n"; }

if ( $fred != $guillaume )
  { print "Fred and Guillaume are not the same person.\n"; }

if ( $a <=> $b )
{ print ( "A and B are not the same." ); }
# Same as 'if ($a != $b)', except it also tells whether $a is
# greater than or less than $b.  If $a = 3 and $b = 5, then
# "print($a<=>$b);" will return -1.

if ( ( $snuffkin = ($a <=> $b) ) == -1 )
  { print "$a is less than $b\n"; }
elsif ( $snuffkin == 1 )
  { print "$a is greater than $b\n"; }
# Expansion of the last example to show full use of <=>.
# The result of $a <=> $b is stored in $snuffkin for quick
# reference (and to show how complex a Perl expression can get).
```

String relational operators

eq	String equality
ne	Inequality
lt	Less than
gt	Greater than
le	Less than or equal to
ge	Greater than or equal to
cmp	Compare; returns -1 if less than, 0 if equal, and 1 if greater than

```
if ( $anne gt $pete )
  { $order{'anne'} = "first"; }
# This tests whether $anne comes before $pete alphabetically.

if ( $author eq "Adam" )
  { print "Hi, Adam!\n"; }
```

File Test Operators

Perl provides many operators to check the status of files, some of which can be used on UNIX systems only. We'll list the more "generic" of these operators;

UNIX users should check the Perl documentation for a complete list. These operators take one argument — either a file name (in quotes) or a filehandle (no quotes) — and test the associated file to see if the specified condition is true.

-e   File exists (can be a plain file or a directory/folder)

-s   File has some content (in UNIX terms, "has non-zero size"); if true, returns the file's size

-d   File is a directory (or folder on a Mac)

-f   File is a plain file (*not* a directory/folder)

-T   File is a text file

-B   File is a binary file

```
if ( -e "filename" )
  { print "The file exists.\n"; }

if ( $size = ( -s "filename" ) )
  { print "The file is $size bytes long.\n"; }

if ( -T "filename" )
  { print "The file is plain text.\n"; }
```

Miscellaneous Operators

Here are a few more useful operators. Except for the negation operator, these operators take two arguments.

!   Negation. For example, !$me means "not me." Negation takes only *one* argument.

.   Concatenation of two strings. Use this the way you would use a plus sign (+) to add two numbers. (See the example below)

&&   Logical AND (Perl 5 synonym: and). When used in an expression, it evaluates as true only if *both* parts of the expression are true. For example, (1<3 && 2<4) is true, but (1<3 && 2>4) is false.

|| Logical OR (Perl 5 synonym: or). When used in an expression, evaluates as true if *either* part (or both parts) of the expression is true; evaluates as false only if *both* parts of the expression are false. For example, (1<3 || 2<4) is true, and (1<3 || 2>4) is also true, but (1>3 || 2>4) is false.

x   Repetition; repeats the *preceding* character or string by the number of times specified by the numerical argument *following* the x. (See below for an example.)

,   Side effect operator; evaluates the first argument and throws away the result, then evaluates the second argument and returns the result (Perl 5 synonym: =>). The comma operator is a C language construct, and we think it is a sloppy programming practice. We include it in this list merely so you can recognize it in existing Perl programs.

..   In array context, this is the range assignment operator. It returns an array of sequential values from the first argument to the second. For example, (1..10) returns the values from 1 to 10. In a scalar context, this is a boolean flip-flop operator, which is too complex for us to describe in a basic guide. If you find it in a program and need to understand what it does, see the Perl man page.

```
if ( !$moisture )
print ( "It's very dry here." );

$good = "Guten";   $day = "Tag";
print ( $good . $day );
# outputs "GutenTag"

print ( "*"x80 , "\n" );
# Outputs 80 asterisks on a line

@one_to_ten = (1..10)
# Sets the array's elements to (1,2,3,4,5,6,7,8,9,10)
```

C.5 SPECIAL VARIABLES, FILEHANDLES, & "HERE" DOCUMENTS

This section contains information on predefined and special entities in Perl, as well as the "here" document method of quoting strings.

Predefined Variables

Perl has a number of predefined variables that can be used to make your programs easier to write and much more difficult to read. (Perl 5.0 contains an "English" module that provides readable synonyms for the most cryptic of these variables; it's worth checking out, although we won't describe it in this book.) Here are the most useful of these predefined variables:

$_   "The default argument" — the default input or searching space; also used as the default iteration variable in a loop (and in several functions, such as grep and chop). The value of this argument changes depending on context. It is often omitted by experienced programmers, because its use is more or less optional. We suggest that you look at several example Perl programs (including the Guest Book script in Chapter 13) to learn how this variable is used.

$*   The number of lines matched within a string; the default value (0) matches a a single line. You can set this variable to 1 to do multi-line matching.

$/   The input line separator; set to a new line (return, or \n) by default. Can be set to specify multi-line input.

$,   The output field separator for the print function (a space, by
              default).

$ARGV   The name of the current file when reading from <> (the default
              input file). $ARGV is also an element in the array @ARGV; see the
              next subsection on "Special Arrays."

Special Arrays

Perl defines a few special arrays for your use:

@_   The array holding parameters for a subroutine.

@ARGV   The array containing the command line arguments (available on
              DOS and UNIX systems).

%ENV   The associative array holding all the environment variables of
              the calling process (primarily on UNIX systems; limited use in
              DOS, and very limited in MacPerl).

Filehandles

Perl calls a reference to a file from within a program a *filehandle*. There are
several predefined filehandles:

STDIN   Represents "standard input" — input read from a terminal, from
              input, or from the files on the command line.

STDOUT   Represents "standard output" — output written to the screen, or
              in the case of the Web, to an HTTP transfer.

STDERR   Represents "standard error" — output written to the standard
              error device (UNIX systems only).

To define your own filehandle, use the open function as in this example,
which creates the filehandle ELOISE to represent a file named plaza:

```
open (ELOISE,"plaza");
```

A filehandle can be used for both input and output. After specifying the filehandle name in open, you use the filehandle, not the file name, to manipulate the
file.

Evaluating a filehandle in angle brackets (for example, <STDIN>) reads the
next input line from that file, including the line break (\n) symbol. The brackets
are not part of the filehandle name; they act as an input function.

The null filehandle is used with angular brackets (<>) as a synonym for
<STDIN>; in fact, you rarely see <STDIN> in Perl programs, but you see <> a lot.
This example shows the syntax of a while loop that prints each line of input until
the end of the file is reached:

```
while ($_ = <STDIN>)  { print ($_); }
```

Ordinarily you must assign the line of input to a variable. However, because the input function is the only statement in the conditional portion of the while loop, the input is automatically assigned to the predefined variable $\_$ (which can be omitted, because it is the default). Note that the following line of code is equivalent to the previous while loop:

```
while (<>) { print; }
```

If you understand this, you're well on your way!

"Here" Documents

Perl has borrowed the concept of "here" documents (also called "here" strings) from the UNIX C shell. A "here" document is a line-oriented form of quoting a multiple-line string. This facility is quite useful for producing HTML tags and text.

The beginning of the string is marked with `<<UNIQUE_STRING`, and the end of the string is marked with `UNIQUE_STRING` on a line by itself, at the beginning of the line. (Note that `UNIQUE_STRING` must not occur in the text used for the "here" document.)

If you've done any of the Perl scripts in Chapters 10 or 13, you've used this trick before. If not, here's a simple example using a "here" document to print two lines with a blank line in between:

```
print <<STOPHERE;
Hello!

Goodbye.
STOPHERE
```

Note that the first occurrence of the `UNIQUE_STRING` is terminated with a semicolon, but the second occurrence is not.

C.6 COMPOUND STATEMENTS AND FLOW CONTROL

By default, a Perl program "flows" in a sequential manner, from one statement to the next. However, you can use compound statements to change this flow.

If Statements

The `if` statement allows conditional execution of statements. There are various versions of `if` statements: if-then, if-then-else, if-then-elsif, and do-if.

Here is an example of each type of `if` statement:

```
# if-then statement:
if ( @oz )
  { print "Toto, we're not in Kansas any more."; }
```

```
# if-then-else statement:
if ( !$water )
   { print ("I'll get you and your little dog too!"); }
else
   { print ("I'm melting!"); }

# if-then-elsif statement - note spelling of "elsif":
if ( $wizard eq "great" || $wizard eq "powerful" )
   { print ("Scarecrow wants a brain.\n"); }
elsif ( $wizard eq "useless" )
   { print ("There's no place like home!\n"); }
else
   { print ("$wizard is neither great nor useless.\n"); }

# do-if statement:
print ("Follow the yellow brick road!\n") if ( @oz );
```

If statements can be *nested*: an if statement can occur as one of the statements in the block of statements between {curly brackets}. The if-then-elsif statement is an example of a single level of nesting, but you can also combine different types of if statements.

While Statements

The while statement continues to execute as long as a specified condition is true. Here is an example that adds up all of the elements in an array:

```
while (@yertle)
   { $turtles = $turtles + $yertle[$_ ];
     shift (@yertle); }
```

The next and last keywords are useful in while loops. The next keyword jumps back to evaluate the condition again, skipping the remaining statements in that iteration of the loop. The last keyword exits the loop and goes to the statement following the loop.

By the way, beware of infinite loops! (An infinite loop is one where the condition is *always* met, so it continues forever.)

Foreach Statements

The foreach statement executes a certain number of times (or until a specified condition is true). Here is an example of foreach that prints each entry in an array:

```
foreach (@maisy) { print ("$_ has a head like a daisy"); }
```

Perl also has a for statement that is equivalent to foreach; its syntax is the same as in the C language. Because foreach has simpler syntax, for is not described here.

Until Statements

The `until` statement executes *until* a specified condition is true; it's like the opposite of `while`. Here is a simple example of the `until` statement that echoes input until a certain string is encountered:

```
# prints each line of TINKER_BELL until a line
# containing only "EOF" is found:
print <TINKER_BELL> until $_ = "EOF";
```

Unless Statements

The `unless` statement executes unless a specified condition is true. Here is an example:

```
print ("I do not like green eggs and ham")
  unless ($in_a_box) ;
```

The `unless` statement can be combined with the `if`, `while`, or `for` statement, as in this example:

```
if ( @night )
  { print "zzzz..." unless ( $not_tired ); }
```

The || Operator as Flow Control

Interestingly enough, the `||` relational operator (logical OR) can be used to provide flow control of an "either-or" type. It has the following format:

```
statement1; || statement2;
```

You can read this line like, "either perform `statement1` or `statement2`." If the first statement is true, the second statement is ignored. In other words, the second statement is evaluated only if the first statement is false. This allows code like the following example:

```
open(PRINCESS,$ozma); || die "Can't open $ozma - exiting";
```

This code checks to see if the file defined by the `$ozma` variable can be opened; if it can, the value returned from the open function is true, and the remainder of the line is ignored. However, if the file cannot be opened, open returns false and the second statement is executed (the `die` function prints out a message and then immediately exits the program).

C.7 STRING OPERATIONS

One of the best features of Perl is that it combines the regular expression and pattern matching capabilities of UNIX tools (such as `sed` and `awk`) with a nice set of string-oriented functions and routines. If you are a UNIX user who knows vi, sed, awk, or shell regular expression syntax, you're well on the way to knowing what Perl has to offer.

There's so much to describe that we can't cover it all here, but we show a few simple examples to get you started.

Pattern Matching

Perl's pattern matching functions are often used to search and replace strings of text. The string to be searched must be in the $_ predefined variable (if it isn't, you can put it there with an assignment statement.) Perl has two pattern matching operators:

/pattern/	Searches through a string for the specified pattern; returns true if the string is found and false if it is not found.
s/pattern/replacement/	Searches through a string for the specified pattern and replaces it with the specified replacement string. This operator also returns true if the string is found and false if it is not found.

Patterns are specified by regular expressions (described below).

Regular Expressions

Perl's regular expressions are often used to specify the patterns used for the pattern matching functions. Regular expressions can be as simple as a text string. For example, /bosco/ searches for the string "bosco". But regular expressions can get complicated fast. If you want to find "bosco", "Bosco", and "BOSCO", you don't have to execute three searches; instead, you can use a regular expression to specify that you don't care about the case of the letters in the string. The following regular expression would accomplish this goal:

/[bB][oO][sS][cC][oO]/

This regular expression also matches "bOsco", "boSco", "bosCo", "boscO", "BOsco", and so on. In this case, additional matches are probably fine, but there may be instances when a too-liberal pattern can be a problem.

The following list illustrates a few of the more useful regular expressions that you can use in Perl:

[abc]	Matches any character that is either a, b, or c.
[Tt]	Matches a capital T or lowercase t.
[a-z]	Matches any lowercase alphabetic character.
[a-zA-Z]	Matches *any* alphabetic character.
[^a-zA-Z]	Matches any *non*-alphabetic character (The ^ symbol denotes the negation of a class of characters).

\d	Matches any digit.
\D	Matches any non-digit.
\w	Matches any "word" (a string of alphanumeric characters with white space on either side).
\W	Matches any non-"word" (non-alphanumeric) character.
\s	Matches any white space character (space, tab, new line, etc.).
\S	Matches any *non*-white space character.
.	Matches any character (except new line).
\n	Matches a new line.
\t	Matches a tab.
\0	Matches a null character.
^	Anchors the match to the beginning of a line or string (as in ^\W, which matches any non-word character at the beginning of a line); note that this is different than the negation character used in [^a-zA-Z], above.
$	Anchors the match to the end of a line or string.

String Functions

Perl has a number of functions that perform useful operations on strings. Here are some of our favorites:

Split This function splits a string into individual "words." The first argument specifies the character in the string that divides the words; the second argument specifies the string to be split. (split is the opposite of the join function, below.) This example uses the split function to divide a sentence into individual words, which are stored in the array @words:

```
$once_upon = 'Once:upon:a:time';
@words = split (":", $once_upon);
```

Join This function joins the individual strings in the second argument, using the first argument to separate the strings. The result, a single string, is returned as the value of this function. For example, you can use the join function to create a sentence out of single words. Assuming the @words array is the same one we used in the split example, the following two lines produce the same result:

```
join (" ", @words);

join (" ", 'Once','upon','a','time');
```

Chop   This function removes the last character of a string and returns that character (which can be ignored, if you want). If you specify an array as chop's argument, every element in the array is "chopped." This function is useful for removing the new line character (\n) from the end of a line of input. Here are some examples:

```
chop(<>);                   # Chops the \n from an input line

$break = chop(<>);          # Sets $break to \n

while (<>) { @oz = $_; }     # Reads each line of input into @oz
chop(@oz);                   # Chops the \n from each line of input
```

C.8 OTHER PERL FUNCTIONS

Perl has many predefined functions — too many to describe in a brief guide. We summarize a few more of our favorites in this section, knowing that you will refer to the Perl documentation to learn about all of the others. Note we have already covered quite a few Perl functions: shift, sort, each, delete, keys, chop, join, and split. The general syntax for a Perl function is as follows:

```
function(arguments);
```

The parentheses are sometimes optional (people usually omit them in print statements, for example), but we recommend using parentheses to help keep your programs easy to understand.

Input/Output Functions

Perl's input and output functions are extremely useful when working with CGI programs and HTML files.

Print   The print function prints, or outputs, the specified argument. The argument can be a variable, a string, a comma-separated list of strings, or a literal value (or any combination of these). The print function also returns the value 1 if successful and 0 if not successful.

By default, print writes its output to the <STDOUT> filehandle. To specify a different file, use the filehandle as the first argument. This example writes the string "Here I am" to the file specified by the filehandle PEEKABOO:

```
print ( PEEKABOO "Here I am" );
```

Note that there is *no comma* between the filehandle and the string (this is a common beginner's mistake).

Open   This function opens a file and assigns it the specified filehandle. After open completes, the file can be manipulated (read from or written to). For example, this code opens the input file wonderland and assigns it the filehandle ALICE:

```
open (ALICE, "wonderland");
```

At this point, input can be read from this file with the specification <ALICE>.

Close   This function closes a file that has been opened with the open function. The filehandle, not the file name, is used to specify the file, as in this example:

```
close(ALICE);
```

It is good practice to close a file when you are done with it, and also to close it before you open it again (although this is not always required).

Miscellaneous Functions

Here are some more Perl functions that are extremely useful:

Defined   The defined function checks to see if the argument is defined. It returns true if the specified expression has a real value and false if it does not.

Die   The die function prints its argument and immediately exits the program. It can be useful for printing error messages and terminating execution when an error is discovered. (If you use die for this purpose, it is handy to include the predefined variable $! in die's argument; $! represents the current error message.)

Reverse   This function reverses the elements in an array or list. It can be used to swap the order of a numbered array, as in this example:

```
@cslewis = ("wardrobe", "witch", "lion");
reverse(@cslewis);
print(@cslewis);
```

Running this code results in lion witch wardrobe.

Return   This function returns the specified value from a subroutine. It can be used (as the last line) when the would-be last statement in the subroutine does not return the desired value. Note that this function cannot be used outside of a subroutine.

Platform-Specific Functions

For users on UNIX systems, Perl provides a very powerful set of functions to interact with the system, and we will mention a few of them here. (There are also a number of functions that can only be used with DOS or Macintosh implementations of Perl; refer to your Perl documentation for details on those functions.) Here are a few UNIX Perl functions to whet your interest:

chmod   This function changes the mode (access permissions) of a file.

kill   This function terminates the specified running process.

mkdir   This function creates a directory.

rename   This function moves, or renames, a file.

sleep   This function waits a specified amount of time before continuing execution of the Perl program.

C.9 SUBROUTINES

Writing subroutines in Perl is easy. A subroutine can go almost anywhere in a Perl program (but we suggest clustering them at the beginning — after the required first line and initial comments — or at the end of your program).

A subroutine is declared as follows:

```
sub MySubroutine {
statement1;
statement2;
etc.;
}
```

Any arguments to the subroutine are passed into the predefined @_ array. (Elements in this array are accessed by $_[0], $_[1], etc.) You can define local variables with the local() function (for example, local($amelia) defines $amelia as a variable which is local to the subroutine). The subroutine returns the value of the last expression evaluated.

To call a subroutine, use the name of the subroutine prefaced by the & character. For example, &Sub4($i); calls the Sub4 subroutine and passes it the value of the variable $i, which is then stored in the @_ array (as $_[0]).

Here's a simple subroutine that prints a magic word when it is called from somewhere in a Perl program with the proper argument:

```
sub MagicWord {
   if ( $_[0] eq "Hocus Pocus" )
   { $word = "abra";
     print ( "$word", "cad", "$word", "\n" ); }
}
```

C.10 DEBUGGING

In general, debugging a Perl program is like debugging a program in any other language: carefully check your spelling, syntax, and use of variables, functions, and keywords. A few "gotchas" include:

- Make sure that each statement is terminated with a semicolon.
- Scalar variables (including elements of arrays) must begin with $.
- Remember to use @ for normal arrays and % for associative arrays.
- Use the correct character for an array's index elements: [square brackets] are for normal arrays; {curly brackets} are for associative arrays.
- Arrays are indexed starting from 0, not 1.
- {Curly brackets} (*both* of them!) are required on if and while statements.
- Remember that single equal signs (=) are only used to assign values to variables; logical expressions must use *double* equal signs (==).
- Know the difference between string comparisons (for example, eq and lt) and numeric comparisons (like == and <).
- The current input line is normally in the variable $_. It generally ends with the new line character (\n).
- You must open your files (except STDOUT and STDERR) before you print to them.
- Spell the "else-if" keyword as elsif rather than else if or elseif.
- Comments begin with #. Anything after the # is ignored.

If you can use command-line options, Perl provides several handy options to help you debug your program. The -c option checks the syntax of a program without actually executing it. The -w option prints warnings about "iffy" Perl code in your script. Among the items -w warns you about are:

- Identifiers (variables and expressions) that are used only once
- Scalar variables that are used before being set
- References to undefined filehandles
- Use of == (numeric equivalence test) for values that look like strings
- Subroutine recursion more than 100 levels deep

The -c and -w options can provide extremely valuable information for novice and experienced Perl programmers alike. We recommend that you get into the habit of testing your Perl programs frequently as you develop them, using the following command:

```
perl -c -w my_perl_program
```

If you're really stuck, you can access a built-in Perl debugger with the -d option, like this:

```
perl -d my_broken_program
```

The Perl man page contains a "Debugging" section that describes the directives that are available in the debugger. Here's a little information to help you get started.

When the debugger starts, it displays a few informational lines, shows the first line of your program, and then prints the debugger prompt (probably DB<1>) and waits for you to type a directive. Most debugger directives are one character. Type h (short for "help") to get a list of directives. Type q (short for "quit") or ^D to exit the debugger. You can also type a Perl statement to be executed by the debugger; this lets you check input lines or print the value of suspect variables during your investigation.

OK, now you're on your own!

C.11 CONVERTING OTHER SCRIPTS TO PERL

If you are an experienced user of the UNIX commands awk, find, or sed, listen up. You can easily convert existing scripts to Perl programs. The a2p utility converts awk scripts into Perl programs. The find2p utility similarly transforms find scripts, and the s2p utility translates sed scripts. The resulting Perl code might not win any beauty prizes, but it's usually an adequate starting place.

These three utilities are included with the UNIX Perl distribution package; see the Perl documentation for more information on them.

C.12 PERL LIBRARIES

Perl has a number of prepackaged libraries — collections of subroutines — that you can use to accomplish complex but common tasks. And because the Web is simply awash with philanthropic Perl programmers, there are many public domain or freeware archives that you can access via the Web or FTP. (And remember that Perl comes with standard libraries that contain many useful subroutines; you can read all about them in the Perl documentation.) This section tells you about some of the libraries of particular interest to CGI programmers. But first, we'll tell you how to install and use Perl libraries.

Installing and Using Perl Libraries

By default, Perl libraries should be installed "in a directory along the @INC path," according to the creator of Perl. This, of course, assumes that the instructions for the standard Perl distribution explain exactly where the @INC path is supposed to be (which they don't!).

But never mind the cryptic documentation; here's the easy solution: All Perl packages come with a directory or folder called lib. Put any new libraries in there, and everything will work.

You can use a routine from a standard or newly installed library by including the following line in your Perl script:

```
require "library.pl";
```

After this declaration has been made, you can use a subroutine in the library simply by calling it as &Subroutine, just like the subroutines you write yourself.

Cgi-lib.pl

The public-domain library `cgi-lib.pl` is a popular and useful library written by S. E. Brenner, who grants permission to use and modify the routines "so long as the copyright is maintained, modifications are documented, and credit is given for any use of the library." The `cgi-lib.pl` library is available from Brenner's page: `http://www.bio.cam.ac.uk/cgi-lib/`.

Cgi-lib.pl contains the following subroutines, which are extremely useful for processing HTML form input and producing HTML output. If you read Chapter 10 or Chapter 13, you've already heard about the magic of the `&ReadParse` subroutine.

ReadParse   Reads HTML form input (GET or POST data), converts it to *unescaped* text, and puts key/value pairs in the associative array `%in`, using `'\0'` to separate multiple selections. This routine returns true if there was input, false if there was no input. ReadParse requires no arguments; almost any form-processing script that you write will include the line `&ReadParse;`.

PrintHeader   Returns an HTTP header that tells a Web browser that the document is an HTML file: `Content-type: text/html\n\n`

HtmlTop   Returns the HTML tags that define the header of a document (including the title) and the beginning of the body (including one `<H1>` heading). You must specify the title (and heading) as a string argument.

HtmlBot   Returns the HTML tags that define the bottom of a document: `</BODY> </HTML>`

MethGet   Tests the method (GET vs. POST) used for an HTML form, and returns true if the form was using the GET request, or false otherwise.

MethPost   This subroutine is the opposite of `MethPost`; it tests the method (GET vs. POST) used for an HTML form, and returns true if the form was using the POST request, or false otherwise.

MyURL   Returns the URL of the CGI script being executed.

CgiError   Formats the specified error message in HTML format (with appropriate headers, markup tags, etc.). If no argument is specified, it produces a generic error message. Otherwise, the first argument is used as a title and the remaining arguments will be formatted as separate paragraphs in the body of the HTML document.

CgiDie   Like `CgiError`, this subroutine formats the specified error message in HTML format, but it also immediately exits the Perl program after issuing the message (unlike `CgiError`, which continues to execute). Arguments are handled as with `CgiError`.

PrintVariables Nicely formats variables in an associative array passed as an argument. The variables are returned in a string of HTML. This subroutine can be useful for debugging.

PrintEnv Nicely formats all *environment* variables as HTML. (This routine is mainly for UNIX systems.)

Other Libraries

There are many Perl libraries on the Net that are yours for the taking. Some programmers are developing possible alternatives to `cgi-lib.pl`, and others are making utilities or subroutines that will simply make your programming life a little easier. Be sure to look around in the following locations for libraries that you may find useful.

- Perl/HTML archives:
  `http://www.seas.upenn.edu/~mengwong/perlhtml.html`
- libwww-perl:
  `http://www.ics.uci.edu/pub/websoft/libwww-perl/`
- Perl- and WWW-related Perl links in Yahoo:
  `http://search.yahoo.com/bin/search?p=perl+scripts`

C.13 SECURITY ISSUES ON UNIX SYSTEMS

Those of you running Web servers on UNIX systems should read this section. The rest of you can return to your Perl programming (or Web surfing), after we mention one thing:

Be careful with scripts that alter files on your hard disk. On a IBM-compatible or Macintosh system, there is little chance that a script will damage anything, but if you don't clean things up every now and then, a small program could fill up your entire disk with script output! Either keep tabs on your disk space, or have your scripts write to a disk partition with a finite size that won't interfere with the rest of your computer. Okay, you Mac and PC people can go now.

But if you are the administrator of a UNIX system, you must protect the system from possible misuse or risky operations; this includes deliberate or unwitting misuse through a Perl program.

External Programs and Shell Meta-Characters

Invoking an external program from within a Perl program can, in certain circumstances, be risking problems. Perl can invoke external programs in several different ways:

- With `backticks`, such as $dir = `pwd`; (which puts the output of the pwd command in $dir)
- Opening a pipe to a program (with the open function and the | character)
- With the system, exec, or eval function

If input to any of these external programs contains UNIX shell meta-characters (* ? . | ` $; [etc.), there is a possibility that a user could perform a system function much different than the one you intended. To protect against this possibility, whenever you invoke the system, exec, or eval functions, you can pass the arguments to the external program as separate members in a list instead of as a single string. If you do this, Perl does not execute the shell when calling the external function; thus, there is no possibility of meta-characters being (mis)interpreted by the shell.

Root Permissions

By default, CGI programs (including Perl programs) run with the permissions of user nobody. Some Web administrators want a certain program to have more permissions than user nobody typically has (for example, if the script needs to write to other users' files), so they increase the permissions on the program by setting the suid ("set user ID"), bit to root (with the chmod command, if you must know).

However, this action can cause problems by increasing the potential for damage if this program is misused by an ignorant or malicious user. We recommend that you *not* give root permission to any CGI program, Perl or otherwise, that users can access from your Web server. An experienced UNIX administrator can usually find a way around a program's permission limitations without resorting to the dangerous suid solutions. If you can't think of a way, find a UNIX guru and beg, bribe, or buy some advice.

Perl Taint Checking

We're happy to report that Perl can help you monitor your programs for potential security problems. The utility to do this is called a "taint checker"; it ensures that your program does not inadvertently pass unsafe user input to the shell.

When the Perl taint checker is used, any variable that is set using data from outside the Perl program is marked as "tainted"; this includes data from the user, the environment, from standard input, and from the command line. The Perl taint checker then prohibits the tainted data from being used to affect anything outside your program.

When a variable is marked as "tainted," any risky operation that involves that variable is marked as tainted as well. For example, if a tainted variable is used to set another value, that value is also marked as tainted. Tainted values cannot be used in functions that perform system operations: eval, exec, system, or piped open calls. (Trying to do so results in a fatal error message from the

Perl taint checker.) Perl also prohibits any attempt to call an external program without setting the PATH environment variable.

In Perl 5.0, use the -T option to run the Perl taint checker, as in the following example:

```
perl -T my_program.pl
```

In Perl 4.0, you must run a separate command, which is included in the standard UNIX Perl distribution, as follows:

```
taintperl my_program.pl
```

We recommend that you use this valuable utility to help ensure the security of any Perl scripts you run on your Web server.

You can learn more about Perl security, and Web security in general, in the comprehensive WWW Security FAQ, which is available at the following URL: http://www-genome.wi.mit.edu/WWW/faqs/www-security-faq.html.

Networks And
TCP/IP

This appendix describes how computer networks function in general, and how the TCP/IP suite of protocols functions in particular. This is pretty detailed material; it's not mandatory to understand datagrams and OSI model layers to set up a Web site, but it helps (especially when something breaks and you're trying to figure out what's wrong!). If you have no interest in learning about the "guts" of the Internet, feel free to stick to the chapters that apply to you and your server. On the other hand, if you want to experience the smug satisfaction of understanding networking better than the amateur Webmaster across the street, read on.

D.1 HISTORY OF NETWORKING

The "Information Superhighway" is not as new-fangled as the media would have us believe. The world's communication infrastructure has simply developed to a point where computer information can be exchanged by users around the world in a simple manner. In fact, this "Infobahn" has existed in some form ever since the first cities were wired for telephone service. This allowed people to communicate without having to personally meet or send a written letter. The biggest advancement, which isn't really new anymore, came when we figured out how to plug computers, rather than telephones, into the electronic infrastructure. The smaller advancements then began to evolve.

The Need for Compatibility

At first, only computers of a common type could communicate with each other. With the same architecture, they didn't need to worry about converting the data to a form the other computer could understand. You had DEC computers talking to other DEC computers, UNIVACs talking with other UNIVACs, and so on. This worked just fine, because computers and modems were very expensive, and organizations tended to buy their systems from a single vendor (most likely IBM).

As the competition intensified and the prices began to drop, more and more computers were purchased by small businesses and individuals, and the big customers themselves began buying from a number of different vendors. Computer users everywhere were not content to hook up only with their systems' siblings. They wanted to be able to communicate with computers of every sort. This gave rise to the huge developments in multi-platform computer networking.

D.2 NETWORKING TODAY

It is the recent evolution of networking technology that has made the Web possible. Over the past 20 years, the world has gone from stand-alone mainframes to computers of all shapes and sizes, all able to communicate with each other seamlessly. Someone using a supercomputer can now send electronic mail to the user of a personal computer halfway around the world as easily as sending a message to a co-worker down the hall.

This evolution is due to three overlapping development phases. First, the development of the technology that allowed physically connected computers with the same architecture to communicate and share resources. Secondly, the ability of dissimilar computers to exchange information over a physical network. Finally, the development of common protocols to connect various networks over the existing telephone infrastructure.

Resource sharing allows certain computers to specialize in various operations, such as file storage or printing, which in turn frees the other computers on that network from having to manage those aspects of their day-to-day operations. More importantly, networked computers can exchange information back and forth. The odds are that the computers at your place of work, your college, or your public library are networked to one degree or another.

To understand general networking concepts, let's take a look at a small Local Area Network (LAN). Most LANs today use the Ethernet standard (although FDDI networks are becoming very popular). This standard describes everything from the type of cables to the data structures that can be used on those cables. Most of this is outside the scope of this book. However, it is important to know that this standard of data communication allows the makers of networking equipment to provide the products that support many different types of networking architectures.

Independent networks connected to the Internet are predominantly hardwired LANs, yet the Internet itself uses the world's telephone and telecommunication infrastructure as its backbone. In a conceptual sense, networking equipment can be looked upon as the computer equivalent of the railroad gauge. There are hundreds of railroad companies in North America. Yet for the most part, any of them can purchase steel rails, box cars, rail ties, and switches from any railroad equipment manufacturer without any customization. The standard equipment in no way dictates what type of railroads they can run (such as passenger or freight), which products they can transport, or the methods they use for switching cars in the rail yard. Like computer networks, these operational specifics are decided upon with the assumption of a standard infrastructure.

D.3   OSI AND TCP

To facilitate multi-platform computer networking, computer scientists from every walk of life — but mostly from the Department of Defense and big corporations — decided to come up with standards that all the computer vendors could live with. To accomplish this goal, they had to design a system where the data coming from one vendor's computer was virtually indistinguishable from the data coming from another vendor's computer. This does not mean that what goes on inside each computer before it hits the network can't be different; in fact, most computers process information in their own unique way. Rather, this means that in order for a PC to exchange information with, say, a supercomputer (or even a Macintosh or an Amiga), some conversion is necessary for the data to appear in the same form once on the network.

Some of the historical developments in the creation of the Internet are covered in Chapter 1 of this book, so we will not repeat them here. Let's just look at the international standards created by the International Standards Organization (ISO) and other associated organizations, like the Institute of Electrical and Electronics Engineers (IEEE). These organizations came up with the Open Systems Interconnection (OSI) Reference Model. Many computer protocols, including all of the ones in the TCP/IP suite, adhere to this type of model.

The OSI Reference Model: Layers

The OSI Reference Model separates the different networking responsibilities into seven defined units, known as *layers* (see Figure D–1). This is simply dividing a problem into smaller pieces to make it easier to address one programming issue or another — computer scientists didn't want to have to worry about network voltage regulation when all they wanted to do was make a customized version of a remote login program. Each layer in the OSI Reference Model can only communicate with the layers immediately above and below it, and has the same responsibility in both the sending and receiving computers.

The following list briefly describes what each layer does. For a detailed discussion on this subject, see Andrew S. Tanenbaum's *Computer Networks*, published by Prentice Hall, Inc.

Let's start at the highest layer, the Application Layer (where your commands are issued), and move down until we reach the physical layer (where computers define what bits and bytes look like in electrical terms).

Application Layer   Defines the operation or function to be performed, such as a file transfer. This is the layer in which commands are issued.

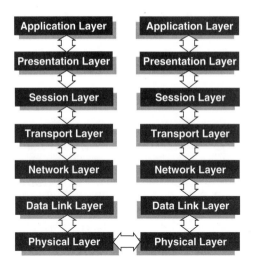

Fig. D–1   The OSI Reference Model. Each layer communicates only with the layers immediately above and below, with the physical layer passing information between systems.

Presentation Layer   Defines the appearance of the information being used by the application. In the case of file transfer, this could be either ASCII (text) or binary information.

Session Layer   Initiates and manages the session between the two computers to move information (which was defined by the presentation layer).

Transport Layer   Takes information (from the session layer), divides it into packets, and propels the packets across a network.

Network Layer   Establishes and manages a network route for packets of data (which came from the transport layer).

Data Link Layer   Facilitates and monitors the physical connection of a network route (determined by the network layer).

Physical Layer   Defines the electrical infrastructure rules for the physical connection (the data link layer).

Using our railroad analogy, this task division frees a rail transport company from having to design a new railroad car for each commodity being moved. Every boxcar gets to its destination on tracks and switches attached to ties and trestles. The designer of the boxcar ensures only that the space between the wheels matches the rail gauge. The steel rail manufacturer only has to worry that the width of the rails match the width of the rail car wheels, and that stan-

dard fasteners can be used to attach the rails to the ties. All of these standardized considerations are necessary for getting the cargo from one location to
another.

TCP and Datagrams

Whether on a hard-wired Ethernet LAN or the Internet itself, data is prepared on your computer for transmission to another computer. Your computer
handles the physical layer of data transmission and reception, and software running on your computer takes cares of the application, presentation, and session
layers. Once the data has been converted to a standardized format, it is then
divided into numbered *datagrams*. (You can think of this as dividing a book into
pages and then numbering them sequentially.) Then, the Transmission Control
Protocol (TCP) implements the transport layer of the OSI Reference Model.
Using TCP, your computer sends the datagrams out across the network to their
destination, where the receiving computer reassembles the pages in a format
that it can use.

Now, how is the receiving computer supposed to know which "pages" to put
where, or even which book they are a part of? The solution is that the sending
computer has tacked a *header* onto each datagram (Fig. D–2). Among other
things, this header identifies the author (continuing with the book analogy), the
title of the book, the page number, and the number of words that are on that particular page. This word count ("checksum") is important because it allows the
receiving computer to request that a message be resent if it appears that some of
the information is missing.

Width in Bits			
Revision	Service Name	Total Length	
Identification		Flags	Offset
Timeout	Protocol	Checksum	
Reserved	Source Address		
Reserved	Destination Address		
Options			Padding
Data ...			

Fig. D–2   This picture illustrates the various data fields in a typical TCP/IP datagram. The header information (everything above the Data field) is used to ensure
proper delivery of the data.

TCP is fast and accurate, so it is used in the vast majority of modern computer networks. It is usually combined with the Internet Protocol (IP), which
handles the remaining layers of the OSI Reference Model.

D.4 IP AND MESSAGE ROUTING

Each electronic datagram has to have a destination address, and it must find a
route to get there. This complex task has been simplified by the networking
developers by dividing the routing problem into many specialized steps. This is
where the Internet Protocol (IP) comes in; it implements the network and data
link layers of the model. IP assumes that TCP is transporting a valid datagram,
then adds another header to each of the datagrams with address information
(among other things); the IP header is added to the existing TCP header.

IP Addresses

The IP address header is similar to the envelope of a regular letter. It has
the destination address, the return address, the name of the sender, and the
name of the recipient. IP addresses are four sets of digits separated by periods
(which are usually called "dots" when people read them aloud). For example, the
address for our ParkWeb test server is 204.246.64.26. You can look at these digits in the same way as street address, city, state, and country (except that, unlike
a postal address, an IP address starts on the left with the broadest classification
and finishes with the smallest on the right).

Each datagram is sent and routed not unlike a letter is. If you sent a letter
from Istanbul, Turkey, to Yakima, Washington, your letter would first go to the
Istanbul post office. The Turkish mail sorter would probably only look at the destination country and throw it into the bin labeled "U.S.A." At the U.S. mail entry
point, an American sorter would only look at the Washington portion of the
address. Once the letter gets to Washington, a sorter there sends it to Yakima,
where it is eventually delivered to the home of the recipient.

IP addresses work in the same way. When the datagram leaves the IP interface, it is routed through the network hierarchy using the series of numbers in
the address. A computer in Istanbul, sending the same letter via e-mail, doesn't
need to know the exact route to the computer in Yakima. It only needs to know
the way to the next number (or numbers) in the IP address. In fact, the IP protocol was specifically designed so that routing would be done dynamically along the
way. This allows for routing redundancies which guarantee the delivery of the
datagram; it may take a different path depending on line conditions, data traffic,
and priority. If a transmission line along the original route goes down, the datagram will be sent along another route.

D.5 SUMMARY

At this point you should be able see how data is conveniently moved from one
location to the next. So what does it all mean? Well, TCP/IP defines the communications format for services like Usenet news (NNTP), electronic mail (SMTP),
remote login (telnet), remote file transfer (FTP), networked file systems (NFS),
and, last but not least, hypertext file transfer (HTTP). In general, both TCP and

IP routines are not concerned with whether the data being sent is a mail message, news article, an HTML file, or whatever; and they do not care what kind of computer the data came from or where it is going. These concerns are left to the other areas of the protocol suite. TCP/IP is what allows you to access all these wonderful new sources of information from your humble PC.

Many of the concepts introduced in this appendix may seem far away from your everyday computing life. But by understanding them, you will be able to more easily diagnose problems, understand the requirements of support software (such as your TCP/IP stack), and be able to understand how your information makes it around the world.

The CD

*T*his book contains hundreds of references to real World Wide Web pages. Rather than make you type in the URL of every single one, we've put together some pages that will take you to all those sites, and we've included them on the CD in the back of this book. The CD also has the source code for all our Perl programs; you *could* read the book and type in all the code by hand, but it'll be a lot easier if you simply copy them from the CD onto your own computer. (Make sure you still read Chapters 12 and 13!)

The CD also includes dozens of freeware and shareware programs for UNIX, Windows, and Macintosh. You are free to copy these from the CD onto your system, but be sure to read all the documentation to find out whether you need to pay for the software or not.

This appendix will tell you how to install the files from the CD onto your computer; read section E.1, "Web Pages and Perl Scripts," then skip to the UNIX, Windows, or Macintosh section for specific instructions.

If You Don't Have a CD-ROM Drive

If your system doesn't include a CD-ROM drive, never fear; all you really need is a modem and Internet access. All the Web pages and Perl scripts are available from our book's corner of Prentice Hall's Web site:

```
http://www.prenhall.com/~palmer/handbook.html
```

As for the software, just follow the links to Chapter 7, 8, or 9 from `handbook.html`, and then download the programs through your Web browser.

E.1 WEB PAGES AND PERL SCRIPTS

The UNIX, Windows, and Mac sections of the CD all contain a directory called `webpages`. It is home to a series of Web pages that correspond to the chapters of this book; each chapter's page contains links to the Web sites discussed therein.

You can read these Web pages locally with your favorite Web browser, but you'll need to be hooked up to the Internet to follow the links. Start out by calling up the file named `handbook.html` (`handbook.htm` in the Windows section). From there you can access any of the other files.

Within `webpages` is another directory called `scripts`. Here you'll find all of the Perl programs — and the associated HTML pages — from Chapters 12 and 13. You can go directly to the `index.html` (or `index.htm`) page in `scripts` for direct access to the programs, or you can get there from the link at the bottom of `handbook.html`.

Because the Internet changes so quickly, it is possible that some of our links may be out of date. You can always find the latest information on our book's Web page at Prentice Hall's site (see above for the URL). Even if all the links on the CD are current, you should still check the pages on `www.prenhall.com` because we will add new information there as it becomes available.

E.2 UNIX

On a UNIX system, just insert the CD into your CD-ROM drive and mount it as you would mount any other filesystem, using the syntax required for your system. For example, on a LINUX system you might use:

```
% mount /dev/scd0 /cdrom -t iso9660
```

On the CD, you will see two top-level directories: `unix` and `windows` (Macintosh files are in a separate partition). Move into the `unix` directory and look at the file listing. As you can see, there are a number of subdirectories, entitled `webpages`, `Perl`, `Servers`, `Helper_Applications`, and `Web_Development_Tools`. The last two correspond to the software categories described at the end of Chapter 7. Some of the software mentioned in the chapter is not included on the CD, due to copyright and distribution restrictions, but you can get them yourself by following the links from the Chapter 7 page on the CD or our book's Web site.

Most of the programs are either in `tar.gz` files (tar files compressed with the `gzip` command) or `tar.z` files (tar files compressed with the `compress` command). To uncompress these files, use the `gzip -d` command (should work for both `.gz` and `.z` files) or the `uncompress` command (only works for `.z` files). Then use `tar xvf` to unpack the resulting tar files.

For example, to install the Apache server software on a LINUX system, move to the directory in which you want to install the software, then execute the following commands (we're assuming you have mounted the CD in a directory called `/cdrom`):

```
% cp /cdrom/unix/servers/apache_1.0.2-linux-ELF.tar.gz .
% gzip -d apache_1.0.2-linux-ELF.tar.gz
% tar xvf apache_1.0.2-linux-ELF.tar
```

For each software package, we tried to include precompiled binaries wherever possible for LINUX, SunOS, and Solaris. For all of the packages (except the Wusage log analyzer), the source code is also included for local compiling.

E.3 WINDOWS

On a Windows PC, just insert the CD into your CD-ROM drive and change to the appropriate drive letter (such as E:). You can do this from the Windows File Manager or the command line prompt.

You will see two top level directories: unix and windows (Macintosh files are in a separate partition). Move to the windows directory and get a file listing. As you can see, there are a number of subdirectories: webpages (described in section E.1), pkzip (PKWARE software), whttpd (Windows httpd server), folkweb (FolkWeb server), website (WebSite server), perl4 (Perl 4 for DOS), help_app (helper applications), inet_app (Internet applications), and webdev (Web development tools). These directories correspond to the software categories described in Chapter 8. Some of the packages mentioned in the chapter are not included on the CD, due to copyright and distribution restrictions. You can get these packages yourself by following the links from our book's Web site.

Most of the programs are in .zip files, which are compressed archives of one or more files. You *must* have PKZIP version 2.04G to uncompress many of the files on our CD. You should always use the -d option if you are using the command line version of this software, so that the original directory structure is maintained. Therefore, even if you have an existing unzip package, it would be prudent to use one of the two distributions included on the CD.

The file pkz204g.exe is a self-extracting archive that creates command line versions of PKZIP and PKUNZIP. Copy the files to a directory on your hard drive (say, C:\ZIP) and run the archive; be sure that this directory is named in the PATH statement in your autoexec.bat file. The file named pkzws201.exe is a Windows zip/unzip program. Simply copy the file to a temporary directory on your hard drive and execute it using the Run utility on the Program Manager's File menu. You will be prompted for the rest of the information.

Once you have installed the PKZIP software on your hard drive, copy the files you want from the CD onto your hard drive. Many of these programs — Windows httpd, for instance — require that you put the .zip files in a certain directory and then extract them from there. Usually, distributions that contain a file called install.exe are installed using the Windows Program Manager.

E.4 MACINTOSH

When you first insert the CD into your Macintosh, you'll see its icon on the right side of your desktop. Double-click the icon; you should see five folders and a file called "READ ME!" (The UNIX and Windows directories are in a separate partition of the CD, so you won't even see them unless you have an unusual system configuration.)

One of the folders is webpages, which we already described in section E.1. You may want to copy the entire webpages folder to your Mac's hard drive for quicker access; you *must* make copies of the Perl scripts if you want to customize them and use them with your server, since you can't alter the CD.

The other four folders in the Macintosh section of the CD are CGI_Stuff, Helper_Applications, Internet_Applications, and Web_Development_Tools. These titles correspond to the sections at the end of Chapter 9, and most of the programs reviewed in Chapter 9 are included on the CD. Just open the folders and look inside to see what's there.

The first thing you should copy from the CD, if you don't already have it, is the freeware utility StuffIt Expander, which is in the Helper_Applications folder. Just double-click the StuffIt Expander installer application, and follow the instructions to place a copy on your hard drive. Once you have this essential tool, you can download almost any Mac file from the Internet; make sure your Web browser knows about StuffIt Expander, so you can use it to automatically decode and extract downloaded files.

Due to copyright restrictions, we were not able to include MacHTTP on our CD, so the second thing you should do, once you have StuffIt Expander, is go to StarNine's Web site and download MacHTTP. You can get there from our Chapter 9 page (on the CD or at prenhall.com), or you can go directly to http://www.starnine.com/machttp/machttp.html.

As for the rest of the Macintosh software on the CD, just try it out and see if you like it. In most cases, you can run the programs directly from the CD for trial purposes, but you should copy them to your hard drive if you decide to keep them. Be sure to use our Chapter 9 Web page to check the programs' home pages to see if more current versions exist.

Index

Symbols

! (Perl operator) 339, 412
!= (Perl operator) 411
. (Perl operator) 412
.. (Perl operator) 413
$! (Perl variable) 350
$_ (Perl variable) 333, 409, 413
&& (Perl operator) 339, 412
** (Perl operator) 410
, (Perl operator) 412
== (Perl operator) 326, 410
@_ (Perl variable) 414
|| (Perl operator) 339, 412, 417
<=> (Perl operator) 411
<> (Perl filehandle) 414
` (Perl) 406
(comment character)
    Macintosh 191
    Perl 325, 404
    UNIX 94, 96
    Windows 138

A

a2p (Perl utility) 424
absolute links 232

access.cnf (Windows httpd configuration file) 138, 145
access.conf (NCSA HTTPd configuration file) 95, 107
AccessConfig (NCSA HTTPd directive) 98
access configuration files
    UNIX 95, 107
    Windows 138
access control
    Macintosh 197
    UNIX 107
    UNIX examples 114
    Windows 145
    Windows examples 153
access counters 288
    Macintosh 208
AccessFileName (NCSA HTTPd directive) 105
AccessFileName (Windows httpd directive) 140
accounts 40
    requirements 45
    shell 41
    SLIP/PPP 42
    testing 50
    types 41

ACFs *see* access control
AddDescription (NCSA HTTPd
    directive) 103
AddDescription (Windows httpd
    directive) 148
AddIcon (NCSA HTTPd directive) 101
AddIcon (Windows httpd directive) 142
AddIconByEncoding (NCSA HTTPd
    directive) 102
AddIconByType (NCSA HTTPd
    directive) 102
<ADDRESS> (HTML tag) 233, 364
AddType (NCSA HTTPd directive) 104
AddType (Windows httpd directive) 141
advertisements on Web pages 279
advertising
    by e-mail 270
    on Usenet 270
    on the Web 27, 33, 273
AgentLog (NCSA HTTPd directive) 98
<A href> (HTML tag) 53, 242, 368
AIFF sounds 251
Alias (NCSA HTTPd directive) 100
Alias (Windows httpd directive) 141
aliases
    Macintosh 185, 187
    security 357
    UNIX commands 355
ALIWEB 283
    site.idx files 283
ALLOW (MacHTTP variable) 198, 201
allow (NCSA HTTPd directive) 111
allow (Windows httpd directive) 150
AllowOverride (NCSA HTTPd
    directive) 109
AllowOverride (Windows httpd
    directive) 147
Alta Vista 281
Amanda the centipede 315
America Online 40
Analog (UNIX and DOS program) 289
analog connections 72
<A name> (HTML tag) 232, 368
Anarchie (Macintosh application) 180,
    211
anchors 232, 368

AND operator (Perl) 339, 412
Andreesen, Marc 9
Annotate (Macintosh application) 209
anonymous FTP *see* FTP
Apache (UNIX Web server) 88
APNIC 76
Apple Macintosh *see* Macintosh
AppleScript (Macintosh extension) 186,
    206
AppleScript (scripting language) 204
<APPLET> (HTML tag) 312
AppleTalk 179
applets 312
application layer (OSI Reference
    Model) 431
Arachnid (Macintosh application) 220
Archie databases 211
<AREA> (HTML tag) 375
arguments *see* CGI programs
$ARGV (Perl variable) 414
ARPA 4
arrays (Perl)
    associative arrays 408
    normal arrays 332, 407
    predefined arrays 414
Asian Pacific Region Internet Registry 76
audio *see* sound
AU sounds 251
authentication *see* user authentication
AuthGroupFile (NCSA HTTPd
    directive) 110
AuthGroupFile (Windows httpd
    directive) 150
AuthName (NCSA HTTPd directive) 109
AuthName (Windows httpd directive) 148
AuthType (NCSA HTTPd directive) 110
AuthType (Windows httpd directive) 149
AuthUserFile (NCSA HTTPd
    directive) 110
AuthUserFile (Windows httpd
    directive) 150
AVI movies 254
    Windows 166

B

<B> (HTML tag) 364
background images 17
backticks (Perl) 406
backups 352
Base64 encoding
    Macintosh 218
<BASEFONT> (HTML tag) 371
.bat files (MS-DOS) 404
BBSs 40
Berners-Lee, Tim 8
<BIG> (HTML tag) 371, 374
BindAddress (NCSA HTTPd
  directive) 99
BinHex 188, 214
<BLINK> (HTML tag) 260, 371
<BLOCKQUOTE> (HTML tag) 366
Bob's HTML Editor (Macintosh
  application) 220
<BODY> (HTML tag) 362
Bourne shell (UNIX) 380

 (HTML tag) 237, 256, 365
    clear attribute 365, 367
browsers 9, 257
    Cello 10
    graphical vs. non-graphical 239, 257
    Internet Explorer 10
    Lynx 10, 46, 50, 256
    Macintosh 180
    MacWeb 10
    Mosaic 9, 256
    Netscape 10, 259, 370, 373
    text-based 46, 50, 239, 257, 368
    UNIX 87
    Windows 130
BSDI 126
bulleted lists 366
bulletin board services see BBSs
Bush, Vannevar 7
button bars 228, 258

C

cables 352
Cailliau, Robert 8

caller ID 360
cat (UNIX command) 384
catalogs 265
cd (UNIX command) 51, 382, 383
Cello browser 10
<CENTER> (HTML tag) 259, 370, 374
CERN 8
CERN httpd see W³C httpd
CGI (Common Gateway Interface) 291,
  292
    Macintosh 204
    Perl 425
    security 357
    UNIX 119
    URLs 294, 296, 347
    Windows 158
cgi-bin directories see CGI programs
cgi-lib.pl (Perl library) 301, 317, 425
    Macintosh 206
    UNIX 120
    Windows 161
CGI programs 291, 292
    archives 298, 328
    arguments 294
    cgi-bin directories 298, 303, 311
    .cgi suffixes 299
    creating 299
    debugging 310
    executing 296
    file naming conventions 299
    finding 297
    HTTP headers 310
    installing 298, 319
    Macintosh 299, 320
    running 296
    security issues 311
    testing 309
    UNIX 298, 319
    uses 291
    Windows 298, 320
    see also Perl
character entities see special characters
  in HTML
chdir (UNIX command) 382, 383
checkboxes 304
    examples 15

in HTML forms 306
checksums 433
Cheetah (Windows 95 server) 169
chmod (UNIX command) 53, 299, 387
chop (Perl function) 420
Clark, Jim 10
"click here" syndrome 232
client pull 261
client-side image maps 375
Clip2gif (Macintosh application) 221
close (Perl function) 421
cmp (Perl operator) 411
<CODE> (HTML tag) 363
.com files (MS-DOS) 404
command environment size
    (MS-DOS) 135
comments
    HTML 330
    Macintosh 191
    Perl 325, 404
    UNIX 94, 96
    Windows 138
commercial use of the Web 263, 360
    encouraging visitors 28
    examples 33, 35
    international 266
Common Gateway Interface see CGI
communication on the Web 36
compatible Web pages 254
comp.infosystems.www.announce 271
comp.infosystems.www.servers.* 354
compression software
    Macintosh 214
    transparent 63
    UNIX 92, 387
    Windows 130, 132, 165
CompuServe 40
computer viruses 354
configuration files
    MacHTTP 191
    NCSA HTTPd 95
    Windows httpd 136
connections see data connections
construction signs 229, 230
Consummate Winsock Apps 162, 175

Content-type (HTTP header) 301, 318,
    425
control key (UNIX) 379
cp (UNIX command) 385
CPUs 64
credit cards 264
csh (UNIX shell) 380
C shell (UNIX) 380
    examples 49
CSU/DSU 74
Cybercash 360

D

DARPA see ARPA
databases
    examples 31, 32, 292
data connections 72
    analog 72
    digital 73
    56k 74
    frame relay 74
    ISDN 74
    T1 74
    traditional phone lines 72
data fork (Macintosh) 188, 223
datagrams 433, 434
data link layer (OSI Reference Model) 432
<DD> (HTML tag) 367
debugging Perl programs 310, 422
DEFAULT (MacHTTP variable) 192, 196
DefaultIcon (NCSA HTTPd
    directive) 103
DefaultIcon (Windows httpd
    directive) 143
default index pages
    Macintosh 189, 193
    UNIX 100
    Windows 140
DefaultType (NCSA HTTPd
    directive) 104
DefaultType (Windows httpd
    directive) 141
defined (Perl function) 421
definition lists 366
delete (Perl function) 409

Denny, Robert 125, 169
DENY (MacHTTP variable) 198, 201
deny (NCSA HTTPd directive) 111
deny (Windows httpd directive) 150
die (Perl function) 421
Digicash 360
digital connections 73
digital money 264, 360
directories (UNIX)
    changing 382
    creating 383
    deleting 383
    home directory 378, 383
    listing contents 381
Directory (NCSA HTTPd directive) 108
Directory (Windows httpd
  directive) 146
directory access control
    UNIX 107
    Windows 145
DirectoryIndex (NCSA HTTPd
  directive) 100
DirectoryIndex (Windows httpd
  directive) 140
disk space 63
    Macintosh 180
    Windows 128
<DIV> (HTML tag) 259, 370, 374
divisions see <DIV> (HTML tag)
<DL> (HTML tag) 366
DocumentRoot (NCSA HTTPd
  directive) 99
DocumentRoot (Windows httpd
  directive) 140
domain names 74, 86
    application form 78
    association with IP addresses 74
    availability 78
    conventions 75
    Macintosh 178
    registration 76
    UNIX 86
    Windows 127, 170
domain name services see DNS
Doug's WWW Mail Gateway 37, 234

DropStuff with Expander Enhancer
  (Macintosh application) 214
<DT> (HTML tag) 366
DUMP_BUF_SIZE (MacHTTP
  variable) 194
dynamic documents 260
dynamic IP addresses 86

E

each (Perl function) 408
edit (MS-DOS command) 138
else (Perl statement) 415
elsif (Perl statement) 415
<EM> (HTML tag) 363
e-mail 45
    Doug's WWW Mail Gateway 37, 234
    as feedback 270, 290
    Macintosh 212
    mail (UNIX command) 50
    protocols 66
    security 358, 359
    UNIX 392
    Windows 164
Emily Postnews 46, 268
EMPs see spam
encryption 359
ENDOFTEXT marker (Perl) 301, 318
%ENV (Perl variable) 408, 414
eq (Perl operator) 326, 411
ERROR (MacHTTP variable) 193, 207
ErrorDocument (NCSA HTTPd
  directive) 105
ErrorLog (NCSA HTTPd directive) 98
ErrorLog (Windows httpd directive) 139
error pages
    Macintosh 193, 207
    UNIX 105
Ethernet 430
etiquette see netiquette
Eudora Light (Macintosh
  application) 212
EWAN 164
examples
    applying for a domain name 80
    connecting to the Internet 47

creating a home page 50
FTP session 389
image maps 30
Perl scripts 299, 315
UNIX login session 49, 378
Web page template 240
execute access *see* file permissions
.exe files (MS-DOS) 404
exit (Perl statement) 336
exit (UNIX command) 380

F

FancyIndexing (NCSA HTTPd
    directive) 101
FancyIndexing (Windows httpd
    directive) 142
FAQs 6, 45, 273
    Perl 403
    WWW security 313, 351
Fast Player (Macintosh application) 217
FDDI 430
Fetch (Macintosh application) 180, 211
56k lines 74
FileError (Perl subroutine) 346, 350
filehandles (Perl) 332, 414, 420
file permissions 52, 299, 356, 386
file servers 59
file test operators (Perl) 411
File Transfer Protocol *see* FTP
file type mapping
    Macintosh 192, 195
    UNIX 104, 106
    Windows 141, 144
    see also MIME types
find2p (Perl utility) 424
finger (UNIX command) 50, 380
firewalls 355
First Virtual 360
flat files (Macintosh) 188, 217, 222
FlattenMooV (Macintosh application) 222
flow control (Perl) 415
FolkWeb (Windows 95 server) 169
<FONT> (HTML tag) 371
fonts
    boldface 363, 364

color 260
italic 363, 364
monospaced 363, 364
size 260, 371, 374
superscripts and subscripts 374
foreach (Perl statement) 332, 416
<FORM> (HTML tag) 302, 303, 316
    action attribute 303, 316
    method attribute 303
forms 302
    actions 303
    checkboxes 304, 306
    default values 305
    examples 299, 304, 316
    GET method 295, 303
    GET vs. POST 295, 303
    hidden elements 305, 320
    HTML source 299, 304
    image maps 305
    input devices 303
    name/value pairs 305
    password boxes 304
    Perl 425
    pop-up menus 306, 320
    POST method 295, 303
    post-query program 308
    radio buttons 304, 306, 323
    reset buttons 305
    selectable lists 306
    submission methods 295, 303, 347
    submit buttons 305
    testing 308
    text boxes 304
    text input areas 307
    variable names 306
    Web resources 302
frame relay 74
frames 262, 374
Free Agent (Windows application) 164
FreeBSD 87
FreeNets 40
free stuff 33, 263
freeware 181, 184
Frequently Asked Questions *see* FAQs
FTP 6, 46, 66
    anonymous 6

commands 389
Macintosh 211
sample session 389
security 358
URL format 12
Web access to 33
Windows 163
ftp (UNIX command) 388
fully qualified domain names *see* domain
names

G

gateway scripts *see* CGI programs
ge (Perl operator) 411
generic.pl (Perl program) 309
GET *see* forms
Ghostview (UNIX application) 122
GIF images 247
compared with JPEG 249
interlaced 221, 247, 262
Macintosh 216, 221
transparent 221, 247, 248
global access control
UNIX 107
Windows 145
Gopher 46
Macintosh 213
security 358
Windows 165
Grandma 300
Grant, Cary 31
graphical counters 288
Macintosh 208
Graphic Converter (Macintosh
application) 220
graphic editors
Macintosh 220
UNIX 121
Windows 168
graphic viewers
Macintosh 216
UNIX 121
Windows 166
GraphX Viewer (Windows
application) 166

Group (NCSA HTTPd directive) 97
groups file
UNIX 113
Windows 152
gt (Perl operator) 411
guest book program 328
gunzip (UNIX command) 388
gzip (UNIX command) 388

H

<H1>–<H6> (HTML tags) 234, 364
#haccess.ctl files (Windows) 145
hardware
base computer 61
disk space 63
Macintosh 179
memory 62
modems 63
processors 64
reliability 352
second-hand 128, 179
testing 47
UNIX 87
Windows 127
<HEAD> (HTML tag) 362
HeaderName (NCSA HTTPd
directive) 103
headings on Web pages 234, 364
examples 235, 365
helper applications
Macintosh 214
UNIX 121
Windows 165
"here" documents 415
hexadecimal numbers (Perl) 406
hidden variables in forms 305, 320
Hide Window in Background (MacHTTP
menu item) 200
High Tea (Macintosh application) 220
hits (HTTP requests) 288
Macintosh 189, 208
see also graphical counters *and*
log files
home directory (UNIX) 42, 378, 383
home pages

creating 50, 189

examples 13, 24

installing on a Macintosh 189

Hoosfoos, Xanzabar 326

horizontal rule lines 260, 365, 371, 372

HoTMetaL Free (UNIX application) 123

HoTMetaL Free (Windows
application) 167

<HR> (HTML tag) 260, 365

align attribute 372

size attribute 371

width attribute 372

.htaccess files (UNIX) 107

HTML 8, 18, 225, 361

buttons 304, 305, 306

capitalization 361, 369

CGI programs 299

checkboxes 15, 304, 306

comments 330

examples 18, 51, 54

forms 302

headers 362

lists 366

logical text styles 362, 374

Netscape extensions 10, 262, 370,
373

page layout tags 364

physical text styles 362

radio buttons 15

reference materials 361

selectable lists in forms 306

source files 8, 9, 18, 51

special characters 369

structural tags 362

text boxes 304

text input areas 307

text style tags 362

titles 362

URLs 54

see also individual tags

<HTML> (HTML tag) 362

HTML.edit (Macintosh application) 220

HTML editors

Macintosh 219

UNIX 123

Windows 167

HTML Pro (Macintosh application) 220

HTML tables *see* tables

HTML Web Weaver (Macintosh
application) 220

htpasswd (MS-DOS program) 151

htpasswd (UNIX program) 112

HTTP 9, 67, 88

Content-type header 301, 318, 425

headers 106, 144, 195, 301, 310, 318,
425

Location header 322

httpd.cnf (Windows httpd configuration
file) 138

httpd.conf (NCSA HTTPd configuration file) 95, 96

httpd software *see* servers

HyperCard 8

hyperlinks *see* links

hypermedia *see* hypertext

hypertext 8

examples 32

hypertext links *see* links

HyperText Markup Language *see* HTML

HyperText Transfer Protocol *see* HTTP

I

<I> (HTML tag) 364

IconsAreLinks (NCSA HTTPd
directive) 101

IdentityCheck (NCSA HTTPd
directive) 97

IEEE (Institute of Electrical and Electronics Engineers) 431

if (Perl statement) 326, 415

image maps 30

client-side 375

examples 28

in forms 305

in HTML 367

Macintosh 208, 221

text alternatives 228, 258

UNIX 120, 123

Windows 159, 168

images 242

alignment 236, 258, 260, 367, 372

alternate text 242, 257, 367
backgrounds 17
borders 373
bullets 243, 248
button bars 228, 258
construction signs 230
formats 247
GIF *see* GIF images
in HTML 367
JPEG *see* JPEG images
"new" icons 229
number 243
organizing 250
placement 258
as replacements for text 242
size 227, 243, 245, 373
textures 17
thumbnails 243
<IMG> (HTML tag) 366, 367
   align attribute 236, 258, 260, 367, 372
   alt attribute 242, 246, 257, 258, 367
   border attribute 373
   height and width attributes 242, 245, 373
   hspace and vspace attributes 373
   ismap attribute 367
   noshade attribute 372
   src attribute 367
$in (Perl variable) 302, 318
%in (Perl variable) 317
INDEX (MacHTTP variable) 193
indexes of Web sites 285
   lists of 285
   regional 287
   topical 285
index.html *see* default index pages
IndexIgnore (NCSA HTTPd directive) 103
IndexIgnore (Windows httpd directive) 143
IndexOptions (NCSA HTTPd directive) 101
Info-Mac archive 181, 207
<INPUT> (HTML tag) 303
   checked attribute 324

name attribute 305
type attribute 304
value attribute 305
other attributes 306
input devices *see* forms
Institute of Electrical and Electronics Engineers (IEEE) 431
Integrated Services Digital Network *see* ISDN
interlacing *see* GIF images
international commerce 266
International Standards Organization (ISO) 431
Internet, the 4
   accessing 47
   management 5
   origins 4
   RFCs (Requests for Comments) 5
   size 5
Internet applications
   Macintosh 210
   Windows 163
Internet Architecture Board 5
Internet Config (Macintosh application) 210
Internet connections 39, 69
   Macintosh 178
   UNIX 86
   Windows 126
Internet Explorer 10
internets 3
Internet service providers 39, 69, 86
   choosing 70
   commercial services 40
   data connections 72
   domain name registration 76
   finding 41, 44, 48
   IP address allocation 83
   local listings 70
   local services 41
   national listing 70
   reliability 353
   testing 50
   using 49
   Web space requirements 46
Internet Society, the 5

InterNIC 5, 76, 86
intruders 359
IP addresses 83, 434
   association with domain names 74
   dynamic 86, 126, 178
   registering 83
   static 86, 127, 178
IP Monitor (Macintosh application) 213
ISDN 74
<ISINDEX> (HTML tag) 294, 362
ISO (International Standards
   Organization) 431
ISPs *see* Internet service providers

J

Jade (Macintosh application) 216
Java 19, 311
JavaScript 19, 312
join (Perl function) 419
JPEG images 247
   compared with GIF 249
   Macintosh 216, 217, 222
   progressive 222, 249, 262
JPEGView (Macintosh application) 216

K

Kelly's Error (Macintosh
   application) 193, 207
keys (Perl function) 409
King, The *see* Presley, Elvis
Korn shell (UNIX) 380
ksh (UNIX shell) 380

L

languages *see* programming languages
layers 431
le (Perl operator) 411
<LI> (HTML tag) 366
Limit (NCSA HTTPd directive) 110
Limit (Windows httpd directive) 150
line breaks 365
links 8, 12, 232
   in HTML 53, 368

mailto 233, 290, 368
   news 368
   relative vs. absolute 232, 250
LINUX 61, 87, 126
   see also UNIX
List, The 70
lists
   in forms 306
   in HTML 366, 367
   using tables to organize 239
Live Objects 20
local area networks (LANs) 2, 430
local ISPs *see* Internet service providers
localtime (Perl function) 336
Location (HTTP header) 322
LOG (MacHTTP variable) 193
log analysis tools 289
log files 98, 289, 359
   analyzing 209, 289
   Macintosh 193, 200, 209
   UNIX 98
logging in/out (UNIX) 49, 378, 380
logical text styles 362, 374
login name (UNIX) 378
LogOptions (NCSA HTTPd directive) 98
logout (UNIX command) 380
Lombard, Carole 31, 54
Lorem Ipsum 231
ls (UNIX command) 43, 381
lt (Perl operator) 411
Lycos 276
   adding your site 277
   searching 277
Lynx browser 10, 256, 257
   examples 50

M

MacBinary 188
MacHTTP 177
   compared to WebSTAR 182
   configuring 191
   connection settings 193
   default files 192
   documentation 186
   downloading 183

File Type Mapping 195
folders 185
installing 184
memory requirements 186
menus 199
MIME types 192, 195
purchasing 184
realms 197, 201
security settings 197
status window 188, 189, 200, 203
testing 188, 203
version 183, 192
MacHTTP.config
comments 191
editing 191
MacHTTP.log 193
MacHTTP Settings 199
Mac-ImageMap (Macintosh
application) 204, 208
Macintosh
CGI 204
CGI applications 207
hardware 179
helper applications 214
Internet applications 210
Internet connection 178
memory 62
multitasking 66
server basics 61
server software 182
software 180
system software 181
Web development tools 219
Web servers 177
MacPerl 205, 206
libraries 206
running scripts 404
see also Perl
MacTCP (Macintosh extension) 186
MacWeb browser 10
mad libs 315, 322
mail see e-mail
mail (UNIX command) 50, 392
mailto links 233, 290
make (UNIX command) 94
man (UNIX command) 397

man pages (UNIX) 397
<MAP> (HTML tag) 375
Mapedit (UNIX application) 123
Mapedit (Windows application) 168
MapServe (Macintosh application) 204,
208
MAXLISTENS (MacHTTP variable) 194
MaxServers (NCSA HTTPd directive) 97
MAXUSERS (MacHTTP variable) 194
memex 7
memory 62
Macintosh 179
UNIX 87
Windows 128
message encryption 359
microprocessors 64
Microsoft Internet Explorer see Internet
Explorer
Microsoft Network 40
Microsoft Windows see Windows
mime.typ (Windows httpd configuration
file) 144
MIME types
Macintosh 192, 195
UNIX 106
Windows 144
see also HTTP headers
mime.types (NCSA HTTPd configura-
tion file) 106
Missing (Perl subroutine) 334, 338
mkdir (UNIX command) 383
modems 63
internal vs. external 64
Macintosh 180
reliability 64, 352
speed 72
Windows 128
Mosaic 9, 256
"What's New" page 282
movie players 122
Macintosh 217, 218
UNIX 122
Windows 166
movies 253
AVI 166
examples 28

formats 253
MPEG 166, 218
QuickTime 122, 166, 217, 222
Mpack (Macintosh application) 218
MPEG-2 sounds 251
MPEG movies 253
    Macintosh 218
    UNIX 122
    Windows 166
Mpegplay (UNIX application) 122
Mpegplay (Windows application) 166
multimedia 28
multitasking 65
multi-user systems 65
    security 311, 355
Murphy's Law 351
mv (UNIX command) 385

N

  see non-breaking spaces
NCSA HTTPd 88
    access configuration file 95, 107
    building from source 93
    configuring 95
    downloading 89
    editing configuration files 96
    installing 92
    log files 98
    main server configuration file 95, 96
    OneStep Downloader 89
    preconfiguring 89
    server resource map 95, 99, 299
NCSA Mosaic see Mosaic
NCSA Telnet (Macintosh application) 211
ne (Perl operator) 411
negation (Perl) 339, 412
Net, the see Internet, the
netiquette 46, 267
net news see Usenet
Netscape
    browser 10, 53, 255, 259
    commerce servers 360
    e-mail 19
    examples 53
    extensions to HTML 10, 259, 262, 370, 373
    frames 262, 374
    JavaScript 311
    origins 10
    reading newsgroups 19
    tables 15, 237, 370
    "What's New" page 282
Netsite (UNIX Web server) 88
network file systems see NFS
Network Information Center see InterNIC
networking 1, 429
    internets 3
    local 2
network layer (OSI Reference Model) 432
Network News Transport Protocol see NNTP
networks 1
newbies 45, 268
"new" icons 229
newsgroups see Usenet
NewsWatcher (Macintosh application) 212
NFS 67
    security 358
NIC handles 81
Nixon, Richard 236, 237
NNTP 67
NO_DNS (MacHTTP variable) 194
NOACCESS (MacHTTP variable) 193
<NOBR> (HTML tag) 371
<NOFRAME> (HTML tag) 262, 375
non-breaking spaces 237, 363, 371
numbered lists 366
numbers (Perl) 405

O

octal numbers (Perl) 406
OneStep Downloader (UNIX) 89
open (Perl function) 332, 420
Open Systems Interconnection (OSI) 431
operators (Perl) 409
    arithmetic 410
    file test 411

miscellaneous 412
relational 410
<OPTION> (HTML tag) 307, 320
Options (NCSA HTTPd directive) 109
Options (Windows httpd directive) 147
order (NCSA HTTPd directive) 111
order (Windows httpd directive) 150
ordered lists 366
order entry program 337
OR operator (Perl) 339, 412
OSAXen (AppleScript extensions) 205
OSI Reference Model 431, 433

P

<P> (HTML tag) 256, 364
align attribute 259, 370, 374
pages 12
compatibility 254
consistency 240
construction signs 229
content 226
divisions 374
forms 302
headings 234, 363, 364
layout 231
proofreading 228
signatures 233
simplicity 231
size 226
tables of contents 232
templates 240
updating 229
white space 236, 365
Paint Shop Pro (Windows
application) 168
passwd (UNIX command) 378
password boxes 304
passwords (UNIX) 378
passwords (WWW authentication)
Macintosh 199, 201
UNIX 112
Windows 146, 149, 151
Passwords... (MacHTTP menu item) 199
path names (UNIX) 381
pattern matching (Perl) 418

PCGI (MacPerl extension) 205, 206
peanut butter 300
Pegasus Mail (Windows application) 164
#!perl 301, 317, 405
Perl 315, 401
arrays 407, 408
comments 325, 404
converting UNIX scripts 424
debugging 310, 422
documentation 402
filehandles 332, 414, 420
file names 404
flow control 415
functions 407, 408, 419, 420
HTTP headers 301, 318
input variables 302
libraries see Perl libraries
location of interpreter 301, 317, 405
logical expressions 409
Macintosh 205, 404
numbers 405
operators 409, 410, 411, 412
pattern matching 418
popularity 296
predefined arrays 408, 414
predefined variables 407, 409, 413
regular expressions 418
running programs 403
security issues 311, 426
statements 404
strings 406
subroutines 324, 326, 422
taint checking 427
time and date 336
UNIX 120, 421
variables 405
versions 402
Web resources 298, 402, 426
Windows 160
perl (UNIX and DOS command) 403
debugging options 423
taint checking 428
Perl libraries 424, 426
cgi-lib.pl 301, 317, 425
Macintosh 206
UNIX 120

Windows 160

permissions *see* file permissions

PGP (Pretty Good Privacy) 359

phone lines 72, 73

physical layer (OSI Reference Model) 432

physical text styles 362

PidFile (NCSA HTTPd directive) 98

PIG_DELAY (MacHTTP variable) 194

ping (UNIX command) 50

PKZIP (Windows application) 35, 130, 132, 165

plug-ins 20

poetry program 299

Point Communications 284
 "Top 5%" awards 284

Point-to-Point Protocol *see* SLIP/PPP

pop-up menus 306
 example script 320

PORT (MacHTTP variable) 194, 202

Port (NCSA HTTPd directive) 97

Port (Windows httpd directive) 139

port numbers
 Macintosh 194, 202
 security 357
 Windows 139

POST method *see* forms

post-query program 308

PostScript files (UNIX) 122

Power Macintosh 187

PPP *see* SLIP/PPP

Practical Extraction and Report Language *see* Perl

<PRE> (HTML tag) 364

presentation layer (OSI Reference Model) 432

Presley, Elvis 236, 237
 impersonators from Pluto 224

Pretty Good Privacy (PGP) 359

print (Perl function) 318, 333, 420

processor speed 64
 Macintosh 179
 Windows 127

Prodigy 40

programming languages
 for CGI programs 296
 object-oriented 311

Progressify (Macintosh application) 222

ProJPEG (Photoshop extension) 222

protocols 66
 FTP 6, 46
 Gopher 46
 HTTP 9
 SLIP/PPP 42, 73
 TCP/IP 4

providers *see* Internet service providers

proxies 355

publicizing your site 267

publishing on the Web 20

pwd (UNIX command) 382

Q

Quarterdeck Internet Suite (Windows) 132

QuickEditor (Macintosh application) 222

QuickTime for Windows (application) 166

QuickTime movies 254
 Macintosh 217, 222
 UNIX 122
 Windows 166

quote characters (Perl) 406

R

radio buttons 304, 306
 checked attribute 324
 examples 15, 323

RAM *see* memory

Random URL 226

read access *see* file permissions

ReadmeName (NCSA HTTPd directive) 103

ReadmeName (Windows httpd directive) 147

ReadParse (Perl subroutine) 317, 425

RealAudio 252

REALM (MacHTTP variable) 197

realms
 Macintosh 197, 201
 UNIX 109
 Windows 148
 see also user authentication

real-time audio 252
`Redirect` (NCSA HTTPd directive) 100
`Redirect` (Windows httpd directive) 141
`RefererLog` (NCSA HTTPd directive) 98
`Refuse New Connections` (MacHTTP menu item) 200
regular expressions (Perl) 418
relative links 232
remote logins (UNIX) 391
`require` (NCSA HTTPd directive) 111
`require` (Perl statement) 301, 317, 424
`require` (Windows httpd directive) 150
ResEdit (Macintosh application) 207, 223
reset buttons 305
`ResourceConfig` (NCSA HTTPd directive) 98
resource fork (Macintosh) 188, 223
`reverse` (Perl function) 421
RFCs (Requests for Comments) 5
RIPE Network Coordination Centre 76
rlogin 6
    security 358
`rlogin` (UNIX command) 391
`rm` (UNIX command) 385
`rmdir` (UNIX command) 383
routers 74
rules of the Web *see* netiquette

S

`s2p` (Perl utility) 424
`satisfy` (NCSA HTTPd directive) 111
`satisfy` (Windows httpd directive) 151
scalars *see* Perl variables
`ScanHTMLTitles` (NCSA HTTPd directive) 101
Schwartz, Randal 403
SCO UNIX 126
scratch 'n' sniff 20
`<SCRIPT>` (HTML tag) 312
`ScriptAlias` (NCSA HTTPd directive) 100
`ScriptAlias` (Windows httpd directive) 141
Script Editor (Macintosh application) 205
scripts *see* CGI programs

ScriptWizard (Macintosh application) 205
searchable index program 345
searching databases *see* databases
searching the Web
    Alta Vista 281
    Lycos 277
    WebCrawler 279
    Yahoo 276
sectioning directives
    UNIX 108
    Windows 146
secure transactions 360
    Macintosh 203
security 351
    aliases 357
    CGI 311, 357
    e-mail 359
    FAQs 351
    file permissions (UNIX) 386
    file space 356
    Internet services 358
    Java and JavaScript 313
    Macintosh 201
    Perl 426
    port numbers 357
    server-generated indexes 357
    server processes 357
    UNIX 359
    user authentication 358
    Windows 145
security realms *see* realms
`<SELECT>` (HTML tag) 306, 320
selling merchandise 264
Serial Line Internet Protocol *see* SLIP/PPP
`ServerAdmin` (NCSA HTTPd directive) 97
`ServerAdmin` (Windows httpd directive) 139
server-generated indexes
    security 357
    UNIX 101
    Windows 142
`ServerName` (NCSA HTTPd directive) 97

ServerName (Windows httpd
  directive) 139
server processes (UNIX) 357
server push 260
server resource maps
    UNIX 95, 99, 299
    Windows 138
server root 242
ServerRoot (NCSA HTTPd directive) 98
ServerRoot (Windows httpd
  directive) 139
servers 23
    Macintosh 182
    overview 59
    security 353, 356
    UNIX 88
    Windows 129, 131
ServerStat (Macintosh application) 209
ServerType (NCSA HTTPd directive) 96
service providers see Internet service providers
session layer (OSI Reference model) 432
SGML 8
sh (UNIX shell) 380
shareware
    Macintosh 181, 184
    Windows 129, 161, 162
shell accounts 41
    advantages 43
shells (UNIX) 379
    default login shell 380
shift (Perl function) 407
Shotton, Chuck 177
signatures
    in Usenet articles 272
    on Web pages 233
Simple Mail Transfer Protocol see SMTP
SimpleText (Macintosh application) 191,
  215
single-user systems 65
    security 354
site.idx files (ALIWEB) 283
SLIP/PPP 73, 86
    accounts 42
    advantages 43
    Macintosh 178

protocols 42
Windows 126
<SMALL> (HTML tag) 371, 374
SMTP 66
software
    distribution on the Web 33, 35
    Macintosh archives 181
    updating 353
    Windows archives 161
software requirements
    Macintosh 180
    operating systems 64
    TCP/IP 66
    Windows 128
Solaris 62
sort (Perl function) 407
SoundApp (Macintosh application) 217
sound editors
    Macintosh 221
    Windows 166
SoundEffects (Macintosh
  application) 221
sound players 251
    Macintosh 217
    Windows 166
sounds 251
    examples 28
    formats 251
    players 251
    real-time audio 252
    sampling rates 252
    size 252
source HTML see HTML source files
spam 273
Sparkle (Macintosh application) 218
special characters in HTML 369
spell checking 228
spiders 277, 279, 281
Spike's Smut Shack 287
split (Perl function) 349, 419
Squeaky T. Parrot 268
srm.cnf (Windows httpd configuration
  file) 138, 140
srm.conf (NCSA HTTPd configuration
  file) 95, 99, 299

Standard Generalized Markup Language 8
StarNine Technologies 177, 182
StartServers (NCSA HTTPd directive) 97
static IP addresses 86
STDERR (Perl filehandle) 414
STDIN (Perl filehandle) 414
STDOUT (Perl filehandle) 414
Stein, Lincoln 313, 351
strings (Perl) 406
<STRONG> (HTML tag) 363
StuffIt Expander (Macintosh application) 180, 214
<SUB> (HTML tag) 374
submit buttons 305
Submit It 281
subroutines (Perl) 324, 326, 422
subscripts 374
Sun Microsystems 311
<SUP> (HTML tag) 374
superscripts 374
SuppressDescription (NCSA HTTPd directive) 101
SuppressLastModified (NCSA HTTPd directive) 101
SupressSize (NCSA HTTPd directive) 101
surfing the Web 12
surveys 290
Suspend Logging (MacHTTP menu item) 200
symbolic links see aliases
syslog (UNIX) 359

T

T1 lines 74
tables 237, 370
    alternatives to 240, 364
    borders 240
    example in Netscape 15
    organizing lists 239
    reference materials 370
tables of contents 232
taint checking (Perl) 427

taintperl (UNIX command) 428
tape archives see tar files
Tar (Macintosh application) 218
tar (UNIX command) 92, 393
tar files
    Macintosh 218
    UNIX 393
Tcl interpreter 380
tclsh (UNIX shell) 380
TCP/IP
    checksums 433
    datagrams 433
    headers 433, 434
    HTTP 67
    IP (Internet Protocol) 434
    message routing 434
    NFS 67
    NNTP 67
    origins 4
    OSI reference model 431, 433
    SMTP 66
    software 435
    telnet 67
    Windows 129
tcsh (UNIX shell) 380
TeachText (Macintosh application) 191, 215
telnet 6, 46, 67
    Macintosh 211
    security 358
    UNIX 390
    Windows 164
telnet (UNIX command) 390
templates for Web pages 240
terminal type (UNIX) 379
terminating devices 74
testing
    CGI programs 309, 311
    hardware 47
    MacHTTP 188, 203
    UNIX Web servers 118
    Windows server 157
Tex-Edit Plus (Macintosh application) 191, 215
text-based browsers see browsers
text boxes 304

text editors
    Macintosh 215
    UNIX 51, 96
    Windows 138
text input areas 307
Thread Manager (Macintosh
    extension) 66, 181
thumbnails 243
time (Perl function) 336
TIMEOUT (MacHTTP variable) 194
Timeout (NCSA HTTPd directive) 97
Timeout (Windows httpd directive) 139
time zones (Windows) 134
<TITLE> (HTML tag) 362
"Top 5%" awards 284
TransferLog (NCSA HTTPd
    directive) 98
TransferLog (Windows httpd
    directive) 139
Transmission Control Protocol see
    TCP/IP
transparency see GIF images
Transparency (Macintosh
    application) 221
transport layer (OSI Reference
    Model) 432
Trojan horse programs 354
Trumpet Winsock (Windows system
    software) 129
truth (Perl) 409
<TT> (HTML tag) 364
TurboGopher (Macintosh
    application) 213
TypesConfig (NCSA HTTPd
    directive) 98

U

<UL> (HTML tag) 366
Umich archive 181
uname (UNIX command) 90
uncompress (UNIX command) 92, 388
Uniform Resource Locators see URLs
UNIX 61, 85, 377
    CGI 119
    compression 387
    directories 381, 383
    documentation 397
    editing files 394
    e-mail 392
    files 380, 384
    hardware requirements 87
    helper applications 121
    home directory 378, 383
    httpd program 87
    LINUX 61
    logging in/out 378, 380
    man pages 397
    memory 62, 87
    multitasking 65
    network commands 388
    passwords 378
    path names 381
    Perl functions 421
    security 359
    server basics 61
    shells 379
    software requirements 87
    Solaris 62
    special characters 379
    terminal type 379
    user ID 378
    versions 377
    Web resources 377
unless (Perl statement) 332
unordered lists 366
unpack (UNIX command) 388
until (Perl statement) 417
unzip (UNIX command) 388
URLs 54
    & character 295
    = character 295
    ? character 294
    CGI 294, 296, 347
    FTP format 12
    plus signs 294
    spaces 294
Usenet 6, 45
    advertising on 270
    buying used computers 128, 179
    commercial newsgroups 270
    etiquette 45, 268

Macintosh 212
news server security 358
origins 4
Perl newsgroup 403
protocols 67
searching 281
security newsgroups 354
Web access 19
Windows 164
User (NCSA HTTPd directive) 97
user authentication 358
    Macintosh 197, 201
    UNIX 112
    Windows 151
UserDir (NCSA HTTPd directive) 100
user ID (UNIX) 378
UUCP 6
    security 358
uudecode (UNIX command) 393
uuencode (UNIX command) 393
uuencoding
    Macintosh 218
    UNIX 393
uuUndo (Macintosh application) 218

V

variable interpolation (Perl) 406
variables
    names in HTML forms 305
    Perl 405, 413
VBRUN300.DLL (Windows system
    software) 135, 158
Verbose Messages (MacHTTP menu
    item) 200
VeriFone 360
VERSION (MacHTTP variable) 192
vi (UNIX command) 52, 394
virtual banking 264, 360
virtual machines (Windows) 159
viruses 354
Visual Basic applications 159
Vromans, Johan 403

W

W³C httpd (UNIX Web server) 88
Wall, Larry 403
WAV sounds 251
<WBR> (HTML tag) 371
Web, the see World Wide Web
Web browsers see browsers
WebCompare 356
WebCrawler 279
    adding your site 279
    searching 279
Web development tools
    UNIX 122
    Windows 167
WebImage (Windows application) 168
WebMap (Macintosh application) 208,
    221
Web pages see pages
WebServer (Windows Web server) 132
Web servers see servers
WebSite (Windows 95 server) 131, 169
    configuring 172
    downloading 170
    installing 170
    network configuration 170
    password files 174
    starting up 175
    testing 175
WebSTAR (Macintosh server) 177, 182
WebSTAR (Windows 95 server) 169
Webster's HTML Dictionary 32
Webtor (Macintosh application) 220
week, thingamajig of the 229
WHAM (Windows application) 166
"What's New" pages 282
while (Perl statement) 416
white space 236
Wiederspan, Jon 204
Windows
    hardware 127
    helper applications 165
    Internet applications 163
    Internet connection 126
    memory 62
    multitasking 65

security 145
server basics 62
server software 129, 131
software 128
Web development tools 167
Windows 3.1 servers
    Chameleon 132
    WebServer 132
    Windows httpd 131
Windows 95 169
Windows 95 servers
    Cheetah 169
    FolkWeb 169
    WebSite 131, 169
    WebSTAR 169
Windows httpd 125
    access configuration file 138
    access control 145
    CGI 158
    configuring 136
    downloading 131
    editing configuration files 138
    groups file 152
    image maps 159
    installing 132
    main server configuration file 138
    MS-DOS command environment
        size 135
    Perl CGI scripts 160
    price 131
    server resource map 138, 140
    starting up 136
    testing 136, 157
    time zone setup 134
    user authentication 151
    VBRUN300.DLL 135
    Visual Basic applications 159
    Windows/DOS system
        configuration 133
Windows NT 169
WinScriptAlias (Windows httpd
    directive) 141
Winsock (Windows system software) 129
Wizbang Widgets 75
word breaks 260, 371
World Wide Web 11

advertising on 27, 33, 273
basic tools 45
browsers 9
finding information 20
origins 7, 8
publishing information 20
rules see netiquette
servers 59
size 27
Wright, Matt 328
write access see file permissions
WS_FTP (Windows application) 163
WS_Gopher (Windows application) 165
WWW see World Wide Web
www-security mailing list 354

X

x (Perl operator) 412
XAnim (UNIX application) 122
Xing StreamWorks 252
XTML (Microsoft Excel extension) 220
XV (UNIX application) 121
X Windows (UNIX) 9, 121

Y

Yahoo 50, 257
    adding your site 276
    as advertising 274
    indexes of Web sites 285
    list of ISPs 70
    "new" icons 230
    Random URL 226
    search interface 276, 296
    Web Launch 276

Z

ZIP files
    Macintosh 219
    Windows 130, 165
ZipIt (Macintosh application) 219